CW01163556

Resale Price Maintenance and Vertical Territorial Restrictions

NEW HORIZONS IN COMPETITION LAW AND ECONOMICS

Series Editor: Steven D. Anderman, *Department of Law, University of Essex, UK*

This series has been created to provide research based analysis and discussion of the appropriate role for economic thinking in the formulation of competition law and policy. The books in the series will move beyond studies of the traditional role of economics – that of helping to define markets and assess market power – to explore the extent to which economic thinking can play a role in the formulation of legal norms, such as abuse of a dominant position, restriction of competition and substantial impediments to or lessening of competition. This in many ways is the *new horizon* of competition law policy.

US antitrust policy, influenced in its formative years by the Chicago School, has already experienced an expansion of the role of economic thinking in its competition rules. Now the EU is committed to a greater role for economic thinking in its Block Exemption Regulations and Modernisation package as well as possibly in its reform of Article 102. Yet these developments still raise the issue of the *extent* to which economics should be adopted in defining the public interest in competition policy and what role economists should play in legal argument. The series will provide a forum for research perspectives that are critical of an unduly-expanded role for economics as well as those that support its greater use.

Titles in the series include:

Collective Dominance and Collusion
Parallelism in EU and US Competition Law
Marilena Filippelli

Cartels, Competition and Public Procurement
Law and Economic Approaches to Bid Rigging
Stefan Weishaar

The Chinese Anti-Monopoly Law
New Developments and Empirical Evidence
Edited by Michael Faure and Xinzhu Zhang

Standardization under EU Competition Rules and US Antitrust Laws
The Rise and Limits of Self-Regulation
Björn Lundqvist

Joint Research and Development under US Antitrust and EU Competition Law
Björn Lundqvist

Monopolies and Underdevelopment
From Colonial Past to Global Reality
Calixto Salomão Filho

Resale Price Maintenance and Vertical Territorial Restrictions
Theory and Practice in EU Competition Law and US Antitrust Law
Barbora Jedličková

Resale Price Maintenance and Vertical Territorial Restrictions

Theory and Practice in EU Competition Law and US Antitrust Law

Barbora Jedličková

TC Beirne School of Law, The University of Queensland, Australia

NEW HORIZONS IN COMPETITION LAW AND ECONOMICS

Edward Elgar
PUBLISHING

Cheltenham, UK • Northampton, MA, USA

© Barbora Jedličková 2016

All rights reserved. No part of this publication may be reproduced, stored in a retrieval system or transmitted in any form or by any means, electronic, mechanical or photocopying, recording, or otherwise without the prior permission of the publisher.

Published by
Edward Elgar Publishing Limited
The Lypiatts
15 Lansdown Road
Cheltenham
Glos GL50 2JA
UK

Edward Elgar Publishing, Inc.
William Pratt House
9 Dewey Court
Northampton
Massachusetts 01060
USA

A catalogue record for this book
is available from the British Library

Library of Congress Control Number: 2015952681

This book is available electronically in the Elgaronline
Law subject collection
DOI 10.4337/9781783477746

ISBN 978 1 78347 773 9 (cased)
ISBN 978 1 78347 774 6 (eBook)

Typeset by Columns Design XML Ltd, Reading
Printed and bound by CPI Group (UK) Ltd, Croydon, CR0 4YY

To my daughter Eliška Marie Barnes

Contents

Preface		ix
List of abbreviations		xiii
Table of cases		xiv
Table of legislation		xxiii
1	Introduction	1
2	Distribution and competition	7
	I Introduction	7
	II Distribution and vertical integration	8
	III Competition and bargaining power	26
	IV Market structure: the application of RPM and VTR	38
	V Conclusion	46
3	US development, case studies and summaries	48
	I Introduction	48
	II The Sherman Act	50
	III The first era (1890s–1930s): the interpretation of the Sherman Act	56
	IV Strict era (1940s–beginning of 1970s): protecting small businesses	71
	V Free era (end of 1970s–1990s): Chicago School influence	91
	VI The rule of reason era (end of 1990s–2010s)	117
	VII Application and enforcement	151
	VIII Conclusion	159
4	EU development, case studies and summaries	162
	I Introduction	162
	II The origin of competition law and the Treaty Framework	163
	III Economic integration (1950s–beginning of 1970s)	172
	IV Overcoming crisis and further integration (1970s–1980s)	182
	V Stability and vertical restraint regulation (1990s–2005)	193
	VI Economic crisis and new vertical restraint regulation	206
	VII Application and enforcement	230
	VIII Conclusion	242

5	Theories and impacts of RPM and VTR on competition	244
	I Introduction	244
	II Procompetitive theories of services, quality certification and exclusivity: free riding	248
	III Procompetitive theory of facilitating entry	268
	IV Procompetitive effects on consumer welfare, output and efficiency	270
	V Empirical studies	277
	VI Anticompetitive effects	281
	VII Anticompetitive theory of supplier (interbrand) cartel	284
	VIII Anticompetitive theory of retailer (intrabrand) cartel	286
	IX Anticompetitive motivations by retailer	287
	X (Anti)competitive motivations by supplier	289
	XI Conclusion	297
6	Jurisprudential arguments and the economic concept of RPM and VTR	300
	I Introduction	300
	II Outcomes: consequentialist approach	301
	III Process: deontological account	305
	IV Conclusion	317
7	Conclusion	320
Bibliography		325
Index		345

Preface

The first time I started to think about vertical restraints beyond their legal doctrine was during my LLM studies in competition law and policy at the University of Glasgow ten years ago. At that time, I had already found the topic of vertical restraints fascinating, primarily because it was difficult to find the right answer as to whether they should or should not be part of competition/antitrust law, why, in what form and to what extent. Despite the fact that vertical restraints form part of the competition/antitrust regimes of many countries, the topic of vertical restraints has always been at the edge of research interest, unlike research in and knowledge of cartels, monopolies and mergers.

However, at the same time, the topic of vertical restraints, in particular resale price maintenance (RPM) and also vertical territorial restraints (VTR), causes significant controversy. Some claim that RPM and VTR restrict competition and are potentially two of the most anticompetitive vertical restraints, while others argue that they are procompetitive and beneficial to consumers. The approach to RPM and VTR in the competition/antitrust law regimes studied in this book, the European Union (EU) and the United States of America (US), also differs. Nevertheless, recent commentators agree that there is a lack of comprehensive studies, and that these studies are desirable in order to understand this issue better and make a qualified judgment regarding the competitiveness or anticompetitiveness of RPM and VTR.

These differences and the calling for more research were the reasons for writing this book. I conceptualized my first ideas at the beginning of my PhD candidature in 2007. That year was a significant milestone for the approach to RPM in the US given that the US Supreme Court delivered its decision in the case of *Leegin* [*Leegin Creative Leather Products, Inc. v. PSKS, Inc, DBA Kay's Kloset … Kays' Shoes*, 551 U.S. 877 (2007)], overruling the previous approach and introducing the rule of reason to all forms of RPM. The rule of reason also applies to VTR in the US, and this rule has led to the de facto legalization of these practices.

Leegin provoked a noticeable debate on the nature and approach to RPM in both US and EU jurisdictions, however, no final conclusion has been made in that regard and the way the rule of reason should apply in practice has not been absolutely clarified and settled in the US. Since *Leegin*, no cases on RPM have reached the US Supreme Court which could assist with specifying the application of the rule of reason to RPM.

The situation in the EU is different. The EU categorizes vertical price fixing, vertical minimum price fixing and some forms of vertical territorial restraints, such as some forms of absolute vertical territorial restrictions, as hard-core restrictions of EU competition law, meaning that it is unlikely that such a practice could be justified under Article 101(3) of the Treaty on the Functioning of the EU, although it would not be impossible.

The differences in the EU and US regimes provide a well-rooted scope for comparison which, together with the reasons behind these differences and the historical development of these approaches, can then assist with providing a detailed understanding of RPM and VTR and their EU and US legal approaches and applications. The essential part of this understanding is not only the law itself but, significantly, the economic theories and economic and marketing knowledge of this area of competition which I discuss in this book. However, I go even further, as I propose other, less conventional, views on this area of competition/antitrust law. In particular, I address a number of questions arising from the legal differences and differences in arguments on these issues arising, primarily, from law, economics and marketing.

The principal objectives of this book are to provide you, the reader, with a detailed understanding of this topic, to inform you whether and to what extent RPM and VTR restrict competition and to outline different angles of understanding for determining the anticompetitiveness and pro-competitiveness of RPM and VTR than the currently used economical account. I identify these different views based on determining the drawbacks of the current economical and legal approaches to RPM and VTR in the US and EU. In order to fulfil these objectives, I divided this book into five substantive chapters. Each chapter plays a specific role, and, at the same time, they form part of the one puzzle, where each assists with determining the principal objectives of this book, serving the overall objective of finding the optimal approach to RPM and VTR.

This brief preface is followed by a general, introductory, chapter, on the operation of RPM and VTR in distribution. That chapter outlines a number of the essential elements of vertical interactions by using knowledge from economics, marketing and other disciplines. In Chapter 2, I commence my argument that it is not only horizontal and interbrand competition which should be considered when evaluating vertical restrictions, but that the nature of vertical restraints requires intrabrand competition and the driving force of vertical restrictions – bargaining power –

to be taken into consideration. Chapters 3, 4 and 5 provide specific examples supporting this argument and, finally, Chapter 6 shows that by using a deontological account all forms of competition need to be considered.

Although this book is based on comprehensive, holistic research, I provide a number of suggestions rather than one answer to this issue and specific legislative suggestions simply because, unlike hard-core cartels, there is no black and white answer to RPM and VTR. The comprehensive research on which this book stands should not imply that this book answers all questions on RPM and VTR, nor that it provides the absolute single correct answer. On the contrary, it confirms that the answer can differ depending on the angle of view. Indeed, the book outlines more than one angle, explains the different opinions on this topic and, by providing a detailed understanding, it should provoke critical thinking in readers and unleash both conservative and new ways for understanding and analyzing RPM and VTR.

I would not have been able to write this book and finish it in August 2015 without the support, assistance and advice from many people I have met since researching this area of competition/antitrust law. I would like to mention at least some of them. First, I am grateful to the publisher Edward Elgar for giving me the opportunity to publish my first monograph and its staff members for being professional and supportive.

The basis of this book rests on my PhD thesis. I would like to acknowledge the support, advice and encouragement I have received since then from my former principal supervisor Prof Mark Furse from the University of Glasgow and also examiners, Prof Alison Jones from King's Colleague in London and Prof Rosa Greaves from the University of Glasgow, for our inspiring discussions and their useful comments during my PhD viva. I have absorbed a lot of knowledge from and was highly inspired by Prof Herbert Hovenkamp during my academic visit to the Faculty of Law at the University of Iowa in 2009 for which I am deeply grateful.

I met a number of practitioners and academics during my academic visits to the US in 2009 and 2014 who challenged and influenced my ideas, understanding and concepts of this topic and related issues. In particular, my recent visit had a significant impact on this book. I had the opportunity to discuss vertical restraints with economists from the Antitrust Division of the US Department of Justice and the US Federal Trade Commission, and for that my special gratitude belongs to Norman Familant, Chief, Economic Litigation Section from the Antitrust Division of the US Department of Justice, and Ken Heyer, Deputy Director, Bureau of Economics at the US Federal Trade Commission. I discussed a number of issues arising from this topic with Prof John E Kwoka from Northeastern University and I had inspiring conversations with solicitor Theodore Voorhees, the former President of the American Antitrust Institute, Albert A Foer and Richard Brunell.

My deep gratitude goes to Prof Keith N Hilton and Boston University for providing me with an office and research materials during my short academic visit in 2014 and likewise to Prof Josef Bejček from Masaryk University. Last year, I was also given an excellent opportunity to undertake part of my research at the Court of Justice of the European Union in Luxembourg. This short visit proved to be extremely inspiring, especially a number of discussions I had with judges from the Court of Justice and the General Court; the one with Prof Koen Lenaerts, Vice-President of the Court of Justice, was the most influential. I would like to thank them for their time and also thank the Library and Documentation and their staff members for providing me with essential materials and for their warm hospitality.

I am grateful to my colleagues from the University of Queensland and the TC Beirne School of Law for their support. In particular, the School for funding my research trips, the UQ librarians for their research assistance and Claire Morris, Xavier Goffinet and Laura Marshall for their editing assistance. I also received partial funding from the Ian Potter Foundation (Travel Grant number 20150242) for my 2014 US and EU research trip, for which I am sincerely grateful. On a personal note, I am extremely fortunate for and would like to thank my family and friends and, in particular, my excellent partner, Matthew Barnes, for his loving support.

The law in this book is up-to-date as at 1 June 2015.

Barbora Jedličková

Abbreviations

AMCHAM EU	American Chamber of Commerce to the European Union
CJEU	Court of Justice of the European Union
DOJ	The United States Department of Justice, Antitrust Division
EC	European Community
ECSC	Treaty Establishing the European Coal and Steel Community
EEA	European Economic Area
EEC	European Economic Community
EFTA	European Free Trade Area
EU	European Union
FTC	Federal Trade Commission (USA)
GSK	GlaxoSmithKline Services Unlimited
GW	Glaxo Wellcome, SA
ICC	International Chamber of Commerce
OECD	Organisation for Economic Co-operation and Development
OJ	Official Journal
R&D	research and development
RPM	resale price maintenance
SSNIP	small but significant non-transitory increase in price
TFEU	Treaty on the Functioning of the European Union
UNIDROIT	International Institute for the Unification of Private Law
US	United States; United States of America
VTR	vertical territorial restraints

Table of cases

EU CASES

Court of Justice of the European Union

Activision Blizzard Germany GmbH v. European Commission (Case C-260/09)
[2011] ECR **216–19**, 237
AEG – Allgemeine Elektricitäts – Gesellschaft AEG – Telefunken AG v. Commission
(Case 107/82) [1983] ECR 3151, [1984] 3 CMLR 325, CMR 14018 185,
259, 268, 293
Allianz Hungária Biztosíto and others v. Gazdasági Versenyhivatal (Case C-32/11)
[2013] ECR 1 187, 238–9
BMW Belgium SA v. Commission of the European Communities (Cases 32/78, 36/78
to 82/78) [1979] ECR 2435 187
Bundesverband der Arzneimittel-Importeure EC and Commission v. Bayer AG
(Cases C-2/01 P, C-3/01 P) [2004] ECR I-23 .... 32, 171, 292, 317
Commission v. Volkswagen AG (Case C-74/04 P) [2006] ECR I-6585 ... 198, **204–7**,
236–7
Costa v. ENEL (Case 6/64) [1964] ECR 585 167
Delimitis (Stergios) v. Henninger Bräu (Case C-234/89) [1991] ECR I-935, [1992]
5 CMLR 210 186
Demo-Studio Schmidt v. Commission (Case 210/81) [1983] ECR 3045, [1984] 1
CMLR 63 185
Deutscher Apothekerverband v. 0800 DocMorris, Jacques Waterval (Case C-322/
01) [2005] 1 CMLR 46 228
Eco Swiss China Time Ltd v. Benetton International NV (Case C-126/97) [1999]
ECR I-3055, [2000] 5 CMLR 816 194
*Établissements Consten S.à.R.L. and Grundig-Verkaufs-GmbH v. Commission of
the European Economic Community* (Cases 56/64, 58/64) [1966] ECR
299 .... **172–81**, 188, 221, 240, 242, 259, 289, **292–5**
Ford Werke AG v. Commission of the European Communities (Cases 25/84, 26/84)
[1985] ECR 2725, [1985] 3 CMLR 528 .... 187, 205
GlaxoSmithKline Services Unlimited v. Commission of the EC (Cases C-501/06 P,
C-513/06 P, C-515/06 P, C-519/06 P) [2009] 4 CMLR 2 ...... 32, 199, 208, **213–
14**, **219–26**, 229, 233, **237–42**
Hoffmann-La Roche & Co. AG v. Commission (Case 85/76) [1979] ECR 461,
[1979] 3 CMLR 211 307
Höfner and Elser v. Macrotron GmbH (C-41/90) [1991] ECR I-1979, [1993] 4
CMLR 306 12

IBM Personal Computer (Case 60/81) [1981] ECR 2639, [1984] 2 CMLR
  347 186
*IHT Internationale Heiztechnik GmbH and Uwe Danzinger v. Ideal-Standard
  GmbH and Wabco Standard GmbH* [1994] ECR 2789 186
Ker-Optika bt v. ANTSZ del-dunantuli Regionalis Intezete (Case C-108/09) [2011] 2
  CMLR 15 228
Lelos kai Sia EE v. GlaxoSmithKline AEVE Farmakeftikon Proionton (Case
  C-468/06 to 478/06) [2008] ECR I-7139, [2008] 5 CMLR 20 .... 209, **215**, **230**,
                                                                                                232, 292
L'Oreal v. De Nieuwe AMCK (C-31/80) [1980] ECR 3775 186
Metro-SB-Grossmärkte GmbH v. Commission (Case 26/76) [1977] ECR 1875,
  [1978] 2 CMLR 1 .... 183, **185**, 191–2
Nungesser (LC) KG and Kurt Eisele v. Commission (Case 258/78) [1982] ECR
  2015, [1983] 1 CMLR 278 .... 183, **186–9**, 240, 259, 269
Parke-Davis v. Probel (Case 24/67) [1968] ECR 55 175
*Pierre Fabre Dermo-Cosmetique SAS v. Président de l'Authorité de la
  Concurrence, Ministre de l'Économie, de l'Industrie et de l'Emploi* (Case
  C-439/09) [2011] 5 CMLR 31 .... 24, 214, 224, **226–32**, 238–9, **259–63**
Polydor Ltd et al. v. Harlequin Record Shops Ltd et al. (Case 270/80) [1982] ECR
  329 183
Pronuptia de Paris GmbH v. Pronuptia de Paris Ismgard Schillgalis (Case 161/84)
  [1986] ECR 353, [1986] 1 CMLR 414 .... 184–5, 259
Remia BV v. Commission (Case 42/84) [1985] ECR 2545; [1987] 1 CMLR 1 186
*Rewe-Zentralfinanz eG and Rewe-Zentral AG v. Landwirtchaftskammer für das
  Saarland* (Case 33/76) [1976] ECR 1989 231
SA Binon & Cie v. SA Agence et Messageries de la Presse (Case 243/83) [1985]
  ECR 2015 185–6
Sandoz prodotti faraceuttici SpA v. Commission of the European Communities
  (Case 277/87) [1990] ECR I-45 .... 32, 187
Sirena v. Eda (Case 40/70) [1971] ECR 69 175
Société La Technique Minière v. Maschinenbau Ulm GmbH (Case 56/65) [1966]
  ECR 234, [1966] CMLR 357, CMR 8047 .... 174–5, **180–82**, 186, 232–3,
                                                                                   237–42, 269–70, 289, 309
*T-Mobile Netherlands BV v. Road van bestuur van de Nederlandse
  Mededingingsautoriteit* (Case C-8/08) [2009] 5 CMLR 11 .... 209, 223,
                                                                                                238–40, 244
*Union Royal Belge des Société de Football Association ASBL & others v. Jean-Marc
  Bosman* (Case 415/93) [1995] ECR I-4921, [1996] 1 CMLR 645 194
United Brands v. Commission (Case 27/76) [1978] ECR 207, [1978] 1 CMLR
  429 307
Van Gend en Loos v Nederlandse Administratie der Belastingen (Case 26/62)
  [1963] ECR 3 .... 167, 173

General Court

Automobiles Peugeot SA, Peugeot Nederland NV v. Commission (Case T-450/05)
  [2009] ECR II-2533 214

Bayer AG v. Commission of the European Communities (Case T-41/96) [2000] ECR
II-3383 .... 171, 198, **201–5**, 215, 236, 292
CD-Contact Data GmbH v. European Commission (Case T-18/03) [2009] ECR
II-1021 .... **217–19**, 237
*Confédération européenne des associations d'horlogers-réparateurs (CEAHR) v.
European Commission* (T-427/08) [2010] ECR II-5865 209
Daimlerchrysler AG v. Commission (Case T-325/01) [2005] ECR II-3319, [2007] 4
CMLR 15 19
Dunlop Slazenger International Ltd. v. Commission (Case T-43/92) [1994] ECR
II-441 187
GlaxoSmithKline v. Commission (Case T-168/01) [2006] ECR II-2969 199,
213–14, 219–26, 237, 241–2
Groupement d'achat Édouard Leclerc v. Commission (Case T-88/92) [1996] ECR II
1961 197
Intel v. European Commission (T-286/09) [2014] ECR 0 207
Nintendo Co., Ltd and Nintendo of Europe GmbH v. Commission of the EC (Case
T-13/03) [2009] ECR II-947 217
Tréfileurope v. Commission (Case T-141/89) [1995] ECR II-791 204
Van den Bergh Foods Ltd v. Commission of the European Communities (Case T-65/
98) [2003] ECR II-4653, [2004] 4 CMLR 14 194
Volkswagen AG v. Commission (Case T-208/01) [2003] ECR II-5141 .... 32, 198,
201, **204–6**

Commission Decisions

Automobiles Peugeot SA and Peugeot Nederland NV (Cases COMP/E2/36623,
36820 and 37275) [2006] OJ L173/20 210
Bayo-n-ox (Case (IV/32.026) [1990] OJ L21/71 187
Commission Decision rejecting the complaints, Case AT.39097 (29 July 2015),
Rejection Decision published on 13 May 2015 212
Eco System/Peugeot (Case 92/154/EEC) [1992] OJ L66/1 187
Grohe (Case IV/30.299) [1985] OJ L19/17 186
Grosfillex Sàrl (Case IV/A-00061) [1964] OJ 58/915 .... **174**
Konica (Case (IV/31.503) [1988] OJ L78/34 187
Nintendo (Cases COMP/35.587 PO Video Games, COMP/35.706 PO Nintendo
Distribution and COMP/36.321 Omega – Nintendo) [2003] OJ
L255/33 .... 198, 216, 233
Novalliance/Systemform (Case IV/35.679)[1997] OJ L47/11, [1997] 4 CMLR
876 .... 197, **199–201**, 237, 239–40, 242
Repsol's motor fuel distribution practices, OJ C258/7, October 20 2004 193
SEP and others/Automobiles Peugeot (COMP/36.623, 36.820 and 37.275) decision
of 5 October 2005 210
Souris-Topps (Case No COMP C-3/37.980), OJ 2006 L353/5 .... 210, 242
Van den Bergh Foods Ltd [1998] OJ L246/1, [1998] 5 CMLR 475 194

US CASES

Supreme Court

Addyston Pipe & Steel Co. v. United States, 175 U.S. 211 (1899) ... 51, 53, 56–8, 63, 64–5, 68
Albrecht v. Herald Co., 390 U.S. 145 (1968) 44, 74, 80–85, 121, 161
American Column & Lumber Co. v. United States, 257 U.S. 377 (1921) 53
Arizona v. Maricopa County Medical Society, 457 U.S. 332 (1982) 53, 134
Atlantic Richfield Co. v. USA Petroleum Co., 495 U.S. 328 (1990) 53
Bell Atlantic Corp. v. Twombly, 550 U.S. 544 (2007) **145–51**, 152
Brooke Group Ltd. v. Brown & Williamson Tobacco Corp., 509 U.S. 209
    (1993) 152
Brown Shoes v. United States, 370 U.S. 294 (1962) 72–3, 140
Brunswick Corp. v. Pueblo Bowl-O-Mat, Inc., 429 U.S. 477 (1977) 151
Business Electronics Corp. v. Sharp Electronics Corp., 485 U.S. 717
    (1988) 2, 14, 22, 32, 43, 48, 95, 113–17, 120–21, 131, 134, 151, 153, 201, 245, 286, 317
California Dental Association v. FTC, 526 U.S. 756 (1999) 158
Chicago Board of Trade v. United States, 246 U.S. 231 (1918) 53, 57, 106, 154
Cline v. Frink Dairy Co., 274 U.S. 445 (1927) 56
Connally v. General Construction Co., 269 U.S. 385 (1926) 56
Continental T.V., Inc. v. GTE Sylvania, Inc., 433 U.S. 36 (1977) ... 14, 49, 55, 72, 75,
    93, 96, 98–111, 114, 125, 127, 131, 142, 151, 154–60, 184, 201, 222, 258, 270
Copperweld Corp. v. Independence Tube Corp., 467 U.S. 752 (1984) 12, 152
Dr Miles Medical Company v. John D. Park & Sons Company, 220 U.S. 373
    (1911) 2, 13, 37, 48, 52, 61–71, 74, 79, 80, 81, 89, 94, 96, 111–12, 124–6, 133, 135, 151, 159–60, 178, 201, 293, 303
Federal Trade Commission v. Beech-Nut Packing Co., 257 U.S. 441 (1922) 71, 73, 79–80, 153
Federal Trade Commission v. Cement Institute 333 U.S. 683 (1948) 60
Federal Trade Commission v. Sperry and Hutchinson Company 405 US 233
    (1972) 60
Flood v. Kuhn 407 U.S. 258 (1972) 133
Frey & Son, Incorporated v. Cudahy Packing Company, 256 U.S., 208 (1921) 62
Illinois Brick Co. v. Illinois, 431 U.S. 720 (1977) 133
International Salt Co. v. United States, 332 U.S. 398 (1947) 73
Kiefer-Stewart Co. v. Joseph E. Seagram & Sons, Inc., 340 U.S. 211 (1951) 74
*Leegin Creative Leather Products, Inc. v. PSKS, Inc, DBA Kay's Kloset ... Kays'
    Shoes,* 551 U.S. 877 (2007) 1–6, 19, 34, 40, 48, 50, 55, 61, 87, 113, 117–19,
    121–3, 124–36, 137–9, 139–46, 151, 154–60, 222, 242–3, 252, 254, 258, 270, 274–5, 279-80, 289–90, 302–7
Maple Flooring Mfrs Ass'n v. United States, 268 U.S. 563 (1925) 53
Monsanto Co. v. Spray-Rite Service Corp., 465 U.S. 752 (1984) 14, 95–6, 110–16, 151–2, 153–4, 201, 275
National Society of Professional Engineers v. United States, 435 U.S. 679
    (1978) 53, 263, 295

xviii   *Resale price maintenance and vertical territorial restrictions*

NCAA v. Board of Regents, 468 U.S. 85, 100, 104 S. Ct 2948, 82 LEd2d 70 (1984) 158
Reiter v. Sonotone Corp., 442 U.S. 330 (1979) 92
Simpson v. Union Oil Co. of California, 377 U.S. 13 (1964) 19, 74, 151–2
Square D Co. v. Niagara Frontier Tariff Bureau, Inc., 476 U.S. 409 (1986) 133
Standard Oil Co. v. United States, 221 U.S. 1 (1911) 53, 56–7, 61–2, 154
Standard Oil Co. of California v. United States, 337 U.S.293 (1949) 73
State Oil Co. v. Khan, 522 U.S. 2 (1997) 48–9, 117, 121, 127–8, 133, 151
Theatre Enterprises, Inc. v. Paramount Film Distributing Corp., 346 U.S. 537 (1954) 152
United States v. American Tobacco Co., 221 U.S., 106, 31 S.Ct. 632 (1911) 56–7, 62
United States v. Arnold Schwinn & Co., 388 U.S. 365 (1967) 75, 88–91, 93, 96, 101–3, 184
United States v. Bausch & Lomb Optical Co., 321 U.S. 707 (1944) 71, 73, 76–80, 85, 89, 153, 252
United States v. Colgate & Company, 250 U.S. 300 (1919) 2, 13, 30, 32, 48, 62, 68, 69–71, 73, 76–80, 81–2, 111, 124, 151, 153, 256, 293, 303–4
United States v. E.I. Du Pont de Nemours and Co., 353 U.S. 586 (1957) 61
United States v. General Electric Co., 272 U.S. 476 (1926) 19, 62, 152
United States v. Griffith, 334 U.S. 100 (1948) 73
United States v. Joint Traffic Assn., 171 U.S. 505 (1898) 52, 57
United States v. McKesson & Robbins, 351 U.S. 305 (1956) 147, 154
United States v. Paramount Pictures, 334 U.S. 131 (1948) 61
United States v. Parke, Davis & Co., 362 U.S. 29 (1959) ... 71, 73–4, 78–80, 81, 111, 153, 175, 293
United States v. Topco Associates, 405 U.S. 596 (1972) 53
United States v. Trans-Missouri Freight Association, 166 U.S. 290 (1897) 52, 53, 56–7, 66, 70, 116, 125, 303
United States v. Von's Grocery Co., 384 U.S. 270 (1966) 72
United States v. Yellow Cab Co., 332 U.S. 218 (1947) 73
White Motor Co. v. United States, 372 U.S. 253 (1963) 74–5, 84–8, 89–90, 93, 270

Court of Appeals

Abadir & Co. v. First Miss. Corp., 651 F.2d 422 (5th Cir. 1981) 97, **100**, 147, 154
Ace Beer Distributors, Inc. v. Kohn, Inc., 318 F.2d 283 (6th Cir. 1963) 98
America Oil Co. v. McMullin, 508 F.2d 1345 (10th Cir. 1975) 75
Assam Drug Co. v. Miller Brewing Co., 798 F.2d 1430 (8th Cir. 1986) 97
Beach v. Viking Sewing Machine Co., 784 F.2d 746 (16th Cir. 1986) 97
Benny Jacobs, Wanda Jacobs v Tempur-Pedic International, Inc., Tempur–Pedic North America, Inc., 626 F.3d 1327 (11th Cir. 2010) 123, **145–7**, 153–4
Blomkest Fertilizer, Inc. v Potash Corp. of Sask., Inc., 203 F.3d 1028 (8th Cir. 2000) 95
Brand Name Prescription Drugs Antitrust Litigation, In re 288 F.3d 1028 (7th Cir. 2002) 150

Brothers v. Monsanto Co., 525 F.2d 486 (8th Cir. 1975), cert. denied, 423 U.S. 1055 (1976) 75
Call Carl, Inc. v. BP Oil Corp., 554 F.2d 623 (4th Cir. 1977) 152
Cayman Exploration Corp. v. United Gas Pipe Line, 873 F.2d 1357 (10th Cir. 1989) 95
Century Oil Tool Inc. v. Production Specialities, Inc., 737 F.2d 1316 (5th Cir. 1984) 152
Chevrolet v. General Motors Corp., 803 F.2d 1463 (9th Cir. 1986), cert. denied, 480 U.S. 947 (1987) 95
Chisholm Bros. Farm Equipment Co. v. International Harvester Co., 498 F.2d 1137, 1141–1142 (9th Cir.), cert. denied, 419 U.S. 1023 (1974) 95
Coca-Cola Company, Pepsi Co. Inc. v. Federal Trade Commission, 642 F.2d 1387 (D.C. Cir. 1981) 46
Copy-Data Systems, Inc. v. Toshiba America, Inc., 755 F.2d 293, (2d Circuit 1985) 97, 100
Cowley v. Braden Indus., Inc., 613 F.2d 751 (9th Cir. 1980), cert. denied, 446 U.S. 965 (1980) 97
Crane & Shovel Sales Corp. v. Bucyrus-Erie Co., 854 F.2d 802 (6th Cir. 1988) ... **97**, 143, 155
Daniels v. All Steel Equip. Inc., 590 F.2d 111 (5th Cir. 1979) 106
Darrell Murphy v. Business Cards Tomorrow, Inc., 854 F.2d 1202 (9th Cir. 1988) 97, 103, **108–10**, 143, 154–5, 157, 184, 222
Dart Industries, Inc. v. Plunkett Co., 704 F.2d 496 (10th Cir. 1983) 97
Davis-Watkins Co. v. Service Merchandise Co., 686 F.2d 1190 (6th Cir. 1982), cert. denied, 466 U.S. 931 (1984) 97
Del Rio Distribution Inc. v. Adolph Coors Co., 589, F.2d 176 (5th Cir.), cert. denied, 444 U.S. 840 (1979) 97
Donald B. Rice Tire Co. v. Michelin Tire Corp., 638 F.2d 15 (11th Cir.), cert. denied, 454 U.S. 822 (1981) 97
Eastex Aviation v. Sperry and Hutchinson Co., 522 F.2d 1299, 1305–1306 (5th Cir. 1975) 75
Edward J Sweeney & Sons v. Texaco, Inc., 637 F2d 105 (3d Cir. 1980) 112, 153
Edwin K. Williams & Co. v. Edwin K. Williams & Co.-East, 542 F.2d 1053 (9th Cir. 1976), cert. denied, 433 U.S. 908 (1977) 75
Eiberger v. Sony Corp. of America, 622 F.2d 1068 (2d Cir. 1980) **97–8**, 103, **104–9**, 155, 158–9
Euromodas, Inc. v. Zanella, Ltd., 368 F.3d 11 (1st Cir. 2004) 22, 32, 43, **121**, 153, 286
Fibreglass Insulators, Inc. v. Dupuy, 856 F.2d 652 (4th Cir. 1988) 152
First Beverages, Inc. of Las Vegas and Will Norton v. Royal Crown Cola Co. and H&M Sales Co., 612 F. 2d 1164 (9th Cir. 1980) 46, 96–7, 225
Fray Chevrolet Sales, Inc. v. General Motors Corp., 536 F.2d 683 (6th Cir. 1976) 97–8
Gordon v. Lewistown Hospital, 423 F.3d 184 (3d Cir. 2005) 138
Gray v. Shell Oil Co., 469 F.2d 742, 747–748 & n.3 (9th Cir. 1972), cert. denied, 412 U.S. 943 (1973) 95

Guzowski v. Hartman, 969 F.2d 211, 214 (6th Cir. 1992), cert. denied, 506 U.S. 1053 (1993) 152
H & B Equip. Co. v. International Harvest Co., 577 F.2d 239 (5th Cir. 1978) 97
Hanson v. Shell Oil Co., 541 F.2d 1352, 1357 n.4 (9th Cir. 1976), cert. denied, 429 U.S. 1074 (1977) 95
Hardwick v. Nu-Way Oil Co., 589 F.2d 806, 808 (5th Cir. 1979) 152
Hershey Chocolate Corp. v. FTC, 121 F.2d 968 (3d Cir. 1941) 76
Hobart Bros. Co. v. Malcolm T. Gilliland, Inc., 471 F.2d 894 (5th Cir. 1973) 146, 154
Illinois Corp. Travel v. American Airlines, 889 F.2d (7th Cir. 1986)
Janel Sales Corp. v. Lanvin Parfums, 396 F.2d 398, 406 (2d Cir.), cert. denied, 393 U.S. 938 (1968) 75
Jayco Systems v. Savin Business Mach. Corp., 777 F.2d 306, 320 (5th Cir. 1985), cert. denied, 479 U.S. 816 (1986) 98
JBL Enters., Inc. v. Jhirmack Enters., Inc., 698 F.2d loll, 1016 (9th Cir.), cert. denied, 464 U.S. 829 (1983) 97
John D. Park & Sons Company v. Samuel B. Hartman, 153 Fed. Rep. 24 (6th Cir. 1907) 52, **62–5**, 66, 69, 178, 249, 293
McDaniel v. Greensboro News Co., 679 F.2d 883 (4th Cir. 1983) 156, 270
Mendelovitz v. Adolph Coors Co., 693 F.2d 570 (5th Cir. 1982) 96–7, 255
Mesirow v. Pepperidge Farm, 703 F.2d 339 (9th Cir.), cert. denied, 464 U.S. 820 (1983) 95, 97
Midwestern Waffles, Inc. v. Waffle House, Inc., 734 F.2d 705 (11th Cir. 1984) ... 147, 154
Morrison v. Nissan Motor Co., 601 F.2d 139 (4th Cir. 1979) 95
Muenster Butane, Inc. v. Stewart Co., 651 F.2d 292 (5th Cir. 1981) 97
Oreck Corp. v. Whirlpool Corp., 579 F.2d 126 (2d Cir. 1978) 106
Ozark Heartland Electronics Inc. v. Radio Shack, 278 F.3d 759 (8th Cir. 2002) 152
Packard Motor Car Co. v. Webster Motor Car Co., 243 F.2d 419 (D.C. Cir.) 17, 75,
Paddock v. Chicago Tribune, 103 F.3d 42 (7th Cir. 1996) 17
Polygram Holding, Inc., v. Federal Trade Commission, 416 F.3d 29 (D.C. Cir. 2005) 158
Quality Mercury, Inc. v. Ford Motor Co., 542 F.2d 466 (8th Cir. 1976) 76
Red Diamond Supply v. Liquid Carbonic Corp., 637 F.2d 1001 (5th Cir. 1981) 100, 147, 154
Redd v. Shell Oil Co., 524 F.2d 1054, 1057-1058 (10th Cir. 1975), cert. denied, 425 U.S. 912 (1976) 75
Russell Stover Candies Inc. v. FTC, 718 F.2d 256 (8th Cir. 1983) 62, 69, 303
Service Merchandise Co. v Boyd Corp., 722 F. 2d 945 (1st Cir. 1983) 97, **99–100**, 154, 285
Susser v. Carvel Corp., 332 F.2d 505 (2d Cir. 1964), cert. dismissed, 381 U.S. 125 95
T'ai Corp. v. Kalso Systemet, 568 F.2d 145 (10th Cir. 1977) 75
Toledo Mack Sales & Service, Inc. v. Mack Trucks, Inc., 530 F.3d 204 (3d Cir. 2008) 22, 32, 34, 43, **122–3**, **136–9**, **141–2**, 154–9, 285
Toys 'R' Us, Inc. V. FTC, 221 F3rd 928 (7th Cir. 2000) 33, **123–4**

United States v. Addyston Pipe & Steel Co., 85 Fed. 271 (6th Cir. 1898), affirmed
175 U.S. 211, 20 S.Ct. 96 (1899) 51
United States v. Aluminum Co. of America, 148 F.2d 416 (2d Cir. 1945) 53, 72
United States v. Brown University, 5 F.3d 658 (3d Cir. 1993) 138, 158–9
United States v. Dentsply International, Inc, 399 F.3d 181 (3d Cir. 2005), cert.
denied, 546 U.S. 1089 (2006) 32
United States v. Microsoft Corp., 253 F.3d 34 (D.C. Cir.), *cert. denied*, 534 U.S. 952
(2001) 53
Valley Liquors v. Renfield Importers, 678 F.2d 742, 745 (7th Cir. 1982) 98, 156
Yentsch v. Texaco, 630 F.2d 46, 53 (2d Cir. 1980) 95

District Courts

Babyage.Com, Inc. v. Toys 'R' US, Inc., 558 F. Supp. 2d 575, (E. D. Pa. 2008) 22,
43, 143, 155
Bell Atlantic Business Systems Services v. Hitachi Data Systems Corp., 849 F. Supp.
702 (N.D. Cal. 1994) 152
Hesco Parts, LLC v. Ford Motor Co., No. 3:02CV-736-S, 2006 WL 2734429
(W.D.Ky. September 22, 2006) 147, 154
McDonough v. Toys 'R' Us, Inc., 638 F.Supp. 2d 461 .... 124, **142–5**, 154, 158, 286
Newberry v. Washington Post. Co., 438 F. Supp. 470 (D.D.C. 1977) 270
In re Online Travel Company Hotel Booking Antitrust Litigation, 2014 WL 626555
(N.D.Tex.) 145, **147–8**, 152–3, 285
Rio Vista Oil, Ltd. v. Southland Corp., 667 F. Supp. 757 (D. Utah 1987) 152
Southeast Missouri Hospital and St. Francis Medical Center C.R. Bard, Inc., Not
Reported in F.Supp.2d, 2008 WL 4372741 (E.D.Mo.), 2009-1 Trade Cases P
76,461 32
United States v. Anchorshade, Inc., 1996-2 Trade Cas. (CCH) 71,640 (S.D.Fla.
1996) 94
United States v. Brush Fibres, Inc., 1997-2 Trade Cas. (CCH) 71,915
(E.D.Pa.1996) 94
United States v. California Sun-Care, Inc., 1994-2 Trade Cas. (CCH) 70,843 (C.D.
Cal. 1994) 94
United States v. Canstar Sports USA, Inc., 1993-2 Trade Cas., (CCH) 70,372 (D. Vt.
1993) 94
United States v. Chicago Tribune-N.Y. News Syndicate, Inc., 309 F. Supp. 1301
(S.D.N.Y. 1970) 76
United States v. Cuisinarts Inc., No. H80-49 (D. Conn. 1980) 94
United States v. Playmobil U.S.A., Inc., 1995-1 Trade Cas. (CCH) 71000
(D.D.C.1995) 94

State Cases

California v. DermaQuest, No. RG10497526 (Sup. Ct. Cal. Feb. 5, 2010) 118
New York v. Tempur-Pedic International, No. 400837/10 (Sup. Ct. Cal. Jan. 14,
2011) 118

FTC Cases/Proceedings/Actions

In re American Cyanamid Co., 123 F.T.C. 1257 (1997) 94
In re *Coca Cola Co.*, No. 8855 (F.T.C. April 25, 1978), Trade Reg.Rep. (CCH)
    Supp. No. 330 .... 96, 225
In re *the Keds Corp.*, 117 F.T.C. 389 (1994) 94
In re *Kreepy Krauly, U.S.A., Inc.*, Dkt. C-3490, 5 TRADE REG. REP. (CCH) P
    23,463 (1991) 94
In re *Kreepy Krauly USA, Inc.*, 114 F.T.C. 777 (1991) 94
In re *New Balance Athletic Shoe, Inc.*, 122 F.T.C 137 (1996) 94
In re *Nine West Group, Inc.*, File No. 981 0386, Docket No. C-3937 (2008) 119
In re *Nintendo of America, Inc.*, FTC File No. 901-0028 (April 10, 1991) 94
In re *Nintendo of America Inc.*, 114 F.T.C. 702 (1991) 94
In re *PepsiCo, Inc.*, No. 8856 (F.T.C. April, 1978) 96, 255
In re *Realcomp II Ltd.*, File No. 061-0088, Docket No. 9320 (2009) 158
In re *Reebok International, Ltd.*, 120 FTC 20 (1995) 94
In re *Toys 'R' Us*, 5 TRADE REG. REP. (CCH) P 24, 516 (1998) 123

UNITED KINGDOM CASES

Mitchel v. Reynolds, 24 E.R. 347, (1711) 1 P. Wms. 181 50
Skyscanner Ltd. v. Skoosh International Ltd., 2014 WL 4636815 147
*Universe Tankships Inc. of Monrovia v. International Transport Workers Federation
    (The Universe Sentinel)*, [1983] 1 A.C. 366, [1982] 2 W.L.R. 803, [1982]
    I.C.R. 262 203
Wickens v. Evans, 148 E.R. 1201, (1829) 3 Y. & J. 318 50

Table of legislation

EUROPEAN TREATIES AND CONVENTIONS

Charter of Fundamental Rights of the European Union [2000] OJ C364/1; currently [2012] OJ C 326/391 169–70
Single European Act [1987] OJ L169/29 183
    Art 13 168
Treaty Establishing the European Coal and Steel Community (adopted 18 April 1951, entered into force 23 July 1952) 261 UNTS 140 (The ECSC Treaty) 166–8
    Preamble 167
Treaty Establishing the European Economic Community (adopted 25 March 1957, entered into force 1 January 1958) 298 UNTS 11 (The Treaty of Rome) 163, 166, 167, 168, 171, 175, 178, 183, 309, 310
    Preamble 163
    Art 2 .... 167, 168
    Art 3 .... 167, 168
    Art 4 168
    Art 8 167
    Art 85 .... 168, 171
    Art 86 .... 168, 171
    Art 87 173
    Art 88 173
    Art 89 173
    Art 164 168
    Art 3(a) ... 194, 309 (post-Maastricht)
    Art 102(a) .... 194, 309 (post-Maastricht)
    Art 105 ... 194, 309 (post-Maastricht)
Treaty of Amsterdam amending the Treaty on European Union, the Treaties establishing the European Communities and certain related acts [1997] OJ C340/01 .... 169, 171
    Art 81 171
    Art 82 171
Treaty of Lisbon amending the Treaty on European Union and the Treaty Establishing the European Community [2007] OJ C306/1 .... 169, **207**
Treaty of Nice amending the Treaty on European Union, the Treaties establishing the European Communities and certain related acts [2001] OJ C80/1 169
Treaty on European Union (Consolidated version 2010) [2010] OJ C83/01 .... 3, 169, 170–71
    Art 3 170
Treaty on European Union (Maastricht Treaty), O.J. C 191 of 29 July 1992 .... 168, 169, 194, 309
    Article G 194, 309
Treaty on the Functioning of the European Union (consolidated) [2010] OJ C83/01 .... **169–70**, 173–81, 183–93, 198, 200–202, 204–7, 211–12, 214–33, 235–43, 259–62, 266, 270, 307, 309, 321, 324
    Art 3 (1)(b) 170, 207
    Art 3(1)(g) 207
    Art 3(2) 170
    Art 3(3) 170
    Art 4(2) 170

xxiii

Art 101 .... x, 171, 173, 175–81, 185–93, 198, 200–202, 204–7, 211–12, 214–33, 235–43, 259–62, 266, 270, 307, 321
Art 101(1) 171, 173–4, 176–7, 180–81, 185–6, 188, 191, 198, 200–202, 204–6, 214, 216, 217–22, 227–9, 232, 235–8, 240, 242–3, 259–62, 266, 307, 321
Art 101(2) 171, 176, 178, 180–81, 236, 240
Art 101(3) .... x, 171, 173, 176, 179–81, 185–6, 188–9, 191, 193, 198, 212, 214, 219, 224–9, 233, 236, 239, 240–43, 259–62, 266, 270
Art 102 .... 171, 173, 176, 183, 207, 209, 211, 215, 230–32, 322
Art 120 .... 170, 208, 309
Art 261 231
Art 263 231
Art 267 .... 226, 232

EU SECONDARY LEGISLATION

Regulations

Council Regulation (EEC) 17/62 implementing Articles 85 and 86 of the Treaty [1959] OJ Spec Ed 87 .... 168, 173
Commission Regulation (EEC) 67/67 of 22 March 1967 on the application of Article 85(3) of the Treaty to certain categories of exclusive dealing agreements [1967] OJ 57/849 175
Commission Regulation (EEC) 1983/83 of 22 June 1983 on the application of Article 85 (3) of the Treaty to categories of exclusive distribution agreements [1983] OJ L173/1 .... 175, 184
Commission Regulation (EEC) 1984/83 of 22 June 1983 applying Article 85(3) to exclusive purchasing agreements [1983] OJ L173/7 .... 175, 184
Commission Regulation (EEC) 4087/88 of 30 November 1988 on the application of Article 85 (3) of the Treaty to categories of franchise agreements [1988] O.J. L359/46 184
Commission Regulation (EC) 2790/1999 of 22 December 1999 on the application of Article 81(3) of the Treaty to categories of vertical agreements and concerted practices [1999] OJ L336/21 .... 196–7, 212, 227, 229
Commission Regulation (EC) 2658/2000 of 29 November 2000 on the application of Article 81(3) of the Treaty to categories of specialisation agreements [2000] OJ L304/3 173
Commission Regulation (EC) 2659/2000 of 29 November 2000 on the application of Article 81(3) of the Treaty to categories of research and development agreements [2000] OJ L304/7 173
Council Regulation (EC) 1/2003 of 16 December 2002 on the implementation of the rules on competition laid down in Articles 81 and 82 of the Treaty [2003] OJ L1/1 .... 170, 173, 193, 207, 210, 230–32
Council Regulation (EC) No 139/2004 of 20 January 2004 on the control of concentrations between undertakings (the EC Merger Regulation) [2004] OJ L24/1 307
Commission Regulation (EC) 772/2004 of 27 April 2004 on the application of Article 81(3) of the Treaty to categories of technology transfer agreements [2004] OJ L123/11 .... 173, 213, 270

Commission Regulation (EU)
330/2010 of 20 April 2010 on the
application of Article 101(3) of
the Treaty on the Functioning of
the European Union to categories
of vertical agreements and
concerted practices [2010] OJ
L102/1 .... 207–8, 212–23, 229,
233–4, 238, 245
Preamble 208, 212
Art 3 213
Art 4 .... 212, 229, 233,
Art 7(g) 213

Decision

Council Decision 88/591/ECSC/EEC of
24 October 1988 establishing a
Court of First Instance of the
European Communities [1988] OJ
L319/1 183

Commission Notices

Commission Notice of 18 December
1978 concerning assessment of
certain subcontracting
agreements in relation to Article
85(1) of the EEC Treaty [1979] OJ
C 1/2 236
Commission Notice (EC) 98/C9/03
Guidelines on the method of
setting fines imposed pursuant to
Article 15 (2) of Regulation No 17
and Article 65 (5) of the ECSC
Treaty [1998] C9/3 214
Commission Notice (EC) 2000/
C291/01 Guidelines on
vertical restraints [2000] OJ
C291/1 .... 197, 237
Commission Notice (EC) 2001/C3/02
Guidelines on research and
development agreements [2001]
OJ C3/2 174
Commission Notice 2004/C31/03
Guidelines on the assessment of
horizontal mergers under the
Council Regulation on the control
of concentrations between
undertakings [2004] OJ C31/
03 .... 208, 307
Commission Notice 2004/C101/02
Guidelines on the application of
Article 81 of the EC Treaty to
technology transfer agreements
[2004] OJ C101/27 270
Commission Notice (EC) 2004/
C101/08 Guidelines on the
application of Article 81(3) of the
Treaty [2004] OJ C101/97 193,
208
Commission Notice (EC) of 20 October
2004 pursuant to Article 27, [4] of
Regulation (EC) No 1/2003,
concerning Case COMP/B-1/
38348 [2004] OJ C258/7 193
Commission Notice 2008/C265/07
Guidelines on the assessment of
non-horizontal mergers under the
Council Regulation on the control
of concentrations between
undertakings [2008] OJ
C265/7 208
Commission Notice 2009/C45/02
Guidance on the Commission's
enforcement priorities in applying
Article 82 of the EC Treaty to
abusive exclusionary conduct by
dominant undertakings [2009] OJ
C45/7 .... 208–9, 307
Commission Notice (EC) 2010/
C130/01 Guidelines on Vertical
Restraints [2010] OJ C130/1 ... 16,
184, 193, 207–8, **212–13**, 229–30,
233–9, 240–42, **258–63**, 270, 281,
285
Commission Notice (EC) 2014/
C291/01 on agreements of minor
importance which do not
appreciably restrict competition
under Article 101(1) of the Treaty
on the Functioning of the
European Union (De Minimis
Notice) [2014] OJ C291/1 237,
245

UNITED STATES LEGISLATION

United States Statutes

Antitrust Criminal Penalty Enhancement and Reform Act, Pub. L. No. 108-237, 118 Stat. 661 (2004) 54
Celler-Kefauver Anti-Merger Act, Pub L. No. 81-899, 64 Stat 1125 (1950) 73
Clayton Antitrust Act (Pub. L. No. 63-212, 38 Stat. 730, enacted October 14, 1914, codified at 15 U.S.C. §§ 12–27, 29 U.S.C. §§ 52–53) 59–61, 73, 151, 307
s 2 59
s 3 59
s 4 151
s 5(a) 151
s 7 .... 59, 61, 307
s 16 151
Federal Trade Commission Act (1914, 38 Stat. 717, 15 U.S.C. §§ 41–58, as amended) 54, 60
s 5 60
Hart-Scott-Rodino Antitrust Improvements Act, Pub. L. No. 94-435, 90 Stat. 1383 (1976) 54
McGuire Act (66 Stat. 632 [1952]) 48, 61, 73, 93, 96, 130
Miller-Tydings Fair Trade Act (50 Stat. 693 [1937]) 48, 61, 73, 77, 93, 96, 130
The Robinson–Patman Anti-Price Discrimination Act of 1936, Pub. L. No. 74-692, 49 Stat. 1526 (codified at 15 U.S.C. § 13) 54, 60–61
Sherman Antitrust Act (July 2, 1890, ch. 647, 26 Stat. 209, 15 U.S.C. §§ 1–7) 48, **50–65**, 66–70, 73–5, 77–81, 83–4, 88–90, 92, 97–8, 101, 104, 106–10, 112–13, 121, 124–5, 129, 133, 137, 140, 145–9, 151–2, 154, 156–9, 161, 164, 170, 222, 245, 249, 258, 307, 310, **321–2**
s 1 .... 50, 52–4, 62–3, 69–70, 74–5, 77–81, 83, 88, 90, 97–8, 101, 104, 106–10, 121, 137, 140, 145–9, 151–7, 161, 222, 245, 258, 321–2, 324
s 2 ...... 50, 52–4, 59–61, 75, 161, 307, 322

OTHERS

UNIDROIT Principles of International Commercial Contracts 2010, <http://www.unidroit.org/english/principles/contracts/main.htm> 203

1. Introduction

> Antitrust is an interdisciplinary field that is best served by acknowledging that a deeper understanding of the issues will result by addressing the subject from several points of view.[1]
>
> (Oliver Eaton Williamson)

Resale price maintenance, vertical territorial restraints and other vertical restraints have the ability to restrict competition in a primarily vertical fashion. They involve arrangements on a vertical chain, such as bilateral agreements between a manufacturer and a retailer.[2] In contrast with horizontal collusion, vertical agreements are common and essential in a market consisting of bilateral or even multilateral arrangements. Nevertheless, such arrangements can include restrictive aspects which can lessen competition, primarily, intrabrand competition. Based on the European Union (EU) approach, some forms of resale price maintenance and vertical territorial restraints have the potential to be the most restrictive forms of vertical restraints. Resale price maintenance (RPM) includes the practice of a seller and her buyers 'agreeing' that the latter will sell her product at, above or below a set price. Vertical territorial restraints (VTR), or vertical market allocation, include territorial arrangements between a seller and her buyers where the buyers are allowed to sell only within certain territories. Throughout this book, I use the abbreviations of RPM for vertical minimum price and vertical price fixing and VTR for absolute territorial restrictions and exclusive territories (thus focusing on the most serious forms of vertical territorial restraints and resale price maintenance) unless expressly stated otherwise.

---

[1] Oliver E Williamson, *Antitrust Economics: Mergers, Contracting, and Strategic Behaviour* (Basil Blackwell, New York, 1987) 158.

[2] In this book, I often use the terms 'supplier' and 'buyer' when describing RPM and VTR and their vertical nature, as well as terms commonly found in the US cases, such as 'manufacturer' and 'retailers', where 'manufacturer' is used in a broader sense in this book including not only manufacturers but also producers of raw materials, farmers and others.

1

Despite the fact that vertical restraints form part of potential anticompetitive practices in many competition/antitrust law regimes, including the EU regime and the regime of the United States of America (US), opinions on their potential anticompetitive effects differ. Indeed, RPM and VTR are controversial topics and their approaches differ in the EU and US.

In the US, the approach to RPM has come under criticism since the introduction of the US per se rule in 1911.[3] This approach was gradually modified[4] and in 2007 completely changed, with only a close majority in the case of *Leegin*.[5] *Leegin* introduced the rule of reason to RPM, which opened a new and intensive debate on RPM not just in the US, but across the globe, including the EU,[6] where the hard-core-restriction approach is present at the EU and partly the Member-State levels. This discussion reached its peak in 2010 with scholars agreeing that there was a lack of research in this area of competition/antitrust law calling for new comprehensive and empirical studies and, with regards to the new US approach based on the rule of reason, calling for clarity and change, most notably urging the courts to provide more detailed instructions and modify the rule of reason.[7] Despite this emphasis on change and clarification, scholars do not agree on an exact solution.

---

[3] *Dr. Miles Medical Co. v. John D. Park & Sons Co.*, 220 U.S. 373 (1911).

[4] See, e.g., *United States v. Colgate & Co.*, 250 U.S. 300 (1919); *Business Electronics Corp. v. Sharp Electronics Corp.*, 485 U.S. 717 (1988).

[5] *Leegin Creative Leather Products, Inc. v. PSKS, Inc, DBA Kay's Kloset … Kays' Shoes*, 551 U.S. 877 (2007).

[6] See, e.g., Craig Callery, 'Should the European Union Embrace or Exorcise Leegin's "Rule of Reason"?' (2011) 32(1) *European Competition Law Review* 43; Alison Jones, 'Resale Price Maintenance: A Debate about Competition Policy in Europe?' (2009) 5(2) *European Competition Journal* 479.

[7] See, e.g., Theodore Voorhees, 'Reasoning Through the Rule of Reason for RPM' (Fall 2013) 28.1 *Antitrust*, 58; Richard M Brunell, 'United States: Dr. Miles' Last House Call' in Barry Rodger, *Landmark Cases in Competition Law: Around the World in Fourteen Stories* (Wolters Kluwer, 2012), 366–7; Francine Lafontaine and Margaret E Slade, 'Transaction Cost Economies and Vertical Market Restrictions – Evidence' (2010) 55 *Antitrust Bulletin* 608; Barak Y Orbach, 'The Image Theory: RPM and the Allure of High Prices' (2010) 55 *Antitrust Bulletin* 277; Pamela J Harbour and Laurel A Price, 'RPM and the Rule of Reason: Ready or Not, Here We Come?' (2010) 55 *Antitrust Bulletin* 227; Pauline M Ippolito, 'RPM Myths that Muddy the Discussion' (2010) 55 *Antitrust Bulletin* 151–65; William S Comanor, 'Antitrust Policy Toward Resale Price Maintenance Following *Leegin*' (2010) 55 *Antitrust Bulletin* 78; Andrew Gavil, 'Resale Price Maintenance in the Post-*Leegin* World: A Comparative Look at Recent Developments in the United States and European Union' (2010) 1 *The*

Furthermore, the dissention to the approach to RPM is also present among legislators within the US, with a number of US states applying the per se rule rather than the new rule of reason at the state level. Nevertheless, since *Leegin*, no significant change has been made to the US federal approach. I consider this situation to be alarming. The last few years show very little, if any, interest by US antitrust authorities in dealing with RPM and a lack of success in proving a violation of US antitrust law in private RPM cases. This indicates that at the federal level, the rule of reason could lead to the same situation as in the case of VTR: ignoring such behavior in practice and de facto legalizing resale price maintenance.

In the case of VTR, its development shows the US approach to be very benevolent and different from the EU approach, which is stricter, particularly when such territorial restriction is absolute. The obvious explanation for this difference lies in the protection of free and internal markets being the main objective of the EU. However, another more key explanation, although not as obvious, is an inconsistency and lack of extensive knowledge of the issue. Therefore, if there is a lack of comprehensive research in the field of VTR, the question arises as to how US antitrust policy can come to the final conclusion that VTR is not, or almost always not, anticompetitive? Or, in contrast, how can the EU state that such forms of vertical restraints are rather anticompetitive and almost as anticompetitive as RPM? Similarly, the question remains open as to whether the change in the US approach to RPM leads to the optimal approach.

These questions provide the principal reason for a comparable and simultaneous analysis of the two forms of vertical restraints, RPM and VTR, in two regimes, the US and the EU. Both regimes have a lengthy experience and are recognized worldwide as being well established. However, the EU regime establishes that vertical price fixing, minimum price fixing and some forms of vertical territorial restraints, such as restriction of passive sale, are 'hard-core' restraints and, thus, have a high potential for being anticompetitive. On the contrary, the US federal

---

CPI Antitrust Journal 1; Robert Steiner, 'Vertical Competition, Horizontal Competition and Market Power' (2008) 53 *Antitrust Bulletin* 252; Michael P Lynch, 'Why Economists Are Wrong to Neglect Retailing and How Steiner's Theory Provides an Explanation of Important Regularities' (2004) 49 *Antitrust Bulletin* 911–40; Pamela J Harbour, 'An Enforcement Perspective on the Work of Robert L. Steiner: Why Retailing and Vertical Relationships Matter' (2004) Winter *Antitrust Bulletin* 997; William S Comanor, 'The Two Economics of Vertical Restraints' (1992) 21 *Southwestern University Law Review* 1277.

approach assumes that RPM and VTR are rather procompetitive, in particular when introduced by the supplier. Moreover, the US approach to RPM changed only recently and without indisputable support. Thus, this approach is lacking in a mutual agreement that there is sufficient grounding for introducing the rule of reason in the form that it has been introduced and applied.

The differences in approaches and scholarly arguments together with the call for comprehensive research provide the basis behind writing this book. Thus, this book is centered on determining the optimal approach to RPM and VTR, which requires a holistic rather than one-issue focused view. Williamson's quote at the start of this chapter reflects well the way this topic is addressed in this book and its content, with the focus being on studying the effects of RPM and VTR on competition and analyzing the existing approaches and their developments.

There are a number of ways to analyze the effects of RPM and VTR. In this book, I discuss the effects as they arise from EU and US cases, the nature of RPM and VTR based primarily on economic and marketing studies and economic theories and theoretical accounts and questions. The questions which accompany the above-discussed issues and which form the principal questions of this book are:

1. The overall, general question is whether and to what extent RPM and VTR restrict competition. This question involves a number of sub-questions, most notably:
   a. What is the nature of VTR and RPM?
   b. What do the theories and practices reveal with regards to the competitiveness and anticompetitiveness of RPM and VTR?
   c. Who and for what reasons introduces RPM and VTR?
2. What are the current US and EU approaches and how have they developed?
3. What approach and/or which policy model should apply to VTR and RPM, particularly in relation to the objective of competition/antitrust law and the nature of RPM and VTR?

The nature of these questions requires a holistic analysis of RPM and VTR in order to provide an overall and detailed understanding. This can be achieved by using legal, historical, economical, theoretical, empirical and other points of view. In that regard, every chapter plays an essential role and forms a part of a jigsaw leading to the book's overall argument and finding, and revealing specific issues arising from different analytical methods and views utilized in different chapters. The argument made in this book is that tolerating RPM and VTR is not the right direction for effective competition/antitrust policies and law. Such a situation is simply a failure to tackle their consequences and to protect competition.

An introductory chapter, Chapter 2, sets vertical restraints, in particular RPM and VTR, within distributive systems explaining how RPM and VTR operate and how they can influence competition. In that context, I discuss the meaning of competition and argue that competition with regards to RPM and VTR must reflect the nature of their vertical and distribution settings. In this introductory section, I divide the approaches to competition in connection with RPM and VTR between two policy models to assist with determining the optimal approach. The first policy model is based on horizontal and interbrand competition, while the second model takes into consideration both horizontal and vertical relationships protecting all forms of competition, including intrabrand competition, and recognizing that even vertically related entities compete in order to obtain better profit and that these competitive tensions are based on bargaining rather than horizontal market power. Indeed, the second model goes as far as protecting vertical competition.

Chapters 3 and 4 contain analysis of the existing two policy and legal approaches, the US and EU, and their development. The current approaches are not only described but are studied from a broader context accompanied by analysis and summaries of important cases and also cases which illustrate arguments and developments of specific eras and potential counterarguments. Both chapters reveal two common issues of the EU and US approaches to RPM and VTR agreements: the proving of (1) an agreement,[8] in particular, in a situation where RPM or VTR is forced by one party, and (2) the restriction of competition. Furthermore, the discussion on the US approach shows that the economic approach based on the rule of reason used for both VTR and RPM is rather overcomplicated leading to the de facto legalization of both forms of vertical restraints.

In Chapter 5, I discuss existing anticompetitive and procompetitive theories and economic effects and provide further explanations for the reasons for using RPM or VTR in practice. I analyse them in connection with the empirical studies and findings from previous chapters. I argue that not all so-called 'procompetitive theories' establish genuine procompetitive explanations for using RPM or VTR and that the traditional anticompetitive theories are based on form (arising from the substance of the first policy model) rather than the analysis of economic effects of RPM and VTR. The essential question of how often the procompetitive

---

[8] Each regime involves different terminology. See, Chapters 3 and 4.

theories apply in practice was raised in the case of *Leegin* and is, in general, addressed in Chapter 5. In particular, the existing empirical studies and cases show that procompetitive theories are not as common as estimated by the Chicago School.[9]

Finally, in Chapter 6, I provide a different view for law and policy on the analysis of RPM and VTR. I argue that the procompetitive economic theories and the current US approach are outcome-based, which involve a number of issues and unanswered questions and do not fully reflect the objective of competition/antitrust law. A different, process-focused approach, which has its roots in a deontological account, can assist with addressing these issues and answering these questions. It is also better suited for the objective of competition/antitrust law, which is centered around the protection of the competitive process including the protection of free and fair competition. The process-focused approach supports the second policy model. Nevertheless, it also provides a limited scope for the procompetitive justifications utilized in the outcome approach.

By the end of reading this book, the reader should have a comprehensive understanding of this topic.[10] Although the book is a research monograph that focuses on a detailed understanding of RPM and VTR, as well as their optimal approach and the issues arising from the current legal and economical approaches, practitioners dealing with VTR or RPM cases could find a number of chapters helpful, in particular, Chapters 3, 4 and 5. Indeed, I have tried to balance the academic research with a practical approach offering not only theories in this field but also explanations of how the law developed and is currently applied, including summaries and analyses of cases and the arguments that can be used regarding procompetitive or anticompetitive explanations for RPM and VTR.

---

[9] The book is not based on an empirical study; it only refers to studies which are available. Therefore, I do not provide an exact frequency of utilizing particular procompetitive theories, but I address this question from the point of analysis of previous chapters, the available data and counterarguments to theories.

[10] However, it is impossible to include every idea and every case. For instance, in Chapter 4, I focus on Brussels policy without comparing the approaches of individual Member States.

2. Distribution and competition

I. INTRODUCTION

Vertical restrictions, unlike horizontal restrictions, take place at the vertical level. They can be introduced in a distribution system if the entities cooperating on the vertical chain are independent and not vertically integrated. Whether and to what extent vertical restraints, in particular RPM and VTR, restrict competition are some of the principal questions of this book. In this chapter, I set this topic in a broader context to assist with answering the questions from a more holistic point of view rather than through the analysis of a situation or a case, which I discuss in the following chapters. Before looking into specific cases, I provide my understanding of how distribution, competition and markets operate in connection with vertical restrictions.

We will see in Chapters 3 and 4 that the EU and US regimes differentiate between intrabrand competition and interbrand competition where interbrand competition plays a primary role. However, in this chapter, I put forward a few arguments explaining that not only interbrand competition but other forms of competition should be considered by antitrust/competition policy in order to effectively determine whether RPM or VTR restricts competition. Indeed, later in this book I offer explanations and recommendations for the approach to vertical restrictions based on two policy models. The first model is conventional as it follows the Chicago School, and assumes that only horizontal competition should be protected by antitrust/competition law and policy. The second model is progressive as it proceeds on the assumption that horizontal competition is not the only form of competition essential for the evaluation of vertical restrictions, as vertical restrictions need to reflect not only horizontal market structure but also vertical market structure and its vertical interaction and vertical relationships.

Therefore, the purpose of this chapter is to set a broader scene for RPM and VTR by outlining the important elements of vertical interactions and addressing knowledge from economics and other disciplines.

I do not comprehensively discuss everything;[1] instead, this chapter surveys a number of the relevant elements in order to explain the nature of vertical restrictions and to a provide basis for the specific analysis of the effects of RPM and VTR contained in Chapter 6. In particular, in the first part of this chapter I discuss the conditions predetermining the potential for introducing vertical restrictions, including the operation of distribution, and I outline briefly the reasons for introducing RPM and VTR.[2] In the second part, I explain the meaning of competition and its driving force in vertical restrictions: bargaining power. Finally, I outline a number of situations where RPM or VTR could have horizontal, harmful effects in order to satisfy the anticompetitive effect required by the first economic-policy model.

II. DISTRIBUTION AND VERTICAL INTEGRATION

Every economic entity, for example a manufacturer, has a choice between being vertically integrated or being specialized in only one activity, such as production. The inclination towards integration or concentration in one activity has been changing over the past decades and centuries. In the Middle Ages, individual manufacturers used to be vertically integrated (within geographically isolated markets): a shoemaker would make shoes, distribute them and sell them to customers. He would also repair shoes. Nowadays, shoe manufacturers focus on the production of shoes and then sell them to distributors who sell them to the final retailers.[3] However, even in the Middle Ages the market would not be absolutely concentrated. The shoemaker would buy leather and other raw materials and tools to make shoes. This means that if vertical integration exists in the market, it is almost never absolute in the broad sense simply because it was not and is not efficient.

But how do manufacturers decide whether to be vertically integrated or whether to specialize in production? Transaction costs and economies of scale offer one possible explanation as to why some markets and/or manufacturers are vertically integrated and others are not. Whether the entity decides to be integrated or specialized depends on cost and profitability; in other words, which alternative is less costly and more

---

[1] Being a lawyer not an economist, I would not even aim to do so.
[2] The reasons are further discussed in the following chapters and analyzed in connection with procompetitive and anticompetitive theories in Chapter 5.
[3] See, e.g., Herbert Hovenkamp, 'The Law of Vertical Integration and the Business Firm: 1880–1960' (2010) 95 *Iowa Law Review* 863, 865–70.

profitable. In his article from 1937, Coase explains this decision-making process by referring to transaction costs,[4] explaining that '[i]t is clear that an alternative form of economic organisation which could achieve the same result at less cost than would be incurred by using the market would enable the value of production to be raised'.[5]

Any business decision and any part of the business process, including bargaining with non-integrated entities or taking responsibility for an integrated part of an entity, has its own transaction costs. Even law and regulations, including competition law and policy, are considered when entities make decisions as to whether they will be vertically integrated. The consideration of these costs then determines the structures of the firms.[6] However, this consideration is not usually faultless. Although firms want to be as efficient as possible to maximize profits, they do not always succeed in doing so simply because strategic decision-making is not perfect. According to Williamson, strategic decision-making based on transaction costs includes bounded rationality and opportunism. Bounded rationality means that firms are not absolutely capable of making the most efficient decisions because there are simply too many aspects and too much information that they must consider. Therefore, their knowledge and obtained information are limited. Opportunism means that it is wrong to presume that firms always tell the truth; if they recognize an opportunity they will do whatever they can not to miss it.[7] Therefore, the information available is not always factual.

Based on a non-perfect consideration of transaction costs and economies of scale, firms consider whether to be vertically integrated or not. If they decide to concentrate on one activity such as production, they would need other entities to distribute their products, such as distributors and retailers. The relationship between these entities would be shaped in a contract and other arrangements, which could include a form of vertical

---

[4] Ronald H Coase, 'The Nature of the Firm' (1937) 4 *Economica* 386.

[5] Ronald H Coase, 'The Problem of Social Cost' (October 1960) III *The Journal of Law & Economics* 1, 16.

[6] Note 4, Coase; Note 5, Coase, 15–28; see also Herbert Hovenkamp, 'Harvard, Chicago, and Transaction Cost Economics in Antitrust Analysis' (2010) 55 *Antitrust Bulletin* 613, 624–5, 628–30.

[7] Oliver E Williamson, *Antitrust Economics: Mergers, Contracting, and Strategic Behaviour* (New York, Basil Blackwell 1987) 126–7; see also, Warren S Grimes, 'A Dynamic Analysis of Resale Price Maintenance: Inefficient Brand Promotion, Higher Margins, Distorted Choices, and Retarded Retailer Innovation' (2010) 55 *Antitrust Bulletin* 101, 101–49; Herbert A Simon, 'Theories of Bounded Rationality' in CB McGuire and Roy Radner (eds), *Decisions and Organizations* (Amsterdam: North-Holland Publishing Company 1972).

restriction, such as RPM or VTR. The firms would introduce vertical restrictions only if they assume it would be more profitable and thus less costly for them to do so. Therefore, on one hand, vertical restrictions restrict competition;[8] on the other hand, they can save costs and lead to profits for their participants.[9]

However, even if the particular vertical restriction increases the profitability of both independent parties involved, such profitability of integrated or non-integrated firms is based on a restriction of competition and, thus, does not necessarily lead to increased social welfare. Cartels are profitable for their participants but there is no disputing the fact that pure cartel behavior leads to lower social welfare in the form of increased prices and decreased innovation. It is true that the impact of cartels and vertical restrictions is generally different as vertical restraints primarily hinder intrabrand competition and not interbrand competition.[10] However, RPM and VTR can also lead to a restriction of interbrand competition, as explained later in this book. Therefore, a case-by-case evaluation is ideal, although not necessarily optimal, for clear and transparent legal rules and enforcement, to determine whether any potential benefits arising from RPM or VTR lead to increased social welfare and outweigh any negative impacts on competition.[11]

Some neoclassical economists (and lawyers) go even further when advocating the benefits for the participants of vertical restrictions in the form of saved costs and increased profits, arguing that RPM and VTR are not anticompetitive, but they can be used as substitute tools for the

---

[8] Whether they restrict competition and to what extent is explained below and further discussed in the following chapters.

[9] Other organizational-economics theories, which explain the existence of vertical restrictions, are the agency theory and property rights theory. The agency theory considers some vertical restrictions, such as RPM and VTR, as contractual arrangements which lower risk jointly with selling certain products; for instance, in situations when a new product is entering a market. See, e.g., G Frank Mathewson and Ralph A Winter, 'An Economic Theory of Vertical Restraints' (1984) 15(1) *RAND Journal of Economics* 27. The property rights theory argues that vertical restrictions, such as RPM, assign rights to consumer information to retailers (in a retailer–manufacturer relationship) for their promotional services. This consumer information includes incentives to determine optimal promotional strategies and to stop free riding. See, e.g., Alan J Meese, 'Property Rights and Intrabrand Restraints' (2003) 89 *Cornell Law Review* 553.

[10] The terms 'intrabrand' and 'interbrand competition' are terms which became part of cases and competition law/antitrust law policy in the US and EU. They are not traditional economic terms.

[11] See the following chapters.

benefits arising from vertical integration.[12] RPM and VTR can substitute the management decisions of a similar nature of an integrated firm. If it is less costly and more profitable for a firm to be specialized in one activity on the vertical chain and utilize RPM or VTR rather than being vertically integrated, RPM or VTR will compensate for the economic benefits arising from vertical integration. This comes in the form of a saved cost from being free to decide and manage her own business as a vertically integrated firm, while saving costs from being a specialized firm in a situation where it is more efficient not to be vertically integrated. Easterbrook described this in 1984 as a form of cooperation similar to one in an integrated firm. He says:

> [r]estricted dealing is a form of cooperation. One firm (the retailer) agrees to do things the way a manufacturer specifies, just as an employee does things within an integrated firm ... Such contracts are the market at work.[13]

There are two problem areas regarding this statement: economics and policy-/law-making. The core of the economic problem is in the goals of firms. The goal of a vertically integrated firm differs from one that is independent from the manufacturer. A vertically integrated firm's goal could serve the purpose of its parent firm, for example a parent firm specializing in production, by maximizing the efficiency, production and profit of the parent firm. Frank explained in his article from 1925 that vertical integration is 'the functional coordination of one or more units in each of the several successive stages of production, so that they are all operated as a single, unified industrial process'.[14] Therefore, the goal is also unified and integrated.

On the contrary, the goal of an independent entity is not to serve the purpose of another firm but to maximize its own profit. It is usually in the interests of the firm with bargaining power to introduce RPM or VTR

---

[12] See, e.g., Shubha Ghosh 'Vertical Restraints, Competition and the Rule of Reason' in K Hylton, *Antitrust Law and Economics* (2010, Edward Elgar Publishing), 221–3; Thibaud Vergé, 'Minimum Resale Price Maintenance and Concentrated Markets' (2008) 54(3) *Applied Economics Quarterly* 161, 172 (footnote no. 21); Victor P Goldberg, 'Featuring the Three Tenors in La Traviata' (2005) 1(1) *Review of Law and Economics*, 55; Frank H Easterbrook, 'Vertical Arrangements and the Rule of Reason' (1984) 53 *Antitrust Law Journal* 135, 140; Robert Bork, 'The Rule of Reason and Per Se Concept: Price Fixing and Market Division' (1966) 75 *Yale Law Journal* 373, 404.

[13] Easterbrook, ibid., 140.

[14] Lawrence K Frank, 'The Significance of Industrial Integration' (1925) 33 *Journal of Political Economy* 179.

and hence such a restriction serves the profitability of this firm but not necessarily both.[15] It is common that one entity is better off and the other is worse off once RPM or VTR is introduced, although this is not always the case.

The policy-making argument is related to the economic welfare and the aim of antitrust/competition law and policy. Policy makers must ask themselves what the aim of the competition/antitrust policy and law should be. The policy is usually focused on the protection of competition and on maximizing consumer or total welfare. If vertical restrictions restrict competition and decrease total or consumer welfare, no matter whether they increase the profits of the participants, they should be prohibited (unless there is a reason as to why they should not). As we explore later in this chapter, the meaning of competition differs; however, it is important to determine whether the term 'competition' also includes intrabrand or vertical competition. If it does, then by protecting intrabrand competition, vertical restrictions would be prohibited if they do not provide competitive incentives (such as increased services, as further discussed in Chapter 5).

Furthermore, from a positivistic point of view, we can see that neither EU competition law nor US antitrust law are concerned with the management within one (integrated) firm and their own setting of prices or geographic areas of sale, but they cover both vertical and horizontal restrictions between independent entities.[16] Therefore, from a competition/antitrust point of view, restricted dealings between the employees of one integrated firm are not the same as restricted dealings between independent vertical entities.

Distribution in General

The example of the shoemaker from the beginning of this chapter illustrated that the usage of vertical integration versus non-integrated distribution has changed rapidly. However, the matter is more complicated than this. It is not only a question of integration, but also of market structure and the way that distribution and all related business, economic and marketing elements interact and have been constantly evolving. These changes are reflected in the theories and research. The most recent changes are due to developments in information technology

---

[15] See below and the following chapters.
[16] See, e.g., EU: C-41/90 *Höfner and Elser v. Macrotron GmbH* [1991] ECR I-1979, [1993] 4 CMLR 306; US: *Copperweld Corp. v. Independence Tube Corp.*, 467 U.S. 752 (1984).

and the creation of new distribution systems that have resulted in ongoing greater concentration and integration, and the decline of traditional distribution channels: manufacturers–wholesalers–retailers.[17] Gundlach divides changes in distribution in the US since the emergence of the neoclassical school into four periods:[18]

Channel distribution
One of the first studies of distribution, the channel distribution, emerged in the 1950s. The theoretical part was influenced by neoclassical economics, which studied distribution as a vertical chain of independent firms, including manufacturers, distributors or wholesalers and retailers, usually dominated by manufacturers.[19] This distribution was governed by contracts and transaction costs without including a relational perspective.

Distribution systems of interdependent firms
In the 1970s, the perspective changed towards the recognition of an overlap of functions performed by manufacturers, wholesalers and retailers. Distribution was viewed more as a system of interdependent firms. Such a system reduces some inefficencies to create a more streamlined, organized system. The manufacturer was still the dominant performer on the vertical chain; however, aside from contracts, she also used other

---

[17] Gregory T Gundlach, Joseph P Cannon and Kenneth C Manning, 'Free Riding and Resale Price Maintenance: Insights from Marketing Research and Practice' (2010) 55 *Antitrust Bulletin* 381, 391–401, 403–10, 412–13; European Commission, 'Green Paper on Vertical Restraints in EC Competition Policy', (Cm 721, 1996) points 20, 40, 41, 44.

[18] Gregory T Gundlach, Yemisi A Bolumole, Reham A Eltantawy and Robert Frankel, 'The changing landscape of supply chain management, marketing channels of distribution, logistics and purchasing' American Antitrust Institute, 2014 Annual Conference: The Inefficiencies of Efficiency (19 June 2014) available at <http://www.antitrustinstitute.org/2014annualconference> accessed 18 May 2015.

[19] The initiation of vertical restrictions by manufacturers (monopolists) is already obvious in the first US cases including *Dr. Miles Medical Firm v. John D. Park & Sons Firm*, 220 U.S. 373 (1911) ('*Dr. Miles*') and *United States v. Colgate & Co.*, 250 U.S. 300 (1919) ('*Colgate*'). Therefore, the practice of channel distribution can be dated from before the 1950s. Furthermore, the first theories of transaction costs, which later influenced the distribution channels, were introduced before the 1950s. See, Note 4, Coase.

forms of vertical integration mechanisms to control the roles of wholesalers and retailers.[20]

Supply chains: dynamically organized distribution

In the 1980s, intensified competition at the manufacturer level arising from globalization and slow growth caused the expansion of the distribution system to include supply as a function. To manage the intensified competition, manufacturers used trade promotions and introduced many new products. At the same time, resellers and retailers focused on a better understanding of their customers, using high technology within the supply chain, and started to dynamically organize their distribution. Such distribution resulted from the creation of a relationship with customers at the retail level by using promotions to appeal to customers and capture them in an ongoing purchase relationship with the retailer. This led to the creation of power at the retail level.

Distribution networks

Most notably in the 2000s, the systems of distribution have become even more complex with relationships involving many firms at the horizontal level interacting with many firms at the vertical level forming distribution networks or distribution ecosystems, which include outsourcing and single sourcing. These are managed interactively and bilaterally across the levels of the distribution systems as well as on the same level. They are governed by sources that go beyond contracting, including standards and norms of the industry and, therefore, can no longer be called 'chains'. This complexity increases the risk of opportunism and bounded rationality, which could be projected in decisions on vertical restrictions.

Competition occurs between systems and within distribution networks. In the US, distribution networks have been formed, for instance, in the

---

[20] It has been proclaimed that vertical restrictions in vertically non-integrated distribution systems subsidized benefits arising from vertical integration. See, e.g., Note 12, Easterbrook, 'Vertical Arrangements', 140. In VTR, this period was reflected in the case of *Continental T.V. v. GTE-Sylvania*, 433 U.S. 36 (1977) and later, in the 1980s, in the cases on RPM: *Monsanto Co. v. Spray-Rite Service Corp.*, 465 U.S. 752 (1984); *Business Electronics Corp. v. Sharp Electronics Corp.*, 485 U.S. 717 (1988) ('*Business Electronics*'). In RPM, procompetitive theories emerged in the early twentieth century and were further developed in the second half of the twentieth century. See, e.g., Thomas H Silcock, 'Some Problems of Price Maintenance' (1938) 48 *Economic Journal* 42; Lester G Telser, 'Why Should Manufacturers Want Fair Trade?' (1960) 6 *Journal of Law & Economics* 86.

grocery and agricultural industries, as well as the healthcare industry.[21] However, this does not mean that distribution networks exist in all industries and that small distribution systems have disappeared completely.

With these changes in distribution new forms of competition have also arisen, such as online shopping and new technologies, which have brought about changes in consumer shopping habits. Large retail stores have developed and have played an important role in the changes by increasing their bargaining power and becoming concentrated and vertically integrated. This is most notable in the grocery industry.[22]

Forms of Distribution Via Independent Distributors

Distribution systems, whether channels or networks, are primarily contractual, relationship-based systems. There is a mutual benefit and need between the supplier and her buyer to cooperate and get the product or service to the final consumer. Suppliers need buyers and buyers need suppliers, unless a supplier or buyer is vertically integrated. If the supplier (or buyer) is vertically integrated then she will not need her distribution partner or, if she does, she will likely be advantaged in negotiations and dealings with her buyers due to increased bargaining power.

Distribution relationships within a particular and complex distribution network or a smaller system, or occasionally on its own, can take a number of different forms, from free/competitive distribution to exclusive, one-on-one distribution. Generally, individual distribution relationships between a particular supplier and her buyer can be divided into open (non-restricted) distribution, which means that a supplier chooses to distribute via as many outlets as possible; or restricted distribution such

---

[21] See, e.g., Diana L Moss and C Robert Taylor, 'Short end of the stick: The plight of growers and consumers in concentrated agricultural supply chains' American Antitrust Institute, 2014 Annual Conference: The Inefficiencies of Efficiency (19 June 2014) available at <http://www.antitrustinstitute.org/2014annualconference> accessed 18 May 2015; Ravi S Achrol and Philip Kotler, 'Marketing in the Network Economy' (1999) 63 *Journal of Marketing* 146.

[22] See, e.g., Pierre Kobel, Pranvera Këllezi and Bruce Kilpatrick (eds), *Antitrust in the Groceries Sector & Liability Issues in Relation to Corporate Social Responsibility* (Springer 2015); Barbora Jedličková, 'Vertical Issues Arising from Conduct between Large Supermarkets and Small Suppliers in the Grocery Market: Law and Industry Codes of Conduct' (2015) 36(1) *European Competition Law Review* 19.

as exclusive distribution, franchising and selective distribution. However, there are different variations of these forms.

Selective distribution occurs when the supplier, usually a manufacturer, chooses her buyers on the basis of set criteria. In a franchising system, a franchisee exploits the know-how and intellectual property rights of the franchiser and sells in a standardized format in an allocated territory. Exclusive distribution can be divided into exclusive selling and buying. In exclusive selling (also referred to as an exclusive supply agreement or exclusive dealership), a manufacturer sells to only one distributor usually in a particular territory, while in the exclusive buying distribution (also referred to as exclusive dealing or single-branding), the distributor takes supplies only from one manufacturer. Exclusive buying is typified by the beer and petrol markets.[23]

If a particular distribution system is not open it includes some form of restriction. Besides these three restrictive forms of distribution (exclusive distribution, franchising and selective distribution), there exist other restrictive arrangements. These restrictive arrangements, including restrictive distribution forms, can be divided into two categories: those aimed at restricting interbrand competition and those aimed at primarily restricting intrabrand competition. The EU and US antitrust/competition-law regimes differ in their terminology and approach to these forms. The US recognizes two forms of vertical restrictions that foreclose interbrand competition: tying and exclusive dealing.[24] The European Commission differentiates four forms of vertical restraints restricting interbrand competition: exclusive sourcing,[25] single-branding[26] (and also category management agreements),[27] tying[28] and franchising.[29] Exclusive dealing and single-branding are synonyms. Both require directly or indirectly that the supplier's buyers do not purchase goods (or services in the EU)[30] from a supplier's competitors and, thus, the buyers are exclusive distributors for the supplier, purchasing and reselling only the supplier's brand. Exclusive

---

[23] The EU – Note 17, European Commission, point 4.

[24] E Thomas Sullivan, Herbert Hovenkamp and others, *Antitrust Law, Policy and Procedure: Cases, Materials, Problems* (7th edn, LexisNexis 2014).

[25] Commission Notice on Guidelines on vertical restraints [2010] OJ C 130/1, [162].

[26] Ibid., [129].

[27] Ibid., [209]–[213].

[28] Ibid., [214]–[222].

[29] Ibid., [189]–[191]; Alison Jones and Brenda Sufrin, *EU Competition Law: Text, Cases, and Materials* (5th edn, Oxford University Press 2014), 771–2.

[30] Or such arrangements limit buyers from purchasing other than the supplier's goods or services.

sourcing is not as restrictive as single-branding because it allows buyers to purchase goods or services from competing suppliers.

Vertical restrictions that primarily restrict intrabrand competition are resale price maintenance, territorial restrictions, including exclusive distribution as one form of an exclusive supply agreement (exclusive dealership), and customer allocations.[31] The European Commission also refers to selective distribution and upfront access payments.[32] Exclusive supply agreement is a term used in the EU, while the US refers to the same practice as exclusive dealership. This refers to situations where the supplier is restricted in that she can only supply to one buyer and not to the buyer's competitors. Usually this is limited to a certain territory and, if it is, the EU would call it exclusive distribution.[33]

Recent Development: Hybrid Distribution Forms

Aside from the types of distribution of non-integrated and vertically integrated firms, there are hybrid distribution forms or systems where a firm or firms are partially vertically integrated. If a firm decides to be partially integrated, it can utilize some forms of vertically combined systems, such as dual distribution systems or 'private labels' – a system which is not de facto partial vertical integration but appears to be because private labels have the trademark of the retailer but are produced by independent manufacturers.[34] If the firm is partially integrated, she combines her specialization with another stage at the vertical level.

In the decision-making process, when a firm is considering whether to be vertically integrated or specialized, the firm decides to be partially integrated if it is more efficient, profitable and less costly for her to do

---

[31] In the US, it is only resale price maintenance, territorial restrictions, customer allocations and exclusive dealership. See, Note 24, Sullivan, et al.

[32] For EU, see, Note 29, Jones and Sufrin, 771; Guidelines on vertical restraints, [2010] O.J. C130/01, [129]–[229].

[33] For US cases on exclusive dealership within certain areas, see, e.g., *Paddock v. Chicago Tribune*, 103 F.3d 42 (7th Cir. 1996); *Packard Motor Car Co. v. Webster Motor Car Co.*, 243 F.2d 419 (D.C. Cir.), cert. denied, 355 U.S. 822 (1957).

[34] For the discussion on private labels, see, e.g., Ariel Ezrachi and Ulf Bernitze, *Private Labels, Brands and Competition Policy: The Changing Landscape of Retail Competition* (Oxford University Press 2009); Organisation for Economic Co-operation and Development, 'Buying power of multiproduct retailers' 7 OECD (Policy Roundtables) (1998) DAFFE/CLP(99)21, Introduction 15–18, available at <http://www.oecd.org/dataoecd/1/18/2379299.pdf> accessed 18 May 2015.

so. One of the advantages of this is the strengthened bargaining power that comes from being partially vertically integrated.

Recently, the number of dual distribution forms has been increasing. Gundlach and Loff argue that 'many dual distribution arrangements expand the reach of a manufacturer's distribution to new markets and new customers'.[35] This is most notably due to the increased usage of the Internet and online social media, which influence customer purchasing habits. For example, consumers research relevant products over the Internet before deciding what product to purchase and where to purchase it. The Internet is an easy option for reaching final consumers directly rather than via the traditional distribution channels. Moreover, customers purchasing products online are not necessarily the same customers shopping in high street stores, therefore, by creating dual distribution, where the manufacturer sells directly to the final customers via the Internet, the manufacturer reaches different kinds of consumers with different preferences.[36]

Distributing via the Internet raises a number of issues and questions, including the facilitation of free riding, which is further explained in Chapter 5, and the legal arrangement between the manufacturer and the webpage owner – the seller. The common relationship between a manufacturer and his retailer and the relationship between the manufacturer and an online retailer usually differ. The webpage owner commonly acts as an agent of the manufacturer (agent's principal) rather than as an independent retailer. Different rights and responsibilities apply between independent entities and an agent and his principal who act together in a similar way to one economic entity, such as a parent firm and its subsidiary. In the agent–principal distribution system, the principal is entitled to provide exact conditions of distribution, including selling price, while at the same time bearing the risks and responsibilities that would belong to an independent distributor in the independent entity distribution system. Indeed, the manufacturer does not violate antitrust/competition law by imposing RPM or VTR on his agents as they are not

---

[35] Gregory T Gundlach and Alex G Loff, 'Dual Distribution Restraints: Insights from Business Research and Practice' (2013) 58(1) *The Antitrust Bulletin* 69, 77.

[36] Ibid., 74–80; Chun Se-Hak, Rhee Byong-Duk, Park Y Seong and Kim Jae-Chleol, 'Emerging Dual Channel System and Manufacturer's Direct Retail Channel Strategy' (2011) 20 *International Review of Economics & Finance* 812; see also, Nicole McGuire, 'An Antitrust Narcotic: How the Rule of Reason is Lulling Vertical Enforcement to Sleep' (2012) 45 *Loyola of Los Angeles Law Review* 1225, 1272–5.

independent retailers.[37] Therefore, different standards apply when imposing RPM, VTR and other vertical restrictions between an online retailer, an agent, and their manufacturer, the agent's principal, and a high street retailer, an independent buyer and their manufacturer.[38]

Why Impose RPM or VTR in Distribution Systems?

We have seen that vertical restrictions are used between non-integrated economic entities. Any decision about price or the market division where the entity is vertically integrated is a business decision of one entity. Indeed, for a vertical restriction to raise any antitrust concern, vertical entities must be independent, not vertically integrated and, under both US and EU regimes, not be in a relationship of agent and principal, as the agent does not act independently but on behalf of the principal.

The fact that entities are independent does not alone mean that they will be interested in utilizing vertical restrictions. Indeed, one of the essential questions for the purposes of this book is to determine who would initiate vertical restrictions, in particular RPM and VTR, and for what reason. In this section, I outline these reasons and in Chapter 5 I analyze them in connection with procompetitive and anticompetitive theories and the facts presented in relevant US and EU cases.

As will follow from the next chapters, theory and practice are not always in agreement as to whether firms would impose vertical restrictions and for what reasons. Dual distribution systems provide a good example for demonstrating the difficulties one might face when determining whether RPM or VTR would be imposed and why. Practice shows, as illustrated by cases such as *Leegin*,[39] that firms can also be motivated to impose vertical restrictions in dual distribution systems. Theoretically, however, there are two opposing opinions as to whether

---

[37] See, e.g., EU: T-325/01 *Daimlerchrysler AG v. Commission*, [2005] ECR II-3319, [2007] 4 CMLR 15; Guidelines on Vertical Restraints [2010] O.J. C130/01, 6–9; US: *Simpson v. Union Oil Co.*, 377 U.S. 13 (1964); *United States v. General Electric Co.*, 272 U.S. 476 (1926).

[38] A question arising from this phenomenon is whether antitrust law and policy should be reshaped due to increased online sales incorporating agents rather than independent entities. However, this is a question for other research. In this book, I focus only on the application of vertical restrictions between independent entities.

[39] *Leegin Creative Leather Products, Inc. v. PSKS, Inc, DBA Kay's Kloset ... Kays' Shoes*, 551 U.S. 877 (2007) ('*Leegin*').

firms with dual distribution systems would impose RPM. These opinions arise from two schools: the neoclassical school and the progressive school.

Areeda and Hovenkamp from the neoclassical school argue that manufacturers of dual distribution systems, who are also distributors, use the same profit-maximizing strategy as they would in non-dual distribution systems. Despite being involved in dual distribution, they focus on setting efficient wholesale prices in order to maximize intrabrand price and non-price competition and thus maximize profits. Introducing vertical restrictions could result in excess profit for their distributors, which is not in the manufacturers' interest. Furthermore, manufacturers in dual distribution systems do not have to introduce RPM to increase their own profits. They are in a position where they can increase profits by increasing wholesale prices. This is further facilitated by the fact that their bargaining power is increased by the existence of dual distribution, which means that they are in a better negotiating position to increase their wholesale prices. The reasons for using RPM do not differ in any way from the reasons arising from independent distribution–production relationships and are thus not related to the reasons arising from horizontal arrangements.[40]

In contrast, the progressive school argues that dual distribution systems provide incentives to restrict competition at the buyer level and thus facilitate the introduction of vertical restraints, increasing profits at the buyer level if the manufacturer operates at the same level.[41] Instead of keeping prices competitive and increasing profit by increasing wholesale prices, which could demotivate buyers other than the vertically integrated manufacturer to buy the manufacturer's product, the manufacturer introduces a vertical restriction to charge higher prices at the buyer level. This allows the manufacturer acting as a retailer to not only increase his own profit through increased retail prices, but also to motivate other retailers to sell his products because of the higher profits that will arise from his products with RPM. Therefore, the manufacturer's profit is increased both from his own retail sales and from increased (or maintained) output from selling to other retailers where the vertical restriction provided an

---

[40] Note 6, Hovenkamp, 641–2; Philip E Areeda and Herbert Hovenkamp, *Antitrust Law: An Analysis of Antitrust Principles and Their Application* (2nd edn, Volume VIII, Aspen Publishers 2004) 68–81.

[41] David Gilo, 'Private Labels, Dual Distribution, and Vertical Restraints – An Analysis of the Competitive Effects' in Ariel Ezrachi and Ulf Bernitze, *Private Labels, Brands, and Competition Policy* (Oxford University Press 2009) 152; see also Note 35, Gundlach and Loff, 87–8.

incentive to sell the manufacturer's products. This situation could even facilitate higher wholesale prices because the final retail price is high.[42] Working on the assumption that a retailer has the choice to sell several competing products, if one manufacturer ensures a higher profit for the retailer by imposing RPM (the retailer knows that others will sell this product for the same [minimum] price), the retailer will be motivated to sell this product over other products because she can earn higher profits from the RPM product than its competitive substitutes.

Indeed, as Gundlach explains by referring to contemporary research on distribution, 'it is conceivable that a manufacturer might adopt strategies that would favor less retail competition among resellers and enhance the sales and profits of its direct channel of distribution'.[43] This is due to a number of reasons:

First, dual distribution constitutes a new channel of distribution which expands the manufacturer's reach to final customers beyond his other established customers and markets, due to the fact that consumer preferences for distribution channels differ. The extra sales that arise from this additional distribution channel increase the profits for the manufacturer; however, by entering the market as a retailer, intrabrand competition increases and the manufacturer in the dual distribution is in direct competition with his retailers. In this situation, he might be motivated to ease intrabrand competition in order to keep the higher profits arising from the higher retail price.

Second, dual distribution can increase the pressure that retailers put on the manufacturer-retailer because they can perceive dual distribution as an unfair way of competing at the retail level. Unlike in non-dual distribution, the manufacturer is less neutral, and is instead in competition with his retailers. Indeed, retailers 'may not view the manufacturer-owned direct channel as helpful to their individual goals'.[44] Therefore, by introducing a vertical restriction and thus restricting intrabrand competition, the manufacturer eases the pressure and keeps his retailers happy.

Finally, the introduction of vertical restrictions is even further stimulated in situations where the retailer(s) has bargaining power and, thus,

---

[42] Note 41 Gilo, 155; see also Ioannis Lianos, 'The Vertical/Horizontal Dichotomy in Competition Law: Some Reflections with Regard to Dual Distribution and Private Labels' in Ariel Ezrachi and Ulf Bernitze, *Private Labels, Brands and Competition Policy: The Changing Landscape of Retail Competition* (Oxford University Press 2009) 174.

[43] Note 35, Gundlach and Loff, 92.

[44] Ibid., 93–4.

pressures his suppliers to decrease their wholesale price. Although dual distribution increases a partially vertically integrated manufacturer's bargaining power, it does not entirely rule out the possibility of the retailer holding stronger bargaining power, especially as the shift of bargaining power from the manufacturer to the retailer has been more and more profound in distribution relationships.[45]

In general, the reasons for using RPM and VTR vary, as follows from EU and US cases and theories to be discussed in Chapters 3, 4 and 5. They not only include the reasons already described by the progressive school in connection with dual distribution, but also other reasons, including procompetitive reasons. The discussion above describes some reasons for manufacturers to introduce RPM; however, buyers (for instance, retailers), can also initiate RPM and VTR. Both retailers and manufacturers are driven by their own profits but, unlike manufacturers, who can initiate RPM or VTR for either anticompetitive or procompetitive reasons, retailers are interested in introducing RPM or VTR for anticompetitive reasons. For example, if retailers are continually decreasing the retail prices of a well-established brand as part of competing, then they are highly motivated to use RPM in order to increase their profit. It can also be in the interest of a strong single retailer or a group of retailers to use RPM to decrease competition and/or restrict smaller but possibly more efficient competitors who have been selling for less. They can then 'persuade' their manufacturer to enforce vertical restraints on the remaining retailers.[46]

Manufacturers may be interested in RPM or VTR either for procompetitive or anticompetitive reasons. The majority of the procompetitive explanations can be summarized under the banner of 'theories on free riding'. These theories explain the procompetitive reasons for the introduction of RPM (and could also apply to VTR) in the following way: in free riding, a discounting retailer is able to discount not because it is more efficient than others, but because it free rides on pre-sale or after-sale services or promotional services offered by other retailers. The manufacturer would introduce RPM or VTR in order to ensure that retailers offering services are not disadvantaged. Furthermore, RPM could be used as an incentive to introduce these services because retailers

---

[45] Ibid., 95.
[46] See, e.g., *Toledo Mack Sales & Service, Inc. v. Mack Trucks, Inc.*, 530 F.3d 204 (2008) ('*Mack Trucks*'); *BabyAge.com, Inc. v. Toys 'R' Us*, 558 F. Supp. 2d 575 (E.D. Pa. 2008) ('*Toys 'R' Us*'); *Euromodas, Inc. v. Zanella, Ltd.*, 368 F.3d 11 (1st Cir. 2004) ('*Euromodas*'); Note 19, *Business Electronics*.

would only be allowed to compete in non-price competition, which includes these services.

Another procompetitive reason for introducing RPM or VTR is to penetrate a new market. A new manufacturer must be able to persuade potential retailers to take risks to sell his new product, which might only succeed if he increases their prospective profits. This could be in the form of restricting intrabrand competition; when implementing the VTR strategy, they will either be the only retailers in their geographic markets, or they will be assured of certain profits per product sold if RPM is imposed.

However, there are other reasons, which are not procompetitive because they do not facilitate procompetitive effects, as to why manufacturers would be interested in introducing RPM or VTR:

- RPM could be a good tool for increasing output and thus profit because it could provide incentive for new retailers to sell RPM products and/or the existing retailers would be motivated to give products with RPM preference because not competing on price will increase their profit. This will lead to increased manufacturer output and therefore profit.
- The manufacturer may be under pressure of losing retailers or an important retailer. In order to make her retailers loyal, she would introduce RPM. She could also introduce VTR if she feared the loss of an important retailer in a certain, geographic market.
- The manufacturer can use RPM to more easily maintain or introduce higher wholesale prices, as RPM guarantees retail margins and thus eases the negotiation of higher wholesale prices.
- RPM or VTR could be used by a manufacturer in order to persuade retailers to maintain another vertical restraint, such as tying. Tying can assist with increasing the sale of the tied product and thus increase the manufacturer's profit, while RPM or VTR can lead to increased retailer profits.

There are other reasons that are questionable as to whether they are procompetitive or anticompetitive. First, vertical restraints can be used by a manufacturer to control the vertical market and adjust his future business strategy because he believes that he will save his own transaction costs and increase profits. Although this can increase the welfare of the manufacturer by maximizing his profit and production, this does not necessarily lead to an increase of total or consumer welfare because this cost-saving concerns only the manufacturer, who, if successful, can generate more profit. In that case, the reason is not procompetitive.

Second, RPM or VTR could be used to introduce or maintain a manufacturer's reputation for a premium, expensive brand. If it does not generate any procompetitive benefits such as services, it is questionable as to whether this could be used as a procompetitive justification.[47]

Whether the particular RPM or VTR strategy will be successful depends on the behavior of the final consumers, among other factors such as market structure, brand reputation and competitors' reactions. For instance, if the majority of existing consumers are price-orientated, RPM will lead to a significant decrease of consumers in a competitive market because they will switch to the cheaper substitutes. However, in general, only some consumers are price-orientated; others choose their products based on quality, services and brand, including those consumers who prefer the image that luxurious brands provide. Every market, product and retailer has a different composition of consumers. For instance, a discount store will attract primarily low-price-orientated consumers. Therefore, consumers can be divided into different groups based on their preferences. For instance, in connection with services and quality, Comanor differentiates between marginal consumers and infra-marginal consumers. Marginal consumers are those who are sensitive to product improvements and are willing to pay more for better quality. If the quality is high but the price is not as high, marginal consumers would be willing to purchase more of this product. Infra-marginal consumers are those who are loyal to a certain brand or products. They will continue to buy these products even if the price increases significantly and the quality only marginally.[48]

Another factor which can result in unsuccessful vertical-restriction strategy is bounded rationality. I have explained that the decision of whether to be vertically integrated can be influenced by opportunism and bounded rationality.[49] This also applies to other strategic decisions, including the application of vertical restrictions. Vertical restrictions are

---

[47] For further discussion, see Chapter 5 and the case of C-434/09 *Pierre Fabre Dermo-Cosmetique SAS v. Président de l'Authorité de la Concurrence, Ministre de l'Èconomie, de l'Industrie et de l'Emploi* [2011] 5 CMLR 31, 1159 in Chapter 4.

[48] William S Comanor, 'Vertical Price-Fixing, Vertical Market Restrictions, and the New Antitrust Policy' (1985) 98(5) *Harvard Law Review* 983, 991.

[49] Note 7, Williamson, 126–7; see research on behavioral economics, which establishes that the decision-making process is not perfect and thus firms do not always operate in an ideally rational way, including when deciding whether to implement vertical restrictions. See, e.g., Avishalom Tor and William J Rinner, 'Behavioral Antitrust: A New Approach to the Rule of Reason after *Leegin*' (February 2010) *Behavioral Antitrust* 805.

not usually profitable to any parties except the party who initiates it and holds the bargaining power. Even the party who initiates it does not necessarily end up being better off due to her bounded rationality and the opportunism of others. For example, assume that a manufacturer initiates RPM to ensure the loyalty of her retailers. Although these retailers will be loyal to the manufacturer and sell her products due to ensured profit margins, from a long-term perspective the manufacturer will lose some customers because they will swap this product for less expensive substitutes. Thus, the manufacturer will be left with less profit.

Another example is a retailer with significant bargaining power: retailer A. Retailer A has been selling the manufacturer's product for a long time and is well established in the market. A new retailer, retailer B, enters the market and starts selling these products for less than retailer A. Obviously, retailer A is unhappy about losing his customers to the lower prices of retailer B, however decreasing his price is not necessarily the best option, as this would still lead to lower profits and margin. Having bargaining power, retailer A turns to the manufacturer and 'persuades' her, by threatening to stop buying from her, to maintain the retail price at the level he has been selling the products for or, even better for retailer A, to agree to VTR in order to exclude retailer B and any other potential retailers. The manufacturer does so in order to keep her business with the established retailer A. The result is that retailer A ends up with higher margins than when he was competing with retailer B. If RPM is imposed, retailer B could be worse off if the margin from RPM does not compensate for his higher volume sold when he was selling below RPM. Customers have to pay more for the product than they would have been paying if the price was competitive. The manufacturer would have to sell more if there was price competition between retailers A and B, and if consumers or some of her consumers were low-price-orientated. However, at the same time, by not losing retailer A, she ensured that she did not lose the volume of products sold to retailer A.[50]

As follows from these examples, RPM and VTR can cause anti-competitive problems, primarily in the form of restricted intrabrand competition. This can lead to the decreased efficiency and welfare of consumers. RPM, in the form of price fixing and minimum price fixing, restricts price competition and in general increases the intrabrand price

---

[50] It is also likely that from a long-term perspective, she would return to the same sales volume or even increase sales volume if she did not maintain the retail price and let retailer A stop buying from her. However, this would only happen if, after some time, the products reached customers and the price remained or became competitive once again.

(and if RPM is legal, the price could be increased across the whole industry),[51] while VTR, especially absolute vertical territorial restrictions, restrict both price and non-price intrabrand competition. Because there are no competitive forces within the brand in question (not at the intrabrand level), the impact could be negative on both the intrabrand price and innovation. If the price is increased, output could decrease. Because the price competition is foreclosed (RPM) or both the price and non-price competition (VTR) are foreclosed, competitors lose the incentive to compete. They also lose the desire to lower costs and become more efficient than others. Therefore, RPM and VTR can restrict the growth of efficient competitors and decrease innovation. Finally, the consumer has less choice. RPM does not allow buyers to sell for less and VTR does not allow other buyers to enter the intrabrand market and thus decrease the price and innovate.

Indeed, RPM and VTR primarily lead to a restriction of intrabrand competition. The issue of whether interbrand competition could also be restricted is discussed in the following section (and further in Chapter 5), where I also explain the meaning of vertical competition and its related force: bargaining power. Both vertical competition and bargaining power play an important role in vertical restrictions.

III. COMPETITION AND BARGAINING POWER

The core problem when determining whether vertical restrictions should be prohibited in general or whether a particular vertical restraint in a specific case violates antitrust/competition law is whether such a vertical restraint restricts competition. This can be determined by evaluating whether the vertical restriction causes economic harm and has a negative or positive impact on consumer or total welfare in a particular case. This theme is reflected throughout the entire book. Before moving to specific cases and theories, as I do in the following chapters, I need to clarify the

---

[51] See Chapter 5. See also, Press Release, Federal Trade Commission, 'Record Firms Settle FTC Charges of Restraining Competition in CD Music Market' (10 May 2000), <http://www.ftc.gov/opa/2000/05/cdpres.shtm> accessed 18 May 2015; Thomas R Overstreet, 'Resale price maintenance: Economic theories and empirical evidence' (1983) Federal Trade Commission Bureau of Economics Staff Report 160; Hearings on S. 408 before the Subcommittee on Antitrust and Monopoly of the Senate Committee on the Judiciary, 94th Cong., 1st Sess., 173 (1975).

meaning of the term 'competition' for the purposes of vertical restrictions, in particular, RPM and VTR.

Competition is a dynamic process; it requires players on the field and the field itself – the market. However, are those players only (horizontal) competitors and consumers or are there other players on the field? And similarly, is the playing field only one relevant (horizontal) market or does it have further layers?

We have seen that distribution is a complex, relationship-based process. This rather indicates that competition could have many layers and players, a situation that is not necessarily fully reflected in EU and US antitrust/competition law and policy. The current (and even previous) legal practice in the EU and the US differentiates between two 'forms' of competition: interbrand[52] and intrabrand,[53] putting the general emphasis on interbrand competition.

Taking into consideration the current approaches in the US and EU, while also reflecting on the recent knowledge of distribution and the way firms compete, in this book I evaluate the restriction of competition for the purposes of vertical restrictions from the perspective of two different economic-policy models. The first model is based on the conventional and accepted existence of horizontal competition. If we assume that only horizontal competition exists, and thus only horizontal competition should be protected, then, under legal terms, what we primarily aim for is the protection of interbrand competition. The restriction of intrabrand competition would concern us only if it significantly harms horizontal competition leading to the restriction of interbrand competition.

The second model follows the idea that it is not correct to analyse vertical restrictions, such as RPM and VTR, merely from the perspective of the horizontal market structure and relationships. Vertical restrictions need to reflect a much broader and more complex market structure, which includes vertical interactions and relationships. Even further, if we accept that vertical relationships in the market are not the same as horizontal ones then we cannot agree that vertical restrictions should be evaluated in the same way as horizontal restrictions and that horizontal competition is the only aspect on which we should determine whether a particular vertical restriction is anticompetitive at the vertical level. Indeed, by accepting the difference between vertical interactions with bargaining power as their driving force and horizontal interactions among firms and the complexity of the market with its vertical and horizontal levels, we

---

[52] Competition among competing substitutes on the horizontal level.
[53] Competition within one brand.

could argue that the determination of anticompetitive impacts in vertical restrictions must be different than the anticompetitive impact of a joint action between horizontal competitors. This different understanding of competition for the purposes of vertical restrictions, which should be considered for the second model, can be referred to as 'vertical competition'.

Currently, the EU and US take different approaches to RPM and VTR. Under the current US approach, unless the market is characterized by the existence of an entity with significant market power, interbrand competition must be restricted in order to prove the restriction of US antitrust law.[54] In contrast, EU anticompetitive provisions can be satisfied if there is a restriction of intrabrand competition. Therefore, the US approach is similar to the first policy model, where only horizontal competition, in particular interbrand competition, should be protected. This policy follows from the US neoclassical school, most notably the Chicago School. The Chicago School recognizes horizontal competition as something that should be protected and thus which should determine whether a particular practice violates US antitrust law.[55] In contrast, the EU approach accepts that intrabrand competition should also be protected, but not to the same extent as interbrand competition.

The complexity of distribution and the differences in approaches to vertical restrictions lead to three general questions: first, does intrabrand competition matter or not? Second, can RPM and VTR restrict interbrand competition?[56] Third, is interbrand or intrabrand competition a sufficient and the only indicator for the analysis of vertical restraints? If the answer to the third question is 'no', then other forms of competition should be recognized.

Intrabrand Competition

In the law of vertical restraints, unless the market is monopolistic or very concentrated, the neoclassical school argues that intrabrand competition does not matter, because in a competitive market consumers can choose between competing products.[57] Therefore, even if the price of one product is increased due to RPM or VTR, consumers can choose to

---

[54] Unless it is a horizontal restriction, then it would be per se illegal and the restriction of interbrand competition does not have to be proved. See Chapter 3.

[55] See, e.g., Robert H Bork, *The Antitrust Paradox: A Policy at War with Itself* (The Free Press, New York 1978).

[56] The answer to the third question is reflected in this whole monograph.

[57] See, e.g., Note 55, Bork, 288–98.

purchase its competing substitutes without price restrictions. Unlike a price-fixing cartel, where the price increases across all products of cartel participants, the primary effect of RPM and one of the effects that VTR can lead to is increased intrabrand price, that is the price of the product with RPM or VTR. The primary impact is only intrabrand and not interbrand, and therefore the competitive harm is believed to be minimal in comparison to cartels, particularly where the market is very competitive. Furthermore, reasons for utilizing RPM or VTR are not only anticompetitive but can be also procompetitive, as explained by various procompetitive theories.[58]

However, the market, and especially the vertical market, other than a monopolistic market, as well as the characteristics of the relevant product can be such that intrabrand competition is more important than is argued by the neoclassical school due to the fact that intrabrand competition lowers the retail margins.[59] This is especially obvious in the retail sector, a sector that is directly correlated with final consumers.

Products in the grocery supermarket chains can be divided into two categories: products with well-established brands and other products, including private labels. Supermarkets compete primarily on price in the market for private labels and products without well-established brands (or all products where a supermarket chain has a reputation as a discounter). Price interbrand competition among these products is intensive and those retailers holding the bargaining power are able to negotiate lower wholesale prices with their suppliers. An important effect of the fact that retailers hold the bargaining power is that consumers tend to switch brands within the one store.[60]

However, the situation is different when consumers are loyal to brands and would rather switch stores than switch brands. Manufacturers of such brands have the bargaining power. The existence of well-established brands became significant with the advent of media advertising. For example, Steiner describes that prior to extensive TV advertising in the US (before 1958), the US market only had a few established toy brands and interbrand competition was intensive. When TV advertising became

---

[58] Procompetitive theories explain that RPM and VTR are utilized procompetitively rather than anticompetitively. See Chapter 5.

[59] Robert L Steiner, 'The Leegin Factors – a Mixed Bag' (2010) 55(1) *Antitrust Bulletin* 25.

[60] Ibid., 31–4; Robert L Steiner, 'The Nature of Vertical Restraints' (1985) 30 *Antitrust Bulletin* 143, 157; see also, Douglas E Hughes and Michael Ahearne, 'Energizing the Reseller's Sales Force: The Power of Brand Identification' (2010) 74 *Journal of Marketing* 81.

common, parents' purchasing habits for toys changed so that they would commonly switch stores in order to pay less for a specific branded product that their children were interested in.[61] This implies that, although theoretically there might be substitutes in the market with specific kinds of toys, in fact well-established brands do not have direct substitutes for a significant number of consumers. Nowadays, well-established brands are common due to different advertising techniques, including Internet and media advertising. Any introduction of RPM or VTR would stop this intensive intrabrand competition leading to higher final prices for consumers who would not switch to other products. Therefore, it is important to evaluate the proportion of brand-loyal customers to determine the effect on consumer welfare, rather than merely focusing on the number of potential substitutes and the market shares of the product concerned.

The reason for intensive intrabrand competition between retailers within a well-established brand is obvious: losing important brands or selling them for a high price could lead to a decreased number of consumers. As Steiner explains, the price cut of a brand that has a well-established reputation, such as Colgate, in one retail store will be noticeable for consumers who favor Colgate over other brands, as they will easily switch to this price-cutting retailer. Such intrabrand competition will be intensive, leading to lower margins for retailers and higher margins for manufacturers. On the other hand, the effect of discounting one product (Colgate) in one retail store and another product (Crest Toothpaste) competing with the first product in another store will be less direct, because consumers loyal to Colgate will not switch to another supermarket to purchase Crest Toothpaste.[62]

Well-established brands and advertising are related because successful advertising increases the popularity of brands. Manufacturers who successfully advertise tend to increase their wholesale prices, while retailers try to keep the retail price low due to intensive intrabrand competition.[63] Besides purchasing their favorite brand(s) in a supermarket that sells them for less, consumers could easily assume that if a retail store has higher prices on well-established brands, such a store will also have higher prices on products in general.[64] This is correlated with the fact

---

[61] Ibid., Steiner, 36–7.
[62] Ibid., 34–5.
[63] Robert L Wills and Willard F Mueller, 'Brand Advertising and Pricing' (1989) 56 *Southern Economic Journal* 383; ibid., Steiner, 39–43.
[64] Ibid., Steiner, 31–4; Robert L Steiner, 'Vertical Competition, Horizontal Competition and Market Power' (2008) 53(2) *Antitrust Bulletin* 251, 258; Robert

that if a manufacturer increases the reputation of her brand, most notably through advertising, the elasticity of the demand curve decreases.[65] Thus, as Lynch's economic model shows, interbrand competition among retailers cannot be as intensive as intrabrand competition among retailers.[66] If retailers are continually decreasing the retail prices of a well-established brand as part of competing, then they are also highly motivated to use RPM or other vertical restrictions in order to stop losing their margins.

Market Power and Bargaining Power

Bargaining power is an essential force in distribution. If a manufacturer establishes his brand, he will have bargaining power in relation to his retailer. In contrast, for private labels, it is the retailers and not the smaller suppliers who have bargaining power. Indeed, a simple form of vertical chain which includes a seller and a buyer is based on two forms of power: the horizontal market power of the seller and the buyer, and the vertical bargaining power consisting of buyer power and seller power.

The term 'buyer power' has been used to describe market power or bargaining power (countervailing power), or both.[67] Although the meaning of horizontal market power is arguably unified, different definitions

---

L Steiner, 'Exclusive Dealing + Resale Price Maintenance: A Powerful Anticompetitive Combination' (2004) 33 *Southwestern University Law Review* 447, 454–5, 464–5; Robert L Steiner, 'How Manufacturers Deal with the Price-Cutting Retailer: When Are Vertical Restraints Efficient?' (1997) 65 *Antitrust Law Journal* 409, 411; see also Pamela J Harbour and Laurel A Price, 'RPM and the Rule of Reason: Ready or Not, Here We Come?' (2010) 55(1) *Antitrust Bulletin* 225, 240–42; Howard Smith and John Thanassoulis, 'Bargaining between Retailers and Their Suppliers' in Ezrachi and Bernitze, *Private Labels*, Note 34, 46–7; Michael P Lynch, 'Why Economists Are Wrong to Neglect Retailing and How Steiner's Theory Provides an Explanation of Important Regularities' (2004) 49(4) *Antitrust Bulletin* 911, 926–40.

[65] Ibid., Steiner, 'Vertical Competition', 258–9; Note 59, Steiner, 'The Leegin Factors', 36–9. Steiner also refers to work of Alfred Marshall (Alfred Marshall, *Industry and Trade* (1920, Macmillan) 301–2), who identified the importance of successful advertising, with the impact of high profits for manufacturers who successfully advertised, while retailers who would refuse to sell their products 'would simply drive away customers' (ibid, 39).

[66] Note 64, Steiner, 'How Manufacturers Deal with the Price-Cutting Retailer', 413–14, 440–41; Note 64, Lynch, 'Why Economists Are Wrong to Neglect Retailing', 926–40; see also Note 17, Gundlach, Cannon and Manning, 418–19.

[67] Yo Sop Choi and Kazuhiko Fuchikawa, 'Comparative Analysis of Competition Laws on Buyer Power in Korea and Japan' (2010) 33 *World Competition*

of bargaining power and buyer (seller) power exist.[68] I use the term 'bargaining power' (including the terms 'buyer power' and 'seller power'[69]) to capture how strong the 'competitor'[70] is in relation to their vertical partner/competitor, thus, at the vertical level. This reflects the definition of the Organisation for Economic Co-operation and Development (OECD), which defines buyer power as 'the ability of a buyer to influence the terms and conditions on which it purchases goods'.[71]

Indeed, bargaining power is a power where one party has such a position that she can effectively threaten other parties on the vertical chain that, for instance, she will terminate their contract or pressure them to deal solely with her.[72] As we will see in cases and examples in the

---

499, 500; Note 64, Smith and Thanassoulis, 46; Zhiqi Chen 'Defining Buyer Power' (2008) 53 *Antitrust Bulletin* 241.

[68] Compare with, Chen, ibid; Roger G Noll, '"Buyer Power" and Economic Policy' (2005) 72 *Antitrust Law Journal* 589; Robert A Skitol 'Concerted Buying Power: Its Potential for Addressing the Patent Holdup Problem in Standard Setting' (2005) 72 *Antitrust Law Journal* 727; John K Galbraith, *American Capitalism: The Concept of Countervailing Power* (first published in 1952, Transaction Publishers 1993).

[69] Such meaning is based on bargaining power and indeed specifies the owner of that power. The reason for the usage of the terms 'buyer power' and 'seller power' is that the terms 'buyer' and 'seller' indicate themselves that this power reflects an interaction on the vertical and not the horizontal chain.

[70] If we accept the existence of vertical competition – see below.

[71] Note 34, OECD, 'Buying Power of Multiproduct Retailers'; see also Warren S Grimes, 'Buyer Power and Retail Gatekeeper Power: Protecting Competition and the Atomistic Seller' (2005) 72 *Antitrust Law Journal* 563, 565.

[72] John B Kirkwood, 'Buyer Power and Exclusionary Conduct: Should *Brooke Group* Set the Standards for Buyer-Induced Price Discrimination and Predatory Bidding?' (2005) 72 *Antitrust Law Journal* 625, 627, 638–44; for instance, monopolists who threatened their dealers: *Southeast Missouri Hospital and St. Francis Medical Center C.R. Bard, Inc.*, Not Reported in F.Supp.2d, 2008 WL 4372741 (E.D.Mo.), 2009-1 Trade Cases P 76,461; *United States v. Dentsply International, Inc*, 399 F.3d 181 (3d Cir. 2005), cert. denied, 546 U.S. 1089 (2006); some form of bargain power plays a role in almost all cases discussed in Chapter 3, see, e.g.: *Mack Trucks*; Note 46, *Euromodas*; Note 19, *Business Electronics*; Note 19, *Colgate*; and in Chapter 4 'Development of the US Law of Vertical Territorial and Price Restraints', see, e.g.: C-501/06 P, C-513/06 P, C-515/06 P, C-519/06 P, *GlaxoSmithKline Services Unlimited v Commission of the EC* [2009] 4 CMLR 2; C-2/01 P and C-3/01 P *Bundesverband der Arzneimittel-Importeure EC and Commission v Bayer AG* [2004] ECR I-00023; C-277/87, T-208/01*Volkswagen AG v. Commission* [2003] ECR II-5141; *Sandoz prodotti faraceuttici SpA v Commission of the European Communities* [1990] ECR I-45; see also Note 64, Smith and Thanassoulis, 57; Paul Dobson,

following chapters and as the aforementioned example of retailers A and B shows, it is bargaining power that determines whether vertical restrictions such as RPM and VTR will be successfully imposed. This is because it is the firm or firms with bargaining power who enforce RPM or VTR and the vertical restriction only sometimes arises from a mutual agreement and with mutual benefit, for example, when two different vertical restrictions are introduced.

However, this does not mean that market power[73] that exists at the horizontal level is not relevant in relation to bargaining power and vertical restrictions. Market power is one of the factors that influences bargaining power. A manufacturer can strengthen her bargaining power by increasing her vertical downstream market share and thus becoming a stronger salesman. However, this is not the only factor. As illustrated earlier, one of the best ways to increase bargaining power is to establish a significant number of loyal customers who would rather switch retailers than products.[74]

Another important factor for bargaining power is transparent and correct information. Market failures in the form of defective information, such as misleading information at any level of the vertical chain, a lack of transparent information among buyers and sellers, and when the arrangements regarding price between sellers and buyers are kept secret, create not only bargaining power but also unfair advantages that are not based on competitive efficiencies.[75] Generally, if the ability of a supplier to find a new vertical partner is low, and risks and costs, such as

---

'Exploiting Buyer Power: Lessons from the British Grocery Trade' 72(2) *Antitrust Law Journal* 529, 532.

[73] Easterbrook defines market power as 'the ability to raise price significantly without losing so many sales that the increase is unprofitable' (Note 12, Easterbrook, 159).

[74] Note 64, Steiner, 'Vertical Competition', 258; Note 64, Lynch, 926–40; Robert L Steiner, 'Does Advertising Lower Consumer Prices?' (1973) 37 *Journal of Marketing* 19; for example in the case of *Toys 'R' Us, Inc. V. FTC*, 221 F3rd 928 (7th Cir. 2000), 20 percent of market share of the buyer created significant bargaining power.

[75] Peter Carstensen, 'Buyer Power, Competition Policy, and Antitrust: the Competitive Effects of Discrimination among Suppliers' (2008) 53(2) *Antitrust Bulletin* 271, 280–81, 288–9; Robert Lande, 'Market Power Without a Large Market Share: The Role of Imperfect Information and Other "Consumer Protection" Market Failures' (8 March 2007) <http://www.justice.gov/atr/public/hearings/single_firm/docs/222102.htm> accessed 18 May 2015; see also Note 7, Grimes, 101–49.

negotiating the cost of switching and finding a new buyer, are high, the buyer(s) has significant bargaining power.[76]

Vertical Competition

We have seen that it is not only interbrand competition that plays an important role in practice, intrabrand competition is also important, particularly in markets with branded products. Furthermore, I have mentioned that competition-law policy, which also protects intrabrand competition, such as the one in the EU, would find the restriction of intrabrand competition satisfactory for an infringement of competition law. Policy focused on interbrand competition such as that in the US, however, would require further analysis to prove a restriction of interbrand competition. The US approach also differentiates between de facto vertical and horizontal intrabrand competition.[77] For instance, RPM does not always occur vertically. Price fixing, including minimum price fixing, can be arranged among retailers in relation to one brand. Despite the fact that it is still intrabrand competition being restricted and therefore the impact can be the same no matter whether it was arranged horizontally among retailers or vertically, horizontal intrabrand competition is prohibited per se in the US.[78]

In both the US and EU, regardless of whether intrabrand competition is arranged vertically or horizontally, the impact on intrabrand competition and the effect on competition is analyzed from the final consumers' angle at the horizontal level, as we will see in Chapters 3 and 4. However, such an impact can also be vertical, especially when we take into consideration bargaining power and its significance for firms competing at the vertical level. Indeed, Robert Steiner argues that an economic model based on a single stage market (horizontal market) is insufficient to make accurate assumptions about vertical restraints.[79] Instead, the vertical process is based on 'dual-stage' factors or 'triple stage effects', where the

---

[76] Ibid., Carstensen, 278–80; Note 40, Areeda and Hovenkamp, 59.
[77] See the most recent federal cases on RPM, e.g., Note 46, *Mack Trucks*, 221; Note 39, *Leegin*, 893.
[78] See Chapter 3.
[79] Note 64, Steiner, 'Vertical Competition, Horizontal Competition and Market Power', 254; Note 64, Lynch, 911–40; Paul Dobson, Michael Waterson and Alex Chu, 'The welfare consequences of exercise of buyer power' (September 1998) Office of Fair Trading, Research Paper Number 16, 6; Note 64, Steiner, 'How Manufacturers Deal with the Price-Cutting Retailer'; Friedrich Hayek, 'The Meaning of Competition' in *Individualism and Economic Order* (Chicago: University of Chicago Press [1948] 1996).

triple stage refers to manufacturers buying from suppliers and selling to retailers who then resell to final consumers.[80]

Competition also takes place between these stages and not just at the horizontal level. If we agree that firms are competitors if they can take sales or profit, margins and market share from each other,[81] then we accept that the competition process also takes place vertically. Although competing at the vertical level is not the same as competition among direct competitors at the horizontal level, because the relationship between firms on the vertical chain is primarily complementary, these firms are able to take sales, profit, margins and even market share from each other at the vertical level.[82] For example, manufacturer X supplies his products to three supermarket chains in the UK: Tesco, Morrisons and Sainsbury's. Tesco decides to stop buying these products from manufacturer X and instead buys more from the manufacturer's horizontal competitors. This would lead to a decrease in sales, profits, margins and market share for manufacturer X because manufacturer X's products would no longer reach Tesco customers. These customers would likely switch to competing substitutes, unless they were willing to switch

---

[80] Note 59, Steiner, 'The Leegin Factors', 30–31; According to Steiner, aspects which influence this dual or triple process are: '(1) retail penetration – which measures the share of retail market held by dealers stocking the brand; (2) dealer support – which measures the additional demand due to display, local advertising, and other promotional efforts by the brand's retailers; and (3) retail gross margin (RGM) – roughly the difference between the brand's retail price and its factory price divided by the former'. (Note 64, Steiner, 'How Manufacturers Deal with the Price-Cutting Retailer', 411.)

[81] Note 60, Steiner, 'The Nature of Vertical Restraints', 158; Note 64, Steiner, 'Vertical Competition, Horizontal Competition and Market Power', 254; see also Note 79, Hayek, 96: competition is 'the action of endeavouring to gain what another endeavours to gain at the same time'.

[82] Not only Steiner but also others identified the existence of vertical competition or conflict. In 1968, Palamountain had already recognized three types of competition: horizontal competition, competing among different types of retailers and vertical competition, which he termed 'vertical conflict'. He stated that the last type had been mostly ignored by antitrust policy and law. Joseph Palamountain, *The Politics of Distribution* (Harvard University Press 1955) 48. The progressive school also accepts the existence of vertical competition law. See, e.g., Alberto Sa Vinhas and Erin Anderson, 'How Potential Conflict Drives Channel Structure: Concurrent (Direct and Indirect) Routs to Market' (2005) 42 *Journal of Marketing Research* 507; Note 41, Gilo, 155; Note 42, Lianos, 174; Note 35, Gundlach and Loff, 88–9.

supermarkets rather than products and potentially travel greater distances to reach those supermarkets.[83]

Therefore, manufacturers compete among themselves, distributors compete among themselves, and manufacturers and distributors, including retailers, also compete among themselves at the vertical level. Distributors attempt to bargain down manufacturers' wholesale prices and decrease selling prices for retailers. There is not only a complementary but also a competitive relationship between firms at different vertical stages.

Indeed, firms aim their strategies not only at horizontal competition but also at 'vertical competition'. Both strategies have an impact on profits. When competing horizontally, firms focus on improving their products (or services) and production. They can also lower their cost and price and/or innovate their products. In comparison, at the vertical level, they focus on improving their bargaining position and distribution. Therefore, some strategies are aimed primarily at one form of competition, for instance, innovation of the product at the horizontal level, bargaining strategies at the vertical level, while others, such as advertising, focus on both levels. For instance, TV advertising sends a direct message to the final customers and thus improves the bargaining position of the advertising manufacturer by strengthening consumer awareness and desire to purchase the advertised products. In other words, it strengthens brand establishment and recognition. Simultaneously, by doing so, the manufacturer attracts more consumers, which subsequently intensifies competition among his competitors, i.e. manufacturers, who could try to introduce a better strategy and a better message.

Vertical restrictions have been perceived by some as vertical strategies and are grouped with advertising.[84] The other view, including the US and EU antitrust/competition law and policy regimes, group them among restrictions or potential restrictions of competition. The second perception reflects better the nature of vertical restrictions. The reason for this is that, unlike advertising, which directly raises consumer demand and in that way increases competition and improves the bargaining position of

---

[83] If they switched supermarkets, it would mean that the brand of manufacturer X is well established and that it is not Tesco but manufacturer X who has the bargaining power. In that situation, it is unlikely (but not impossible) that Tesco would stop buying manufacturers X's products, as explained above.

[84] Elizabeth M Bailey and Gregory K Leonard, 'Minimum Resale Price Maintenance: Some Empirical Evidence from Maryland' (2010) 10 *The B.E. Journal of Economic Analysis & Policy* 1, 1–6; see also Note 17, Gundlach, Cannon and Manning, 410–11.

the manufacturer, the primary effect of RPM and VTR is to restrict intrabrand competition.[85] While RPM and VTR can improve the bargaining position of the manufacturer, they do not do so competitively by directly increasing demand but by primarily restricting intrabrand competition, most notably in the form of increased intrabrand prices.

Furthermore, not only are some strategies aimed at both vertical and horizontal competition, but other aspects of vertical and horizontal competition also coexist in a close relationship, as they influence each other. It is likely that if a manufacturer increases her horizontal market power she could also, by the same process, gain a stronger bargaining power at the vertical level. Lower vertical bargaining power could lead to lower horizontal power and a lower market share.[86] The key factors that influence both processes, as well as bargaining and market power, are market structure and the nature of the product. Market structure is determined by many aspects generally centered around the nature of the product. For example, the market for the production of jet planes will be naturally more concentrated and geographically wider than the hair salon market in a city. The market structure, most notably the concentration of the markets, then influences the effect of RPM and VTR on competition. For example, RPM or VTR imposed by a monopolist will restrict the whole market because there is no substitute available, while RPM imposed by one manufacturer in a competitive production market will primarily influence the final price of that manufacturer while consumers would still be able to choose from a broader range of substitutes. Because, in practice, significant emphasis is placed on the restriction of horizontal competition, in the following section I discuss a number of situations, occurring from different dual market structures, that have an extensive horizontal effect on competition, harming consumers significantly.

---

[85] As Brunell summarizes it, advertising and other strategies 'raise demand directly, and only indirectly raise prices, while resale price maintenance raises prices directly and only indirectly may lead to the hoped-for benefits'. (Richard M Brunell, 'Overruling *Dr. Miles*: The Supreme Trade Commission in Action' (2007) 52 *Antitrust Bulletin* 475, 511–12.)

[86] Note 64, Steiner, 'Vertical Competition, Horizontal Competition and Market Power', 252, 257, 260, 268; Note 59, Steiner, 'The Leegin Factors', 35–6.

IV. MARKET STRUCTURE: THE APPLICATION OF RPM AND VTR

Nothing is static in competition, including the distribution of products and services at the vertical level. Markets, entities and distribution channels are constantly evolving as illustrated by the shoemaker example at the beginning of this chapter. Williamson goes one step further stating that 'neither firms nor markets come in predetermined shapes'.[87] This statement has its limitations in the nature of the market. For example, some markets will be naturally more concentrated than others. The jeans production market will not be as concentrated as a railway from point A to point B or the production of commercial airplanes. Although the nature of the market, as well as the related nature of the products, limits dramatic changes in the market, the nature can still change to a certain extent if other conditions change, for example, cost of production, demand, deregulation or regulation of the markets. Nevertheless, market structure is the essential element that predetermines whether RPM or VTR could restrict competition at the horizontal level to a noticeable or even significant extent. As VTR and RPM emerge on the vertical chain, it is necessary to understand the structure of and the interactions on the dual markets to determine the impacts of VTR and RPM on competition. Those market structures which predetermine that RPM or VTR could have an extensive horizontal impact on competition are monopolies and oligopolies, monopsonies and oligopsonies; and dual monopolies and oligopolies.[88]

Monopolies and Oligopolies

If manufacturers are oligopolists or monopolists and the buyer's market is competitive, the manufacturers will most likely have the bargaining power. If the manufacturer is a monopolist, RPM would have the same effect as setting monopolistic prices and whole absolute territorial restrictions will restrict competition completely, having a negative impact on both price and non-price competition because there will only be one manufacturer and one retailer. In this situation, the retailer has no incentive to compete because there is no one to compete with. Even if the

---

[87] Note 7, Williamson, 124.
[88] The market can be monopolistic, oligopolistic or competitive at the manufacturer level. At the buyer level, we would refer to monopsony, oligopsony and competitive market.

manufacturer has a dominant position in the market competing with only a few smaller manufacturers, the impact on the market when using vertical restrictions would be much greater than if the market was competitive.

In oligopolies, the situation is more complicated. Game theory could assist us with further predictions on the impact of vertical restraints on interbrand competition. There are two basic assumptions that would lead to two different outcomes. If one oligopolist introduces RPM or VTR, others (or the second one in a duopoly) could decide to follow or not follow. In both situations, the others will be better off but only in the first situation will the initiator be better off.

In the first situation, others follow the initiator in the form of increased RPM or increased wholesale price, which could then increase the final retail price. They would do so because this would lead to increased profit for the other manufacturers without increasing production and thus their output. If RPM does not lead to a drastic increase of the final price, and particularly in situations where the products have an inelastic demand curve, the output of each competitor could remain the same while price and profit would increase. Additionally, others could also be motivated to introduce RPM as that could provide an incentive for retailers to favor the products with RPM because those products would lead to higher profits for retailers than those products without RPM. If a retailer has a choice between a product where she does not have to compete with other retailers on price and minimum profit (in minimum price fixing) is ensured due to RPM, or a product where she has to compete with other retailers and such competition would decrease the final price and her profit, she would most likely, based on the profit maximization motivation, prefer the product with RPM. This first assumption would indeed lead to a restriction of interbrand competition.

Under the second assumption, the other manufacturers would not make any changes in order to increase their output by attracting more consumers due to having lower retail prices than the retail price of the product with RPM. This would increase their profit by increasing output while, at the same time, decreasing the output of the manufacturer with RPM. Therefore, if it was the manufacturer who initiated this change, perhaps in the hope that others would follow or that his retailers would promote his products over others, his strategy was unsuccessful. However, there is still a chance that retailers will increase the retail price of other manufacturers' products in order to receive a higher profit for these other products. In this situation, the profits of retailers and manufacturers with RPM would increase while the profits of the other manufacturers would remain the same. Furthermore, if the brand was strongly established, the introduction of RPM and the subsequent increase of the retail price would not lead to a lower number of consumers even if the price of the other products remained the same.

The situation is different with VTR. Taking into consideration observations from studies of current distribution behavior, in particular that manufacturers try to use different distribution channels in order to reach different groups of consumers, it is unlikely that a manufacturer would, on her own initiative, divide the market among a few retailers if she already has an established network of retailers or distributors. By introducing VTR, she would become less competitive as she would not reach all potential consumers. Furthermore, VTR would lead to an increased bargaining position for her exclusive retailers.

However, if the nature of the product is such that, for example, VTR leads to decreased distribution costs, or if the manufacturer wishes to create a specific image, particularly where a franchising system is established, she could still be motivated to introduce VTR. This would restrict intrabrand competition, including price competition, as the exclusive retailer could dictate the retail price without intrabrand competing restraints. The above two assumptions could be then applied, where the first assumption would foreclose entire interbrand competition.

Monopsonies and Oligopsonies

A market structure can be such that at the seller/manufacturer level, the market is competitive, however, at the buyer/retailer level, the market is based on a monopsony or oligopsony. In such situations, buyers may have the bargaining power and can dictate the conditions of the vertical market.[89] A monopsony can have a negative impact on consumer welfare in a similar way to a monopoly.[90] If the retailer is an absolute monopsonist, he is not restricted by competitive forces, he can set monopolistic

---

[89] Note 39, *Leegin*, 2733 (Breyer, J., dissenting); Note 40, Areeda and Hovenkamp, 48–9; Note 85, Brunell, 499–500; Note 72, Kirkwood, 638–44; Thomas A Piraino, 'A Proposed Antitrust Approach to Buyers' Competitive Conduct' (2004–2005) 56 *Hastings Law Journal* 1121, 1125; Note 34, OECD; William S Comanor, 'The Two Economics of Vertical Restraints' 21 *Southwestern University Law Revue* 1265, 1265, 1277; Roger Blair and Jeffrey Harrison, 'Antitrust Policy and Monopsony' (1990–1991) 76 *Cornell Law Revue* 297, 308; George Stigler, *The Theory of Price* (4th edn, Prentice Hall College Div. 1987) 216–18.

[90] Note 79, Dobson, Waterson and Chu, 9–16; Note 89, Blair and Harrison, 303; see also Note 40, Areeda and Hovenkamp, 33–4.

prices and, in general, is not motivated to make improvements due to a lack of competition.

If an upstream market is competitive because there is no monopoly or oligopoly, however buyers are oligopsonists or monopsonists and thus have the bargaining power, buyers could lower upstream-market/ wholesale prices by using their bargaining power. This could lead to either positive or negative effects for final consumers. The relationship between large oligopolistic retailers and their private label manufacturers, where low retail prices are key to their business, can illustrate a positive effect in the form of decreased prices.[91] For instance, in the private label market, big retail chains have bargaining power and can thus negotiate low wholesale prices. Because of intensive competition among private labels of different supermarket chains, retailers pass these low prices on to the final consumers while still making a significant profit.[92] Furthermore, private labels increase horizontal competition by providing substitutes, private label products, with lower prices than other brands.

However, a lowering of supply prices by powerful buyers is not necessarily positive for competition for two reasons. First, in an extreme circumstance, monopsonies and oligopsonies can lead to situations where suppliers are forced to sell their products to buyers below the competitive price because they lack bargaining power.[93] As argued by Blair and Harrison, even the conduct of monopsonists or oligopsonists, which decreases wholesale prices, can cause inefficiencies in the form of decreasing the quantity and innovation on the side of suppliers.[94] Second, it is not always the final consumers who will benefit from this situation. Retailers are driven by profit maximization, and lower wholesale prices would be more beneficial to them in the form of increased profits rather than to final consumers if the lower wholesale price is not projected into the final retail price. Monopsonistic or oligopsonistic retailers with

---

[91] Note 64, Smith and Thanassoulis, 47–8. This is typified in Australia where the market for food supermarket chains is oligopolistic. For more, see, Barbora Jedlickova and Julie Clarke, 'Antitrust in the Groceries Sector: Australia' in Pierre Kobel, Pranvera Këllezi and Bruce Kilpatrick (eds), *Antitrust in the Groceries Sector & Liability Issues in Relation to Corporate Social Responsibility* (Springer 2015).

[92] Note 89, Piraino, 1121–4, 1137; Note 34, OECD; Note 79, Dobson, Waterson and Chu, 13; Note 89, Blair and Harrison, 301–6, 310–17; Note 64, Steiner, 'How Manufacturers Deal with the Price-Cutting Retailer', 414; Note 64, Smith and Thanassoulis, 52–7.

[93] This has its limits because buyers need suppliers unless they are vertically integrated.

[94] Note 89, Blair and Harrison, 298–340.

bargaining power can pressure manufacturers to lower wholesale prices, while keeping the retail price the same or even increasing it.[95] This scenario is illustrated by one of the oldest recorded antitrust cases in the world – a case from ancient Greece in 388BC – involving the grain market, which was one of the basic and the most important food commodities. In Athens, grain was imported from abroad and sold to wholesalers who then sold to retailers and final consumers. Due to Spartan raids, many grain ships did not reach Athens. One Athenian grain commissioner suggested to wholesalers to bid collusively for the grain in the hope that they would pay less for the grain and pass the savings on to Athenians in the form of lower prices. Although this strategy lowered the wholesale price, it did not lower the retail price. The wholesalers hid their grain in warehouses, spreading rumors of war and loss of grain in order to make customers panic and pay more. The final consumer price increased up to six times the legal limit.[96] This case shows that if there are no competitive forces, buyers do the maximum to keep their profits as high as possible, rather than passing the benefits on to their final consumers.

In terms of vertical restrictions, in oligopsonies or in situations with a dominant retailer, increased buyer power assists with the successful negotiation of some forms of vertical restraints, such as RPM or VTR.[97] As illustrated in the example of retailers A and B and well recognized in both the US and EU antitrust/competition law regimes, it can be in the interest of a single retailer or a group of retailers to use RPM or VTR to decrease competition and in that way increase their profits and potentially restrict smaller but possibly more efficient competitors.[98] In oligopsonies and situations where a retailer has a dominant position, a retailer or retailers have such strong bargaining power that they are able to

---

[95] Ibid., 306.

[96] Lambros E Kotsiris, 'An Antitrust Case in Ancient Greek Law' (1988) 22(2) *International Lawyer* 451.

[97] See, e.g., William S Comanor, 'Antitrust Policy toward Resale Price Maintenance Following *Leegin*' (2010) 55 *Antitrust Bulletin* 59, 60–63, 67–9, 75–7; Roger Blair and Jessica Haynes, 'The Plight of Online Retailers in the Aftermath of *Leegin*: an Economic Analysis' (2010) 55(1) *Antitrust Bulletin* 245, 260; Kenneth G Elzinga and David E Mills, 'The Economics of Resale Price Maintenance' in *Competition Law and Policy*, Collins W (ed.) (2008) American Bar Association, Chapter XX, 5; Note 40, Areeda and Hovenkamp; Note 34, OECD; Greg Shaffer, 'Slotting Allowances and Resale Price Maintenance: A Comparison of Facilitating Practices' (1991) 22 *Rand Journal of Economics* 120, 120–36; Note 7, Williamson, 123–60.

[98] See the following chapters for further discussion.

'persuade' their suppliers to enforce vertical restraints on the remaining retailers.[99] For instance, it is in the interests of a dominant retailer with significant bargaining power who charges higher prices than his competitors not to lose customers to those competitors selling below his price.

Bilateral Monopoly and Oligopoly

In bilateral monopolies and oligopolies, both suppliers and buyers have balanced bargaining power; therefore, both parties need to find a way to maximize their own profits. This will likely set prices high in a way that will be beneficial for each party but not for consumers. Bilateral monopolies, in particular, could lead to double marginalization, and thus a restriction of efficiencies, a situation where there is no competition in either downstream or upstream markets and participants on both sides are trying to maximize their profits.[100] Due to the creation of concentrated distribution networks, it is possible that marginalization is more common than it used to be.

Marginalization can also be triple or any other 'multiple' depending on the market power of all the players on the vertical chain or network, which can include more vertical layers and entities than just a buyer and a seller. Although the occurrence of multiple marginalization would seem to be a significant problem, such phenomena are limited by consumer demand. Depending on the elasticity of the demand curve, consumers would start decreasing their purchasing if prices were too high. In other words, each price has its own monopolistic peak; if players go beyond it, their profits start to decrease rather than increase.

Nevertheless, as with other market structures, even markets based on bilateral monopolies and oligopolies must be analyzed case by case as they can lead to different outcomes, which are not always anti-competitive. Indeed, an OECD study from 1998 shows that it is impossible to make exact predictions of results in each market on the vertical chain or network if there is a bilateral (multilateral) monopoly or oligopoly. Unlike single monopolies/oligopolies or monopsonies/

---

[99] Note 46, *Mack Trucks*; Note 46, *Toys 'R' Us*; Note 46, *Euromodas*; Note 19, *Business Electronics*; Note 40, Areeda and Hovenkamp, 35–41, 59; Note 89, Comanor, 'The Two Economics of Vertical Restraints', 1280; Chapter 4 'Development of the US Law of Vertical Territorial and Price Restraints' and Chapter 5 'Development of the EU Law of Vertical Territorial and Price Restraints'.

[100] See, Note 6, Hovenkamp, 635–8; Note 34, OECD; Nikolaos Vettas, 'Developments in Vertical Agreements' (2010) 55(4) *Antitrust Bulletin* 843, 855–7.

oligopsonies, where the bargaining power is on one side of the vertical chain, in a bilateral monopoly or oligopoly the relationship and bargaining power between suppliers and buyers is more balanced and the profit is not concentrated within one party. Buyer power will leave the produce surplus, including buyer surplus, unchanged and high or even increase it up to its maximum as each player seeks to gain the highest possible profit for herself. Nevertheless, this does not always lead to monopolistic prices. For example, in certain cases manufacturers can be motivated to maximize their outputs.[101] Another result is that a bilateral strong market power and neutralized bargaining power will neutralize the effects on the final consumers because it can lower the retail price, in comparison to situations where a monopoly power exists at only one end of the vertical chain.[102]

Hovenkamp identified three options that firms have in situations with double marginalization:

1. accept the consequences of double marginalization, which might be the best alternative if internal production is costly and alternative 3 is unavailable; for example, a manufacturer selling to a market-dominating local dealer may have no choice but to accept that dealer's high markups as a cost of doing business;
2. the neoclassical solution, which is to integrate by ownership with the other production level, whether by merger or new entry; or
3. the 'bargaining' solution, which is to enter into one of many types of contractual arrangements under which the two vertically related firms increase output and cut prices to the joint maximizing level.[103]

The first option creates the marginalization problem with monopolistic prices and decreased output, while options two and three would instead lead to higher output and lower prices.[104]

If double marginalization occurs, maximum price fixing at the vertical level could improve efficiencies and the negative impact that marginalization has on final consumers.[105] Basically, a manufacturer could be concerned about the monopolistic retail prices because these lead to a

---

[101] Note 34, OECD; see also Note 6, Hovenkamp, 638–9, 651.
[102] Note 64, Steiner, 'Vertical Competition', 262; see also ibid., Hovenkamp, 635–6, 638–9.
[103] Ibid., Hovenkamp, 638–9.
[104] Ibid., 639.
[105] Ibid., see the factual situation in the case of *Albrecht v. Herald Co.*, 390 U.S. 145 (1968).

lowering of the final output. If the prices are lower, a higher number of consumers would be interested in buying his products. The manufacturer could persuade his retailers to agree to the maximum price setting policy which will prevent the retailer from charging monopolistic prices. If the retailer has a reason to agree to this policy, the final consumers will pay less and would therefore be interested in buying more of those products.[106]

Unlike vertical maximum price fixing, RPM and VTR would have an anticompetitive effect because both the buyer's and the supplier's markets are concentrated or monopolistic. Thus, final consumers would not have substitutes to purchase from a different retailer or directly from a different manufacturer and, thus, even horizontal competition would be restricted. The manufacturer could be motivated to introduce vertical restrictions because RPM and potentially VTR can ease the bargaining tension in oligopoly-oligopsony or monopoly-oligopsony vertical markets as it prevents downstream players from pressuring upstream players to decrease wholesale prices.[107] However, VTR can, at the same time, increase the buyer's (retailer's) bargaining power because it can create an exclusive position in relation to the buyer's manufacturer (supplier).

Restriction of Interbrand Competition in Other Market Structures

Similar to monopolies and oligopolies, in any market with more than one player and especially in a market that is concentrated, there is the possibility of the existence of follow-the-leader strategies. As Williamson explains, vertical restraints are of a restrictive nature when considering transaction costs in situations where a vertical restraint enhances strategic purposes or oligopolistic interdependence.[108] Such situations occur when, for example, other manufacturers and/or retailers follow the retail prices of a leader using RPM. They do not necessarily have to impose RPM as well, they could decide to increase the wholesale price or more likely

---

[106] The maximum price setting for their distributor(s) could be also utilized by a monopolistic manufacturer if the downstream market is more competitive. In that situation, it would be easier for the manufacturer to persuade their retailer(s) to do so, as they could switch to other retailer(s).

[107] Paul W Dobson and Michael Waterson 'The Competition Effects of Industry-Wide Vertical Price Fixing in Bilateral Oligopoly' (2007) 25 *International Journal of Industrial Organization* 935, 935–62.

[108] Note 7, Williamson, 130; see also Patrick Rey and Joseph Stiglitz, 'Vertical Restraints and Producers' Competition' (1988) 32 *European Economic Review* 561.

retailers themselves could simply follow the rise of the retail price of this particular brand. Steiner observes that others tend to follow well-established brands. He discusses the example of Levi Strauss jeans in the US, explaining that the price of jeans dropped significantly and a consumer surplus in men's jeans grew by approximately $203 million across the jeans market in the US after one manufacturer, leading brand Levi Strauss, stopped using RPM.[109]

The reasons for others following the 'leader' do not necessarily arise from a situation where the leader is the leading dominant brand; the manufacturer in question could, in fact, be less prominent. When considering game theory, this strategy could be attractive to others because it would be more profitable for them to increase their prices while maintaining the same output but receiving a higher profit per item, as explained further in the 'Monopolies and Oligopolies' section.

V. CONCLUSION

The understanding of how vertical restrictions operate in the market and their impact on competition is a complex matter, as outlined in this chapter and explored further in the rest of the book. This understanding involves an evaluation of the market at the vertical level, where recent developments reveal the introduction and/or facilitation of new forms of distribution, such as concentrated, partially integrated and online distributions. In order to understand vertical restrictions and determine their effect, it is useful to evaluate them from the individual, dual or triple vertical stages or relationships while considering the entire market, especially the reaction of other competitors, once VTR or RPM is introduced. Indeed, the effects of RPM and VTR differ based on a

---

[109] Note 64, Steiner, 'Vertical Competition, Horizontal Competition and Market Power', 260–61; Note 64, Steiner, 'Exclusive Dealing + Resale Price Maintenance', 451; see also Note 60, Steiner, 'How Manufacturers Deal with the Price-Cutting Retailer', 415; Note 60, Steiner, 'The Nature of Vertical Restraints', 178–83; see also Note 97, Comanor, 77; Note 97, Blair and Haynes, 245, 262; Matthew Bennett, Amelia Fletcher, Emanuele Giovannetti and David Stallibrass, 'Resale price maintenance: Explaining the controversy, and small steps towards a more nuanced policy' (2010) MPRA Paper No. 21121 (4 March 2010) <http://mpra.ub.uni-muenchen.de/21121/> accessed 18 May 2015; see also *Coca-Cola Firm, Pepsi Co. Inc. v. Federal Trade Commission*, 642 F.2d 1387 (1981); *First Beverages, Inc. of Las Vegas and Will Norton v. Royal Crown Cola Co. and H & M Sales Co.*, 612 F. 2d 1164 (1980).

number of conditions. If the horizontal effects are considered, it is not advisable to generalize because the effects are difficult to predict with certainty.

The understanding of competition in connection with vertical restrictions should not be narrowed to a mere evaluation of interbrand competition; other forms of competition should also be considered. First, the restriction of intrabrand competition, which is primarily effected by vertical restriction, could have a significant harmful effect even in a competitive market if the vertical restriction is used on a well-established brand or in situations where others follow the example of the firm restricting the market vertically. Second, firms compete by focusing their strategies not only on horizontal competition but also at the vertical level by bargaining for better conditions for themselves and strengthening their bargaining power. Vertical restrictions can then further facilitate the bargaining power of certain firms and, as I explain and show in a number of examples in the following chapters, it is the firm with bargaining power who will succeed in introducing RPM or VTR, unless vertical restrictions are introduced with mutual benefits for both parties on the dual vertical chain.

3. US development, case studies and summaries

I. INTRODUCTION

The US was one of the first (arguably the first) countries to introduce modern antitrust (competition) law. An important piece of US legislation, the Sherman Act,[1] was enacted in 1890. It created the most important basis for the law of vertical restraints. However, it would be wrong to suppose that antitrust law and policy, including the law of vertical restraints, has not changed since 1890. US antitrust policy has been constantly evolving, in some areas, such as vertical restrictions, more than others.

The first important milestone for the approach to RPM was the case of *Dr. Miles*,[2] which introduced the per se rule in 1911. Since then many changes have been adopted, with the *Colgate*[3] doctrine from 1919 and *Business Electronics*[4] arguably limiting the per se approach in 1988. The Miller-Tydings Act in 1937 and McGuire Act in 1952 allowed RPM under state statutes, both of which were repealed by the Consumer Goods Pricing Act in 1975. *Khan*[5] introduced the rule of reason to vertical maximum price fixing in 1997 and, ten years later, the Supreme Court overruled *Dr. Miles* in *Leegin*,[6] which changed the per se rule to the rule of reason.

---

[1] Sherman Antitrust Act 15 USC §§1–7, 26 Stat 209 (1890) ('Sherman Act').
[2] *Dr. Miles Medical Co. v. John D. Park & Sons Co.*, 220 U.S. 373 (1911) ('*Dr. Miles*').
[3] *United States v. Colgate & Co.*, 250 U.S. 300 (1919) ('*Colgate*').
[4] *Business Electronics Corp. v. Sharp Electronics Corp.*, 485 U.S. 717 (1988) ('*Business Electronics*').
[5] *State Oil Co. v. Khan*, 522 U.S. 2 (1997) ('*Khan*').
[6] *Leegin Creative Leather Products, Inc. v. PSKS, Inc, DBA Kay's Kloset … Kays' Shoes*, 551 U.S. 877 (2007) ('*Leegin*').

The situation with VTR is different. Since the judgment of *Sylvania*[7] was delivered in 1977, the rule of reason has applied to VTR. *Sylvania* is an important milestone not only for VTR cases but for vertical restrictions in general. Additionally, the cases that changed the per se rule for RPM and vertical maximum price fixing, *Khan* and *Leegin*, referred to the economic arguments presented in *Sylvania*. The Supreme Court in *Sylvania* started the (modern) economic approach based on the rule of reason, requiring the balancing of procompetitive and anticompetitive effects, later implemented for RPM in *Leegin*.

RPM has been a controversial topic in the US to a certain extent. Despite the long-established per se rule, there have been many arguments put forward as to why RPM can have procompetitive benefits.[8] However, since changing the strict per se rule to the rule of reason in *Leegin*, many have advocated a less lenient approach.[9] This was especially prominent immediately after the judgment in *Leegin* was delivered. Currently, this voice is becoming less profound, in particular, among the policy makers.

Indeed, any change in the development of US antitrust law has its reason(s). This also applies to policy and the application of the law of vertical restraints. These reasons are centered on aspects of the social environment, such as knowledge of economics and economic theories and, indeed, the ideology of relevant judges and officials of the Federal Trade Commission (FTC) and the Antitrust Division of the Department of Justice (DOJ). To describe RPM and VTR without the social context would not provide a coherent picture of the development of these practices in the US. Therefore, in this chapter, I do not merely intend to describe the law of vertical restrictions, in particular RPM and VTR, but, in order to provide a more holistic picture of the law of RPM and VTR in the US, I survey its development in connection with other factors that have influenced antitrust law while analyzing significant and selected

---

[7] *Continental T.V. v. GTE-Sylvania*, 433 U.S. 36 (1977) ('*Sylvania*').

[8] See the discussion in Chapter 5.

[9] See, e.g., Theodore Voorhees, 'Reasoning Through the Rule of Reason for RPM' (2013) 28(1) *Antitrust* 58; Adrian Kuenzler, 'Presumptions as Appropriate Means to Regulate Resale Price Maintenance: in Defence of Structuring the Rule of Reason' (2012) 8(3) *European Competition Journal* 497; Gregory T Gundlach, 'Overview and Contents of the Special Issue: Antitrust Analysis of Resale Price Maintenance after *Leegin*' (2010) 55 *Antitrust Bulletin* 1, 4–7; Andrew I Gavil, 'Resale Price Maintenance in the Post-*Leegin* World: A Comparative Look at Recent Developments in the United States and European Union' (2010) 1 *The CPI Antitrust Journal* 1, 2–3; Richard M Brunell, 'Overruling *Dr. Miles*: The Supreme Trade Commission in Action' (2007) 52 *Antitrust Bulletin* 475, 528.

cases. By examining these cases, I illustrate in detail the changes in approach to RPM and VTR and their application.

II. THE SHERMAN ACT

Modern antitrust law as introduced by the Sherman Act[10] by the US Congress in 1890 has its roots in the common law.[11] Indeed, the US courts adopted a number of common law terms during the interpretation of the Sherman Act and many are still used by US antitrust law today. Examples of these include the rule of reason, the doctrine of conspiracy, the restraint of trade and the per se rule.[12]

Contrary to current US antitrust law, the common law did not create a complex system of antitrust law.[13] It tolerated most anticompetitive practices, including vertical restrictions, with the reasoning based on freedom of contracting and the understanding that the market could regulate competition itself.[14] Even cartels were not considered illegal if all they did was increase prices and did not control the markets by dividing territories to avoid competition.[15]

This approach changed significantly with the enactment of the Sherman Act by Congress. It seems that Congress wished to weaken the power of some strong combinations and monopolists, such as railway and oil companies, and thus protect small businesses. Those big companies obtained their monopolistic power due to conditions throughout and after the Civil War.[16] The content of the anti-collusion Section 1 and anti-monopoly Section 2, as well as the title Sherman *Antitrust* Act indicate that the purpose of the Act was to prevent the creation of big enterprises

---

[10] Note 1.

[11] Senator John Sherman, 21 *Congressional Record* 3: 2457, 2456 (21 March 1890).

[12] Herbert Hovenkamp, *Federal Antitrust Policy, The Law of Competition and Its Practice* (4th edn, Thomson West, St. Paul 2011) 62; Hans B Thorelli, *The Federal Antitrust Policy: Origination of an American Tradition* (PA Norstedt & Söner, Stockholm 1954) 9–35.

[13] Keith N Hylton, *Antitrust Law: Economic Theory and Common Law Evolution* (Cambridge University Press 2003) 31–7.

[14] Note 12, Hovenkamp, 69.

[15] See, e.g., *Wickens v. Evans*, 148 E.R. 1201, (1829) 3 Y. & J. 318; *Mitchel v. Reynolds*, 24 E.R. 347, (1711) 1 PWms 181; Note 12, Hovenkamp, 65.

[16] Alan D Neale and Dan G Goyder *The Antitrust Laws of the United States of America: A Study of Competition Enforced by Law* (3rd edn, Vermont 1980) 15; Note 12, Thorelli, 54–163.

in order to protect small businesses. Companies with strong market and political power brokered fear and their existence went against the American ideology, which proposes that anybody can enter and compete in the US market. In addition, the protection of small businesses can be detected from the fact that during the discussion of the Sherman Act in Congress, associations of independent and small businesses were among the most effective lobbying organizations, as their existence was threatened by large, vertically integrated competitors. Indeed, Senator Sherman most likely acted on behalf of independent oil manufacturers competing with the Standard Oil Company.[17] Since the enactment of the Sherman Act, the protection of small businesses was the principal ideology of US antitrust law, and this sentiment lasted until the 1970s. However, although the statute should have been used as a tool against (anti) trusts, it started more as a process of protecting competition.

Finally, the purpose of the Sherman Act was to 'federalize' and make the common law more effective by creating a statute with jurisdiction over more than one state, a purpose stated by Senator Sherman, who proclaimed that this new Act should have been governed by common law principles.[18] This was further confirmed in the case of *Addyston Pipe*.[19] Even at the beginning of the twenty-first century, the Supreme Court linked the Sherman Act with the common law by referring to the Act as 'a common-law statute'.[20] The courts, when interpreting the Act, adopted some common law terminology such as the per se rule. However, they found some standards of the common law improper for the purposes of the Sherman Act. Most obviously, the Supreme Court rejected the common law standard of reasonableness and introduced a new standard

---

[17] Note 12, Hovenkamp, 59–61; Note 13, Hylton; Note 12, Thorelli, 164–234; George W Stocking and Myron W Watkins, *Monopoly and Free Enterprise* (Twentieth Century Fund, New York 1951) 80.

[18] Senator John Sherman, 21 *Congressional Record* 2455 (21 March 1890): the Senator stated that this bill 'does not announce a new principle of law, but applies old and well recognized principles of the common law to the complicated jurisdiction of our State and Federal Government'; see also Senator John Sherman, 20 *Congressional Record* 1167 (25 January 1889).

[19] *United States v. Addyston Pipe & Steel Co.*, 85 Fed. 271 (6th Circuit 1898) 278–91, affirmed 175 U.S. 211, 20 SCt 96 (1899) ('*Addyston Pipe*'); see also Note 12, Hovenkamp, 61; Note 16, Neale and Goyder, 17; Note 12, Thorelli, 9.

[20] Note 6, *Leegin*, 899.

of unreasonable restriction of trade in two of the oldest cases of *Trans-Missouri*[21] and *Joint Traffic*.[22]

Content

The core substance provisions of the Sherman Act are Sections 1 and 2, where Section 1 prohibits collusion that restricts trade or commerce, and Section 2 prohibits unlawful monopolization, which primarily takes a unilateral form. Both groups of conduct addressed under Sections 1 and 2 of the Sherman Act were unenforceable under the common law.[23] Therefore, one of the obvious elements of novelty was that collusion restricting trade and monopolization were declared to be public offences under the Sherman Act. The Act also allowed for the aggrieved party to obtain damages or injunctions.

As well as horizontal collusion and monopolization, vertical restraints were also not enforceable under the common law. Despite the fact that the Sherman Act does not contain any provision specifically drafted for vertical restrictions,[24] it has been applied to them. In particular, the courts have been applying Section 1 of the Sherman Act to RPM since the beginning of the twentieth century[25] and later to VTR.[26] This section prohibits '[e]very contract, combination in the form of trust or otherwise, or conspiracy, in restraint of trade or commerce among the several States, or within foreign nations'. Therefore, two aspects must be proven: first, the existence of multilateral/bilateral conduct, commonly referred to as 'an agreement' by the US courts, and, second, the restriction of trade.

Despite the fact that the Act refers to terms such as 'combination' and 'conspiracy', these terms have not been individually defined by the US courts. Instead, all terms commune with each other and the broad definition of the term 'agreement', including tacit agreements, has been

---

[21] *United States v. Trans-Missouri Freight Association*, 166 U.S. 290 (1897) ('*Trans-Missouri*').

[22] *United States v. Joint Traffic Association*, 171 U.S. 505 (1898) ('*Joint Traffic*').

[23] At least not to the same extent.

[24] This is understandable when we consider the reason for the existence of the Sherman Act: it was introduced to protect small businesses and to weaken powerful trusts by prohibiting restrictive collusion and harmful monopolizations.

[25] See Note 2, *Dr. Miles*; *John D. Park & Sons Co v. Samuel B. Hartman*, 153 Fed. Rep. 24 (6th Circuit 1907) ('*Park & Sons*').

[26] See below.

applied by the courts for all.[27] An agreement is illegal if it restrains trade or commerce as stated in the Sherman Act, however, the Supreme Court specified that not all restraints are prohibited, only those that are considered unreasonable.[28]

Section 2 of the Sherman Act can also apply to vertical restrictions. This section is based primarily on unilateral conduct and also prohibits multilateral/bilateral conduct in the form of 'every person who shall ... combine or conspire with any other person or persons'. This conduct, which is either unilateral or multilateral/bilateral, must have a form of monopolization or be an attempt to monopolize under Section 2. It prohibits the process of monopolization, not a static situation, as is obvious from the language used in the Act ('monopolization or attempt to monopolize') and from relevant cases.[29] The courts further specified that not all monopolization is illegal, only that which is harmful, in other words based on anticompetitive and not competitive practices.[30]

Aside from horizontal forms of anticompetitive practices, a person can become a monopolist or use her monopolistic power unreasonably by restraining competition at the vertical level, for example, through her buyers. This could also include vertical collusions between the manufacturer and her retailers, for instance, to maintain a high price or, on the contrary, to maintain low, predatory prices, which would then create boundaries for other competitors wishing to join the market. The retailers have little choice but to cooperate with the monopolist if they wish to stay in the market. If such conduct is based on collusion both Section 1 and Section 2 could apply, and both sections have been applied in reality to these cases; however, Section 2 only rarely.[31] It is primarily Section 1

---

[27] Compare: Note 21, *Trans-Missouri*; Note 19, *Addyston Pipe*; *Chicago Board of Trade v. United States*, 246 U.S. 231 (1918) ('*Chicago Board of Trade*'); *American Column & Lumber Co. v. United States*, 257 U.S. 377 (1921); *Maple Flooring Manufacturers Association v. United States*, 268 U.S. 563 (1925); *United States v. Topco Associates*, 405 U.S. 596 (1972); *National Society of Professional Engineers v. United States*, 435 U.S. 679 (1978); *Arizona v. Maricopa County Medical Society*, 457 U.S. 332 (1982) ('*Maricopa County*').

[28] See following section 'The First Era of the Sherman Act'.

[29] See, e.g., *Standard Oil Co. v. United States*, 221 U.S. 1 (1911) ('*Standard Oil*'); *United States v. Aluminum Co. of America*, 148 F.2d 416 (2nd Circuit 1945) ('*Aluminum Co.*').

[30] Since the case of Note 29, *Standard Oil*.

[31] Compare: *Atlantic Richfield Co. v. USA Petroleum Co.*, 495 U.S. 328 (1990), Section 1; *United States v. Microsoft Corp.*, 253 F.3d 34 (D.C. Circuit), cert. denied, 534 U.S. 952 (2001), Section 2. However, some forms of vertical

that applies to vertical restrictions and it has only been Section 1 that has been applied to RPM and VTR.

Changes in Policy and Law

The political influence on antitrust law based on the Sherman Act is limited. The brief character of the Sherman Act indicates that the US Congress preferred to leave it to the courts to introduce a precise interpretation and specific rules on Sections 1 and 2 rather than providing long and detailed legislation. Indeed, Senator Sherman stated, when commenting on the bill: 'I admit that it is difficult to define in legal language the precise line between lawful and unlawful combinations. This must be left for the courts to determine in each particular case.'[32] Congress has respected this characteristic and although it has passed new laws and many statutory exemptions from antitrust law,[33] it has left the substance of Sections 1 and 2 of the Sherman Act untouched, creating one of the most stable antitrust/competition Acts in the world.

Nevertheless, the courts' interpretation, priorities of antitrust agencies and, thus, antitrust policy and the application of the Sherman Act by the courts, have been changing and have differed in different eras. They have been influenced by economic theories and law and, to a certain limited extent, by politics.[34] Pitofsky, Handler and Baker compare changes in US antitrust policy to *'pendulum narrative'* dividing US antitrust law and policy into three core eras: the 1960s and 1970s were active eras, which were replaced by passive eras in the 1980s and a moderate era in the 1990s. According to them, the two extreme periods helped to create the

---

restrictions, such as tying, can typically violate both sections if used for the purposes of 'monopolization'.

[32] Senator John Sherman, 21 *Congressional Record* 2455 (21 March 1890) 2460.

[33] For instance, Federal Trade Commission Act 15 USC §§ 41–58 38 Stat 717 (1914) ('Federal Trade Commission Act'); The Robinson-Patman Anti-Price Discrimination Act 15 USC §§13–13b, 21a 49 Stat 1526 (1936) ('Robinson-Patman Act'); Hart-Scott-Rodino Antitrust Improvements Act, PubL No 94-435, 90 Stat 1383 (1976); Antitrust Criminal Penalty Enhancement and Reform Act, PubL No 108-237, 118 Stat 661 (2004); see also, Theodore Voorhees, 'The Political Hand in American Antitrust – Invisible, Inspirational, or Imaginary?' (2014) 79 *Antitrust Law Journal* 557, 558.

[34] Regarding the politics see, e.g., Steven C Salop, 'What Consensus? Why Ideology and Elections Still Matter to Antitrust' (2014) 79(2) *Antitrust Law Journal* 601.

'golden middle way' moderate era.[35] Although this categorization involves a number of useful observations,[36] any attempt to divide eras based on certain characteristics is never perfect. Indeed, Kovacic criticized this division claiming that it does not reflect the real historical development of antitrust policy precisely and simplifies some historical and current issues.[37]

Despite the imperfections, any scholarly work that intends to track and explain changes in historical development, as this chapter does, must characterize certain periods and divide them in accordance with these characteristics. I have divided this chapter primarily based on the interpretation of the Sherman Act and its application to RPM and VTR by the courts, taking into consideration other influential aspects. I have used this approach because it is primarily the interpretation by the courts and their application of the Sherman Act that have changed the approach to VTR and RPM. Therefore, the First Era explains the first interpretation of the Sherman Act and the creation of relevant rules to antitrust cases. The Strict Era is characterized by a strict enforcement of RPM and VTR based on the protection of small businesses. The Free Era, being influenced by the Chicago School, eased the previous strict enforcement. The Rule of Reason Era is characterized by the application of the rule of reason to both VTR and RPM, as, in this era, the Supreme Court 'gradually'[38] established the rule of reason for all forms of RPM.[39]

---

[35] Robert Pitofsky, 'Proposals for Revised United States Merger Enforcement in a Global Economy' (1992) 81 *Georgetown Law Journal* 195, 195–6; Milton Handler, 'Introduction' (1990) 35 *Antitrust Bulletin* 13, 13–21; early changes – before World War II: see Jonathan B Baker, 'Competition Policy as a Political Bargain' (2005–2006) 73 *Antitrust Law Journal* 483.

[36] For example, I would agree that the 1980s were more passive in terms of the number of cases brought by antitrust agencies than the previous and following eras.

[37] William E Kovacic, 'The Modern Evolution of U.S. Competition Policy Enforcement Norms' (2003–2004) 71 *Antitrust Law Journal* 377, 377–478.

[38] It is possible that not everybody would argue that the development was gradual; however, looking at several factors, I characterize this change as gradual rather than sudden. Consider, for instance, the application of the Sherman Act to RPM and VTR by the Supreme Court, which first introduced the rule of reason to VTR, and later it made it harder to apply the per se rule to RPM. Following this, it introduced RPM to maximum price fixing with the final important change in Note 6, *Leegin*, which established the rule of reason to the rest of resale price maintenance.

[39] The courts continued to apply the rule of reason to VTR, which was first introduced at the beginning of the Strict Era in Note 7, *Sylvania* in 1977.

III. THE FIRST ERA (1890s–1930s): THE INTERPRETATION OF THE SHERMAN ACT

Antitrust law and policy began to hold an important position in US society soon after the enactment of the Sherman Act. The first task important for the existence of a vibrant antitrust law was to interpret and clarify the Sherman Act. The DOJ undertook this role seriously, bringing a number of important cases to the courts. The courts, and especially the Supreme Court, introduced a number of rules essential for the interpretation of the Sherman Act, which have been applied ever since. Although the courts referred to the common law in early cases of the Sherman Act,[40] they differentiated the Sherman Act and its antitrust law from the common law doctrine, which assisted with the creation of a new field of law: antitrust law.[41]

In the case of *Trans-Missouri*,[42] the Supreme Court differentiated between the common law doctrine of prohibiting only some restraints of trade (unreasonable restraints of trade), stating that the wording of the Sherman Act referred to all restraints of trade and therefore it differs from the common law.[43] It held that the effect of the agreement and not its intent had to be evaluated in order to determine whether the agreement violated the Sherman Act.[44]

In *Addyston Pipe*, the Court referred back to the common law term 'ancillary restraints' and differentiated between ancillary and naked restraints for the purposes of the Sherman Act.[45] This division of restraints laid the foundation for the differentiation and application of the rule of reason and the per se rule, where the per se rule is only applied to naked restrictions and not ancillary restrictions.[46] In *Addyston Pipe*, the

---

[40] See, e.g., Note 19, *Addyston Pipe*; *Connally v. General Construction Co.*, 269 U.S. 385 (1926); *Cline v. Frink Dairy Co.*, 274 U.S. 445 (1927).

[41] See the discussion above. See Note 29, *Standard Oil*; *United States v. American Tobacco Co.*, 221 U.S. 106, 31 S.Ct. 632 (1911) ('*American Tobacco*').

[42] Note 21, *Trans-Missouri*.

[43] Ibid., 328.

[44] Ibid., 342.

[45] A restraint of trade, for instance a price-fixing arrangement, can be ancillary to a joint venture agreement aiming to develop a new product if such price fixing is necessary for the purposes of the joint venture. This could result in a greater social benefit than detriment.

[46] The per se rule means that a particular restriction is always illegal, while under the rule of reason the plaintiff has to prove that the restriction is unreasonable and thus that it restricts competition.

Supreme Court ruled that if the agreement was ancillary, the Court would then have to decide whether it was reasonable.[47] The Court held that the term 'reasonable' did not mean whether the prices in the market were reasonable but whether the practices, such as setting the prices, were reasonable.[48]

This standard of reasonableness was later challenged in *Standard Oil*, which introduced the rule of reason approach. The Supreme Court stated that the Sherman Act condemned not all restraints but only unreasonable restraints of trade.[49] Unlike the ruling in *Addyston Pipe*, the Supreme Court broadened the application of reasonableness to all restraints of trade. Under this standard, an agreement can be unreasonable by its nature,[50] its purpose or its effect, and the nature, purpose or effect has to have had a negative impact on competition. This approach was well summarized two weeks later in *American Tobacco*,[51] where the Supreme Court stated:

> Applying the rule of reason to the construction of the statute, it was held in the *Standard Oil Case* that, as the words 'restraint of trade' at common law and in the law of this country at the time of the adoption of the anti-trust act only embraced acts or contracts or agreements or combinations which operated to the prejudice of the public interests by *unduly restricting competition*, or unduly obstructing the due course of trade, or which, either because of their inherent nature or effect, or because of the evident purpose of the acts, etc., *injuriously restrained trade*, ... It was therefore pointed out that the statute did not forbid or restrain the power to make normal and usual contracts to further trade by resorting to all normal methods, whether by agreement or otherwise, to accomplish such purpose ... the term 'restraint of trade,' required that the words 'restraint of trade' should be given a meaning which would not destroy the individual right to contract, and render difficult, if not impossible, any movement of trade in the channels of interstate commerce,-the free movement of which it was the purpose of the statute to protect.[52]

In the case of *Chicago Board*,[53] the Supreme Court stated that the restriction had to have an appreciable effect on the market. Significantly, it confirmed that the restriction concerned had to restrict competition

---

[47] See also Note 22, *Joint Traffic*.
[48] Note 19, *Addyston Pipe* 235–6; see also Note 21, *Trans-Missouri*, 339.
[49] Note 29, *Standard Oil*, 3–4; see also Note 27, *Chicago Board of Trade*.
[50] Here, the per se rule would apply.
[51] Note 41, *American Tobacco*.
[52] Ibid., 179, emphasis added.
[53] Note 27, *Chicago Board of Trade*.

unreasonably and that 'the rule of reason does not support a defense based on the assumption that competition itself is unreasonable'.[54] It also explained that when applying the rule of reason, parties must include all information about themselves, the market and their business. It set the test for the rule of reason as follows:

> [T]he court must ordinarily apply: its condition before and after the restraint was imposed, the nature of the restraint and its effect, actual or probable. The history of the restraint, the evil believed to exist, the reason for adopting the particular remedy, the purpose or end sought to be attained . ...[55]

During the time of the interpretation of the Sherman Act, important economic bases were introduced, such as the measurement of welfare, the marginalist theory and the theory of transaction costs. However, it took a number of decades before these concepts were adopted into US antitrust policy in the late 1970s. For example, in 1937, Coase published an influential article 'The Nature of the Firm' where he developed the marginalist theory of firm organization and structure. He also explained firms' decision-making processes by referring to transaction costs.[56] In connection with VTR and RPM, this neoliberal idea of the Coase Theorem was further implemented in free riding theory on procompetitive services later in the 1960s, where it was presumed that the manufacturer is better placed to determine what services should be offered with the product, thus resolving the information problem arising from free riding.[57]

In 1906, Italian scholar, Pareto, had already introduced a mechanism for measuring welfare: the Pareto optimality. The Pareto model promoted consumer rather than total welfare as it argued that the transferring of wealth from consumers to manufacturers was harmful.[58] In 1939, the Kaldor-Hicks efficiency introduced the concept of measuring total welfare. The Kaldor-Hicks model is based on the principle that an outcome is efficient not just if there are no losers, as in the Pareto optimality, but also when the winners win more than the losers lose. Thus, winners can compensate for losers and still have an extra part of the surplus left for them.[59]

---

[54] Ibid., 238.
[55] Ibid.
[56] Ronald H Coase, 'The Nature of the Firm' (1937) 4 (16) *Economica* 386.
[57] See Chapter 5.
[58] Vilfredo FD Pareto, *Manuale d'economia politico* (Milan, 1906).
[59] John Hicks, 'The Foundations of Welfare Economics' (1939) 49(196) *Economic Journal* 696, 696–712; Nicholas Kaldor, 'Welfare Propositions in Economics and Interpersonal Comparisons of Utility' (1939) 49(195) *Economic*

Soon after the first Supreme Court cases and still during the continuing period of the first interpretation of the Sherman Act, politics became 'significantly' involved in formulating antitrust law and policy.[60] This is reflected first in presidency campaigns and the presidential influence at the beginning of the twentieth century and later in the enactment of new antitrust legislation. For example, antitrust law and policy were the center of attention throughout the presidential election of Theodore Roosevelt and William Howard Taft who promised stronger and stricter antitrust law. In particular, during the presidency of William Howard Taft (1909–13), who later became the tenth Chief Justice of the US (1921–30), the US experienced aggressive antitrust enforcement, most notably aimed at the most powerful companies in order to protect small businesses.[61]

At the end of Taft's presidency and the beginning of Woodrow Wilson's, Congress established a Commission on Industrial Relations. Partly influenced by its proceedings, but most notably influenced by President Wilson,[62] Congress introduced two new Acts. These Acts represented the preference of Congress for a stricter approach and stronger antitrust enforcement. First, the Clayton Act (1914)[63] reflected Congress's belief that the Court should accommodate a stricter approach. The Act focuses on 'unfair competition' and the prohibition of, for instance, mergers and acquisitions which 'may substantially lessen competition' or 'tend to create a monopoly' (Section 7) and some forms of vertical restraints, including tying, exclusive dealing (Section 3) and price restraints, such as price discrimination (Section 2) and other unfair methods of competition.

Journal 549, 549–52; see also Robert L Steiner, 'The *Leegin* Factors – a Mixed Bag' (2010) 55(1) *Antitrust Bulletin* 25, 44–5, 51.

[60] In contrast with more recent eras, the presidential campaigns promised strong antitrust laws and the involvement of presidents has been well documented. See, James F Rill and Stacey L Turner, 'Presidents Practicing Antitrust: Where to Draw the Line?' (2014) 79 *Antitrust Law Journal* 577. Furthermore, the beginning of the twentieth century is characterized by the enactment of a number of antitrust acts. This is incomparable to any more recent periods in antitrust history.

[61] See ibid.

[62] See, e.g., E Thomas Sullivan, Herbert Hovenkamp, Howard A Shelanski and Christopher R Leslie, *Antitrust Law, Policy and Procedure: Cases, Materials, Problems* (7th edn, LexisNexis 2014) 34–5.

[63] Clayton Antitrust Act PubL 63-212, 15 USC §12–27, 29 USC §52–53, 38 Stat 730 (1914) ('Clayton Act').

The second act, the FTC Act (1914),[64] established another antitrust agency, the Federal Trade Commission (FTC). The FTC Act protects not only competition, but also consumers, against unfair practices, thereby giving the FTC the authority to enforce both antitrust and unfair-practices law. Section 5 of the FTC Act prohibits 'unfair methods of competition'. The Supreme Court confirmed that practices which violated the Sherman Act were also unfair methods of competition under Section 5 of the FTC Act.[65] Therefore, the FTC has the power to enforce the Sherman Act in connection with Section 5 of the FTC Act. This means that the antitrust agenda is split between the Antitrust Division of the DOJ and the FTC.[66] Both agencies have concurrent jurisdiction over the enforcement of the Clayton Act, while the Sherman Act is the principal jurisdiction of the DOJ. The FTC is the only agency responsible for the enforcement of the FTC Act.

The period which followed, the 1920s and the 1930s, is characterized by many contradictions. On one hand, the ideology that advocated primarily the protection of small businesses continued to play an important role.[67] On the other hand, Congress was inclined to allow a number of exceptions to antitrust law.

The protection of small businesses is very obvious in the enactment of the Robinson-Patman Act in 1936. This Act amended Section 2 of the Clayton Act, which forbade various forms of price discrimination. The Robinson-Patman Act[68] became a far more complex statute. It was passed to protect small firms against unfair, price discriminative competition from vertically integrated, multi-location chain stores which, Congress

---

[64] Note 33, Federal Trade Commission Act, notably Section 5.

[65] See, e.g., *Federal Trade Commission v. Cement Institute*, 333 U.S. 683 (1948); *Federal Trade Commission v. Sperry and Hutchinson Co.*, 405 U.S. 233 (1972).

[66] The split agenda and the five Commissioners of the FTC, where no more than three can belong to one political party, assists with the independence of the agencies; however, politics continued to influence antitrust policy to a certain extent. For instance, particularly in the early stages of US antitrust law, Rill and Turner described a number of cases and investigations where the US President successfully or unsuccessfully intervened using his constitutional right (such as intervention on the basis of foreign policy) or other means (appointing an Attorney General or direct lobbying). Note 60, Rill and Turner; see also Note 33, Voorhees.

[67] Note 12, Hovenkamp, 60, 66–7; Ellis Hawley, 'Herbert Hoover and the Sherman Act, 1921–1933: an Early Phase of a Continuing Issue' (1989) 74 *Iowa Law Revue* 1067.

[68] Note 33, Robinson-Patman Act.

believed, could dominate markets through predation and other forms of economic advantages.[69]

Only one year later, in 1937, Congress introduced the Miller-Tydings Act, which permitted states to authorize resale maintenance agreements by fair-trade state laws. The exception was broadened in the McGuire Act[70] in 1952. The Act allowed states to create laws which would permit manufacturers to enforce RPM as unilateral conduct or even in an agreement with dealers. These Acts and their authorizations were withdrawn by the Consumer Goods Pricing Act[71] in 1975. Furthermore, throughout the New Deal era, Congress also allowed for government regulation to take place and began to regulate several industries, creating various degrees of antitrust immunity.

The beginning of the twentieth century, particularly the year 1911, was an important milestone for the formulation of the approach to vertical restraints. First, merging, including vertical integration, was seen as suspicious and was consequently considered to be unwanted and illegal.[72] In 1911, the DOJ used Section 2 of the Sherman Act to attack vertical integrations in *Standard Oil*.[73] This trend continued in later periods and was prohibited under Section 7 of the Clayton Act (1914).[74] Secondly, and most importantly for the purposes of this book, in 1911, for the first time, the Supreme Court applied the Sherman Act to an RPM case in *Dr. Miles*,[75] deciding to apply a strict approach, the per se rule, to RPM cases. The Court concluded that vertical agreements fixing prices were against public interest, were illegal and were without reasonable justification.[76] This started a long period of the per se rule approach, which was stopped entirely by the case of *Leegin*[77] in 2007.

---

[69] Secretary of the Federal Trade Commission Donald S Clark, 'The Robinson-Patman Act: General Principle, Commission Proceedings and Selected Issues, Retail Channel Conference for the Computer Industry' (San Jose, 7 June 1995) <https://www.ftc.gov/es/public-statements/1995/06/robinson-patman-act-general-principles-commission-proceedings-and-selected>, accessed 7 May 2015.

[70] 66 Stat 632 (1952).

[71] 89 Stat 801 (1975) section 11.5a.

[72] Herbert Hovenkamp, 'The Law of Vertical Integration and the Business Firm: 1880–1960' (2010) 95 *Iowa Law Review* 863, 879–80.

[73] Note 29, *Standard Oil*.

[74] Note 63, Clayton Act; see *United States v. Paramount Pictures*, 334 U.S. 131 (1948); *United States v. E.I. Du Pont de Nemours & Co.*, 353 U.S. 586 (1957).

[75] Note 2, *Dr. Miles*.

[76] Ibid., 408.

[77] Note 6, *Leegin*.

However, this was not the first case on RPM. Already in 1907, the Court of Appeals had decided a case on RPM: *Park & Sons*. Because this case was decided before the cases of *Standard Oil* and *American Tobacco*, the Court referred to the standard of reasonableness as applied in *Addyston Pipe* in 1899.

The main argument for the per se illegality of RPM in *Dr. Miles* was based on ownership rights, in that only the owner of the product in question can determine the price of the product and other sales conditions. The supplier cannot dictate the resale price to his retailer when selling his products, as the supplier no longer owns the product.[78] The Sherman Act protects the rights of owners to determine their business and to compete.[79]

Although the US case of *Dr. Miles* introduced the per se prohibition of RPM, such prohibition was not absolute, it had its limits. First, an IP owner was free to maintain resale prices as confirmed in the case of *General Electric*.[80] Secondly, another limit followed from the fact that Section 1 of the Sherman Act requires the existence of an agreement. In 1919, in the case of *Colgate*,[81] the Supreme Court held that the buyer, the retailer, was free to do whatever she wanted after she had purchased the product. However, it also explained that the supplier could refuse to sell his products if the retailer did not respect the supplier's price policy, as such refusal constituted unilateral conduct.[82] The Court stated that the Sherman Act did not restrict the rights of a person, in this case the supplier, to freely choose his business partners, in other words, with whom he would deal. This also included the announcement of conditions, such as resale price, under which the supplier will sell.[83]

Two years after *Colgate*, the courts fully applied the *Colgate* doctrine on price fixing in the case of *Frey & Son*, stating that letters issued by a manufacturer from time to time urging her distributors to apply her fixed prices constituted unilateral conduct.[84]

---

[78] Note 2, *Dr. Miles*, 404–5.
[79] Ibid., 406.
[80] *United States v. General Electric Co.*, 272 U.S. 476 (1926) ('*General Electric*').
[81] Note 3, *Colgate*.
[82] Ibid., 305–6.
[83] Ibid., 307; the *Colgate* doctrine was confirmed in the case of *Russell Stover Candies Inc. v. FTC*, 718 F. 2d 256 (8th Circuit 1983) ('*Russell Stover*').
[84] *Frey & Son, Incorporated v. Cudahy Packing Co.*, 256 U.S., 208 (1921), 213.

Park & Sons[85] and the Theory of Free Riding

The cases of *Park & Sons* and *Dr. Miles* share a very similar factual scenario. Both dealt with fixing or minimum fixing of retail prices by a manufacturer. In both cases, when applying Section 1 of the Sherman Act, the courts referred to the manufacturer as the initiator of RPM restricting competition despite the fact that Section 1 of the Sherman Act is based on bilateral/multilateral conduct in the form of a 'contract, combination ... or conspiracy' (an agreement) requiring evidence of the existence of an agreement.[86]

However, the case of *Park & Sons* only reached the Court of Appeals while *Dr. Miles* got as far as the final appeal to the Supreme Court, where the Court laid down the basis for future RPM cases. The judgment in *Park & Sons* by the Court of Appeals is older, being delivered four years before the final judgment of the Supreme Court in *Dr. Miles*. Importantly, it introduced the theory of free riding in RPM, which was not utilized in RPM cases for almost a century.[87]

As in *Dr. Miles*, in *Park & Sons*, the manufacturer controlled the sales and resale of medicine through her distribution system. This distribution system maintained minimum prices for wholesalers and retailers and controlled the sales of proprietary medicines. This was initially just for patented products or products protected by copyrights, but later included other products under the protection of trade secrets.[88]

The Court of Appeals first considered whether the manufacturer was entitled to maintain prices for wholesalers and retailers, arriving at the same conclusion as the Supreme Court in *Dr. Miles*. It concluded that she was not entitled in situations where the products only involved the trade secret. Then, by referring to the case of *Addyston Pipe* and applying the standard of reasonableness, the Court analyzed whether RPM was ancillary in order to protect the trade secret and Park & Sons' business. It concluded that it was not, stating that this form of RPM constituted an absolute elimination of competition.[89]

---

[85] Note 25, *Park & Sons*.

[86] In both cases, RPM was part of a contract, therefore the requirement of the agreement under Section 1 of the Sherman Act was met; however, the language used by the Court of Appeals in Note 25, *Park & Sons*, and by the Supreme Court in Note 2, *Dr. Miles*, was such that it predominantly pointed at the manufacturer as the entity initiating and maintaining RPM.

[87] See below.

[88] Note 25, *Park & Sons*, 26, 41–2.

[89] Ibid., 42.

IP rights as entitlement to vertical restraints
Like the Supreme Court in *Dr. Miles*, the Court of Appeals explained that trade secret owners were not free to create 'exclusive monopolies'. Therefore, they are prohibited from controlling trade, in the form of, for example, fixing prices, because the existence of the trade secret only protects the process of manufacturing.[90] The common law rule explains that once a product is sold, the buyer is free to do whatever he wants with it; patents and copyrights, however, are exempt from this rule.[91] The patent statute gives an advantage only to the patentee in the form of an 'exclusive monopoly'. If the owner of the secret process cannot bring the process under the protection of the patent statute, based on the complete publication of the invention, he also cannot claim the advantages from this statute.[92] Therefore, the trade secret does not have any impact on, and cannot be used as a justification for, restrictions on trade.

The application of *Addyston Pipe* to RPM
The Court of Appeals referred to *Addyston Pipe* and its standard of reasonableness and the differentiation between ancillary and naked restraints. The court found that the system of contracts in question had restrained trade but it admitted the possibility that this system could have been ancillary to the purpose of protecting the secret process and the complainant's business and, therefore, if this conduct was ancillary, the standard of reasonableness would have applied. To succeed with the claim that this conduct was ancillary the complainant would have to prove that this conduct was necessary for the protection of her business. In that respect, the court analyzed 'whether the restraint was necessary to the retained business and therefore ancillary to the principal purpose of the agreement'.[93]

The court held that the complainant failed to justify the restriction on this basis.[94] However, the court itself, not the complainant, offered a potential justification, expressing the possibility of using such a restraint to avoid price-cutting, in other words to protect the business and businesses of its retailers against free riding. Nevertheless, this was not proven in this case.[95]

---

[90] Ibid., 29.
[91] Ibid., 39.
[92] Ibid., 32.
[93] Ibid., 40–41.
[94] Ibid., 44–5.
[95] Ibid., 45.

Indeed, the court found this conduct to be unreasonable and not justified, and thus it was not ancillary because the only purpose of the contract was the restriction of competition.[96] The court highlighted the importance of protecting competition under the Sherman Act, stating that 'competition is desirable'[97] and partial restriction of competition can only be allowed under reasonable and necessary circumstances. While such restriction must only be ancillary to require protection, the restraint is not ancillary if the only purpose of the contract is the restriction of competition, as it was in this case.[98]

Dr Miles:[99] Per Se Rule in RPM

The Dr. Miles Medical Company (Dr. Miles) sold medicines in the US and abroad that were protected by trade secret, distinctive packages and labels and trademarks.[100] The company fixed minimum prices for both wholesale and retail prices, where the minimum price setting was part of agreements signed between Dr. Miles and over 400 US wholesalers and 25,000 US retailers.[101]

The complainant, Dr. Miles, claimed that she fixed wholesale and retail prices in order to ensure fair profit for her retailers and wholesalers. She alleged that without fixing prices some retailers were not willing to sell her products due to the 'undercut' prices of other retailers or did not 'urge or favor sales' of her products. She stated that this had a negative effect on the reputation of her products.[102] Dr. Miles argued that by fixing wholesale and retail prices she 'established a method "of governing, regulating, and controlling the sale and marketing" of [her] remedies'[103] in order to protect her 'trade sales and business' and of conserving her 'goodwill and reputation'.[104]

The defendant, wholesaler John D. Park & Sons Co., refused to enter into a price-fixing wholesale contract with Dr. Miles and was discounting

---

[96] Ibid.
[97] Ibid.
[98] Ibid.
[99] Note 2, Dr. Miles.
[100] Ibid., 374.
[101] Ibid., 374–81.
[102] Ibid., 374–5.
[103] Ibid., 375.
[104] Ibid.

Dr. Miles Medical Co.'s products.[105] Dr. Miles was seeking equitable relief for this.

By ruling on equitable relief, the courts considered the validity of the contract in question. The Supreme Court by referring to both the common law and the Sherman Act found the contract to be invalid.[106] The Supreme Court disagreed with the complainant, holding that vertical agreements fixing prices and thus restricting competition were against the public interest, were illegal and were without reasonable justification.[107] The Court based its reasoning on three important aspects. First, it differentiated different IP rights as entitlements to vertically fixed prices. Second, it stated that it is the right of the owner of the products in question to determine prices and thus the owner should be free to do so. Finally, the Court emphasized the fact that the contract concerned foreclosed the entire retailers' competition without differentiating between interbrand and intrabrand competition (a concept used in later cases).

Unlike the Court of Appeals in *Park & Sons*, the Supreme Court did not evaluate the intent of the complainant to protect her brand, to avoid under-cutting of retail prices and ensure fair profit for her retailers, stating that for this form of price fixing there is no reasonable justification, thus making it clear for future RPM cases that the per se rule and not the rule of reason should apply. Instead of analyzing the individual intent of the complainant, the Court surveyed objective criteria by referring to the arguments presented, as is obvious from the above-named three aspects. In the first two aspects, the Court set certain boundaries for determining prices. It is only the owner of the product or the owner of the statutory IP rights, such as a patent, who should determine prices. The last aspect, which discussed the foreclosure of competition, shows that the Court was concerned with the effect of this conduct on competition and not with the intentions of the participants. The analysis of this effect is in agreement with *Trans-Missouri*, where the Supreme Court held that the effect of the contract and not its intent must be evaluated in order to determine a violation of the Sherman Act.[108]

IP rights as entitlement to vertical restraints

By addressing the complainant's argument that her trade secret protection allowed her to determine wholesale and retail prices, the Supreme Court

---

[105] Ibid., 393.
[106] Ibid., 373, 409.
[107] Ibid., 408.
[108] Note 21, *Trans-Missouri*, 342.

first differentiated statutory IP rights, such as patents and copyrights, from other rights, including trade secrets. The Court stated that the patents were granted statutorily; it recognized that an owner of the patent could use the benefit of market control arising from exclusive manufacturing with the aim to promote invention.[109] However, this case was not based on a statutory grant and, therefore, could not benefit from the same privileges as in the case of patents.[110]

The Court then analyzed whether there was any difference between the products produced by a manufacturer with a trade secret and without.[111] In that respect, it held that trade secrets protected the process of manufacturing and not the products and, therefore, a trade secret did not entitle the holder to have 'monopolist's rights' over her products and thus to freely restrict competition, including the restriction of competition via RPM.[112]

The Court stated that the trade secret allowed the owner to sell licenses. It was also a subject of confidential communication and concerned the process of manufacturing. However, the minimum prices were fixed for the products not for the manufacturing process, while the process was not communicated to the wholesalers, retailers and consumers and thus remained a secret. Therefore, it cannot be concluded that the trade secret entitled the manufacturer to control sales through minimum price setting.[113]

The theory of ownership and freedom to compete
The Supreme Court confirmed that the previous doctrine established by the common law, which had regulated contracts restricting trade, was 'substantially modified' by the Sherman Act. The Supreme Court recognized public interest as the most important goal, holding that it was in the interests of both individuals and the public that every person be free and not restricted in their own business.[114]

In this regard, the Supreme Court ruled that the manufacturer lost her ownership rights when she sold her products to wholesalers and retailers, and was therefore not entitled to determine resale prices and other sales conditions because only the owners of the products were entitled to do so. The owners of the products must be free to determine their business

---

[109] Note 2, *Dr. Miles*, 401–2.
[110] Ibid., 402.
[111] Note 2, *Dr. Miles*, 400–401; the Court cited a case on patents: *Bement v. National Harrow Co.*, 186 U.S. 70 (1902) 92–3.
[112] Note 2, *Dr. Miles*, 400–403.
[113] Ibid., 402–3.
[114] Ibid., 406.

and to compete. In this case, the wholesalers and retailers should have been free to do whatever they wanted to with the products they owned.[115]

Mr. Justice Holmes's dissenting opinion overturned the theory of freedom. He argued that it was the manufacturer who should have been free to determine the retail prices of the products she manufactured, as this was part of the manufacturer's business.[116] He explained that the company had tried to set profitable, and for consumers affordable, prices, which were therefore fair prices. If the price was not affordable for the consumers, they would choose different products.[117] Justice Holmes's dissenting argument reflects the old common law doctrine rather than the Sherman Act. This doctrine had already been refused in *Addyston Pipe*, where the Supreme Court held under the Sherman Act that the question was not whether the prices in the market were reasonable but whether the practices, such as setting the prices, were reasonable.[118]

The question of ownership and the right to determine business was reopened eight years later in the case of *Colgate*,[119] as discussed further below. This question has its own jurisprudential value and as such I explore it further in Chapter 6. However, to outline a possible answer in connection with the case of *Dr. Miles*, the question as to who has the right to determine retail prices, the manufacturer or the retailers, can be looked at from two angles. First, the *Dr. Miles* angle of ownership clearly argues that the owner should be free to determine his/her prices. In this case, the owners of the products were the retailers and the wholesalers, and so they should have been free to determine the prices rather than the manufacturer. Second, competition, as an essential value of antitrust law, indicates that free competition should determine the retail prices and not the manufacturer or other individuals. This value was recognized and highlighted by the Supreme Court in *Dr. Miles* when the Court stated that the owners of the product must be free to compete. Indeed, Peritz rightly observed that the Court, when applying the Sherman Act, favored free competition.[120]

A correlated and rather economic question is whether the manufacturer or retailers know the product and customers better to determine the final prices. The argument based on the ruling in *Dr. Miles* could be that the

---

[115] Ibid., 404–6.
[116] Ibid., 412.
[117] Ibid., 412.
[118] Note 19, *Addyston Pipe* 235–6.
[119] Note 3, *Colgate*.
[120] Rudolph J Peritz, 'A Genealogy of Vertical Restraints Doctrine' (1988–89) 40 *Hastings Law Journal* 511, 516–29.

wholesalers and the retailers know their own customers and should hence be free to make their own business decisions and determine the best and fairest prices for themselves. The manufacturer already does this when setting the wholesale prices and selecting her wholesalers.

Foreclosure of intrabrand competition
The Supreme Court did not differentiate between different forms of competition such as intrabrand and interbrand competition in *Dr. Miles*. However, by holding that the entire retailer's competition was completely foreclosed because the manufacturer controlled the prices of all sales by reaching restrictive agreements,[121] it established indirectly that intrabrand competition must be protected and restrictions of trade which would foreclose intrabrand competition have the potential to violate Section 1 of the Sherman Act. In this regard, it cited *Park & Sons*,[122] where the Court of Appeals explained that the kind of practice that set minimum prices and did not allow retailers to sell to other retailers had destroyed all of the retailers' competition.[123]

Colgate:[124] **Unilateral Conduct and Ownership Rights**

Only eight years after the delivery of the judgment in *Dr. Miles*, the Supreme Court set limits to the *Dr. Miles* ownership doctrine in the case of *Colgate*. By doing so, it differentiated between unilateral conduct and bilateral/multilateral conduct, an agreement, establishing that the Sherman Act did not restrict the rights of a person, in this case the supplier, to freely choose his business partners, in other words, with whom he would deal. This also included the announcement of conditions, such as resale price maintenance, under which the supplier would sell.[125]

This case involved Colgate & Co., a US manufacturer producing soap and toiletries. At that time, Colgate sold his products through distributors and wholesalers throughout the US.[126] Colgate circulated letters, telegrams and other lists to dealers requiring uniform prices, stating that sales would be cancelled to those who did not follow this policy. He requested assurances and promises from his dealers to follow the price

---

[121] Note 2, *Dr. Miles*, 394, 399.
[122] Note 25, *Park & Sons*.
[123] Note 2, *Dr. Miles*, 399; Note 25, *Park & Sons*, 42.
[124] Note 3, *Colgate*.
[125] Ibid., 307; the *Colgate* doctrine was confirmed in the case of Note 83, *Russell Stover*.
[126] Note 3, *Colgate*, 302.

policy, many of which were given. In cases where the promise was not given, the manufacturer refused to sell, while sales were unrestricted to all dealers who complied with the new price policy and gave their assurances. Dealers who did not follow the policy were put on a suspended list and business with them was terminated.[127]

Ownership and freedom to deal constituting unilateral conduct

The Supreme Court based its decision primarily on the control and disposal of property.[128] It confirmed that the buyer, a retailer, a distributor or a wholesaler, was free to do whatever she wanted after she had purchased the product. However, it also explained that the supplier could refuse to sell his products if his buyer did not respect the supplier's price policy, as such refusal constituted unilateral conduct.[129]

The Court referred to the case of *Trans-Missouri*,[130] where the Supreme Court had confirmed that traders were free to sell to whomever they wished. It explained in *Colgate* that, with the exception of creating and/or maintaining a monopoly, the Sherman Act did not restrict the rights of a person, in this case the manufacturer, to freely choose his business partners, in other words, with whom he would deal. This also included the announcement of conditions under which the manufacturer would sell.[131] The Court shifted its view from the buyer's freedom to conduct her business to the manufacturer's freedom to trade. By applying this limit based on ownership and the freedom to deal, it found Colgate's conduct to be unilateral and therefore legal under Section 1 of the Sherman Act, which requires the existence of an agreement.[132]

Despite the Court's logical reasoning, the exact boundary between multilateral and unilateral conduct is not clear in this case as the prices could not have been maintained if the dealers did not agree and/or comply with the price policy. Dealers had to promise to follow the prices and they did so; therefore, an argument could be put forward that RPM was based on multilateral conduct not on unilateral actions. In agreement with this argument is the judgment by the lower court, the District Court, which found this conduct illegal under Section 1 of the Sherman Act, claiming that the defendant, together with the dealers, did not conclude an agreement but instead engaged in a combination with wholesalers and

---

[127] Ibid., 302–3.
[128] Ibid., 305.
[129] Ibid., 305–6.
[130] Note 21, *Trans-Missouri*, 320.
[131] Note 3, *Colgate*, 307.
[132] Ibid., 305–6.

retailers to maintain fixed prices.[133] The Supreme Court had to deal with this issue in the cases which followed (in particular, *Bausch & Lomb*,[134] *Beech-Nut*[135] and *Parke, Davis*[136]), where it clarified the boundary between unilateral conduct and an agreement under the *Colgate* and *Dr. Miles* doctrines.

IV. STRICT ERA (1940s–BEGINNING OF 1970s): PROTECTING SMALL BUSINESSES

This era is characterized by rather a strict legal and policy approach to antitrust law and the boom of economic theories in the US. Two theoretical schools were formed: the Harvard School, which had already formed in the 1930s and the Chicago School in the 1950s. First, the Harvard School theory, which was based on the empirical studies of American industries, preferred a structural approach. Its first scholarly works were introduced in the 1930s and its boom continued until the 1960s. Harvard School scholars were suspicious of any situation other than what they believed were competitive conditions, claiming that competitors would choose non-competing over competing.[137]

The Chicago School established its own theory as a reaction to the Harvard School. The School argued that many of the imperfections of competition were a result of competing and from competitors finding ways to be more efficient than their rivals. The Chicago School introduced a revolutionary approach to antitrust theory, which was, unlike the Harvard School theory, theoretical rather than empirical. Its scholars argued that economic efficiency was the antitrust goal and was the result of a free market. The Chicago School believed that inefficiency occurred only randomly in the market, arguing that monopolists had no interest in facilitating a monopoly or in narrowing access in vertically related

---

[133] Ibid., 303–4.

[134] *United States v. Bausch & Lomb Optical Co.*, 321 U.S. 707 (1944) ('*Bausch & Lomb*').

[135] *Federal Trade Commission v. Beech-Nut Packing Co.*, 257 U.S. 441 (1922) 455 ('*Beech-Nut*').

[136] *United States v. Parke, Davis & Co.*, 362 U.S. 29 (1959) ('*Parke, Davis*').

[137] See, e.g., Joe S Bain, *Essays on Price Theory and Industrial Organization* (Little, Brown and Company, Boston 1972); Edward S Mason, *Economic Concentration and the Monopoly Problem* (Harvard University Press 1957); Joe S Bain, *Barriers to New Competition* (Harvard University Press 1956); Ward S Bowman Jr, 'Toward Less Monopoly' (1953) 101 *University of Pennsylvania Law Review* 577.

markets. Like vertical monopolies, vertical restrictions were usually efficient at facilitating efficiencies rather than inefficiencies resulting from vigorous competition and innovation.[138]

RPM procompetitive theories are advocated on the basis of some of these Chicago School views and they started to play their role in economic thinking in this era. For example, the theory of pre-sale services was well explained by Telser[139] in 1960. He argued that discounting retailers free ride on pre-sale services offered by other retailers. In other words, free riding retailers steal profits from retailers who offer pre-sale services. By applying RPM, the manufacturer encourages retailers to promote manufacturers' products and protects them from free riders who benefit from the services of other retailers by charging low prices. If RPM sets the minimum price at such a level that includes the manufacturer's price, retailers' profits and the cost of services, then no retailer can benefit from the services of other retailers because it is not allowed to charge such low prices that would not include the cost of pre-sale services.

However, the application of antitrust law was different to the Chicago School, as this era was characterized by a strict rather than lenient approach to potential restrictions and imperfections of competition, including vertical restrictions.[140] Indeed, cases from this period, particularly Supreme Court cases, had obvious similarities with the Harvard School, as both the cases and the Harvard School identified the imperfections of competition as ways that firms avoid competing rather than the way firms try to compete more efficiently, as argued by the Chicago School. In accordance with the theory of the Harvard School, the central ideology of this era continued to be the protection of small businesses and their 'right' to compete with larger firms.[141] For example, the

---

[138] Note 12, Hovenkamp, 71–2; Richard Posner, 'The Rule of Reason and the Economic Approach: Reflections on the *Sylvania* Decision' (1977) 45 *University of Chicago Law Revue* 1; Robert Bork, 'The Rule of Reason and Per Se Concept: Price Fixing and Market Division' (1966) 75(2) *Yale Law Journal* 373; further see Chapter 6 'Theories'.

[139] Lester G Telser, 'Why Should Manufacturers Want Fair Trade?' (1960) 6 *Journal of Law & Economics* 86. Telser was not the first one but since his article, this theory has often been advocated in the US.

[140] The Chicago School became more important in the 1970s and antitrust policy became noticeably influenced by it in the next, free era, as discussed later in this chapter.

[141] See, e.g., *United States v. Von's Grocery Co.*, 384 U.S. 270 (1966) 274–5; *Brown Shoes v. United States*, 370 U.S. 294 (1962) 344 ('*Brown Shoes*'); Note 29, *Aluminum Co.*; Note 12, Hovenkamp, 60, 66–7; Herbert Hovenkamp, *The*

Celler-Kefauver amendment,[142] which passed in the 1950s and strengthened the merger provisions in the Clayton Act, confirmed that market imperfections had become a priority, increasing the strictness of antitrust policy.[143]

However, not all legislation followed this ideology. For instance, the per se prohibition of RPM continued to be loosened by legislation when the exception introduced in the Miller-Tydings Act in 1937, which permitted states to authorize resale maintenance agreements, was broadened in the McGuire Act[144] in 1952. These Acts and their authorizations were subsequently withdrawn by the Consumer Goods Pricing Act[145] in 1975.[146]

In accordance with this era, US antitrust agencies and courts were suspicious of any restrictive activity in the area of vertical distribution practices and vertical mergers.[147] The Supreme Court explained and arguably limited the *Colgate* doctrine and clarified that the *Colgate* doctrine included a simple refusal to sell to distributors who did not resell at the price suggested by the supplier. However, RPM in the form of 'agreements', such as a situation where a supplier goes beyond the refusal to sell, were illegal under the Sherman Act.[148] Three cases were important in that sense: *Parke, Davis*[149] from 1959, *Bausch & Lomb*[150] from 1944 and an old case of *Beech-Nut*[151] from 1922.

In the RPM case of *Parke, Davis*, the Supreme Court explained that the seller exceeded the *Colgate* doctrine and fulfilled conditions set in the cases of *Bausch & Lomb* and *Beech-Nut* as Parke, Davis required from their distributors (and also offered them) assurances of compliance.

Antitrust Enterprise: Principles and Execution (Harvard University Press, London 2005) 1–6; Note 37, Kovacic, 464.

[142] Celler-Kefauver Anti-Merger Act, PubL No 81-899, 64 Stat 1125 (1950).
[143] Note 12, Hovenkamp, 68.
[144] 66 Stat 632 (1952).
[145] 89 Stat 801 (1975) section 11.5a.
[146] At the time, 36 out of the 56 US states had implemented legislation authorizing RPM.
[147] See, e.g., *United States v. Yellow Cab Co.*, 332 U.S. 218 (1947); *International Salt Co. v. United States*, 332 U.S. 392 (1947); *United States v. Griffith*, 334 U.S. 100 (1948); *Standard Oil Co. of California v. United States*, 337 U.S. 293 (1949); Note 141, *Brown Shoes*; Note 37, Kovacic, 383–4, 402.
[148] Note 134, *Bausch & Lomb*, 723.
[149] Note 136, *Parke, Davis*.
[150] Note 134, *Bausch & Lomb*.
[151] Note 135, *Beech-Nut*, 455.

Without this, they would not have been able to change their policy.[152] Later, in the case of *Simpson v. Union Oil*,[153] the Supreme Court fully applied the *Dr. Miles* approach to a situation where the agreement between the Union Oil Company selling gasoline and their retailer fixed the price of gasoline, among other things. Simpson, one of the retailers, sold gasoline below the fixed price. Union Oil then refused to renew their lease with Simpson.[154] The Supreme Court confirmed *Dr. Miles*'s theory of ownership, and found the agreements illegal, claiming that independent dealers should have been free to make their own decisions on prices.[155]

The Supreme Court, applying the per se rule, also found that vertical maximum price fixing violated Section 1 of the Sherman Act in the case of *Albrecht*[156] in 1968. Before *Albrecht* (the first Supreme Court vertical maximum price-fixing case) reached the Supreme Court, the Court found horizontal maximum price fixing illegal under Section 1 of the Sherman Act in *Kiefer-Stewart*[157] in 1951. Although the Court of Appeals found this kind of conduct legal and beneficial for competition applying the rule of reason,[158] the Supreme Court ruled that horizontal maximum price fixing restricted competition and was illegal because agreements to fix maximum prices 'cripple[d] the freedom of traders and thereby restrain[ed] their ability to sell in accordance with their own judgment'.[159]

While the Supreme Court reached for a stricter approach in RPM cases, including maximum price fixing, and applied the per se rule during this era, it used a more lenient approach for vertical territorial restrictions and exclusive dealerships. Although this could appear to be against the ideology of this era, this is only an impression because the lenient approach was applied in order to protect small businesses in cases that involved small firms.

In 1963, territorial restraints were addressed by the Supreme Court in *White Motor*.[160] In this case, the Supreme Court protected a small company – manufacturer White Motor – which was in agreement with

---

[152] Note 136, *Parke, Davis*, 46.
[153] *Simpson v. Union Oil Co. of California*, 377 U.S. 13 (1964) ('*Simpson*').
[154] Ibid., 14–15.
[155] Ibid., 16, 20.
[156] *Albrecht v. Herald Co.*, 390 U.S. 145 (1968) ('*Albrecht*').
[157] *Kiefer-Stewart Co. v. Joseph E. Seagram & Sons, Inc.*, 340 U.S. 211 (1951).
[158] Ibid., 212.
[159] Ibid., 213.
[160] *White Motor Co. v. United States*, 372 U.S. 253 (1963) ('*White Motor*').

the antitrust policy of that era. It declared that it did not have a good knowledge of this kind of restraint from previous cases, therefore, it did not declare it per se illegal but it did not confirm that the rule of reason should apply to VTR either.[161] A few years later, territorial restraints were declared to be per se illegal in *Schwinn*,[162] a case where the alleged party was a manufacturer of bicycles with significant market power. However, the Court also held in this case that the per se rule would not apply in a very competitive market if VTR was the only restriction utilized.[163] Furthermore, the cases that followed in this era (and which were older than *Sylvania*[164] from 1977) distinguished between VTR in franchising and non-franchising systems, applying the per se rule only to some territorial restraint situations where VTR was not utilized in franchising systems.[165]

The VTR case of *Schwinn* involved not only territorial restrictions but also RPM. Furthermore, its distribution system was part of an exclusive dealership. In the earlier case of *Packard Motor*[166] from 1957, which involved an exclusive dealership agreement between a car manufacturer and his dealer, the Court of Appeals held that the exclusive dealership did not violate Section 1 or Section 2 of the Sherman Act because there were other manufacturers and their dealers competing in the same territory and because this agreement did not monopolize the market. Unlike *Schwinn*, where the alleged party was a well-established manufacturer, Packard was a small manufacturer competing with big manufacturers of cars.

---

[161] Ibid., 263.
[162] *United States v. Arnold, Schwinn and Co.*, 388 U.S. 365 (1967) ('*Schwinn*').
[163] Ibid., 381.
[164] Note 7, *Sylvania*.
[165] *T'ai Corp. v. Kalso Systemet*, 568 F.2d 145 (10th Circuit 1977); *America Oil Co. v. McMullin*, 508 F.2d 1345 (10th Circuit 1975); *Eastex Aviation v. Sperry and Hutchinson Co.*, 522 F.2d 1299 (5th Circuit 1975) 1305–6; *Redd v. Shell Oil Co.*, 524 F.2d 1054 (10th Circuit 1975) 1057-58, *cert. denied*, 425 U.S. 912 (1976); *Brothers v. Monsanto Co.*, 525 F.2d 486 (8th Circuit 1975), *cert. denied*, 423 U.S. 1055 (1976); *Edwin K. Williams & Co. v. Edwin K. Williams & Co.-East*, 542 F.2d 1053 (9th Circuit 1976), *cert. denied*, 433 U.S. 908 (1977); *Janel Sales Corp. v. Lanvin Parfums*, 396 F.2d 398, 406 (2nd Circuit), *cert. denied*, 393 U.S. 938 (1968); see Phillip E Areeda and Herbert Hovenkamp, *Antitrust Law: An Analysis of Antitrust Principles and Their Application* (2nd edn, Volume VIII, Aspen Publishers 2004) 387–8.
[166] *Packard Motor Car Co. v. Webster Motor Car Co.*, 243 F.2d 418 (DC Circuit 1957).

Packard entered into an exclusive dealership and thus terminated dealership contracts with other dealers in a particular territory, Baltimore, in order to retain the dealership with the most significant, and the largest, dealers in Baltimore. The court directly expressed the ideology of this era when it stated that penalizing a 'small manufacturer for competing in this way not only fails to promote the policy of the antitrust laws but defeats it'.[167]

Other exclusive dealership cases of this era also established some boundaries of prohibition for this form of distribution. Exclusive distributorships were subject to challenge when the territory was unreasonably broad,[168] if their duration was unreasonably long[169] and if either the distributor or the supplier had a dominant market position.[170]

RPM: *Bausch & Lomb*:[171] The Complex Restriction and *Colgate* Doctrine

The case of *Bausch & Lomb* involved complex vertical restrictions including RPM. Soft-Lite, an exclusive distributor of pink tinted lenses, sold the non-patented lenses under her trade name, Softlite. She purchased the lenses exclusively from the manufacturer Bausch & Lomb and sold them on to wholesalers who sold to retailers. Bausch & Lomb was exclusively selling its pink tinted lenses in the US to Soft-Lite. Their long-running, integrated distribution plan was based on a two-sided exclusive relationship, including both exclusive selling and buying.[172]

Soft-Lite dealt only with wholesalers who distributed to retailers who held licenses from Soft-Lite. If a wholesaler had delivered to a retailer without the licence, Soft-Lite would have excluded the wholesaler from her distribution.[173] The retailers were only allowed to sell to final consumers or patients. They were required under the licence agreement 'to promote the sale of Soft-Lite lenses and to do nothing to injure their

---

[167] Ibid., 8.
[168] *United States v. Chicago Tribune-N.Y. News Syndicate, Inc.*, 309 F.Supp 1301 (1970) 1308–9.
[169] *Quality Mercury, Inc. v. Ford Motor Co.*, 542 F.2d 466 (8th Circuit 1976) 471–2.
[170] *Hershey Chocolate Corp. v. FTC*, 121 F.2d 968 (3rd Circuit 1941).
[171] Note 134, Bausch & Lomb.
[172] Ibid., 709–13.
[173] Ibid., 714.

prestige',[174] where it was stated in the agreement that 'the substitution of other lenses for Soft-Lite would adversely affect that prestige'.[175]

Furthermore, Soft-Lite published a list of prices for wholesalers and retailers where, without providing any written agreement, she indicated the prices via price lists and price schedules, which were maintained by retailers and wholesalers.[176] In 1940, after the Miller-Tydings Act introduced an exception for states to legalize minimum price fixing between manufacturers and distributors, Soft-Lite concluded her RPM contracts in those states. The District Court called these contracts 'a patch upon an illegal system of distribution of which they have become an integral part',[177] meaning that RPM was part of complex restrictive conduct including, among other things, exclusive distribution and customer allocations, which had been going on across the US for decades and started well before the Miller-Tydings Act was passed.

In that regard, the Supreme Court analyzed RPM in the context of the whole distribution system. It explained that each illegal practice in this case, including RPM, had to be considered in context and as part of the Soft-Lite distribution system.[178] Therefore, different aspects were recognized as parts of one illegal conduct and not as separate restrictions. Although the Court agreed that choosing customers was essential for Soft-Lite due to the luxurious nature of her products and her aim to achieve 'the highest standard of service', it did not classify this as sufficient justification for vertical restrictions, especially for this complex vertical-restriction conduct.[179]

The appellants based their arguments on the *Colgate* doctrine, claiming that a simple refusal to sell in cases where the buyer does not follow RPM did not violate Section 1 of the Sherman Act. The Supreme Court replied that although the case of *Bausch & Lomb* did not include written agreements, except for contracts that followed after the Miller-Tydings Act was passed, it went beyond the *Colgate* doctrine saying that Soft-Lite illegally conspired with at least some of her wholesalers.[180]

Nevertheless, this case, as well as the previous cases of *Colgate* and *Frey & Son*, did not sufficiently clarify the boundary between unilateral and bilateral/multilateral prohibited actions if there was no written

---

[174] Ibid., 716.
[175] Ibid.
[176] Ibid., 715, 717.
[177] Ibid., 716.
[178] Ibid., 720.
[179] Ibid., 728.
[180] Ibid., 723.

agreement between the manufacturer and his distributors about fixing prices. Although, in *Bausch & Lomb*, the Supreme Court disagreed with the appellants that this was unilateral conduct and thus legal under Section 1 of the Sherman Act, the Court referred to the seller as the one who made others comply.[181] The same language was used in the aforementioned older cases on RPM. This language assumes the existence and imposing of the seller's power and a lack of free will on the part of the participants. The *Colgate* doctrine was again discussed in the later case of *Parke, Davis*.

RPM: *Parke, Davis*:[182] Clarification of the *Colgate* Doctrine

This case dealt with an allegation against the appellee, the Parke, Davis Co., that they and their retail and wholesale druggists illegally conspired and violated Section 1 (and Section 3) of the Sherman Act by maintaining prices of around 600 different Parke, Davis pharmaceutical products marketed nationally through wholesalers and retailers.[183] This conduct included informing retailers and wholesalers that they would lose their supply from Parke, Davis if they did not maintain the suggested minimum retail prices. Furthermore, wholesalers were prohibited from selling to retailers who did not follow the suggested minimum retail prices.[184] Each wholesaler and retailer was interviewed individually by Parke, Davis and was informed that every other wholesaler and retailer had been told the same. Some retailers refused to assure the company that they would comply with the suggested resale prices and continued selling below these prices. These retailers lost their supply from Parke, Davis and wholesalers refused to supply to them also.[185]

Following this, one of the retailers announced that it was willing to stop advertising but would not necessarily keep selling under the suggested minimum prices. Other retailers followed saying they would cease advertising; their supplies were not cancelled. After a month, one retailer started to advertise again and others followed.[186]

The District Court applied the *Colgate* doctrine, stating that the Sherman Act was not violated because the actions concerned appeared to

---

[181] Ibid., 721.
[182] Note 136, *Parke, Davis*.
[183] Ibid., 30–32.
[184] Ibid., 33.
[185] Ibid., 33–4.
[186] Ibid., 35–6.

be unilateral.[187] However, the Supreme Court held that the basic difference between the case of *Colgate* and the case of *Dr. Miles* was that *Dr. Miles* was based on written contracts between distributors and the manufacturer, whereas *Colgate* did not involve an agreement, it merely protected the manufacturer's right to deal with whomever it chooses.[188] The Supreme Court, by referring to the cases of *Bausch & Lomb* and *Beech-Nut*,[189] stated that the *Colgate* doctrine only involved a simple refusal to sell to distributors who did not resell at the prices suggested by the manufacturer. It explained that Section 1 of the Sherman Act includes not only explicit agreements but also any other combination, such as when a manufacturer goes beyond the refusal to sell.[190] To decide whether the manufacturer exceeded the *Colgate* doctrine and went beyond the mere refusal to sell, the court must primarily evaluate the actions of the parties and not only the language, phrases and words used.[191]

The Supreme Court then applied this to *Parke, Davis* holding that this case exceeded the *Colgate* doctrine and fulfilled the conditions clarified in *Bausch & Lomb* and *Beech-Nut*, as Parke, Davis had not only announced retail prices and stopped supplying to retailers who were not willing to follow the price policy, but they had cooperated with wholesalers to avoid the possibility that retailers would buy from them directly and sell below the price.[192] Moreover, they were willing to make exceptions for larger retailers.[193] Parke, Davis also discussed the subject with Dart Drug and other retailers. Indeed, Parke, Davis required and offered assurances of compliance and, without this, they would not have been able to change their policy. Therefore, Parke, Davis went beyond the announced refusal to deal. These actions established 'an agreement' prohibited under Section 1 of the Sherman Act.[194]

Mr. Justice Harlan, Mr. Justice Frankfurter and Mr. Justice Whittaker jointly dissented because they believed that in this case the Supreme Court de facto overruled *Colgate*. They argued that in *Colgate*, the distributors were also made to promise the manufacturer that they would follow its price policy, but the Court ruled that unilateral conduct was not

---

[187] Ibid., 36.
[188] Ibid., 38–9.
[189] Note 135, *Beech-Nut*, 455.
[190] Note 136, *Parke, Davis*, 43.
[191] Ibid., 44.
[192] Ibid., 45–6.
[193] Ibid., 45.
[194] Ibid., 46.

prohibited by Section 1 of the Sherman Act.[195] Therefore, one way to look at this case, together with *Bausch & Lomb* and *Beech-Nut*, is that it not only clarified, but also narrowed, the boundaries between legal unilateral conduct and prohibited bilateral/multilateral conduct, an agreement, in that anything more than a pure announcement of the price policy and its uncompromised application went beyond the *Colgate* doctrine.

Vertical Maximum Price Fixing: *Albrecht*[196]

In this case, the Supreme Court dealt with vertical maximum price fixing, for the first time applying *Dr. Miles* and the per se rule. The case involved a publisher of the morning newspaper, the *Globe-Democrat*, which was distributed by independent carriers (the respondent). Each carrier was granted its own exclusive territory on the condition that the carrier would not exceed the suggested price printed in the newspapers.[197] In 1961, the petitioner, Albrecht, increased the price above the maximum level. The respondent responded to this by sending a letter to the petitioner stating that she would deliver the newspaper for customers who did not want to pay the overcharged price. She also warned the petitioner that she would terminate his contract if he did not stop selling at the overcharged price.[198]

The respondent offered the lower price and direct delivery to customers over the phone through a company, Milne Circulation Sales, Inc. Roughly 300 out of the 1200 petitioner's customers switched to the direct delivery from the publisher. Following this, the respondent granted her 300 customers to another carrier, George Kroner.[199] The petitioner argued that this constituted a prohibited agreement under Section 1 of the Sherman Act in the form of fixing prices.

Complex restriction
This case was based only on vertical maximum price fixing. Exclusive territories were not part of the petition and hence they were not discussed before the jury at the lower court.[200] In accordance with the ruling in *Bausch & Lomb* on complex restrictions, the Supreme Court expressed that if exclusive territories had been part of the petition and these

---

[195] Ibid., 49–57.
[196] Note 156, Albrecht.
[197] Ibid., 147.
[198] Ibid.
[199] Ibid.
[200] Ibid., 153.

exclusive territories had had a negative impact on the public, then the Court of Appeals would have had to find the entire scheme, including both the exclusive territories and the maximum prices, illegal under Section 1 of the Sherman Act.[201]

The *Dr. Miles* doctrine

In connection with vertical maximum price fixing, the Supreme Court, by applying *Dr. Miles*, evaluated two essential requirements of Section 1 of the Sherman Act. First, it analyzed whether there was 'an agreement', followed by whether this agreement restricted trade for the purposes of Section 1 of the Sherman Act and whether the per se rule was the appropriate rule to apply. Both parts of the analysis involved some significant drawbacks, well pointed out by a dissenting judge, Justice Harlan.

First, the Supreme Court, agreeing with the District Court, observed that the District Court and the Court of Appeals disagreed on the fulfilment of both requirements of Section 1 of the Sherman Act. The District Court applied the *Dr. Miles* doctrine, in which it found a violation of Section 1 of the Sherman Act based on a combination to fix resale prices between the respondent and the plaintiff's customers and/or Milne Circulation Sales, Inc. and/or George Kroner, and stated that this conduct was per se illegal.[202] On the contrary, the Court of Appeals applied the *Colgate* doctrine and ruled that there was no violation of the Sherman Act as, first, this was unilateral conduct and, secondly, maximum price fixing did not establish a restraint of trade.[203]

The Supreme Court held that there was a combination because the respondent had gone beyond the 'mere announcement of his policy and the simple refusal to deal ...' as quoted in *Parke, Davis*.[204] The reason for the existence of an 'agreement' was, according to the Supreme Court, the fact that the petitioner was pressured by the respondent and by Milne and Kroner.[205]

Mr. Justice Harlan dissenting disagreed with the existence of a combination between the respondent and Milne and Kroner. As Justice Harlan argued, Milne and Kroner had no special interest in the respondent's reason for setting a maximum price because they were both hired for a specific reason and they themselves had not generated any power to

---

[201] Ibid., 154.
[202] Ibid., 148.
[203] Ibid., 149.
[204] Note 156, *Albrecht*, 149; Note 136, *Parke, Davis*, 44.
[205] Note 156, *Albrecht*, 149–50.

pressure the petitioner.²⁰⁶ Milne was simply asked by the petitioner to advertise by telephone another delivery option to the final consumers, while Kroner was asked to deliver newspapers for consumers who wanted to pay less than what Albrecht was charging. Justice Harlan concluded that these jobs could have been done by the respondent herself.²⁰⁷

Indeed, Justice Harlan rightly observed that the pressure to comply with the maximum price fixing was generated by the respondent only and not by the other two companies. Milne was not even in competition, nor was he a potential competitor of, the petitioner, he merely advertised on behalf of the respondent. Therefore, he had no interest in taking over the business of the petitioner. Although Kroner's business was similar to Albrecht's, delivering newspapers, he got involved and delivered to customers who were not willing to pay Albrecht's price only after he was directly asked by the respondent to do so. He did not generate any pressure prior to being asked to deliver newspapers to those customers. Therefore, the Court of Appeals was right when it applied the *Colgate* doctrine, as this situation involved only announcements and follow-up actions conducted by the respondent.

With regard to the second requirement, the Supreme Court held that the maximum price fixing restricted competition and should be prohibited despite the fact that, as the Supreme Court acknowledged, maximum and minimum price fixing can have different impacts on trade. The Court provided two anticompetitive reasons as to why it should be prohibited per se. First, vertical maximum price fixing restricts the ability of buyers to compete. Second, if the price is set too low, the dealer does not have the ability to furnish services for customers or to compete at all.²⁰⁸

Both reasons raise issues. The second reason constitutes the paradox that by applying the per se rule in RPM, the Supreme Court refused the service-theory justification and by applying the per se rule in maximum price fixing, the Court agreed with this theory. In RPM, one of the potential justifications is that it can assist with ensuring that buyers provide certain services for their customers and that no buyer is free riding on such a service. By applying the per se rule, the courts base their reasoning on the fact that RPM always, or almost always, unreasonably restricts trade and thus no justification, including the justification based on the theory of services, is allowed. However, in this case on vertical

---

[206] Ibid., 160.
[207] Ibid., 161.
[208] Ibid., 152–3.

maximum price fixing, the Supreme Court accepted this theory by arguing that maximum price setting can set prices so low as to prevent the existence of services. It did not explain why services should be preserved, but we could assume that in this part of the case the Court acknowledged that services increase non-price competition and are beneficial to consumers given the fact that the Court recognized their lack as negative for competition.[209]

The Supreme Court's first reason, the restriction of buyers from competing, was dismissed by dissenting Justice Harlan. He also claimed that vertical minimum and maximum price fixings differed. He said that RPM had its effect in 'higher prices, less efficient use of resources and an easier life for resellers'.[210] He argued that RPM lessened intrabrand competition, and there was no difference in this impact whether distributors horizontally agreed among themselves on this practice or whether it was vertically dictated by a manufacturer.[211] The reasons for imposing RPM or vertical maximum price fixing differ. Minimum price fixing is in the interest of buyers as they 'may treat the product better if they have a secure high margin of profits';[212] however, maximum price setting is in the interest of the supplier in avoiding the anticompetitive actions of her distributors.[213]

He continued that the mere statement of the Court that both practices 'cripple the freedom of traders' to sell under their own judgment does not justify the application of the per se rule. Even if one of the objectives of the Sherman Act is to protect freedom and multiplicity of traders, this itself does not justify the application of the per se rule.[214] The price ceilings have a justification in the prevention of distributors charging monopoly prices and receiving monopoly profits in situations where the manufacturer assumes that there is insufficient competition. Therefore, this practice sets prices closer to those that would arise from intense

---

[209] Sherman Act: Section 1 prohibits restrictions of trade. Therefore, the reduction of services was recognized as a restriction of trade because it was applied as a justification for prohibiting vertical maximum price setting per se.

[210] Note 156, *Albrecht*, 157.

[211] Ibid., 156–7. He continued his argument explaining that these actions including RPM presented as vertical unilateral policy created combinations because they were in the interest of distributors and not that of manufacturers. The per se rule is the correct approach as there is no acceptance of the proffered justification as price floors are fixed in such cases.

[212] Ibid., 157–8.

[213] Ibid., 158.

[214] Ibid.

competition and does not lessen competition unless both parties miscalculate the maximum price.[215]

Even if the supplier sets the maximum prices so low that buyers would lose their ability to stay in the market, as included in the reasoning of the Supreme Court, it would be in the interest of the supplier to increase the maximum price because by losing buyers, the supplier would lose his output and profit. If the price is as low as the perfect-competition price, in other words, the price at which buyers would be able to remain in the market but would lose their ability to compete on price and at the non-price level by generating no profit, Justice Harlan's reasoning would apply. He explained that maximum price fixing is in the interest of the supplier to prevent the existence of high ('monopolistic') prices while RPM usually ensures higher profit for buyers. Justice Stewart's dissenting argument supports Justice Harlan's differentiation of motivations for introducing RPM and vertical maximum price fixing and thus the wrongness of applying the per se rule to maximum price fixing. Justice Stewart stated that the respondent could not be liable under antitrust law for not allowing his distributor to hold a complete monopoly. Indeed, the Supreme Court made the respondent liable for such conduct and, therefore, Justice Stewart concluded: 'The Court today stands the Sherman Act on its head.'[216]

VTR: *White Motor*[217]

In this case, the Supreme Court dealt with vertically restricted trade based on VTR, further supported by consumer allocation and vertical price fixing. Two important parts of this case show the Court's intent to protect small businesses as an ideology of this era:[218] the different ruling to previous Supreme Court cases on a complex restriction and the unwillingness of the Supreme Court to set a precedent on exclusive territorial restraints in order to protect a small manufacturer, the appellant, White Motor Co. The appellant was a manufacturer of trucks and spare parts for trucks. She sold her products to distributors, dealers and directly to large users. Distributors then sold the products to users and dealers selected by the appellant.[219]

---

[215] Ibid., 159.
[216] Ibid., 170.
[217] Note 160, White Motor.
[218] Ibid., 263, 276.
[219] Ibid., 255.

The appellant instituted agreements with her distributors and dealers, limiting exclusive territories and persons or classes of persons for each distributor and dealer.[220] The consumer clause restrained distributors and dealers from selling to public entities. Therefore, the only company who could sell trucks and White Motor's spare parts directly to public entities was the manufacturer.[221] Moreover, distributors agreed to charge the same price to dealers as the appellant charged when selling her products directly to dealers. This type of agreement constituted 5 percent of White Motor Co. sales.[222]

Complex restriction
The price fixing was not challenged under this appeal to the Supreme Court. The Court confirmed that the per se rule applied in the case of price fixing,[223] but it refused to consider it in connection with VTR as a complex restriction. Instead, it considered different forms of vertical restrictions, in particular exclusive territories that were part of this complex restriction, on their own because, as the Court argued, the percentage of price fixing was low. Therefore, the Supreme Court distinguished this case from *Bausch & Lomb*, stating that price fixing and other restraints did not create 'an integral part of the whole distribution system'.[224] Indeed, the Court changed its direction on the question of whether a number of vertical restraints applied in one distribution system should be evaluated as one restrictive system; in *Bausch & Lomb* and *Albrecht* the Court held that they should. Arguably, even in *Bausch & Lomb*, RPM was a supportive vertical restriction to the distribution system based on exclusive selling and buying, but this did not prevent the Court from analyzing different forms of vertical restriction as one complex restriction.

If the Supreme Court had applied the complex restriction approach to the case of *White Motors*, it would have likely applied the per se rule because part of the distribution system was RPM. Although RPM created only a minor percentage of White Motors' sales, the reason behind differentiating this case from others could have been the fact that White Motors was a small rather than a well-established manufacturer. As we know, in this era the Supreme Court tended to protect small firms rather than 'punish' them.

---

[220] Ibid., 255–6.
[221] Ibid., 256.
[222] Ibid., 260.
[223] Ibid., 264.
[224] Ibid., 260.

Exclusive territorial restraints introduced by a small manufacturer
In connection with VTR, the Supreme Court refused to state whether the rule of reason or the per se rule should apply to territorial restraints because, as it stated, there was not enough knowledge about this form of vertical restraints. The Supreme Court accepted the appellant's argument that the restrictions in question were 'fair, reasonable and necessary to effectively compete against large competitors'[225] and thus it did not deny that such a practice was a practicable means for a small company to compete with aggressive competitors.[226]

Mr. Justice Brennan concurring applied the principle of proportionality by stating that this mere justification of conduct was not enough. It had to be proved that the restriction concerned was necessary or proportionate. Therefore, a comparison must be made between the restrictive anticompetitive effects, including any possible disadvantages, that the distributors must bear, and the benefits arising from the restriction. Moreover, the Court must also consider whether there are no other means, such as franchising systems, that are less anticompetitive and would introduce the same benefits as the restriction.[227]

Mr. Justice Brennan also added another potential justification, arguing that VTR could allow the manufacturer to penetrate a market if the manufacturer was a small company, or if she started with a 'risky product, or in order to ensure that [her] products were promoted and/or serviced'.[228] He claimed that these justifications distinguished VTR from horizontal territorial restraints and from RPM.[229] However, as I explain further in Chapter 5, RPM can be utilized for the same procompetitive purpose by providing incentives to buyers to take the risk and sell a new product or a product in a new territory.

Another argument made by Mr. Justice Brennan as to why VTR should be differentiated from RPM centered around the impact of RPM and VTR on intrabrand and interbrand competition. He compared territorial restraints to RPM stating that the intrabrand effect could be the same in territorial restrictions. However, he argued that this was not necessarily true of the interbrand effect, as RPM restricts interbrand and intrabrand

---

[225] Ibid., 256–7.
[226] Ibid., 263.
[227] Ibid., 270–72.
[228] Ibid., 269.
[229] Ibid., 270.

competition.[230] He did not explain why he believed so; he only highlighted the appellant's general claim that her restriction fostered interbrand competition.[231] As I discuss below, later US cases on RPM, especially *Leegin*, denied that RPM also restricted interbrand competition.

The Supreme Court, as in previous cases, aimed its focus on the manufacturer by stating that 'a vertical arrangement by one manufacturer [was] restricting the territory of his distributors or dealers'.[232] Mr. Justice Brennan further explained that, unlike in a franchising system, the agreement disadvantaged distributors and dealers and, therefore, served the manufacturer's interests exclusively.[233] This statement has some drawbacks. First, this distribution system in general did not necessarily disadvantage distributors and dealers, because less efficient distributors and dealers, in particular, profit from this situation. Second, VTR itself would be primarily beneficial for buyers due to lessened competition.

We know that White Motors was selling to distributors who then sold products to dealers who were selling directly to the final consumers. We also know that White Motors was selling directly to dealers, thus competing with her distributors, and to public entities. Let's assume that, prior to introducing this distribution system, White Motors had three dealers in the State of Alabama: A, B and C. Dealers A and B were competing vigorously and effectively, in that they were able to lower their costs and final price and promote the products effectively. The third dealer, dealer C, was not as efficient and, was therefore losing customers and profit. Similarly, distributors A and B operating in the US were lowering their costs and prices for dealers, while distributor C was not as efficient and struggled to remain in the market. Both distributors and dealers were considering terminating the sale with White Motors due to intensive intrabrand competition and instead wished to sell other products produced by White Motors' competitors who had higher market shares.

White Motors was forced to lower her price for her customers, the public entities, in order to remain competitive with her dealers. White Motors wanted to increase the profit she generated from selling to the public entities and to dealers, thus she decided that she would set prices for distributors to sell to dealers, to prevent others from selling to public entities. In order to make others comply, she offered distribution based on exclusive territories. Because exclusive territories eliminated intrabrand

---

[230] Ibid., 268.
[231] Ibid., 268.
[232] Ibid., 261.
[233] Ibid., 267.

competition among dealers and distributors, and distributors had assurance of their profit per product due to RPM, they were inclined to agree with this distribution system. Although the eased competition among dealers and distributors was appealing to all of them, distributors and dealers who benefited from this arrangement the most were distributor C and dealer C because their position in the market was strengthened by the existence of assigned territories and ensured prices. White Motors' direct sales to dealers and to public entities increased and she earned the loyalty of her distributors and dealers who were motivated to sell as many of her products as possible due to the ensured profits arising from the changed distribution policy.

VTR: *Schwinn*[234]

This case, together with the previous case of *White Motors*, illustrates how the Supreme Court would use a different approach in its analysis depending on whether the alleged entity was a small or well-established firm. Unlike White Motors, Schwinn was a well-established manufacturer, producing bicycles and spare parts for bicycles.[235] In 1951, it was the largest manufacturer of bicycles in the US with a market share of 22.5 percent. Its market share decreased to 12.8 percent in 1961 and the largest bicycle company became Murray Ohio Manufacturing Company, whose market share increased from 11.6 percent in 1951 to 22.8 percent in 1961. However, Schwinn's production increased throughout these ten years, despite the reduced market share.[236]

Schwinn introduced a new distribution system, including the alleged restrictive practices, during the time it had the majority of the market share in 1952. These practices consisted of three 'forms' of restrictions of competition which were held to violate Section 1 of the Sherman Act:

1. Conspiracy involving price fixing;
2. Conspiracy involving allocation of exclusive territories; and
3. 'Confinement of merchandise to franchised dealers.'[237]

The government's appeal concerned only the last restriction, the distribution limitations (not price fixing), which included territorial restraints in a

---

[234] Note 162, Schwinn.
[235] Ibid 374.
[236] Ibid 368–9.
[237] Ibid., 367.

franchising system.[238] These distribution limitations arose from the so-called 'Schwinn Plan', which covered more than half of Schwinn's distribution, around 75 percent, in 1962. It was based on a form of 'franchising' which did not prevent the franchisees from selling other brands but required the promotion of Schwinn products and purchasing only from a distributor authorized to sell in that exclusive territory. The distributors with exclusive territories were authorized to sell only to the franchisees and not to other dealers.[239]

In contrast to *White Motors*, the Supreme Court followed the *Bausch & Lomb* approach to complex restrictions, considering territorial and price restrictions as part of one illegal conduct. The Court stated that there was no need to examine the reasonableness and competitive effect in the situation when VTR was 'ancillary to the price-fixing'[240] or if it was 'an integral part of the whole distribution system' with price-fixing.[241]

Ownership and the per se rule
However, the Supreme Court went even further than merely stating that VTR was prohibited per se when it formed one complex restriction with RPM. It discussed VTR on its own, agreeing with the government's argument and the District Court ruling that once distributors purchased goods from the manufacturer, they could not be territorially restricted in their sales because the distributors owned the goods.[242] By applying the same reasoning based on ownership as applied in the RPM case of *Dr. Miles*, the Court stated that the distributors should have been free to decide who they would deal with.[243]

The Court also distinguished, indirectly, between situations where the manufacturer had a small business and was competing with others and when he was not. The Court held that VTR was per se prohibited in two situations. First, if it was used together with RPM, as explained above. Second, if it was used on its own when the market was not very competitive. The Court stated: 'In the absence of price-fixing and with an adequate source of alternative products to meet the needs of the unfranchised, the vertically imposed distribution restraints may not be held to be per se violations of the Sherman Act.'[244]

---

[238] Ibid., 368.
[239] Ibid., 370–71.
[240] Ibid., 375–6.
[241] Note 162, *Schwinn*, 375–6; Note 134, *Bausch & Lomb*, 720.
[242] Note 162, *Schwinn*, 377, 379.
[243] Ibid., 378.
[244] Ibid., 378; see also, ibid., 381.

The Court further held that under Section 1 of the Sherman Act, the outcome was different regarding whether the manufacturer completely retained ownership and the risk of loss or not.[245] The per se rule applied only in situations where the buyers became the owners of the products in question, and did not apply in territorial vertical restrictions in franchising systems in cases where the manufacturer remained the owner of the products.[246] In situations when the manufacturer remained the owner, there is no unreasonable restraint of trade and no violation of Section 1 of the Sherman Act.[247]

Mr. Justice Stewart and Mr. Justice Harlan dissented. Mr. Justice Stewart provided two reasons as to why the rule of reason would have been a more appropriate choice in this case. First, the government asked the Court to judge this under the rule of reason and not the per se rule. Despite this, the Court found the conduct per se illegal.[248] Second, Mr. Justice Stewart believed that this case overruled the four-year-old case of *White Motors* despite not providing any new data supporting this change.[249] However, it is arguable to state that the case of *White Motors* was overruled, because although the per se rule was not applied in *White Motors*, the Court stated there that it did not have enough knowledge to make a judgment as to what rule should have been applied.

Efficiency arguments

Another reason as to why Mr. Justice Stewart dissented was that he believed Schwinn was merely using a more efficient distribution system and thus his principal intention was not to restrict competition. Mr. Justice Stewart claimed that, according to studies, Schwinn's previous distribution system had been ineffective and had restricted the promotion of Schwinn's products. For that reason, Schwinn created a new qualitative, 'active and stable' distribution system which included maintaining services and promotions.[250] Schwinn chose his distributors based on qualitative requirements, and hence required his distribution to be provided by small companies. By choosing small companies, Schwinn was able to compete with giant chain distributors. This was shown through increased sales, even though profits decreased.[251] Mr. Justice Stewart's

---

[245] Ibid., 378–9.
[246] Ibid., 379–80, 382.
[247] Ibid., 378, 381.
[248] Ibid., 388.
[249] Ibid., 389.
[250] Ibid., 383.
[251] Ibid., 384.

argument on efficiency was influenced by the ideology of that era, as is further illustrated by his statement that a franchising system was a way for smaller companies to compete effectively and efficiently with larger, integrated companies.[252]

Williamson supports Justice Stewart's position on efficiency. He argues that Schwinn's system was effective in the sense that it assisted the manufacturer to target his consumers, provide them with information and services and simplify the way consumers located Schwinn's bicycles. The distribution system thus resulted in a saving in transaction costs.[253]

V. FREE ERA (END OF 1970s–1990s): CHICAGO SCHOOL INFLUENCE

In this era, antitrust policy became influenced by the Chicago and Post-Chicago School theory and the courts began to implement more economic aspects of competition. Hovenkamp describes this period as 'the antitrust counterrevolution' with antitrust law and policy concentrating on consumer welfare and an economic understanding of competition as a process that should maintain low prices, high output and innovation.[254] Rather than the protection of small businesses, economic welfare, as promoted by many economists including Williamson,[255] became an influential ideology. However, this does not mean that from now on all antitrust law cases were based on proper economic studies and economic efficiency; their usage was still arguably insufficient.[256]

A highly influential work of that time was Bork's *The Antitrust Paradox*. In his book, Bork promoted the view that economics and economic efficiency should play an essential role in antitrust policy.[257] He also proposed that the underpinning principle of antitrust law should

---

[252] Ibid., 386–7.

[253] Oliver E Williamson, *Antitrust Economics: Mergers, Contracting, and Strategic Behaviour* (Basil Blackwell, New York, 1987) 143–8.

[254] Note 141, Hovenkamp, 2.

[255] Oliver Williamson proposed in 1968 that the efficiency defence should have been incorporated in antitrust policy. Oliver E Williamson, 'Economies as an Antitrust Defense: The Welfare Tradeoffs' (1968) 58 *The American Economic Review* 18.

[256] See, e.g., Eleanor M Fox, 'The Modernization of Antitrust: A New Equilibrium' (1980–1981) 66 *Cornell Law Review* 1140, 1140–92.

[257] Robert H Bork, *The Antitrust Paradox* (New York: Free Press 1978). See Kenneth Heyer, 'Consumer Welfare and the Legacy of Robert Bork' (2014) 57 *Journal of Law and Economics* 1, 2, 5.

be consumer welfare.[258] Although he was not the first to use this term,[259] it was Bork's *Paradox* and his proposed goal of antitrust law and policy that influenced both the courts and antitrust agencies, with the DOJ and FTC applying the term 'consumer welfare' in their analysis and policy statements,[260] and by referring to Bork's *Paradox*, the Supreme Court utilized the term 'consumer welfare' in *Reiter v. Sonotone* in 1979.[261]

Despite the references to Bork's work, the term 'consumer welfare' as applied in US antitrust policy does not follow Bork's understanding of its meaning but, rather, refers to consumer surplus and the definition of the term by Brodley. Bork, when referring to the term 'consumer welfare', described a form of total/social welfare related to the general equilibrium concept that is based on economics-allocative efficiency and the Pareto optimality.[262] He used it as a synonym for welfare of the nation by saying that '[c]onsumer welfare ... is merely another term for the wealth of the nation'.[263]

Brodley, on the other hand, argued in his 1987 article that the term 'consumer welfare'

> must refer to the direct explicit economic benefits received by the consumers of a particular product as measured by its price and quality. Using the more precise language of economics, consumer welfare can be defined as consumer surplus ...[264]

Thus, the consumer welfare standard as it has developed in US policy is indeed focused on end users, as summarized by Heyer:

---

[258] He had already referred to consumer welfare as the only value of antitrust law in his previous articles: Robert H Bork, 'The Goals of Antitrust Policy' (1967) 57 *American Economic Review* 242, 243; Robert H Bork, 'Legislative Intent and the Policy of the Sherman Act' (1966) 9 *Journal of Law & Economics* 7, 8.

[259] See Gregory J Werden, 'Antitrust's Rule of Reason: Only Competition Matters' (2014) 79(2) *Antitrust Law Journal* 713, fn 25. He refers to Joe S Bain, 'The Sherman Act and "the Bottlenecks of Business"' (1941) 5 *Journal of Marketing* 254, 255 as the first US article where the term 'consumer welfare' was used.

[260] See ibid., Heyer.

[261] *Reiter v. Sonotone Corp.*, 442 U.S. 330 (1979) 343.

[262] Note 259, Werden; Note 257, Heyer.

[263] Note 257, Bork, 90.

[264] Joseph F Brodley 'The Economic Goals of Antitrust: Efficiency, Consumer Welfare, and Technological Progress' (1987) 62 *New York University Law Review* 1020, 1033 in Note 259, Werden.

Cost savings retained by the manufacturer and not passed through to end users of the product would receive no weight under this standard, which is perhaps more accurate referred to as an end-user standard.[265]

The application of the economic approach is well-reflected in cases on vertical restraints, especially VTR. The arguments of dissenting judges, Mr. Justice Stewart in the case of *Schwinn* from 1967 and Mr. Justice Brennan in *White Motors* from 1963, already show the first attempts to apply economic reasoning in cases on vertical restrictions. However, an important milestone case was that of *Sylvania*,[266] where the US courts introduced the rule of reason to VTR and began to adopt 'modern antitrust economic analysis' to vertical restraint cases, including the consumer welfare goal.[267]

Since *Sylvania*, the approach to vertical restraints has been clearly differentiated between vertical price and non-price restraints. While RPM remained under the per se rule, VTR was proclaimed to be ruled under the rule of reason. The stricter approach to RPM was most likely influenced by the view of Congress.[268] For example, the Supreme Court, when discussing the per se rule approach to RPM agreements in *Sylvania*, referred to the repeal of the Miller-Tydings Act and McGuire Act by the Consumer Goods Pricing Act of 1975 by Congress.[269]

This differentiation in *Sylvania* between non-price and price vertical restraints was followed in later cases and also by antitrust agencies' policies. In 1985, the DOJ issued the Vertical Restraints Guidelines (Guidelines 1985),[270] which also distinguished between non-price and per se illegal price vertical restraints. Guidelines 1985 pointed out that

---

[265] Note 257, Heyer, 8.

[266] Note 7, *Sylvania*.

[267] Note 9, Voorhees. Commissioner Wright refers to it as 'a consumer welfare-based antitrust regime' in Joshua D Wright, 'The economics of resale price maintenance and implications for competition law and policy' (Speech, 9 April 2014, British Institute of International and Comparative Law, London, UK) 2.

[268] See Note 34, Salop; Richard M Brunell, 'United States: Dr. Miles' Last House Call' in Barry Rodger, *Landmark Cases in Competition Law: Around the World in Fourteen Stories* (Wolters Kluwer, 2012) 345, 346.

[269] Note 7, *Sylvania*, 51.

[270] Guidelines on vertical restraints, issued 23 January 1985 and published 50 Fed Reg 6, 263 (14 February 1985) and 4 Trade Reg Rep (CCH) 13, 105 (1988) ('Guidelines 1985').

any vertical restraint could have an impact on price, but that was not a reason for the application of the per se rule.[271]

These guidelines did not have much practical influence. In 1985, Congress had already stated that Guidelines 1985 should not be treated as an 'accurate expression of the Federal antitrust laws or of congressional intent with regard to the application of such laws to resale price maintenance and other vertical restraints of trade'.[272] They were withdrawn by the Assistant Attorney General Anne Bingaman eight years later, in 1993.[273] New guidelines were introduced in 1995, in which the DOJ explained the meaning of RPM as any vertical collusion where independent entities 'agree to fix, raise, lower, maintain or stabilize the price at which goods or services will be resold'.[274]

Unlike in the 1980s, when antitrust agencies significantly decreased antitrust cases on RPM, the 1990s was a period where the FTC and the DOJ began to be active in RPM cases. This is not surprising as the Bush Administration (1989–93) promised the enforcement of *Dr. Miles*. The only case enforced by the DOJ in the 1980s was *Cuisinarts* from 1980, which is, paradoxically, the only RPM criminal case.[275] In 1991, the FTC and the DOJ brought their first RPM cases after a decade[276] and more followed, with the 1990s being a very active decade in the enforcement of RPM.[277]

---

[271] Ibid., 2.3.

[272] Section 605 of Public Law No 99-180, 99 Stat 1169 (13 December 1985).

[273] Guidelines on vertical restraints, issued 27 March 1995, reprinted 4 Trade Reg Rep (CCH) 13, 400; section 605 of Public Law No 99-180, 99 Stat 1169 (13 December 1985) ('Guidelines 1995').

[274] Ibid., 2.1.

[275] *United States v. Cuisinarts Inc.*, No H80-49 (D. Conn. 1980).

[276] FTC cases: In re *Kreepy Krauly, U.S.A., Inc.*, Dkt. C-3490, 5 Trade Reg Rep (CCH) 23, 463 (1991) – it finished as a consent order; In re *Nintendo of America, Inc.*, F.T.C. File No. 901-0028 (10 April 1991) – proposed consent order; DOJ cases: *United States v. Playmobil U.S.A., Inc.*, 1995-1 Trade Cas (CCH) 71000 (D.D.C. 1995) ('*Playmobil*'); *United States v. California SunCare, Inc.*, 1994-2 Trade Cas (CCH) 70, 843 (CD Cal 1994) 7.

[277] DOJ cases: *United States v. Brush Fibres, Inc.*, 1997-2 Trade Cas (CCH) 71, 915 (E.D.Pa. 1996); *United States v. Anchorshade, Inc.*, 1996-2 Trade Cas (C.C.H.) 71, 640 (S.D.Fla. 1996); Note 276, *Playmobil*; *United States v. Canstar Sports USA, Inc.*, 1993-2 Trade Cas (C.C.H.) 70, 372 (D. Vt 1993); FTC cases: In re *American Cyanamid Co.*, 123 F.T.C. 1257 (1997); In re *New Balance Athletic Shoe, Inc.*, 122 F.T.C. 137 (1996); In re *Reebok International, Ltd.*, 120 F.T.C. 20 (1995); In re *the Keds Corp.*, 117 F.T.C. 389 (1994); In re *Kreepy Krauly USA, Inc.*, 114 F.T.C. 777 (1991); In re *Nintendo of America Inc.*, 114 F.T.C. 702 (1991).

Despite the lack of public RPM cases in the 1980s, the courts dealt with a number of private RPM cases. The courts ruled in many cases that the mere suggestion of retail prices without an obligation to maintain them did not create RPM agreements and were legal.[278] Although the 1980s cases on RPM were ruled under the per se rule, there were obvious tendencies by the Supreme Court in *Monsanto*[279] and *Business Electronics*[280] to limit this scope, which also influenced horizontal price-fixing cases by raising the bar for proving such cases.[281] In *Monsanto*, the Court held that the plaintiff must prove the existence of conspiracy between the manufacturer and his distributors to maintain prices in order to rule out potential individual conduct. Similarly, *Business Electronics* required the plaintiff to show that the defendants had agreed to set a specific or minimum price. The Court specifically excluded from the group of intrabrand price restrictions indirect ways of maintaining prices. Vertical collusion with the aim of terminating supply to a price cutter was not enough to establish an RPM case but, instead, should be determined under the rule of reason as a non-price vertical restraint. The Court of Appeals went even further, stating in *Chevrolet*[282] and *Caymen*[283] that the per se rule of RPM applied only to retail prices and not to prices at different vertical levels, such as wholesale prices.

These cases, especially *Monsanto*, also reflect the tension in the opinions on RPM between the DOJ and Congress. In *Monsanto*, the DOJ

---

[278] *Mesirow v. Pepperidge Farm*, 703 F.2d 339 (9th Circuit), *cert. denied*, 464 U.S. 820 (1983) ('*Pepperidge Farm*'); *Yentsch v. Texaco*, 630 F.2d 46, 53 (2d Circuit 1980); *Morrison v. Nissan Motor Co.*, 601 F.2d 139 (4th Circuit 1979); *Hanson v. Shell Oil Co.*, 541 F.2d 1352, 1357 n4 (9th Circuit 1976), *cert. denied*, 429 U.S. 1074 (1977); *Umphres v. Shell Oil. Co.*, 512 F.2d 420, 422 (5th Circuit), *cert. denied*, 423 U.S. 929 (1975); *Chisholm Bros. Farm Equipment Co. v. International Harvester Co.*, 498 F.2d 1137, 1141–2 (9th Circuit), *cert. denied*, 419 U.S. 1023 (1974); *Gray v. Shell Oil Co.*, 469 F.2d 742, 747–8 n3 (9th Circuit 1972), *cert. denied*, 412 U.S. 943 (1973); *Susser v. Carvel Corp.*, 332 F.2d 505 (2nd Circuit 1964), *cert. dismissed*, 381 U.S. 125.

[279] *Monsanto Co. v. Spray-Rite Svc. Corp.*, 465 U.S. 752 (1984) ('*Monsanto*').

[280] Note 4, *Business Electronics*.

[281] Note 34, Salop, 'What consensus?'. Salop referred to the case of *Blomkest Fertilizer, Inc. v. Potash Corp. of Sask., Inc.*, 203 F.3d 1028 (8th Circuit 2000), where the Court of Appeals cited Note 279, *Monsanto*, when determining whether a horizontal agreement existed.

[282] *Chevrolet v. General Motors Corp.*, 803 F.2d 1463 (9th Circuit 1986), *cert. denied*, 480 U.S. 947 (1987).

[283] *Cayman Exploration Corp. v. United Gas Pipe Line*, 873 F.2d 1357 (10th Circuit 1989).

expressed its view to overturn the *Dr. Miles* per se rule in its amicus brief.[284] However, during the oral hearing, the DOJ remained silent on the question of overruling the per se rule as it was prohibited by Congress from doing so.[285] Therefore, likely influenced by Congress, the Court declined to overrule the per se rule.[286] Congress expressly prevented the DOJ from repeating the same initiative by passing measures in 1983, 1985, 1986 and 1987.[287] Congress's strict view on RPM is also obvious from the enactment of the Consumer Goods Pricing Act, which emulated the *Dr. Miles* per se doctrine and repealed the Miller-Tydings Act and the McGuire Act in 1975.

In VTR cases, the most important milestone case was that of *Sylvania*. By overruling *Schwinn*, the Supreme Court in *Sylvania* proclaimed the rule of reason as the right approach to VTR. It differentiated between non-price and price vertical restraints keeping the per se rule for RPM. The Court referred to a number of procompetitive justifications, which could be applied by respondents under the rule of reason. Although it acknowledged that intrabrand competition was restricted, it held that such restriction could lead to the enhancement of interbrand competition, with interbrand competition (and not intrabrand competition) being the primary concern in antitrust law.[288]

After the change to the rule of reason in *Sylvania*, a number of industries implemented VTR.[289] Since then, antitrust agencies have

---

[284] Brief for the United States as Amicus Curiae in Support of Petitioner, *Monsanto Co. v. Spray-Rite Svc. Corp.*, 465 U.S. 752 (1984) (No 82-914), 1983 U.S. S.Ct Briefs LEXIS 375, 32–47.

[285] Note 34, Salop.

[286] Note 279, *Monsanto*; see also ibid., Salop.

[287] Note 268, Brunell, 347.

[288] Note 7, *Sylvania*, 51–2, 65.

[289] For example, exclusive territories became typical practice for all major soft drink manufacturers. See, *First Beverages, Inc. of Las Vegas and Will Norton v. Royal Crown Cola Co. and H & M Sales Co.*, 612 F.2d 1164 (9th Circuit 1980) 1166; In re *Coca Cola Co.*, No 8855 (F.T.C. 25 April 1978), Trade Reg Rep (CCH) Supp No 330; In re *PepsiCo, Inc.*, No 8856 (F.T.C. April, 1978); also the beer industry is typified by VTR. See, *Mendelovitz v. Adolph Coors Co.*, 693 F.2d 570 (5th Circuit 1982) ('*Mendelovitz*'). However, this is further implemented due to state legislation that allows VTR and other vertical restrictions in the beer industry.

ceased enforcing VTR cases. However, a significant number of unsuccessful private cases on VTR followed,[290] where, except for one successful case, *Eiberger v. Sony*,[291] the Court of Appeals usually requires proof of the restriction of interbrand competition if there was a vertical rather than a horizontal agreement in order to prove a violation of Section 1 of the Sherman Act.

For example, in *Business Cards Tomorrow*,[292] the Court of Appeals stated that the restriction of intrabrand competition was irrelevant because, according to the court, interbrand competition was intense and thus Section 1 of the Sherman Act was not violated. In *Crane & Shovel*, the Sixth Circuit of the Court of Appeals held that the Sherman Act could only be violated if the practice in question led to the monopolization of the market or if it caused 'anticompetitive effect at the interbrand level'.[293] *Crane & Shovel* was one of few cases that dealt with the termination of a distributor and his replacement. The Sixth and the Fifth Circuits of the Court of Appeals ruled that such a practice did not constitute a violation of Section 1 of the Sherman Act[294] because this '[did] not eliminate or materially diminish the existing competition'.[295]

---

[290] See, *Darrell Murphy v. Business Cards Tomorrow, Inc.*, 854 F.2d 1202 (9th Circuit 1988) (*'Business Cards Tomorrow'*); *Assam Drug Co. v. Miller Brewing Co.*, 798 F.2d 1430 (8th Circuit 1986); *Beach v. Viking Sewing Machine Co.*, 784 F.2d 746 (16th Circuit 1986); *Dart Industries, Inc. v. Plunkett Co.*, 704 F.2d 496 (10th Circuit 1983); *Service Merchandise Co. v. Boyd Corp.*, 722 F.2d 945 (1st Circuit 1983) (*'Boyd'*); Note 278, *Pepperidge Farm*; *JBL Enters., Inc. v. Jhirmack Enters., Inc.*, 698 F.2d 1011, 1016 (9th Circuit), cert. denied, 464 U.S. 829 (1983); Note 289, *Mendelovitz*; *Davis-Watkins Co. v. Service Merchandise Co.*, 686 F.2d 1190 (6th Circuit 1982), cert. denied, 466 U.S. 931 (1984); *Abadir & Co. v. First Mississippi Corp.*, 651 F.2d 422 (5th Circuit 1981) (*'Abadir'*); *Muenster Butane, Inc. v. Stewart Co.*, 651 F.2d 292 (5th Circuit 1981); *Donald B. Rice Tire Co. v. Michelin Tire Corp.*, 638 F.2d 15 (11th Circuit), cert. denied, 454 U.S. 822 (1981); *Cowley v. Braden Indus., Inc.*, 613 F.2d 751 (9th Circuit), cert. denied, 446 U.S. 965 (1980); *First Beverages, Inc. v. Royal Crown Cola Co.*, 612 F.2d 1164, cert. denied, 447 U.S. 924 (1980); *Del Rio Distribution Inc. v. Adolph Coors Co.*, 589 F.2d 176 (5th Circuit), cert. denied, 444 U.S. 840 (1979).

[291] *Eiberger v. Sony Corp. of America*, 622 F.2d 1068 (2nd Circuit 1980) (*'Eiberger v. Sony'*).

[292] Note 290, *Business Cards Tomorrow*.

[293] *Crane & Shovel Sales Corp. v. Bucyrus-Erie Co.*, 854 F.2d 802 (6th Circuit 1988) 810 (*'Crane & Shovel'*).

[294] See, e.g., ibid., *Crane & Shovel*; *Copy-Data Systems, Inc. v. Toshiba America, Inc.*, 755 F.2d 293, (2d Circuit 1985) (*'Copy-Data'*); *H & B Equipment Co. v. International Harvester Co.*, 577 F.2d 239 (5th Circuit 1978) (*'H & B Equipment'*); *Fray Chevrolet Sales, Inc. v. General Motors Corp.*, 536 F.2d 683

However, the Second Circuit had a different view on showing 'anticompetitive effect at the interbrand level' in the case of *Eiberger v. Sony* from 1980. In this case, the court was satisfied with the evidence that intrabrand competition was restricted, as the respondent did not prove that this restraint enhanced interbrand competition. This case clearly shifted the burden of proof from the plaintiff to the respondent, as the court did not require the plaintiff to prove that interbrand competition was restricted, rather it held that if intrabrand competition was restricted the respondent could show that such a practice increased interbrand competition in order to justify her conduct under the rule of reason.

Following this era and the previous era, market power still played a significant role. However, this era was influenced by the Chicago School's economic approach and was connected with proving the restriction of interbrand competition and/or significant restriction of competition. Therefore, the defendant's lack of market power would lead to the presumption that the conduct in question did not violate Section 1 of the Sherman Act. For example, in *Sylvania*, the Supreme Court held that interbrand competition was likely enhanced, despite the restriction of intrabrand competition, because the manufacturer had 'a small market share' and faced vigorous interbrand competition.[296] In the case on an exclusive dealership in *Valley Liquors*,[297] the Court of Appeals required the plaintiff to show that the defendant held significant market power, adopting the opinion that a firm with no market power would act for the benefit of his consumers and that without market power the defendant 'is unlikely to adopt policies that disserve its consumers'.[298]

A general and clear exception from proving the restriction of interbrand competition where intrabrand competition is restricted is the situation where there is a horizontal rather than a vertical agreement, because a horizontal agreement allocating markets is prohibited per se. If the court found that the agreement was between buyers and was thus horizontal, the court applied the per se rule and did not evaluate the impact on interbrand competition despite the fact that such a restriction

---

(6th Circuit 1976) ('*Fray Chevrolet*'); *Ace Beer Distributors, Inc. v. Kohn, Inc.*, 318 F.2d 283 (6th Circuit 1963); see also, *Jayco Systems Inc. v. Savin Business Machines Corp.*, 777 F.2d 306, 320 (5th Circuit 1985), cert. denied, 479 U.S. 816 (1986) ('*Jayco*').

[295] Note 294, *Fray Chevrolet*, 686.
[296] Note 7, *Sylvania*, 65.
[297] *Valley Liquors, Inc. v. Renfield Importers, Ltd.*, 678 F.2d 742 (7th Circuit 1982) ('*Valley Liquors*').
[298] Ibid., 745.

was an intrabrand restriction and, therefore, primarily restricted intrabrand competition. This was obvious in the case of *Boyd*,[299] where the Court of Appeals applied the per se rule to a situation with a horizontal territorial restriction, which involved only one brand. Therefore, there is no difference between a multi-brand, horizontal market allocation and a one-brand, horizontal territorial restriction in the court's approach.

For instance, in *Boyd*, it was alleged that distributors of microwave ovens produced by one manufacturer, Amana Refrigeration, divided their territories. If a retailer wanted to purchase Amana Refrigeration microwave ovens from a distributor distributing in a different territory, she was refused supply. The Court of Appeals focused on whether competition between distributors at the horizontal level was restricted and not whether the intrabrand or interbrand competition among distributors was hindered, stating that the effect of this arrangement 'was to minimize competition among the Amana distributors'.[300]

As I discuss in Chapters 2 and 5, the effect on competition is the same notwithstanding whether it was a manufacturer together with her retailers who introduced the restriction or only retailers, in that situation only the intent differs. An approach that claims to be based on the economical evaluation of the effects on competition should ideally differentiate between intrabrand and interbrand competition. Indeed, the argued difference between the two led to the introduction of the rule of reason for VTR in *Sylvania*. Because the Court of Appeals applied the per se rule in *Boyd*, the court did not evaluate one of the distributor's arguments that this territorial restriction increased efficiency in the form of 'product service, public relations and customer education programs',[301] none of which differ from the procompetitive theories of vertical restriction.

Besides intrabrand vertical and horizontal agreements, the Court of Appeals also dealt with an agreement on VTR between a 'dealer' and a vertically integrated firm that operated as a supplier and a buyer (a dealer) in a dual distribution. It had to decide whether such an agreement was horizontal or vertical and thus whether the rule of reason for VTR or the per se rule, in the case of horizontal territorial restrictions, applied. The court ruled that when a vertically integrated firm initiated and was involved in a territorial restriction, such a restriction constituted VTR

---

[299] Note 290, *Boyd*.
[300] Ibid., 950.
[301] Ibid., 947.

rather than a horizontal restriction and thus the rule of reason applied.[302] In the case of *Abadir*, the court clarified that a territorial restraint has a form of VTR when the party who initiated the restraint has the same 'potential economic advantage' as a supplier that is not vertically integrated in VTR.

> A particular market-distributing agreement is treated as a vertical agreement if the party imposing the agreement has the potential economic advantages typically available to a supplier in a vertical market-distributing agreement. If these potential economic advantages are absent, then the agreement is horizontal.[303]

This ruling is in agreement with the Chicago School, as further explained in Chapter 2.[304]

VTR: *Sylvania*:[305] Rule of Reason

In this case, the respondent, GTE Sylvania Inc., a manufacturer of television sets, adopted a new franchise plan in 1962 selling directly to his smaller, franchised retailers and granting each retailer one non-exclusive territory. Sylvania hoped that this new distribution system would increase his market share. The new franchise plan was a success with Sylvania's market share increasing approximately 5 percent between 1962 and 1965.[306]

In 1965, Sylvania decided to franchise Young Brothers, an established television retailer in San Francisco, as an additional retailer because Sylvania was not satisfied with the existing retailers' sales in that geographical market. The proposed location for Young Brothers was approximately one mile from a retail outlet operated by the petitioner, Continental T.V., Inc., which was a successful Sylvania franchisee. Continental did not agree with the location for the new retailer, claiming

---

[302] Note 290, *Abadir*; *Red Diamond Supply, Inc v. Liquid Carbonic Corp.*, 637 F.2d 1001 (5th Circuit 1981) ('*Red Diamond*'); see also, Note 294, *Copy-Data*.

[303] Note 290, *Abadir*, 427.

[304] As I discussed in Chapter 2 in connection with RPM, a more recent school, the progressive school, argues that a vertically integrated manufacturer has anticompetitive and not procompetitive reasons. In general, a vertically integrated firm benefits from less intensive intrabrand competition for additional reasons than a non-integrated manufacturer.

[305] Note 7, Sylvania.

[306] Ibid., 38.

that this went against Sylvania's marketing policy, with which Sylvania disagreed. Continental then replaced a large order of Sylvania's products with televisions from Phillips.[307] At the same time, Continental was negotiating with Sylvania for the opening of a new store in Sacramento, California. Sylvania refused and terminated Continental's franchises.[308] Among other complaints, Continental claimed that Sylvania had violated Section 1 of the Sherman Act by entering into franchise agreements,[309] including territorial restraints.[310]

As was the case in *Schwinn*, the manufacturer, Sylvania, was a well-established company, although not as dominant as Schwinn. At the time, Sylvania was the eighth largest manufacturer of color television sets in the US.[311] However, unlike *Schwinn*, where the Supreme Court applied the per se rule in order to protect small companies, in *Sylvania*, the Court overruled the per se rule and introduced the rule of reason to VTR cases, applying some observations from the Chicago School theories, including an emphasis on interbrand competition and procompetitive justifications of VTR. Indeed, the case of *Sylvania* has been referred to as a case on vertical restraints where the Supreme Court adopted the economic analysis framework in the form of the rule of reason.[312]

Intrabrand and interbrand competition
First, the Court discussed whether VTR can restrict competition. In this regard, the Court held that vertical restrictions including VTR could reduce intrabrand competition and simultaneously stimulate interbrand competition.[313] The Court then placed great emphasis on interbrand competition and defined both interbrand and intrabrand competition, stating that:

> [i]nterbrand competition is the competition among the manufacturers of the same generic product – television sets in this case – and is the primary concern of antitrust law. The extreme example of a deficiency of interbrand competition is monopoly, where there is only one manufacturer. In contrast,

---

[307] Ibid., 39.
[308] Ibid., 39–40.
[309] The Court did not define the term 'franchising system' in Note 7, *Sylvania* or in Note 162, *Schwinn*. In comparison with the EU approach and its Vertical Guidelines, it is not clear what the term 'franchising system' means under the US approach to VTR.
[310] Note 7, *Sylvania*, 40.
[311] Ibid., 38–9.
[312] Note 9, Voorhees; Note 267, Wright, 2.
[313] Note 7, *Sylvania*, 51–2.

intrabrand competition is the competition between the distributors – wholesale or retail – of the product of a particular manufacturer.[314]

Hence, 'intrabrand competition', as understood by the Supreme Court in *Sylvania*, is a downstream version of vertical competition, while 'interbrand competition' is a form of horizontal competition. This understanding of intrabrand competition differs from my explanation of its meaning in Chapter 2, where I defined vertical competition as upstream and/or downstream (vertical) competition and intrabrand competition as competition within one brand which can take place vertically but also horizontally, for instance among retailers. Interbrand competition, as explained in Chapter 2, is then competition within competing brands which takes place horizontally, usually at the production level, but can also occur at a downstream market, for instance among retailers. This is important to bear in mind when reading the US cases because later US cases also use the term 'intrabrand competition' in a narrow meaning as a form of downstream vertical competition where vertical entities compete within the one brand.

The Supreme Court then discussed the facts of *Sylvania* finding that intrabrand competition had been reduced because the number of retailers had been limited by and within VTR.[315] However, the Court held that, unlike in *Schwinn*, in *Sylvania*, the manufacturer had 'a small market share' and was competing with a number of substitutive TV sets and consumers were able to switch to other products easily. Therefore, the Court stated that because of the small market share and the existence of other competitors in the competitive market the practice potentially promoted interbrand competition.[316] It must be noted that the Court did not analyze interbrand competition in the relevant market. Its assumption of increased interbrand competition is not necessarily correct as, for instance, an analysis of interbrand competition in connection with the VTR in question would be necessary to make findings of whether interbrand competition was, by this conduct, increased, decreased or unchanged.

Procompetitive justifications
Second, in *Sylvania*, the Court listed several benefits of VTR, dividing them between justifications of new and established manufacturers. First, a manufacturer who wishes to penetrate the market can use VTR to motivate retailers to sell his products and to cover investments. Secondly,

---

[314] Ibid., 52.
[315] Ibid., 54.
[316] Ibid., 65.

the court utilized the knowledge of procompetitive services theories, stating that established manufacturers can use VTR to facilitate promotion and/or services which influence the competitiveness of his products and eliminate free riders.[317]

Based on its arguments of increased interbrand competition and procompetitive justifications of VTR, the Court overruled *Schwinn* explaining that the per se rule was not justified and returned to the rule of reason as the appropriate approach to VTR.[318] However, the Court did not clarify how the rule of reason should apply to VTR.

The application of the rule of reason can take different forms, as illustrated by the cases of *Eiberger v. Sony* and *Business Cards Tomorrow*. In the first case, the Court of Appeals was satisfied with the restriction of intrabrand competition, shifting the burden of proof to the respondent to show an enhancement of interbrand competition as a potential justification under the rule of reason. The second case required the plaintiff to prove not only the restriction of intrabrand competition but also interbrand competition. Subsequent VTR cases followed this heavy burden of proof on the plaintiff. As predicted by Judge Posner in an article from 1981, such an application of the rule of reason made it unfeasible for plaintiffs to win their cases, leading to the de facto legality of VTR in the US.[319] And, indeed, reality confirms this. Since this era, cases on VTR have disappeared from both public and private litigation. There are a number of reasons that could explain this. First, rule of reason litigation, including the heavy burden of proof, is too expensive and complicated for private parties, primarily small companies, to sue and win the case. Second, the justification of the rule of reason in *Sylvania* and its application in later cases is set in a way that presumes these restraints increase efficiency and should thus be legal.[320] Indeed, in *Sylvania*, the Court believed that the restriction of intrabrand competition allowed for the enhancement of interbrand competition, and provided a

---

[317] Ibid., 55–6; Note 138, Bork; William S Comanor, 'Vertical Territorial and Customer Restrictions: *White Motor* and Its Aftermath' (1968) 81(7) *Harvard Law Revue* 1419; Almarin Phillips, '*Schwinn* Rules and the "New Economics" of Vertical Relations' (1975) 44 *Antitrust Law Journal* 573.

[318] Note 7, *Sylvania*, 57–9.

[319] Richard A Posner, 'The Next Step in the Antitrust Treatment of Restricted Distribution: *Per Se* Legality' (1981) 48 *University of Chicago Law Revue* 6.

[320] Jean W Burns, 'Vertical Restraints, Efficiency, and the Real World' (1993) 62 *Fordham Law Revue* 597, 615–6; Douglas H Ginsburg, 'Vertical Restraints: De Facto Legality under the Rule of Reason' (1991) 60 *Antitrust Law Journal* 67.

number of procompetitive justifications as to why the manufacturers would introduce VTR.

VTR: *Eiberger v. Sony*:[321] **Protection of Intrabrand Competition**

The Second Circuit of the Court of Appeals found that the restriction of intrabrand competition in the form of VTR would constitute an unreasonable restraint of trade and thus violate Section 1 of the Sherman Act, provided the restraint did not enhance interbrand competition and could not be in any other way justified. *Eiberger v. Sony* involved the sale of Sony office dictation equipment in the 1970s produced by Sony Kabushiki Kaisha of Japan, a leading manufacturer of electronic equipment, instruments and devices. The Japanese manufacturer established a wholly-owned subsidiary in the US, Sonam. Sonam started to sell the dictation equipment in question in the US in 1971 and by 1975 she had created a dealership network and was a well-established manufacturer, the fifth largest in the US, of office dictation equipment, with a market share of 12 percent. ABP was one of the authorized dealers selling Sonam's products from 1972 to 1976.[322]

Sonam based her dealership network on identical written contracts, where each dealer was assigned a specific geographic area in which he could sell. However, each dealer was also allowed to sell beyond his own territory. Dealers were fully responsible for repairs, replacement and servicing. Thus, the dealership contracts also included provisions on warranty service. Furthermore, based on the contract, it was expected that instructions in the use of the products for customers would be provided by the dealers, a cost borne by the dealers. However, Sonam agreed to reimburse her dealers for warranty replacement of parts. Prior to the beginning of 1975, dealers were allowed to transfer warranty responsibilities to other dealers for a fee in situations where the product was sold in a territory not assigned to the selling dealer.[323]

In 1974, ABP started to sell Sonam's products to another authorized dealer, Williges, who had a network of subdealers in Florida; however, his dealership was terminated by Sonam in the same year and Sonam instead began to sell directly to Williges' subdealers. Williges established a new subdealership network and was competing vigorously with his old network of dealers, who were now authorized to sell Sonam's products. Williges was selling below the prices for which the products were sold

---

[321] Note 291, *Eiberger v. Sony*.
[322] Ibid., 1070.
[323] Ibid., 1070–71.

by his former dealership network. The authorized dealers began to send Sonam letters of complaint and met with Sonam's Regional Sales Manager.[324]

In 1975, Sonam changed her dealership contracts, in particular the warranty fee system provisions. In practice, this led to Sonam keeping written records of the serial numbers of her products. Sonam would automatically charge a particular dealer a warranty fee for any product sold beyond their assigned territory even if the machine was not sold to a final customer or was not even under warranty. The authorized dealers would check their territories and contact Sonam in case they identified that that particular piece of office dictation equipment was not sold by them in their assigned geographical market.[325]

ABP continued to sell to other dealers. Sonam, due to her new warranty fee system, was able to track machines sold by ABP to independent dealers who were selling beyond ABP's territory and usually for less than authorized dealers. Sonam charged ABP warranty fees, which ABP refused to pay, asking Sonam to prove that those machines were rendered by authorized dealers. Sonam did not provide any evidence but instead refused to renew the contract with ABP.[326]

The District Court found that non-authorized dealers purchasing Sonam's products from ABP were providing warranty services and therefore the warranty fees charged by Sonam to ABP had no basis in the warranty system itself, their real purpose was to penalize dealers for products sold outside their territories. Hence, the purpose of the warranty fee scheme was to eliminate intrabrand competition and prevent price-cutting, with the amount of the warranty fee being so high as to eliminate any profit an authorized dealer could make from reselling the products to other dealers.[327] On this basis, the District Court believed that the scheme 'did not enhance interbrand competition but did eliminate intrabrand competition'.[328]

Sonam appealed, referring to the rule of reason in *Sylvania*. She argued that VTR was justifiable because her warranty scheme had a legitimate goal which could increase the intrabrand competitiveness. Its purpose was to ensure the warranty service, prevent free riding and assist with penetrating the market.[329] She further argued that, under the rule of

---

[324] Ibid.
[325] Ibid., 1072–3.
[326] Ibid., 1074.
[327] Ibid., 1074–5.
[328] Ibid., 1075.
[329] Ibid., 1075, 1078–80.

reason, it must be proved that interbrand competition (and not only intrabrand competition) was restricted and that a termination of a dealership contract did not constitute a violation of Section 1 of the Sherman Act.[330]

The Court of Appeals disagreed with Sonam. By applying the rule of reason, it addressed Sonam's justification of the practice and focused its analysis on the evaluation of whether there was an enhancement of interbrand competition, which would outweigh the restriction of intrabrand competition. It referred to the provision in *Chicago Board* that states that for the determination of whether a particular practice 'promotes competition or whether it is such as may suppress or even destroy competition'[331] the court must consider the:

> condition [of business] before and after the restraint was imposed; the nature of the restraint and its effect, actual or probable. The history of the restraint, the evil believed to exist, the reason for adopting the particular remedy, the purpose or end sought to be attained, are all relevant facts. This is not because a good intention will save an otherwise objectionable regulation or the reverse; but because knowledge of intent may help the court to interpret facts and to predict consequences.[332]

By evaluating the purpose and effect of the 1975 warranty scheme, the court then analyzed the reasoning of the District Court and the presented evidence of both parties. It concluded that the District Court was correct in its finding of a violation of Section 1 of the Sherman Act because the warranty scheme as introduced in 1975 led to an unreasonable restraint of trade in the form of exclusive vertical territories.[333]

The court declined Sonam's argument that the 1975 warranty scheme was set up in order to ensure warranty services. It agreed with the District Court that the purpose of the warranty scheme was to enforce an exclusive territorial restriction with the effect of the new scheme being the elimination of intrabrand competition. The presented evidence, including witness testimony, supported the claim that the so-called 'warranty fee' was de facto 'interterritorial commissions', as referred to by a number of authorized dealers, for two reasons. First, the amount of

---

[330] Ibid., 1075–6, 1081. However, Sonam did not refer to VTR cases when arguing that a mere termination of a dealer did not violate the Sherman Act, but it referred to *Oreck Corp. v. Whirlpool Corp.*, 579 F.2d 126 (2d Circuit 1978) and *Daniels v. All Steel Equip. Inc.*, 590 F.2d 111 (5th Circuit 1979).
[331] Note 291, *Eiberger v. Sony*, 1076.
[332] Ibid., 1076 quoting Note 27, *Chicago Board of Trade*, 238.
[333] Ibid., 1076.

the warranty fee was such that it exceeded profits made by ABP when selling to other dealers. Second, Sonam, when charging this fee, did not require information as to whether the product in question needed or would need a warranty service and not even whether the product was already sold.[334]

Sonam's reference to free riding was also not supported by the presented facts because the evidence provided showed that unauthorized dealers were experienced and provided any services needed, including the warranty service.[335] The Court of Appeals also refused Sonam's argument about penetrating the market, stating that with a 12 percent market share combined with a few years of operation in the market and a reference to herself as a 'leader', she was not a newcomer entering the market.[336]

When analyzing the effect on competition, the Court of Appeals also found that the prices charged by the authorized dealers were artificially high in comparison with the prices charged by unauthorized dealers. Therefore, prior to the 1975 warranty scheme, Sonam was constantly pressured by a number of authorized dealers about price-cutting. This had a tendency 'to exert downward pressure on price levels'[337] giving Sonam a reason to address this pressure by eliminating intrabrand competition. Indeed, in comparison to the old system, the new system discouraged competition among dealers without increasing customer services. The system as introduced in 1975 thus led to the reduction of intrabrand competition.[338]

The Court of Appeals did not require evidence of the restriction of interbrand competition. It explained that it was not correct to argue that the restriction of intrabrand competition could not alone violate Section 1 of the Sherman Act. It referred to *Sylvania*, claiming that there was no basis for the claim that the restriction of interbrand competition must be proved.[339] Indeed, in *Eiberger v. Sony*, the plaintiff did not prove, and as the court said did not even have to prove, that interbrand competition was restricted.

This approach differs to the one applied in other post-*Sylvania* VTR cases because it did not require proof of the restriction of interbrand competition under the rule of reason. It shows how the difference

---

[334] Ibid., 1076–80.
[335] Ibid., 1078–9.
[336] Ibid., 1080.
[337] Ibid.
[338] Ibid.
[339] Ibid., 1075–81.

between the emphasis on interbrand competition, which is typified for the first economic-policy model based on the Chicago School, and the protection of both intrabrand as well as interbrand competition, which is in agreement with the second economic-policy model,[340] leads to different results. If the court had required evidence of the restriction of interbrand competition for ABP to succeed, it is unlikely he would have been able to produce it, either because there was no restriction of interbrand competition or, even if there was, it is unlikely that ABP would be able to prove it.[341] Instead, the court applied a reverse approach, placing the burden of proof for the enhancement of interbrand competition on Sonam. Here, Sonam was required to show that this increased interbrand competition because she failed to justify her practice and prove that intrabrand competition was not restricted.

VTR: *Business Cards Tomorrow*:[342] Protection of Interbrand Competition as Test for VTR Cases

The approach utilized by the Ninth Circuit differed to the one applied in *Eiberger v. Sony* by the Second Circuit eight years earlier, in that the Ninth Circuit focused on the 'significant' restriction of competition in the form of interbrand competition and intention to harm competition. Like the previous case, *Business Cards Tomorrow* involved the existence of exclusive territories. This was not disputed. The main question, however, was whether this VTR violated Section 1 of the Sherman Act under the rule of reason, as the court determined that this was a vertical rather than horizontal territorial restriction.[343] The plaintiff argued that the exclusive

---

[340] In Chapter 2, I set forward two models. The first is a conventional, Chicagonist model with the aim of protecting horizontal competition and emphasizing interbrand competition. The second model, on the other hand, accepts the existence of intrabrand and vertical competition protecting not only interbrand competition, but also intrabrand competition.

[341] This case was based on a vertical restriction. To prove the restriction of interbrand competition, ABP would have to obtain data from other brands' manufacturers and their dealers and would have to come with an economic explanation (an economic harm theory) as to why any decrease of interbrand competition was due to Sonam's restriction of intrabrand competition and not due to any other phenomenon in the market.

[342] Note 290, *Business Cards Tomorrow*.

[343] Ibid., 1204.

territories were unreasonable and thus violated Section 1 of the Sherman Act because VTR led to a situation where some prices were artificially high.[344]

The Court of Appeals applied a three-element test, which included the importance of intention as well as the actual restriction, in order to determine an unreasonable restriction under Section 1 of the Sherman Act:

1. the existence of an agreement;
2. intention to harm or restrict competition;
3. actual restriction or injury of competition that had an impact upon competition in a relevant market.[345]

The court found that there was a vertical agreement and, thus, it further focused its judgment on the second and third elements. The court did not find that this 'franchising system', in particular VTR, affected the competitiveness of the entire relevant market, the wholesale thermography market. First, it stated that the prices charged due to VTR, which were not shown to be artificially high in general but only some instances indicated higher prices, showed that the franchising system was in Business-Cards-Tomorrow and his franchisees' economic interests. Therefore, the plaintiffs did not prove the existence of anticompetitive effects.[346]

Second, the court discussed the actual restriction of competition. It stated that the effect on intrabrand competition was irrelevant, and focused instead on the restriction of interbrand competition. It was satisfied with the fact that even the plaintiff agreed that interbrand competition was intense and faced substantial competition with low barriers to entry in the local wholesale thermography market. The court held that this intensive interbrand competition meant there was no significant restriction on competition.[347]

Despite the fact that the plaintiff's main argument of artificially high intrabrand prices was weak, even with strong arguments it would have been difficult to prove unreasonable restriction of competition under this application of the rule of reason. In *Eiberger v. Sony*, the court was satisfied that the VTR in question restricted intrabrand competition. In *Business Cards Tomorrow*, the plaintiff tried to persuade the court that

---

[344] Ibid., 1205.
[345] Ibid.
[346] Ibid.
[347] Ibid.

VTR led to high prices. The court determined higher prices to be in the business interests of the parties involved, requiring evidence of a restriction of interbrand competition. Thus, without proving that interbrand competition was restricted, no plaintiff would succeed with his case under this application of the rule of reason.

RPM: *Monsanto*:[348] Existence of an Agreement

In *Monsanto*, the Supreme Court explained how to establish the existence of an RPM agreement prohibited under Section 1 of the Sherman Act, and how to distinguish such prohibited conduct from legal conduct in the form of unilateral conduct and from a non-price restraint agreement.

Monsanto was a manufacturer of agricultural herbicides and other chemical products. One of her authorized wholesale distributors was Spray-Rite, who alleged that Monsanto and a few other distributors conspired in order to fix the resale price of agricultural herbicides produced by Monsanto. Monsanto's distribution system had been based on a number of criteria since 1967, which, among other things, included the employment of trained salesmen on technical aspects of Monsanto's products.

Spray-Rite was Monsanto's wholesale distributor from 1957 until 1968, when his supply of Monsanto products began to decline. Monsanto claimed that they declined to renew the supply to Spray-Rite because he did not comply with their criteria, in particular the employment of a trained salesman and adequate promotion of sales. However, Spray-Rite claimed that it was due to a conspiracy between Monsanto and other distributors on RPM.[349]

The lower courts agreed with Spray-Rite. The Court of Appeals ruled that a violation of Section 1 of the Sherman Act in the form of RPM is proven if it is shown that the termination of a price-cutting distributor by his supplier is due to complaints by other distributors.[350] Although the Supreme Court also found the violation of Section 1, it disagreed with the Court of Appeals' motion and based its reasoning on a different standard.

The Supreme Court referred to four previous milestone cases when determining the existence of a prohibited agreement on RPM under Section 1 of the Sherman Act:

---

[348] Note 279, *Monsanto*.
[349] Ibid., 756–7.
[350] Ibid., 758–9.

- *Dr. Miles*, which established the per se rule standard for RPM cases;
- *Colgate*, which differentiated between legal unilateral and prohibited collusive conduct on RPM;
- *Parke, Davis*, which clarified the *Colgate* doctrine; and
- *Sylvania*, which established the rule of reason for 'non-price restrictions'.

The Court explained that to correctly analyze a potential violation in the form of RPM, the courts must distinguish between 'concerted and independent action' and concerted action must be distinguished between 'concerted action to set prices and concerted action on nonprice restrictions'.[351] The Court observed that these distinctions are difficult to apply in practice because *'the economic effect* of ... unilateral and concerted vertical price setting, agreements on price and nonprice restrictions ... is in many, but not all, cases *similar or identical*'.[352] This observation is indeed interesting as it supports the argument that despite the different legal approaches utilized for unilateral and collusive actions and for price and non-price vertical agreements, the economic effects of these actions advocate for one, unilateral approach to vertical restraints in general.

The Court then reflected upon the facts from the case explaining the difference between independent and collusive actions. The Court argued that even the disclosure of an intention to set retail prices and marketing strategy did not prove the existence of collusion, and that exchanging this kind of information was legitimate.[353] The Court explained that manufacturers and their distributors need to discuss prices and marketing strategies in order to ensure that the products reach final consumers 'persuasively and efficiently'. This is particularly obvious in situations where the manufacturer implements non-price restrictions and wants to motivate her distributors to utilize services. In these situations, the Court said, the manufacturer will be interested in ensuring that her distributors earn sufficient profit and that nobody free rides on these activities. Thus, the Court argued, communication between the manufacturer and her distributors about prices and their compliance is reasonable and legitimate and does not, on its own, constitute an agreement on RPM.[354]

---

[351] Ibid., 761.
[352] Ibid., 762 (emphasis added).
[353] Ibid.
[354] Ibid., 762–4.

However, what has to be proved is 'a conscious commitment to a common scheme designed to achieve an unlawful objective'.[355] Thus, the evidence presented must show activities towards collusion from both parties.[356] The Court believed that there was enough evidence, including direct evidence on RPM, to conclude that there was an agreement on RPM (and also terminating price cutters). In particular, these were:

1. Monsanto's threats against Spray-Rite to terminate the contract if he did not raise prices;
2. threatening actions against other price cutters shortly after the plaintiff's termination, followed by maintaining prices by distributors;
3. evidence of discussions between Monsanto and Spray-Rite on maintaining prices;
4. a newsletter of one of the distributors based on the meeting between Monsanto and the distributor, published prior to the termination of Spray-Rite, about the existence of RPM and the understanding among distributors to follow RPM.[357]

The Court specifically discussed whether the termination of Spray-Rite was 'part of or pursuant to' the anticompetitive agreement.[358] The Court stated that for RPM to function well there must be a termination of distributors who do not comply. It evaluated that the above-mentioned evidence proved the existence of an agreement on RPM further facilitated by the termination of distributors who did not comply, and thus it agreed with the findings (but not with the standard) of the lower courts.[359]

The concurring judge, Justice Brennan, referred to Congress's standpoint of not overruling the approach of the per se rule set in *Dr. Miles* which the Court followed despite the fact that the DOJ was of a different opinion. However, Congress later prevented the DOJ from supporting the overturning of the *Dr Miles* per se rule in the amicus brief. This would indicate that the Supreme Court treated the Sherman Act as a legislative

---

[355] Ibid., 764. The Supreme Court was quoting *Edward J Sweeney & Sons v. Texaco, Inc.*, 637 F.2d 105 (3d Circuit 1980) 111.
[356] Ibid., 764.
[357] Ibid., 765–8.
[358] Ibid., 767.
[359] Ibid., 767–8.

statute rather than a common law statute as later in the case of *Leegin* the Sherman Act was referred to by the Supreme Court.[360]

RPM: *Business Electronics*:[361] Termination of a Price Cutter as a Non-price Restraint

Four years later, in *Business Electronics*, the Supreme Court applied the rule of reason to an agreement between a supplier and his distributor with bargaining power on the termination of supply to a price-cutting distributor. It ranged this kind of agreement among non-price, vertical restrictions. The Court, applying the rule of reason, stated that the simple cancellation of distribution to a 'price cutter' based on an agreement between the supplier and his second distributor without the existence of an agreement on price or minimum price setting did not demonstrate a restriction of competition or a reduction of output.[362]

We may recall that in *Monsanto* the Supreme Court also ruled that the mere termination of a price cutter, which was not a consequence of an RPM agreement, did not constitute a prohibited RPM agreement. However, in *Business Electronics*, the Court evaluated the presented facts in such a way that it found an agreement on the termination of supply but no agreement on RPM. Therefore, it held that the agreement on termination could not be a consequence of an agreement on RPM.

The respondent, the Sharp Electronics Corp., produced electronic calculators. The petitioner, Business Electronics, became the exclusive retailer of Sharp Electronics calculators in the Houston area, Texas, in 1968. The respondent appointed another retailer, Gilbert Hartwell, in the same territory in 1972.[363]

The respondent published a list of suggested retail prices but there was no evidence to suggest that retailers were obliged to follow these prices. The petitioner's prices were often below the suggested prices and, generally, her prices were lower than Hartwell's prices, which were only seldom below the suggested minimum prices. Hartwell complained to the respondent about the petitioner's prices several times, giving the respondent an ultimatum in June 1973, claiming that she would terminate the contract unless the respondent stopped dealing with the petitioner within

---

[360] For further information, see the discussion in 'RPM: *Leegin*: the rule of reason' below.
[361] Note 4, *Business Electronics*.
[362] Ibid., 726–7.
[363] Ibid., 721.

30 days. The respondent terminated the contract with the petitioner in July 1973.[364]

The Court of Appeals ruled that the evidence presented in this case (in particular, the fact that the retailer, Hartwell, followed the suggested prices and pressured the manufacturer to terminate the contract with the second distributors due to the cutting of prices by Business Electronics) established the existence of a prohibited agreement.[365] However, the Supreme Court disagreed with the Court of Appeals. By evaluating the alleged collusion, it first explained the application of the per se rule, then it distinguished the per se and the rule of reason agreements, deciding that the subject matter had to be ruled by the rule of reason. Thus, by applying the rule of reason, it discussed the effect of the conduct in question.

When explaining the per se rule, the Court argued that certain categories of agreements were illegal per se because they were 'manifestly anti-competitive' and tended to 'always or almost always restrict competition and decrease output'.[366] The restriction, which is the subject of the agreement, must have an obvious, demonstrable economic impact on trade to apply the per se rule.[367] It then related this impact to horizontal competition, stating that 'all competitive effects are, by definition, horizontal effects'.[368] This understanding of competition reflects well the Chicago School (and the first economic-policy model set out in Chapter 2).

The Court then distinguished between price and non-price vertical restrictions. The Supreme Court believed that there was 'a significant distinction between non-price and price vertical restrictions' in that the price restrictions tended to 'reduce interbrand price competition because they "facilitate[d] cartelizing"'.[369] Therefore the Court linked RPM collusion with the restriction of horizontal competition. However, it did so without supporting its argument and without referring to any economic or market study. It then explained by citing *Sylvania* and *Monsanto* that, unlike collusion, in RPM, where the per se rule applied and was justified on the basis of facilitating cartelization, with regards to

---

[364] Ibid.
[365] 780 F.2d 1212, 1219 (CA5 1986).
[366] Note 4, *Business Electronics*, 723.
[367] Ibid., 723–4.
[368] Ibid., 730.
[369] Ibid., 725.

collusion on non-price vertical restraints, a presumption in favor of a rule-of-reason standard always existed.[370]

The Supreme Court then found that the per se rule was not justified in this case because the simple cancellation of distribution to a 'price cutter' based on an agreement between the manufacturer and his second distributor without the existence of an agreement on price or minimum price setting did not demonstrate a restriction of competition or a reduction of output.[371] Therefore, the Court required a demonstration of the existence of 'economic effect, such as the facilitation of cartelizing'.[372] Indeed, by applying the rule of reason, the Court did not find the facilitation of cartels. Instead, it assumed that the manufacturer's reason for termination was to ensure adequate services.[373]

The Court also raised a question as to whether the respondent had been free riding on Hartwell's educational and promotional services; however, it did not examine this further.[374] The Court said that it is also possible that the manufacturer simply disliked cutting prices.[375] The Supreme Court acknowledged that this conduct and non-price vertical restraints in general can lead to higher prices but it also stated that such non-price restraints have the aim of ensuring services and stopping free riders. The Court believed that this was the true motivation for terminating supply in this case.[376]

However, any evidence of free riding or increased services was not provided and these reasons were simply assumed as possibilities by the Supreme Court. Taking into consideration the facts from the case, it is likely that the reason for the termination was that the price cutter did not maintain the suggested prices. Maintaining suggested prices was enforced by the retailer with bargaining power, Hartwell, who pressured Sharp Electronics to terminate supply to Business Electronics.[377] Such situations were well described by Steiner, who claimed that they resulted from a significant bargaining power on the part of the retailers and that

---

[370] Ibid., 726.
[371] Ibid., 726–7.
[372] Ibid., 726.
[373] Ibid., 727–8.
[374] Ibid., 721.
[375] Ibid., 728.
[376] Ibid., 728, 731.
[377] There are similarities between this case and the example provided in Chapter 2 in 'Why Impose RPM or VTR in Distribution Systems?' In both situations, one retailer has the bargaining power and pressures the manufacturer to terminate the contract with the retailer without the same bargaining power and/or maintain retail prices.

they were common in practice.[378] He also argued that, in this case, the market data indicated that Business Electronics Corp. had had lower prices not because she had been free riding but because she had been more efficient than Hartwell. Because Hartwell possessed significant bargaining power, Sharp decided to comply with Hartwell's demand to keep a higher profit from the Hartwell purchase.[379]

Dissenting Justice Stevens disagreed with the majority on two essential points. First, both Justice Stevens and Justice White refuted that this conduct constituted a non-price vertical restraint; they classified this as a boycott by the manufacturer.[380] Second, Justice Stevens argued that this conduct had the same effect as a price-fixing agreement and that it eliminated price competition.[381] He then explained that eliminating price competition did not absolutely assure the increase of service competition and, therefore, 'a better marketplace for consumers' but what was certain was that price competition was eliminated.[382]

Although this is not in line with the majority argument and findings in *Business Electronics*, it does not contradict what the Supreme Court stated in *Monsanto*: that the economic effect of unilateral conduct on maintaining the same retail price and vertical non-price agreements can have the same or similar economic effect.[383] It also supports the petitioner's theory that the agreement had the same effect as a price-fixing agreement.[384] As already stated in *Trans-Missouri*, what must be evaluated by the court is the effect and not the intent of the agreement in question. One way of interpreting this is that it is the effect of the agreement that establishes whether it is a price or non-price restraint, as reflected in the argument of the petitioner and Justice Stevens. Instead, in *Monsanto* and *Business Electronics*, the courts focused on the purpose of the agreements in question to determine whether the agreement was on RPM or whether the agreement was a non-price agreement. It focused on

---

[378] Robert L Steiner, 'How Manufacturers Deal with the Price-Cutting Retailer: When Are Vertical Restraints Efficient?' (1997) 65 *Antitrust Law Journal* 409, 414–16; see also William S Comanor, 'Antitrust Policy toward Resale Price Maintenance Following *Leegin*' (2010) 55(1) *Antitrust Bulletin* 59, 67–9.
[379] Ibid., Steiner, 418–19.
[380] Note 4, *Business Electronics*, 736.
[381] Ibid., 744–5.
[382] Ibid., 756.
[383] Note 279, *Monsanto*, 762.
[384] Note 4, *Business Electronics*, 751.

the effect of the agreement, in particular, the effect on competition, only when the rule of reason applies.

Justice Stevens also focused on the effect on competition in connection with potential justifications as applied under the rule of reason. He argued that the increased services argument was not an effective justification because this was just a theoretical possibility and not a proven fact.[385] He then concluded that this practice had its sole object in the restriction of trade, thus it was not a procompetitive, vertical, non-price restraint.[386] The purpose of this practice was to 'eliminate price competition at Hartwell's level' and, thus, it was, according to Justice Stevens, a naked restraint.[387]

VI. THE RULE OF REASON ERA (END OF 1990s–2010s)

The recent era of antitrust policy has been characterized by the dominance of the Chicago School, most notably, the Post-Chicago School, which opposes the application of the per se rule to vertical restraints. In agreement with the Post-Chicago School, the US antitrust approach to RPM changed during this era to the rule of reason. The rule of reason was first implemented in agreements on vertical maximum price fixing in the case of *Khan*[388] in 1997 and later, in 2007, to the remaining forms of RPM agreements in the case of *Leegin*.[389] This is rather a logical development as the previous era had already, under the influence of the Chicago School, introduced the rule of reason to VTR. Additionally, the per se rule was weakened further by the Supreme Court's ruling in *Business Electronics*, which stated that a termination of supply to a price cutter arising from an agreement between a manufacturer and one of her retailers had to be judged under the rule of reason as it did not constitute a vertical price restraint agreement.

A more lenient approach to vertical restraints, including RPM, was further facilitated by the fact that throughout the Clinton and, most notably, Bush Junior presidencies, antitrust policy and its possible changes were not considered top priorities, nor did presidential elections

---

[385] Ibid., 756.
[386] Ibid., 757.
[387] Ibid., 757–8.
[388] Note 5, *Khan*.
[389] Note 6, *Leegin*.

highlight antitrust policy in their discussion points.[390] During the Bush Junior presidency, there was not even any interest in bringing RPM cases by the FTC.[391]

However, the interest in RPM cases increased with the judgment in *Leegin*. Indeed, the case of *Leegin* aroused significant controversy in the US, sparking intensive discussions on the application of the rule of reason to RPM.[392] Furthermore, several states have overturned or lessened the impact of *Leegin* by statutes reintroducing per se illegality, primarily because retailers have complained that it is impossible to win a case if the rule of reason is applied.[393] Additionally, the immediate reaction to the antitrust agencies was to lessen the impact of the rule of reason. The FTC attempted to introduce a structural approach to RPM, including burden shifting between two parties.[394] The DOJ seemed to be of the same opinion as the FTC in thinking that it was necessary to create alternatives to the traditional rule of reason.[395]

This tendency to change the rule of reason approach to RPM was further facilitated at the beginning of Obama's presidency when the Federal Government tried unsuccessfully to overturn the rule of reason in the US Congress.[396] This is a reflection of Obama's presidency campaign, as he promoted more vigorous enforcement of antitrust law and appointed an Assistant Attorney General who also promised vigorous

---

[390] Note 35, Baker; Note 37, Kovacic, 377.

[391] See Note 34, Salop.

[392] See, e.g., Note 9, Gavil, 2–3; W Todd Miller and Kimberly N Shaw, 'Pricing Practices: A Comparative Perspective' (2009) *The Antitrust Review of the Americas* 14; Alison Jones, 'Completion of the Revolution in Antitrust Doctrine on Restricted Distribution: *Leegin* and Its Implications for EC Competition Law' (2008) 53(4) *Antitrust Bulletin* 903, 903–65; Note 9, Brunell, 475–529.

[393] See, e.g., Note 9, Gavil, 6–7; this is reflected in relevant state cases, for instance: *California v. DermaQuest*, No RG10497526 (Sup.Ct. Cal. Feb. 5, 2010); *New York v. Tempur-Pedic International*, No 400837/10 (Sup.Ct. Cal. Jan. 14, 2011).

[394] Note 9, Gavil, 4–5; The American Bar Association, Section of Antitrust Law, 'The Antitrust Fall Forum' (12–13 November 2009) Washington DC.

[395] Assistant Attorney General, Antitrust Division, DOJ, Christine A Varney, 'Antitrust Federalism: Enhancing Federal/State Cooperation' (speech 7 October 2009) <http://www.justice.gov/atr/public/speeches/250635.pdf> accessed 28 June 2015; Note 9, Gavil, 5–6.

[396] The most recent Bill proposal was introduced in 2011 – the Discount Pricing Consumer Protection Act (2011) s. 75; its predecessor was the Discount Pricing Consumer Protection Act (2009) s. 148 – neither ever became law; see also Note 9, Gavil, 3; Note 392, Miller and Shaw.

enforcement of antitrust law.[397] However, this was not necessarily projected into reality.[398] Due to economic crises, the government stopped hiring new officials and the political influence of the President on antitrust law and its enforcement has not been as far reaching as expected.[399] Indeed, after the first few years of the new approach 'shock', which followed immediately after the *Leegin* judgment, the antitrust agencies seemed to have accepted the rule of reason and lost interest in enforcing RPM.[400]

The new, lenient approach to RPM was reflected, for example, in 2008, when the FTC allowed for the modification of a 2000 FTC Order that prohibited Nine West Footwear Corp. (previously, Nine West Group, Inc.) from maintaining retail prices with dealers. It granted Nine West's petition, agreeing that her RPM was unlikely to harm consumers because, among other things, the market share of Nine West was 'modest', despite the fact that Nine West was one of the largest manufacturers of women's footwear in the US and she did not provide any specific procompetitive-effect justifications.[401]

The beginning of the Obama Administration brought another change: policy focus began to turn towards behavioral economics. Behavioral economics show, based on empirical evidence, that individual decisions are systematically irrational rather than being based on rationality arising from neoclassical theories. Behavioral economics suggests that law and policy should provide the means to navigate individual decisions in a way to maximize individual and social welfare while leaving individuals the

---

[397] See, e.g., Senator Barack H Obama, 'Statement of Senator Barack Obama for the American Antitrust Institute' (27 September 2007) <www.antitrust institute.org/node/10883> accessed 28 June 2015; Christine A Varney, Remarks for the United States Chamber of Commerce, 'Vigorous antitrust enforcement in this challenging era' (12 May 2009) <www.justice.gov/atr/public/speeches/245777.pdf> accessed 28 June 2015.

[398] See, e.g., Note 33, Voorhees.

[399] Ibid.

[400] See, e.g., The American Antitrust Institute, 'Action needed to address resale price maintenance in contact lenses – and countless other markets' (letter sent to FTC and DOJ 24 October 2014) <http://www.antitrustinstitute.org/content/aai-urges-action-minimum-price-policies-contact-lens-industry> accessed 28 June 2015; Note 267, Wright.

[401] Federal Trade Commission, 'Order granting in part petition to reopen and modify order issued 11 April 2000 (Nine West Group Inc., Docket No. C-3937)' (6 May 2008).

ability to make their own final decisions.[402] The Obama Administration has been applying behavioral economics most notably in areas where business profits can arise from consumer and individual irrationality such as consumer credit and labor law[403] and it also had some supporters in antitrust-law policy.[404] However, at the beginning of Obama's presidency this influence did not facilitate any important change in antitrust law and policy. The application of behavioral economics in US antitrust law has had many critics (including FTC and DOJ officials), predominantly from supporters of the Chicago and Post-Chicago Schools,[405] arguing that it 'fails to offer *any* clear policy implications'[406] and policy and law guidance because of its focus on individuals and their individual irrationality.

Indeed, as mentioned above, antitrust agencies and the courts have been significantly influenced by the Chicago and Post-Chicago Schools despite the promotion of behavioral economics and the emergence of new ideas, such as the progressive school's ideas on distribution.[407] This is reflected in RPM cases of this era and the application of the rule of reason.

The courts have followed the rule of reason justifications from *Business Electronics* in situations where a price cutter was terminated.

---

[402] The first ideas emerged in the 1970s, see, e.g., Daniel Kahneman and Amos Tversky, 'Prospect Theory: An Analysis of Decision Under Risk' (1979) 47 *Econometrica* 263; Daniel Kahneman, Jack L Knetsch and Richard H Thaler 'Experimental Tests of the Endowment Effect and the Coase Theorem' (1990) 98 *Journal of Political Economy* 1325. The new policy was suggested by Richard H Thaler and Cass R Sunstein, *Nudge: Improving Decisions about Health, Wealth and Happiness* (Yale University Press, 2008).

[403] See, Joshua D Wright and Judd E Stone II, 'Misbehavioral Economics: The Case against Behavioral Antitrust' (2012) 33 *Cardozo Law Review* 1517, 1519–21.

[404] For example, the former Federal Trade Commissioner, John Thomas Rosch. See, John Thomas Rosch, 'Managing irrationality: Some observations on behavioral economics and the creation of the Consumer Financial Protection Agency' (remarks at the Conference on the Regulation of Consumer Financial Products, New York, 6 January 2010) <http://www.ftc.gov/public-statements/2010/01/managing-irrationality-some-observations-behavioral-economics-and-creation> accessed 28 June 2015.

[405] See, e.g., Note 403, Wright and Stone; Jonathan Klick and Gregory Mitchell, 'Government Regulation of Irrationality: Moral and Cognitive Hazards' (2006) 90 *Minnesota Law Review* 1620.

[406] Note 403, Wright and Stone, 1526.

[407] See Chapter 2.

For instance, in the case of *Euromodas*,[408] the Court of Appeals fully applied the judgment of *Business Electronics*. In *Euromodas*, a retailer, Clubman, with market power in Puerto Rico, was interested in maintaining high prices for Zanella's trousers. He tried first to persuade Euromodas, another retailer, to maintain the prices of Zanella's products. As Clubman did not succeed, he successfully pressured the manufacturer, Zanella, to stop selling to Euromodas, a so-called 'price cutter'.

Citing *Business Electronics*, the Court of Appeals held that the termination of the price cutter and his subsequent replacement with another dealer was not per se a violation of Section 1 of the Sherman Act.[409] Despite the facts showing that Clubman attempted to reach a horizontal agreement on intrabrand price fixing with Euromodas and when he did not succeed he contacted the manufacturer, the court did not find, based on the evidence presented, an agreement on RPM.[410] The court summarized that showing that Clubman pressured the manufacturer to deal with the under-cutting retailer was not satisfactory evidence to prove that there was illegal price-maintaining collusion. This, as the court said, could be nothing more than Zanella's unilateral decision not to supply to the plaintiff.[411] Indeed, the fact that the manufacturer took sides between the two retailers was, according to the court, a legitimate business decision.[412]

The Supreme Court has continued replacing the per se rule with the rule of reason. In 1997, in the case of *Khan*, the Supreme Court overruled *Albrecht*. The Court explained that there was not sufficient economic justification for the application of the per se rule in vertical maximum price fixing, as there was no obvious reason to believe that vertically imposed maximum prices could harm consumers or competition, emphasizing the importance of protecting interbrand and not intrabrand competition.[413]

In 2007, the case of *Leegin*[414] changed the per se rule approach to the remaining RPM forms, establishing the rule of reason for all forms of

---

[408] *Euromodas, Inc. v. Zanella, Ltd.*, 368 F3d 11 (1st Circuit 2004) ('*Euromodas*').
[409] Note 4, *Business Electronics*, 726–7.
[410] Note 408, *Euromodas*, 19.
[411] Ibid., 19.
[412] Ibid., 20.
[413] Ibid., 15, 18.
[414] Note 6, *Leegin*.

RPM agreements.[415] The Supreme Court stated that the high probability of unreasonably restricting competition and decreasing output was key for the application of the per se rule. However, as the Court argued, the economic procompetitive theories and justifications regarding RPM and the importance of interbrand competition and consumer-welfare-enhancing efficiency disprove that minimum resale price maintenance and vertical price-fixing agreements always, or almost always, restrict competition and decrease output.[416] In that context, the Supreme Court explained that the motivation for imposing RPM differs between suppliers and distributors. Suppliers' reasons are usually procompetitive as they wish to minimize distribution costs and improve competition among distributors to attract consumers. Therefore, the supplier will usually introduce RPM to eliminate price competition to motivate distributors/retailers to focus on the quality of their sales and services for consumers. In contrast, distributors introduce RPM to increase their own profits and/or facilitate a distributors' cartel.[417]

Reasoning in the cases on RPM of this era, including that in *Leegin*, promoted both interbrand competition and horizontal competition. Interbrand competition and not intrabrand competition is core for the evaluation of effects when the rule of reason applies, while the restriction of horizontal competition in the form of dividing territories or fixing prices is prohibited per se at both the intrabrand and interbrand level. If buyers of a specific product, one brand, agree to fix the price of this branded product (restriction of intrabrand competition), the per se rule approach would apply, as it would in situations when manufacturers collude to fix prices (restriction of interbrand competition). The horizontal per se rule approach was applied by the Court of Appeals in *Mack Trucks*[418] one year after the delivery of the judgment in *Leegin*, in 2008.

In *Leegin*, the Supreme Court did not give much guidance for the exact application of the rule of reason to RPM cases, pleading future cases decided by lower courts to provide specific rules for its application.[419] Unfortunately, recent RPM cases that have reached the Court of Appeals,

---

[415] This was decided with a close majority: five justices agreeing and four dissenting.

[416] Note 6, *Leegin*, 889; the court cites among others Note 141, Hovenkamp, 184–91; Note 263, Bork, 288–91.

[417] Note 6, *Leegin*, 890, 896, 898.

[418] *Toledo Mack Sales & Service, Inc. v. Mack Trucks, Inc.*, 530 F.3d 204 (3d Circuit 2008) ('*Mack Trucks*').

[419] Note 6, *Leegin*, 899.

for example, *Mack Trucks* and *Leegin 2*,[420] have not necessarily clarified the application of this rule. For example, in *Leegin*, the Supreme Court suggested that the existence of significant market power could indicate a restriction of competition in RPM.[421] The Third Circuit of the Court of Appeals discussed the importance of significant market power in the case of *Mack Trucks* in 2008, where it was of the opinion that rather than proving any anticompetitive effects, which could be complicated and even impossible for the plaintiff, alternatively, the plaintiff could show that the defendant(s) had sufficient market power in order to prove the restriction of competition in the form of RPM.[422] However, the later case of *Leegin 2*, decided by the Fifth Circuit, does not appear to be consistent with *Mack Trucks*. In this case, the court indicated that the plaintiff must always prove that the defendant possesses sufficient market power to allege a vertical claim successfully, unless it is proved that the alleged RPM agreement restricted interbrand competition.[423] In addition, the Eleventh Circuit sought evidence of the existence of market power in order to establish potential harm to competition in situations where actual harm was not proven.[424]

Aside from the traditional RPM cases, the case of *Toys 'R' Us*,[425] where buyer power played an important role in successfully dictating restrictive conditions to her suppliers, reached the Court of Appeals, and had a judgment delivered in 2000. This case dealt with vertical price restrictions and buyer power, and was investigated by the FTC, who challenged the purchasing practices of Toys 'R' Us as preventing price competition. The allegation was based, amongst other things, on direct evidence of vertical collusion between the retailer and at least ten toy manufacturers. Toys 'R' Us, the largest toy retailer in the US, was free to dictate which toys were not allowed to be sold to chain discounters and club stores.[426] The FTC applied the rule of reason to vertical collusion and found that these practices restricted price competition between Toys

---

[420] *PSKS, Inc. v. Leegin Creative Leather Products, Inc*, 615 F.3d 412 (5th Circuit 2010) (*'Leegin 2'*); Petition for a Writ of Certiorari, No. 10-653 (15 November 2010) was denied by the Supreme Court in February 2011.
[421] Note 6, *Leegin*, 896, 898.
[422] Note 418, *Mack Trucks*, 226.
[423] Note 420, *Leegin 2*, 419.
[424] See, *Benny Jacobs, Wanda Jacobs v. Tempur-Pedic International, Inc., Tempur-Pedic North America, Inc.*, 626 F.3d 1327 (11th Circuit 2010) (*'Tempur-Pedic'*).
[425] *Toys 'R' Us*, 5 Trade Reg Rep (CCH) P24, 516 (FTC 1998); *Toys 'R' Us, Inc. v. FTC*, 221 F.3d 928 (2000).
[426] Ibid 24, 383–5.

'R' Us's holding market power and her competitors – the discounters.[427] Toys 'R' Us, however, continued with her restrictive practices. This case was followed by class actions after the delivery of the judgment in *Leegin*.[428]

RPM: *Leegin*:[429] Rule of Reason

In the case of *Leegin*, the Supreme Court introduced the rule of reason to agreements on vertical price fixing and minimum price fixing, overruling the *Dr. Miles* doctrine, which set the per se rule for vertical minimum price collusion. *Leegin* involved RPM in the form of minimum price setting. Leegin, a manufacturer, designer and distributor of leather goods and accessories, started to sell women's belts and other products under the brand name, Brighton, via small, independent boutiques and specialized stores across the US in 1991. Leegin's policy was based on promoting better and more personal treatment, more services and a satisfactory experience for consumers. Leegin believed that smaller retailers were more suitable for her policy rather than large stores such as Wal-Mart.[430]

In 1997, Leegin wrote letters to her retailers announcing a new policy, which included minimum price fixing, refusing to sell to retailers who would sell below these prices. In December 2002, Leegin found out that her retailer, PSKS, was selling her products at 20 percent below the minimum prices. PSKS explained to Leegin that other nearby retailers were doing the same, therefore, he had dropped his retail prices in order to compete.[431] PSKS refused to increase his prices of Brighton products and thus Leegin terminated the contract.[432]

Losing his sale, PSKS sued Leegin for a violation of the Sherman Act. At the District Court, Leegin based her arguments on the *Colgate* doctrine, claiming that she had acted unilaterally. Nevertheless, the jury found the existence of an illegal agreement. Leegin appealed, contending that the rule of reason should be applied to this agreement. The District

---

[427] Ibid., 24, 411.
[428] See, *McDonough v. Toys 'R' Us, Inc.*, 638 F. Supp. 2d 461 (EDPa 2009) ('*McDonough v. Toys 'R' Us*').
[429] Note 6, *Leegin*.
[430] Ibid., 882.
[431] Ibid., 882–3.
[432] Ibid., 884.

Court and the Court of Appeals applied the per se rule in accordance with the Supreme Court case *Dr. Miles*.[433]

The case reached the Supreme Court, which overruled the *Dr. Miles* per se rule by a close majority of judges (five agreeing and four dissenting). In its judgment, the Supreme Court first criticized a few aspects of the *Dr. Miles* decision, then provided grounds for overruling the *Dr. Miles* per se rule and, finally, indicated a few key elements which could play an important role in the application of the rule of reason in future cases on RPM agreements.

The Supreme Court's criticism of *Dr. Miles* was based on economic arguments. First, the Supreme Court explained that *Dr. Miles* was missing a genuine economic analysis because the Court had applied the common law rule in the case.[434] This led to the introduction of a 'formalistic' legal doctrine to RPM rather than a real economic analysis.[435] Second, the Supreme Court criticized *Dr. Miles* for not analyzing the possible motivations for using vertical price restraints.[436] At the same time, the Court stated that '*Dr. Miles* treated vertical agreements a manufacturer makes with her distributors as analogous to a horizontal combination among competing distributors'.[437]

In this chapter, I explained that it is understandable that the Supreme Court focused on objective criteria, in particular the effect of the foreclosure of competition, in *Dr. Miles* rather than on intent, because one of the key antitrust cases of that time, *Trans-Missouri*, ruled that the determination of the effect of the contract was essential in order to determine a violation of the Sherman Act.[438] Indeed, the case of *Dr. Miles* must be understood in accordance with its era, where the courts were influenced by the common law while introducing applicable rules to the Sherman Act. That includes the fact that *Dr. Miles* was based on equitable relief typical for that era. From this point, the evaluation of the change in knowledge, especially knowledge of economics, of RPM since 1911 is reasonable, although the criticism needs to be understood in connection with the era that the *Dr. Miles* judgment was delivered in.

The issue of economic knowledge and policy is one of two grounds on which the Supreme Court overruled the *Dr. Miles* per se rule. The second ground is stare decisis. With regard to economic knowledge and policy,

---

[433] Ibid., 884.
[434] Note 6, *Leegin*, 887 citing Note 2, *Dr. Miles*, 404–5.
[435] Ibid., 887 citing Note 7, *Sylvania* 58–9.
[436] Ibid., 888.
[437] Ibid., 887, 888 citing Note 2, *Dr. Miles*, 407–8.
[438] Note 21, *Trans-Missouri*, 342.

the Court said that the per se rule means that minimum resale price agreements always, or almost always, restrict competition and decrease output. However, this is contradicted by the economic procompetitive theories and justifications and by limited empirical evidence that suggests the efficient use of minimum resale price agreements is not hypothetical. Under the stare decisis analysis, the majority of judges delivering the judgment believed that stare decisis did not prevent them from overruling the per se rule.

Justifications of RPM based on effects and theories
When the Supreme Court set its arguments for overruling the per se rule, it did not rely on the facts from *Leegin*. As Brunell correctly points out, 'the facts of the case were irrelevant to the Court's decision [but] [t]he logic of overturning *Dr. Miles* was simple enough'.[439] Indeed, the facts of the case do not necessarily lead to the conclusion that this situation is not anticompetitive and thus should be legal.

As explained above, PSKS was a small, specialized retail store that complied with Leegin's qualitative conditions. Nevertheless, it was able to decrease prices and thus compete on price, while still promoting Leegin's products. Because retailers were already selected based on qualitative criteria, and minimum price fixing of Leegin's products did not introduce any service or other consumer benefits, RPM did not enhance but, rather, restricted price competition. Indeed, the nature of those particular products, being women's accessories, presumes zero demand for genuine consumer services if promotion is not included, which was already assured by the original Leegin policy based on selective distribution. Therefore, interbrand competition and competition in services had not increased, but the price of Leegin's products had.

Steiner explained that distributors selling Leegin's products did not face vigorous competition because they specialized in the Brighton brand. The lack of interbrand competition and the importance of intrabrand competition were also obvious from the fact that the petitioner went out of business after Leegin stopped her supplies and Leegin's confirmation that Brighton consumers would switch distributors to find Brighton products rather than switch products.[440] Furthermore, Steiner highlighted that Leegin did not argue that PSKS was free riding nor did he refuse to furnish pre-sale services.[441] Nevertheless, free riding and

---

[439] Note 268, Brunell, 348.
[440] Note 59, Steiner, 47–9.
[441] Ibid., 48.

theories on pre-sale services played a key role in the arguments of the Supreme Court for overruling the per se rule.

The Court supported its justification arguments using economic literature. The Court stated that the practice of RPM most likely has no anticompetitive effect because economic literature offers procompetitive justifications for RPM based on the promotion of interbrand competition and consumer-welfare-enhancing efficiency.[442] The Court most notably referred to literature on transaction costs economics based on the Coase Theorem, which focuses on solving information problems between the manufacturer and her distributors.[443]

The Court recognized three principal procompetitive justifications for overruling the per se rule:

1. the 'free riding' theory;
2. new entrant justification; and
3. increasing interbrand competition by providing services.

First, the Supreme Court maintained that without the existence of vertical restrictions there might be a lack of services due to the free riding of retailers.[444] RPM, according to the majority of the Court, solved this free riding 'problem' by preventing 'the discounter from undercutting the service provider'.[445] The Court also argued that even without the problem of free riding, a manufacturer could introduce RPM in order to encourage retailers to provide services. It said that by:

> [o]ffering the retailer a guaranteed margin and threatening termination if it does not live up to expectations may be the most efficient way to expand the manufacturer's market shares by inducing the retailer's performance and allowing it to use its own initiative and experience in providing valuable services.[446]

The Court's second example of a procompetitive effect of RPM was that it can assist new companies in entering the market and thus increase interbrand competition, as previously expressed in *Sylvania* in connection with VTR.[447] Finally, by referring to *Khan*, the Supreme Court stated that

---

[442] Note 6, *Leegin*, 889; the Court cites among others Note 141, Hovenkamp, 184–91; Note 263, Bork, 288–91.
[443] Note 6, *Leegin*, 889–93.
[444] Ibid., 890–92.
[445] Ibid., 892.
[446] Ibid., 893.
[447] Ibid., 892; Note 7, *Sylvania* 55.

the primary purpose of antitrust law is to protect interbrand competition.[448] It then argued that RPM may increase interbrand competition by decreasing intrabrand competition,[449] stating that:

> A single manufacturer's use of vertical price restraints tends to eliminate intrabrand price competition; this in turn encourages retailers to invest in tangible or intangible services or promotional efforts that aid the manufacturer's position as against rival manufacturers.[450]

The Court continued, by saying:

> Resale price maintenance also has the potential to give consumers more options so that they can choose among low-price, low-service brands; high-price, high-service brands; and brands that fall in between.[451]

These arguments are based on procompetitive theories of services. The Court was referring to a situation where the manufacturer, by applying RPM, intends to stimulate services and promotion while her retailers comply with this intention. This further assumes that this will facilitate competitive incentives of competing manufacturers who will then try to improve their price or non-price intrabrand competition. This would lead to more options for consumers. However, this situation could work only if the conditions in the market and the reactions of competitors, including manufacturers and retailers, are such that

(1) other competing manufacturers do not decide to facilitate RPM, as this would lead to a reduction of price competition across the industry;
(2) RPM introduces services beneficial to consumers; and, at the same time, RPM restricts intrabrand price competition,
(3) other competing manufacturers decide to innovate, introduce services or decrease their prices in order to compete with the increased intrabrand non-price competition of the manufacturer with RPM.

It is questionable as to how often such a situation occurs in practice, the issue of which was presented to the Supreme Court. Twenty-five economists who acted as *amici curiae* expressed their disagreement, a stance that is supported in the economic literature, as to how often RPM has

---

[448] Note 6, *Leegin*, 890, referring to Note 5, *Khan*, 15.
[449] Ibid., 890.
[450] Ibid.
[451] Ibid.

procompetitive or anticompetitive effects.[452] Justice Breyer, dissenting, criticized the majority of the Supreme Court in that sense. He stated that the ultimate question is not whether distributors free ride on services nor is it a question of the quality or reputation of another distributor, but rather how often free riding occurs and how often the possible benefits outweigh the potential harms. This is difficult to determine.[453] He reminded the Court of the fact that the Sherman Act's objective was to 'maintain a marketplace free of anticompetitive practices ... [which] will tend to bring about the lower prices, better products, and more efficient production process that consumers typically desire'.[454] However, as is obvious from the delivered judgment of *Leegin*, rather than balancing all of the procompetitive and anticompetitive arguments in order to determine the best approach to RPM, the Supreme Court decided to focus on the procompetitive arguments in order to justify the change from the per se rule to the rule of reason.

Empirical studies supporting procompetitive theories
The Supreme Court supported its procompetitive arguments with reference to two empirical FTC studies: Overstreet's study and Ippolito's study.[455] It referred to these studies as 'recent'; however, they were published in 1983. The studies involved 203 litigated cases reported between 1975 and 1982.

In her study, Ippolito found that between 42 percent and 50 percent of analyzed cases on RPM concerned 'complex products', which, according to the author, are products where quality and information are important attributes. Based on this finding, she concluded that the majority of RPM cases could be explained by the services theory.

This conclusion has two issues. First, 42–50 percent cannot be referred to as the majority; rather, it means that at least half of the analyzed cases did not include services and/or other non-price procompetitive benefits.

---

[452] Brief for William S Comanor and Frederic M Scherer as Amici Curiae Supporting Neither Party, *Leegin Creative Leather Products, Inc. v. PSKS, Inc, DBA Kay's Kloset ... Kays' Shoes*, 551 US 877 (2007), No 06-480, section I.C.4.
[453] Note 6, *Leegin*, 917.
[454] Ibid., 910.
[455] Note 6, *Leegin*, 890, 894; Pauline M Ippolito, 'Resale Price Maintenance: Empirical Evidence from Litigation' (1991) 34 *Journal of Law & Economics* 263, 292–3; Pauline M Ippolito, 'Resale price maintenance: Empirical evidence from litigation' (economic report, FTC, 1983); Thomas R Overstreet, 'Resale price maintenance: Economic theories and empirical evidence' (Bureau of Economics Staff Report, FTC, 1983) 170.

Second, even this percentage of 42–50 percent of analyzed cases does not ensure that free riding and the incentive of services was the motivation for introducing RPM and that RPM itself led to such results. As Brunell points out: 'This can hardly be described as "evidence" that free riding was involved in any of these cases; at most it suggests that free riding could not be ruled out.'[456]

Overstreet, in his study, focused on determining whether the analyzed cases included horizontal collusion of buyers. He concluded that 80 percent of the analyzed cases could not have involved collusion of buyers due to the high number of buyers in those cases. Moreover, he stated that it is not likely that the cases included anticompetitive intentions where the market was structurally competitive.[457]

These conclusions are mere assumptions arising from the study. Although a highly concentrated market can facilitate collusion, there does not have to be a high concentration and/or manufacturers do not have to have a high market share for a cartel to exist or for anticompetitive intentions to occur, as Overstreet himself recognized and wrote in an article two years later, in 1985.[458] Moreover, Overstreet did not exclude in his study that RPM in these cases simply restricted competition without facilitating any procompetitive effect.[459]

As with its procompetitive arguments supporting the rule of reason, the Supreme Court did not balance these two empirical studies (with arguable findings) with the existing studies showing the negative effects on competition. As dissenting Justice Breyer pointed out, there is evidence that RPM increases prices. Justice Breyer referred to Overstreet's study to support his argument stating that the FTC study from 1983 concluded that resale price maintenance led to higher prices in most cases.[460] Furthermore, Justice Breyer referred to the abolition of the Miller-Tydings Fair Trade Act[461] and the McGuire Act.[462] During the existence of these Acts, 36 states had permitted minimum resale price

---

[456] Note 9, Brunell, 509–10.
[457] Note 455, Overstreet, 73, 78–80.
[458] Alan A Fisher and Thomas R Overstreet, 'Resale Price Maintenance and Distributional Efficiency: Some Lessons from the Past', (1985) 3 *Contemporary Policy Issues* 43, 49–50; see also Note 9, Brunell, 510–11.
[459] As I explain in Chapter 5, the form, whether vertical or horizontal, does not, in general, influence the final effect on competition. However, the form can lead to an assumption about the intention of the initiators.
[460] Note 6, *Leegin*, 913–14; see Note 455, Overstreet, 160.
[461] 50 Stat 693 (1937), abolished in 1975.
[462] 66 Stat 632 (1952), abolished in 1975.

maintenance and 14 states had not.[463] Throughout that time, prices rose from 19 to 27 percent.[464] Although there was and still is a lack of empirical studies on the impact of RPM, there were other studies at the time of the ruling on *Leegin* showing the increase in retail prices if RPM is introduced.[465]

Anticompetitive effect
Despite the fact that the Supreme Court focused on procompetitive justifications of RPM and empirical studies which could support its arguments of procompetitive justifications, it acknowledged that RPM could also have anticompetitive effects in the form of increased prices. It limited this anticompetitive argument by linking it with a manufacturer and retailer (buyer) cartel. The Court said that the primary reason for the existence of RPM is to obtain monopoly profits, because, for instance, particular price fixing facilitates and assists a manufacturer cartel or a retailer/distributor cartel.[466] The retailer cartel, as the Court argued, is unlikely in a situation 'when only a single manufacturer in a competitive market uses resale price maintenance'[467] because of the existence of interbrand competition which 'would divert consumers to lower priced substitutes and eliminate any gains to retailers from their price-fixing agreement over a single brand'.[468] This argument dismisses the importance of intrabrand and vertical competition (discussed in Chapter 2). This is not surprising given that in *Leegin*, and also in many important cases starting with *Sylvania*, the Court stated that it was concerned with interbrand and not intrabrand competition.

---

[463] Note 6, *Leegin*, 913; see Assistant Attorney General, Antitrust Division, Thomas E Kauper's statement, hearing on s408 before the Subcommittee on Antitrust and Monopoly of the Senate Committee on the Judiciary, 94th Congress, 1st Session, 173 (1975).

[464] Note 6, *Leegin*, 913; see Deputy Assistant Attorney General, Antitrust Division, Keith I Clearwater's statement, hearing on HR 2384 before the Subcommittee on Monopolies and Commercial Law of the House Committee on the Judiciary, 94th Congress, 1st Session, 122 (1975).

[465] For example, in 2000, the FTC estimated that the restriction of the resale prices of CDs had brought an extra $480 million in three years for 85 percent of US music companies. See Press Release, Federal Trade Commission, 'Record companies settle FTC charges of restraining competition in CD music market' (10 May 2000) <http://www.ftc.gov/opa/2000/05/cdpres.shtm> accessed 28 June 2015; for more studies, see Chapter 5.

[466] Note 6, *Leegin*, 892–3 quoting Note 4, *Business Electronics*, 725–6.
[467] Ibid., 897.
[468] Ibid.

The Supreme Court further justified the anticompetitive effect of increased prices on two bases. First, it said that the increase of prices can be justified by the increase of other procompetitive effects or even a decrease of prices within interbrand competition.[469] The question is how likely is it that RPM would lead to such a situation. As explained above, this argument could only apply if:

(1) other competing manufacturers decide not to facilitate RPM, as this would lead to the reduction of price competition across the industry and thus anticompetitive effects for interbrand competition;
(2) RPM introduces services beneficial to consumers; and, at the same time
(3) other competing manufacturers decide to innovate, introduce services or decrease their prices in order to compete with the increased intrabrand non-price competition of the manufacturer with RPM.

Furthermore, there is no empirical study to prove that other competing brands decrease their prices due to the introduction of RPM for one brand. As Pitofsky argued when justifying the per se rule for RPM agreements, procompetitive justifications are only theoretical but the anticompetitive results of minimum price fixing are 'virtually certain'.[470]

The second argument the Court used to justify the increased price arising from RPM is that other practices that increase the price of products or services, such as advertising and increasing quality, are not illegal under antitrust law.[471] As explained in Chapter 2, although both RPM and advertising improve a supplier's bargaining position and provide a competitive advantage, there is a substantive difference between them. Successful advertising directly raises consumer demand and in that way increases competition and improves the bargaining position of the manufacturer without restricting intrabrand competition. On the other hand, the primary effect of RPM is to restrict intrabrand competition and increase prices, which can provide incentive to retailers to offer such a product to consumers because the retailers' profit is ensured.

---

[469] Ibid., 895–6.
[470] Robert Pitofsky, 'Are Retailers Who Offer Discounts Really "Knaves"?: The Coming Change to the *Dr. Miles* Rule' (2007) *Antitrust Law Journal* 61, 64.
[471] Note 6, *Leegin*, 897.

Overruling *Dr. Miles*: stare decisis analysis
This part of the judgment is brief in comparison to the policy grounds. Indeed, it seems that the stare decisis doctrine was perceived by the Supreme Court as an obstacle that must be overcome in order to change the approach to RPM.[472] The US stare decisis doctrine in statutory interpretation is based on two principles. First, the primary principle says that, unlike in common law, in statutory interpretation, stare decisis is governed by the principle that the applicable rule of law in the form of the interpretation of legislation should remain settled. This was also recognized as a general principle by the Court in *Leegin*.[473] Therefore, as pointed out by dissenting Justice Breyer, under the stare decisis doctrine, the precedent arising from the interpretation of a statute should bear a heavier burden of proof if overruled than in common law.[474]

Nevertheless, the Court held that '[s]tare decisis is not as significant in this case'[475] because the Sherman Act is 'a common law statute' with the need to meet changes in the economic conditions.[476] The Court's standpoint of applying different standards to the interpretation of the Sherman Act than to the interpretation of other statutes is not convincing, as argued by Brunell. By referring to cases where the Court applied strict statutory-interpretation stare decisis and a heavy burden of proof to the Sherman Act,[477] he first dismissed the application of a different standard to the Sherman Act in this case. By referring to the case of *Khan*, where the Supreme Court applied a similar standard to stare decisis as in *Leegin*, he then argued that even under common law, stare decisis is applied more strictly than was the case in *Leegin*, as the Court must have firmly entrenched grounds upon which it decides to overrule its previous precedent in common law.[478]

However, as Brunell pointed out, the right approach in this situation should have been stare decisis based on statutory interpretation where it is required that the Court respects the will of Congress as the legislature. He then argued that Congress had not expressed the will to overrule the per se rule, despite the fact that the per se rule approach to RPM had

---

[472] See also Note 268, Brunell, 348.
[473] Note 6, *Leegin*, 899.
[474] Ibid., 918.
[475] Ibid., 899.
[476] Ibid., 899.
[477] *Square D Co. v. Niagara Frontier Tariff Bureau, Inc.*, 476 U.S. 409 (1986) 424; *Illinois Brick Co. v. Illinois*, 431 U.S. 720 (1977) 736; *Flood v. Kuhn*, 407 U.S. 258 (1972) 282.
[478] Note 268, Brunell, 349–50.

applied for nearly 100 years. On the contrary, Congress favored the per se rule, as is obvious from, for example, Congress's interventions in the 1980s, starting with the intervention in connection with *Business Electronics* preventing the DOJ from supporting the overturning of the per se rule.

Guidance for future cases
The Supreme Court did not provide much guidance for litigation for subsequent RPM cases. It noted that future practice would provide more specific rules for the use of the rule of reason in RPM cases, stating generally that the scope of operation and the existence of an agreement were important elements.[479] As part of the scope of operation, the Supreme Court indicated three elements which could assist with evaluating RPM under the rule of reason: (1) different treatment between vertical and horizontal collusion; (2) importance of market power; and (3) the reasons for introducing RPM.

In connection with vertical and horizontal collusion, the Supreme Court refused analogous treatment between vertical and horizontal combinations because vertical restraints are more defensible than horizontal restraints.[480] The Court confirmed that price fixing among manufacturers or among retailers at the horizontal level is per se illegal, while if parties collude vertically to fix prices, the case must be ruled under the rule of reason.[481] Despite the fact that the Supreme Court promoted interbrand competition as the primary competition for the analysis of restrictive effects under the rule of reason, it did not differentiate between an intrabrand horizontal agreement among retailers maintaining the price of one brand and retailers' horizontal collusion covering more than one brand.

When discussing market power, the Supreme Court highlighted that the market power of a manufacturer or retailer is important in RPM because both parties can abuse their power to pressure others to facilitate RPM.[482] However, the Court indicated that such power needs to be significant because, at the same time, the Court held that using the manufacturer's or retailer's power to introduce RPM need not concern the courts, as there are still other competing retailers and manufacturers, unless the power is seriously monopolistic.[483]

---

[479] Note 6, *Leegin*, 899.
[480] Ibid., 888 citing Note 27, *Maricopa County*, 348.
[481] Ibid., 893.
[482] Ibid., 885, 893–4.
[483] Ibid., 898.

Finally, the Supreme Court differentiated between the interest of retailers and that of consumers and manufacturers. According to the Court, consumers generally desire lower prices,[484] while the manufacturer wants to minimize distribution costs and not overcompensate retailers, who are the ones that gain from the higher retailer prices.[485] Therefore, as the Court stated, it is important to identify the initiators of RPM. If the initiator is a powerful retailer (or retailers), it can constitute evidence of an abuse of a dominant position or the facilitation of a retailer cartel, which is anticompetitive conduct. On the other hand, a manufacturer would most likely use RPM to increase services.[486]

Besides discussing these potential important elements for the application of the rule of reason to RPM agreements, the Supreme Court did not provide any further guidance on the exact way that RPM based on the rule of reason should operate in practice. This lack of guidance has been criticized ever since. For example, Hovenkamp identified three difficulties in applying the rule of reason, one of them being little guidance from the Supreme Court and other two being the complexity of economic understanding of RPM and the *Dr. Miles* doctrine's baggage.[487]

Dissenting Justice Breyer also identified the difficulty when applying economics to RPM cases, pointing out that the law differs from the economy. Litigation is an administrative system applying rules and precedents and, as such, must be balanced to be workable for all parties.[488] Proving market share is highly costly, highly technical and time-consuming in litigation. This is true even more so for RPM over a major monopoly or merger case because RPM cases can include a lot of parties.[489] Indeed, this is especially true if the plaintiffs have to prove a restriction of interbrand competition, which, as stated by the Supreme Court, is the primary concern of US antitrust law, because the plaintiff needs to collect evidence from the whole industry.

Justice Breyer summarized the *Leegin* judgment in the following way:

---

[484] Ibid., 896.
[485] Ibid.
[486] Ibid., 898.
[487] Phillip E Areeda and Herbert Hovenkamp, *2009 Supplement to Antitrust Law: An Analysis of Antitrust Principles and Their Application* (Aspen Publishers, 2009) 238–9, 243; see also Note 378, Comanor; and Frank H Easterbrook, 'Vertical Arrangements and the Rule of Reason' (1984) 53 *Antitrust Law Journal* 135, 163.
[488] Note 6, *Leegin*, 916.
[489] Ibid., 918.

The only safe predictions to make about today's decision are that it will likely raise the price of goods at retail and that it will create considerable legal turbulence as lower courts seek to develop workable principles.[490]

The following cases discuss how the rule of reason based on the *Leegin* judgment has been interpreted and applied by the lower courts.

RPM and VTR: *Mack Trucks*[491]

One year after *Leegin*, the Third Circuit of the Court of Appeals delivered its ruling on RPM and horizontal price restrictions and other restrictions in *Mack Trucks*.[492] Although the court applied *Leegin*, the facts of the case indicate that this was de facto a combination of price restriction and VTR. The facts were as follows.

The company, Mack Trucks, had 'significant power' in the market of heavy trucks in the US. His distribution system was based on a network of authorized dealers, with each dealer being assigned their own territory.[493] Under this distribution system, if a potential customer called a dealer of Mack Trucks giving their specifications and requirements for a product, the dealer would submit a list of these specifications to Mack Trucks. Mack Trucks would then inform the dealer of the price, which usually included a discount called 'sales assistance'. Sales assistance was calculated based on a number of different factors, such as the amount of ordered trucks or potential competition in the market.[494] If the dealer did not agree with the amount of sales assistance, it could negotiate further.[495] However, sales assistance was offered only if the product concerned was sold within the dealer's own territory.[496]

Toledo, one of Mack Trucks' dealers, had aggressively focused on a low price policy for her customers since 1982 and had, therefore, been competing on price against other Mack Trucks dealers.[497] Mack Trucks and his other dealers tried to prevent her from lowering prices in a number of ways. First, in the mid-1980s, as claimed by Toledo, individual Mack Trucks dealers concluded a horizontal 'gentleman's

---

[490] Ibid., 931.
[491] Note 418, *Mack Trucks*.
[492] I focused only on the Court ruling in connection with RPM and VTR and no other elements, such as price discrimination, were discussed.
[493] Note 418, *Mack Trucks*, 209.
[494] Ibid., 209.
[495] Ibid., 209–10.
[496] Ibid., 213.
[497] Ibid., 210.

agreement' not to compete with each other on price. Secondly, in 1989, Mack Trucks and his dealers vertically agreed that Mack Trucks would delay or deny sales to dealers who wished to sell outside their territories in order to protect dealers selling in their own territories. This de facto arrangement created exclusive territories.[498]

Toledo claimed that Mack Trucks and his other dealers violated Section 1 of the Sherman Act because they illegally conspired which resulted in artificially high prices. She supported her claim using several pieces of evidence, such as witness testimonies, Mack Trucks bulletins and various telephone conversations.[499]

It appears that in this case the manufacturer was partly pressured by the other dealers and that the restrictions in question were in the interests of both dealers and the manufacturer. The presented evidence illustrates these points. In one of the bulletins, '[t]he express purpose of the policy [to protect territories] was to create "increased profit margins for Mack distributors as well as the Company"'.[500]

A telephone conversation and bulletins between Mack Trucks and Toledo point out: '[T]here are certain dealers that are sending glider kits in other people's backyards and we are getting calls on it.'[501]

Examples of further telephone conversations are as follows:

> If there is ever a manufacturer that protected their distributor organisation … It's the Mack Trucks Company, to a fault.[502]
>
> [Dealers] constantly want Mack to get involved in these territorial disputes … and to protect them from one another.[503]

The Court of Appeals identified two potential restrictive agreements. First, the claim of the existence of a horizontal 'gentleman's agreement' not to compete with each other on price, the court qualified as a horizontal agreement among dealers to control price. The court stated that the per se rule applies to such horizontal agreements between dealers.[504] This is in agreement with *Leegin*, where the Court held that any horizontal agreement including (intrabrand) horizontal agreement among buyers is analyzed under the per se rule.

---

[498] Ibid.
[499] Ibid., 211–15; 220–21.
[500] Ibid., 212.
[501] Ibid., 214.
[502] Ibid.
[503] Ibid.
[504] Ibid., 221.

Second, the vertical agreement between Mack Trucks and his dealers to delay or deny sales to dealers who wished to sell outside their territories was qualified by the court as vertical conspiracy to control prices, which caused a de facto ban on out-of-territory sales and price competition.[505] Here, the court referred to the case of *Leegin*, a vertical price restraint case. The court applied the rule of reason stating that this rule applies even when it is alleged that the purpose of the vertical collusion is to assist with the facilitation of restrictive horizontal collusion between dealers.[506] It referred to two factors essential for the consideration of vertical price collusion identified in *Leegin*: motivation of the parties involved and market power.[507]

First, the court said that evidence such as the interest of dealers can lead to the assumption of the existence of a retailer cartel rather than that of vertical collusion.[508] Indeed, in *Leegin*, the Supreme Court expressed the opinion that RPM initiated by retailers will usually have anticompetitive reasons and if the initiator was a group of retailers, it can be used for the facilitation of a retailer cartel.

Secondly, a vertical restraint concerns the court if the conspired entities have market power.[509] In that regard, the court explained that there are several ways to prove anticompetitive effects. For instance, it can be demonstrated that 'the restraint is facially anticompetitive or that its enforcement reduced output, raised prices or reduced quality'.[510] By referring to its own case from 2005, the case of *Gordon*,[511] the court held that it could be very difficult to prove these effects. Therefore, it stated that, alternatively, it would be acceptable to prove that the defendants had sufficient market power.[512] The court explained, without providing further guidance on, for example, the minimum of market power and its boundaries, that market power is 'the ability to raise prices above those that would prevail in a competitive market'.[513] The court then referred to the expert testimony presented by Toledo which argued that Mack Trucks had market power in two different product markets.

---

[505] Ibid., 221.
[506] Ibid., 221, 225.
[507] Ibid., 225.
[508] Ibid., 225 citing Note 6, *Leegin*, 2719.
[509] Ibid., 225, citing Note 6, *Leegin*, 2720.
[510] Ibid., 226.
[511] *Gordon v. Lewistown Hospital*, 423 F.3d 184 (3d Circuit 2005) 210.
[512] Note 418, *Mack Trucks*, 226.
[513] Ibid., quoting *United States v. Brown University*, 5 F.3d 658 (3d Circuit 1993) 668 ('*Brown University*').

This ruling raises the question as to whether the Third Circuit applied *Leegin* to a complex vertical-restraint case involving both VTR and RPM. *Leegin* was a case dealing with RPM. Here, in *Mack Trucks*, the Third Circuit was discussing a distribution system based on a network of authorized dealers with assigned territories. From the facts of the case, it appears that the protection of assigned territories was facilitated, originally, by providing discounted wholesale prices (sales assistance) only in situations when the product was sold within the dealer's own territory. Later, VTR was further facilitated by the arrangement between dealers and Mack Trucks, where Mack Trucks allegedly agreed that he would delay or deny sales to dealers who wished to sell outside their territories. This created absolute territorial restrictions with control mechanisms for their protection. It meant that dealers who followed the VTR arrangement did not compete on price and could set their own retail prices because absolute vertical restriction restricts both intrabrand price and non-price competition.

Therefore, the fact that VTR had an impact on retail price does not constitute a price restriction. As explained by Areeda and Hovenkamp, both vertical non-price and price restraints can affect price and be used for the same purpose, for instance to prevent free riding.[514] Indeed, a dealer involved in an absolute vertical territorial restriction distribution system would not welcome another dealer selling in her territory, especially for a lower price, because of the decreased profit and number of potential customers, and would thus be motivated to pressure the supplier to enforce conditions on his distribution system. The claim that Mack Trucks and his dealers allegedly conspired resulting in artificially high prices does not mean they conspired in the form of RPM. On the contrary, the presented facts indicate that this alleged vertical conspiracy was a form of VTR.

RPM: *Leegin 2*:[515] Horizontal and Vertical Minimum Price Setting

Leegin 2 is the remand of the case of *Leegin*. In *Leegin 2*, PSKS filed a second amended complaint claiming that Leegin, as a vertically integrated manufacturer selling her products to final consumers, colluded both horizontally and vertically with some of her retailers to set minimum retail prices. The horizontal conspiracy was a new complaint that was not included in the first allegation in *Leegin*. In this context,

---

[514] Note 165, Areeda and Hovenkamp, 247.
[515] Note 420, *Leegin 2*.

PSKS claimed that Leegin was the largest single retailer of her products. PSKS highlighted the existence of horizontal intrabrand collusion and the importance of Leegin's intrabrand competition on consumers.[516]

The Court of Appeals dismissed the claim on anticompetitive horizontal collusion as this claim was refused previously. Nevertheless, the court explained that any potential anticompetitive effects were illogical. Leegin, as the strongest retailer of the Brighton brand and simultaneously a dual distributor, could have achieved a higher profit by increasing wholesale prices and not by using RPM.[517] This is in agreement with the arguments of the Chicago School and the Post-Chicago School on dual distribution, but contradicts the arguments of the progressive school, as discussed in Chapter 2, which would support PSKS' arguments.

The Court of Appeals also held that PSKS failed to prove a violation of Section 1 of the Sherman Act on the basis of the alleged RPM collusion because PSKS failed to determine the relevant market and prove any anticompetitive harm. By applying the rule of reason to RPM, PSKS identified two alternative relevant markets: 'the retail market for Brighton's women's accessories' and the 'wholesale sale of brand-name women's accessories to independent retailers'. The Court of Appeals refused the petitioner's determination of the relevant product markets.[518] Despite a number of facts showing the exclusive position of Brighton products within the retail market,[519] the court held that Brighton products did not constitute 'the retail market for Brighton's women's accessories' because, as the court believed, Brighton products did not form one single-branded market as there was 'no structural barrier to the interchangeability of Brighton products',[520] nor did they form one submarket. Although the court recognized the submarket doctrine, it stated that submarkets exist within broader markets and, thus, in these situations, pleading must include this broader market and not just a submarket.[521]

---

[516] Ibid., 416.

[517] Ibid., 420–21.

[518] Ibid., 416.

[519] Steiner argued that retailers selling Brighton's products did not face vigorous competition because they specialized in the Brighton brand. The lack of interbrand competition and the importance of intrabrand competition were also obvious from the fact that the petitioner went out of business after Leegin stopped its supplies and Leegin's confirmation that Brighton consumers would switch retailers to find Brighton products rather than switch products. Note 59, Steiner, 47–9.

[520] Ibid., 418.

[521] Ibid., submarkets were recognized and explained in the case of Note 141, *Brown Shoes*, 325.

In regard to the second market, the court argued that 'wholesale sale' is not an adequate definition of a relevant market because it is not focused on the product market but instead on distribution. Furthermore, the court believed, without providing further explanation, that part of the relevant market 'women's accessories' was 'too broad and vague a definition to constitute a market'.[522]

With respect to the harm on competition, the Court of Appeals criticized PSKS for ignoring interbrand competition, which overcompensates for any possible anticompetitive harm as it assures competition in both services and price, stating that 'nothing in its complaint plausibly alleges a harm to interbrand competition'[523] and/or that 'PSKS has never asserted that a cartel of retailers or one dominant retailer is the "source" of Leegin's RPM program'.[524]

We may recall that in the case of *Mack Trucks*, the Third Circuit ruled that proving anticompetitive effect under the rule of reason could be complicated and thus proving the existence of the market power of the defendant could be sufficient to prove harm under RPM collusion. Here, in *Leegin 2*, the court required evidence of harm to interbrand competition. However, in *Leegin 2* the court could potentially have been satisfied if it was proved that a powerful retailer initiated RPM,[525] unlike in *Mack Trucks*, where the court referred to any defendant, meaning both buyers and suppliers.

Therefore, *Mack Trucks* shows a preference for the Supreme Court statement in *Leegin* where the Court highlighted that the market power of a manufacturer or retailer is important in RPM because both parties can abuse their power to pressure others to facilitate RPM.[526] However, at the same time, it does not go as far as to refer to another statement in *Leegin*, where the Supreme Court said that such power should concern the courts if it is seriously monopolistic.[527]

It could also appear that in *Mack Trucks* the court did not pay attention to the initiator of the alleged conduct; however, the fact that it considered the potential existence of two forms of price fixing, an RPM agreement and a horizontal price-fixing agreement among dealers, indicates that it was concerned with dealer collusion and their interests to maintain prices. Moreover, the Court of Appeals said that evidence such as the

---

[522] Ibid., 418.
[523] Ibid., 419.
[524] Ibid.
[525] Ibid.
[526] Note 6, *Leegin*, 885, 893–4.
[527] Ibid., 898.

interest of dealers, can lead to the assumption of the existence of a retailer cartel rather than that of vertical collusion.[528] Indeed, it differentiated between a horizontal price agreement and a vertical RPM agreement, where in *Mack Trucks* the significant market power of either a retailer(s) or a manufacturer played an important role and could have substituted the evaluation of the effect on competition.

On the other hand, in *Leegin 2*, the Court of Appeals expressly referred to the retailer's dominant position and collusion among retailers. Thus, it paid attention to the differentiation between the manufacturer's and the retailer's reasons for introducing RPM in *Leegin* and, in that respect, the statement made by the Supreme Court that if the initiator is a powerful retailer (or retailers), it can constitute evidence of the abuse of a dominant position or the facilitation of a retailer cartel, which is anticompetitive conduct. On the other hand, a manufacturer would most likely use RPM to increase services.[529]

The Application of *Leegin* by the District Court: *McDonough v. Toys 'R' Us, Inc*[530]

The District Court in Pennsylvania dealt with a class action case where consumers alleged that Toys 'R' Us, a retailer of baby and juvenile products, forced their suppliers, manufacturers of these products, to, among other things, prevent Internet retailers competing with Toys 'R' Us from discounting. Toys 'R' Us had such power (the court was referring to market power and not bargaining power) that it was able to dictate the conditions of vertical restraints to manufacturers. These conditions involved different vertical methods of preventing discounting, including enforcing RPM.[531]

In this case, Judge Anita Brody applied and referred to the reasoning in *Leegin*. She discussed, among other things, the motivations of the initiators of RPM, differentiating between buyers and suppliers and harm on competition stating (unlike in *Leegin 2*) that intrabrand competition is also important, despite the fact that interbrand competition is of primary concern.

---

[528] Note 418, *Mack Trucks*, 225, citing *Leegin*, 127 S.Ct. 2705, 2719.
[529] Ibid., 898.
[530] Note 428, *McDonough v. Toys 'R' Us*.
[531] Ibid.

As part of the application for an interlocutory order,[532] Judge Brody explained that the alleged actual harm is proven if the conduct leads to increased retail prices, reduction of output and/or of quality and services. This and previous cases did not exclude the reduction of intrabrand competition from anticompetitive harm, particularly if such reduction had been caused by a retailer with market power.[533] She said:

> binding precedent gives no indication that harm only to interbrand – as opposed to intrabrand – competition may suffice. Indeed, the U.S. Supreme Court and the leading treatise in the field expressly recognize that harm to intrabrand competition is cognizable when brought about by the demands of a 'dominant' retailer, one that has market power in the retail sales market and one upon whom each manufacturer depends for a large portion of its sales ... *Leegin* expressly recognized that abuse of minimum resale price maintenance procured at the behest of a 'dominant retailer' is one of the very types of anticompetitive conduct cognizable in a Sherman § 1 claim.[534]

Therefore, unlike what was stated in the previous cases of *Crane & Shovel* or *Business Cards Tomorrow*, Judge Brody, by referring to *Leegin*, held that antitrust law also protects vertical intrabrand competition if it is restricted by a retailer (or a manufacturer) with market power.[535] Although antitrust law prioritizes interbrand competition, it protects both forms, intrabrand and interbrand competition. However, the rule of reason applies to RPM because RPM can have a positive impact on interbrand competition.[536]

In finding whether the plaintiffs had the motion for class action certification, she relied on and referred to the two crucial arguments of *Leegin*. First, the Supreme Court in *Leegin* differentiated between the procompetitive motivations of manufacturers and the anticompetitive motivations of retailers. Second, the Supreme Court expressed that the market power of a retailer (or a manufacturer) is an important factor to consider when finding anticompetitive, unreasonable restriction of competition. As the Court said, a retailer with market power can pressure its manufacturer to maintain retail prices and such a retailer is driven by

---

[532] Made under §1292(b) of 28 USC in the case of *Babyage.Com, Inc. v. Toys 'R' US, Inc*, 05-6792 and 06-242 (15 July 2008), 2008 BL 156554, US District Court, Eastern District of Pennsylvania ('*Babyage.Com v. Toys 'R' Us*').
[533] Note 532, *Babyage.Com v. Toys 'R' Us*.
[534] Ibid., where Judge Anita B Brody refers to *Leegin*, 127 S.Ct. 2705, 2717, 2719–20.
[535] Ibid.
[536] Note 428, *McDonough v. Toys 'R' Us*.

anticompetitive motivations to increase competition, in order to minimize the losses it can have from competing on price with more efficient retailers.[537] In that respect, Judge Brody quoted an extract from *Leegin*, which says that in situations where the manufacturer is forced to impose RPM by a retailer with market power

> the manufacturer does not establish the practice to stimulate services or to promote its brand but rather to give an inefficient retailer[] higher profits. Retailers with better distribution systems and lower cost structures would be prevented from charging lower prices.[538]

The Supreme Court then said 'that a dominant ... retailer can abuse resale price maintenance for anticompetitive purposes may not be a serious concern unless the relevant entity has market power'.[539]

Despite the fact that Judge Brody explained that US antitrust law also protects intrabrand competition while giving preference to interbrand competition, the meaning of intrabrand competition differs to the one used in Chapter 2 and is very limited. First, by stating that the upstream restrictive conduct of a dominant retailer is of concern only if the retailer has market power, the Court emphasizes horizontal competition because the focus is placed on how much of the horizontal market is taken by the retailer enforcing the vertical restrictive conduct, in comparison with other competing retailers.

If the retailer was dominant (which, here, probably means the most important form to suppliers; thus, the dominancy likely refers to bargaining power) but lacked significant market power, her conduct 'may not be a serious concern' for US antitrust law. It is more likely that a retailer will be dominant on the vertical chain if she has market power but, as explained in Chapter 2, it is not always the case that a retailer who is dominant, or in other words has bargaining power, also has market power. In this case, Toys 'R' Us had significant bargaining power, which allowed her to dictate the vertical restraints her suppliers should impose on other retailers. This leads us to the second, different, understanding of intrabrand competition: although this conduct was initiated by a 'dominant' retailer, it restricted not only intrabrand competition but also interbrand competition because the retailer persuaded more than one manufacturer to maintain retail prices. Therefore, this is an example of the restriction of vertical interbrand competition as a consequence of the

---

[537] Ibid.
[538] Ibid., quoting *Leegin*, 127 S.Ct. 2705, 2719.
[539] Ibid., quoting *Leegin*, 2720.

multiple restrictions of intrabrand competition, where the retailer managed to influence the policy and introduction of RPM not only within one brand (this would constitute the restriction of intrabrand competition) but also persuaded a number of manufacturers to maintain retail prices and thus interbrand competition was restricted.

RPM Allegations and the Application of the Case of *Twombly*

In 2007, another important judgment besides *Leegin* was delivered: the case of *Twombly*.[540] This case dealt with the question of proving an anticompetitive agreement under Section 1 of the Sherman Act, and the standard set in this case has been applied in subsequent RPM cases. In the case of *Tempur-Pedic*,[541] the Court of Appeals applied the requirements set in *Twombly* to evaluate whether plaintiffs had a claim for relief and whether there was horizontal collusion between a manufacturer with a dual distribution system and his retailers. In *Online Travel Company Hotel Booking*,[542] the District Court applied the strict standards from *Twombly* when evaluating circumstantial evidence in order to determine whether two forms of collusion, RPM and horizontal price fixing, existed. The court evaluated the circumstantial evidence showing parallel prices, factors in the form of regular annual meetings of parties involved in the alleged conduct and private communications between them and also potential enforcement mechanisms, and held that these did not satisfy *Twombly*'s standards as they could indicate merely the existence of parallel conduct.

Tempur-Pedic[543]
In this unsuccessful class action motion on RPM, the Court of Appeals applied the case of *Twombly* in order to determine whether the plaintiffs had a claim for relief, in particular whether the plaintiff's legal conclusions were supported by the facts. The plaintiffs alleged that Tempur-Pedic, a manufacturer of a visco-elastic foam mattress, violated Section 1 of the Sherman Act in the form of an RPM agreement and a horizontal price-fixing agreement. Tempur-Pedic North America produced and sold the mattress in the US via retailers and also directly via his own website. Thus, his distribution model was dual distribution.

---

[540] *Bell Atlantic Corp. v. Twombly*, 550 U.S. 544 (2007) ('*Twombly*').
[541] Note 424, *Tempur-Pedic*.
[542] In re *Online Travel Company Hotel Booking Antitrust Litigation*, 2014 WL 626555 (N.D. Tex.) ('*Online Travel Company Hotel Booking*').
[543] Note 424, *Tempur-Pedic*.

Twombly requires that facts must 'plausibly suggest' that legal conclusions made by the plaintiff are correct. The court stated that in the rule of reason cases, in their claim for relief, the plaintiffs must show, as required under Section 1 of the Sherman Act, actual or potential harm to competition. It then referred to *Leegin*, requiring proof of the restriction of *interbrand* competition.[544] To do so, the plaintiffs must first establish the relevant market, then they must show potential or actual harm and establish that this harm resulted from a prohibited RPM agreement. In *Tempur-Pedic*, the plaintiff failed to establish all of these elements.

In case of potential harm, the plaintiff should show that the defendant possesses market power. However, the plaintiffs had already failed to satisfactorily establish the relevant market. Although the plaintiffs claimed that the relevant market was for the visco-elastic foam mattress, they did not provide any elaboration as to why it was this market and not the market for all mattresses. *Twombly* requires plaintiffs to at least indicate that they could provide the court with evidence to suggest that the relevant market was the visco-elastic foam mattress market. However, the plaintiffs failed to indicate that they would be able to provide this evidence. The Court of Appeals agreed with the District Court's reasoning that the relevant market was the market for mattresses in general, as all of these are products 'on which people sleep'.[545]

With regard to the allegation of the existence of a tacit horizontal agreement on fixing prices, the court again applied *Twombly*. It evaluated whether it was more plausible that uniform prices resulted from horizontal tacit collusion and not from 'rational profit-maximizing behaviour'.[546] It concluded that any price-fixing actions were '"fully explained" by their "own interests"' and therefore it was not more plausible that this conduct was based on horizontal tacit collusion.[547] The court also repeated the District Court's argument that 'courts generally have viewed manufacturer-distributor chains as vertical, not horizontal, in nature'[548] and observed that the majority of cases based on dual distribution were found to be vertical-restraint rather than horizontal-restraint cases.[549] This

---

[544] Note 424, *Tempur-Pedic*, 1335–6.
[545] Ibid., 1338.
[546] Ibid., 1342 referring to Note 540, *Twombly*, 1963.
[547] Ibid.
[548] Ibid., 1340.
[549] Ibid. The court referred to the following cases on dual distribution: (1) horizontal in character: *Hobart Bros. Co. v. Malcolm T. Gilliland, Inc.*, 471 F.2d 894 (5th Circuit 1973) 899 ('*Hobart Bros*'); *United States v. McKesson & Robbins*, 351 U.S. 305 (1956) 313 ('*United States v. McKesson*'); (2) vertical in

is in agreement with the above-discussed non-price vertical cases from the previous era, where the courts ruled that these agreements were vertical and not horizontal agreements.

Online Travel Company Hotel Booking[550]

A number of class actions were registered with the District Court alleging the existence of both horizontal and vertical minimum price fixing in the form of the most-favored-nation clause between the major online accommodation reservation sites and major US hotel chains.[551] This conduct has also been investigated in other jurisdictions.[552] In the US, the District Court applied the standards of *Twombly* to determine whether the alleged collusion existed.

In this case, the plaintiffs alleged that a number of online travel agencies and US hotel chains adopted RPM via agreements, including most-favored-nation clauses in the market for 'direct online sale of hotel room reservations' and in that way violated Section 1 of the Sherman Act and state consumer protection laws.[553] The plaintiffs claimed that the conduct had two parts. First, it included vertical collusion on RPM in the form of individual written agreements between each hotel chain and online travel agency. Each vertical agreement typically provided that a hotel chain would establish and publish the 'Best Available Rate' and the 'Lowest Rate' not allowing for discounting below such price, and that the

---

nature: *Hesco Parts, LLC v. Ford Motor Co.*, No 3:02CV-736-S, 2006 WL 2734429 (W.D.Ky 22 September 2006) 4–5; *Midwestern Waffles, Inc. v. Waffle House, Inc.*, 734 F.2d 705 (11th Circuit 1984) 720; Note 302, *Red Diamond*, 1005–7; Note 290, *Abadir*, 427–8; Note 294, *H & B Equipment*, 245. Note, that cases on dual distribution systems, which are vertical in nature, are the most recent ones.

[550] Note 542, *Online Travel Company Hotel Booking*.

[551] See, *Turik v. Expedia Inc.*, (NDCal 2012) JSW C 12-05234 EDL; *Wagner v. Expedia, Inc.*, (2012) JSW C 12-05353 LB; *Stevenson v. Expedia, Inc.*, (2012) JSW C 12-05444 EDL; *Shames v. Expedia, Inc.*, (2012) JSW C 12-05573 MEJ; *Winkelstein v. Expedia, Inc.*, (2012) JSW C 12-05709 MEJ; *Williamson v. Orbitz Worldwide, Inc.*, (2012) C 12-05816.

[552] For instance, in the UK, the former Office of Fair Trading (OFT) investigation commenced in 2010. Commitments were made to the OFT by Expedia and others. On 26 September 2014, the Competition Appeal Tribunal (CAT) upheld an appeal against the OFT's decision of 31 January 2014 accepting these commitments: *Skyscanner Ltd v. Skoosh International Ltd*, 2014 WL 4636815.

[553] Note 542, *Online Travel Company Hotel Booking*, 1, 5.

published rates were guaranteed to be the same rate offered to any other competing online travel agency (so called, 'the most-favored-nation clause').[554] The second part was horizontal conspiracy across the whole industry among online travel agencies.

The plaintiffs stated that although this conduct restricted intrabrand competition and not interbrand competition, it was industry-wide.[555] They tried to prove these agreements entirely on circumstantial evidence.[556] They claimed that the collusion was facilitated through annual industry conferences held by the UK company EyeforTravel, Ltd since 2003. During these conferences and also via private communications, defendants had opportunities to collude in the form of an express or tacit agreement.[557] This argued collusion allegedly included enforcement mechanisms in the form of monitoring, penalty systems, threats of legal action and refusing to supply if an online travel agency did not want to follow the RPM policy.[558]

The court applied the standards from *Twombly*[559] when evaluating whether collusion in the form of a contract, combination or conspiracy existed based on the circumstantial evidence.[560] In that context, *Twombly* explains that a situation where 'facts that are "merely consistent with" a defendant's liability'[561] is not enough. If the presented circumstantial evidence and the facts of the case show that the allegation of conspiracy and the explanation by the defendant point to parallel conduct or the possibility of other unilateral conduct, the presented circumstantial evidence is not enough to prove violation of Section 1 of the Sherman Act.[562]

What has to be proved under *Twombly* is that the presented circumstantial evidence points to the existence of a meeting of the minds or 'further factual enhancements' which would show, for instance, that parallel behavior would not have occurred without the existence of restrictive collusion (an agreement).[563] The plaintiffs referred to a number of presented facts as 'further factual enhancements', such as individually

---

[554] Ibid., 2–3.
[555] Ibid., 2, 5.
[556] Ibid., 5.
[557] Ibid., 1–2, 5.
[558] Ibid., 3.
[559] Note 540, *Twombly*.
[560] Note 542, *Online Travel Company Hotel Booking* 4, 6–7.
[561] Note 540, *Twombly*, 557.
[562] Note 542, *Online Travel Company Hotel Booking*, 4–7.
[563] Ibid., 7 quoting Note 540, *Twombly*, 556–7, 565.

imposed enforcement mechanisms and the existence of RPM across the industry, which, according to them, prove the existence of both forms of collusion. However, the court held that these only prove the existence of parallel behavior.[564] The existence of government investigation in European countries[565] as a form of 'factual enhancement' was also dismissed by the court on the basis of establishing no linkage between the conduct investigated in Europe and the conduct in question, and that other investigations in other jurisdictions were irrelevant for establishing the requirements under Section 1 of the Sherman Act.[566]

The plaintiffs also introduced other alleged factual enhancements: communication among the firms in question, price competition and online travel agencies' market power. First, the court held that the fact that the firms communicated during the conferences and also privately does not on its own constitute the existence of conspiracy as it does not show that illegal conspiracy (in the form of pricing policy) was discussed. This evidence can only point to the existence of 'an opportunity to conspire' but not that the firms in question conspired beyond conscious parallelism.[567] Although the defendants discussed prices, this discussion was about different pricing strategies in the online hotel booking industry, which could assist with the existence of conscious parallelism but did not prove illegal conspiracy.[568]

Second, the change in price competition was also dismissed by the court as a piece of evidence proving conspiracy. The court stated that the gradual adopting of the same price strategy across the industry was the result of adapting to a new form of distribution – online booking via agencies – and a rational adjustment to such a change. Therefore, this also does not prove that the defendants illegally conspired.[569]

Third, although a small number of online booking agencies allegedly involved in this practice possessed a high market share of 94 percent (2011), the court said that without more evidence this did not prove they asserted their 'market power vertically' to conspire horizontally on price fixing among themselves. The court observed that they did not hold this share in 2003, when the alleged collusion was supposed to have taken place, as they built their market share gradually.[570]

---

[564] Ibid., 10.
[565] Ibid., 3.
[566] Ibid., 10.
[567] Ibid., 11.
[568] Ibid., 12.
[569] Ibid.
[570] Ibid., 13.

With regard to the reasons for using **RPM** among individual online hotel booking entities and hotels providing rooms, the court agreed with the defendants and stated that the motivation for this conduct was unsuspicious and was as follows: the hotel chains merely wanted to control prices to, first, establish the price which they believed customers would be willing to pay for their hotel rooms, second, to protect their brands' high-end images[571] and, third, to eliminate price discrimination strategies, which are strategies to 'sell the same product, costing the same to make and sell, at different prices to different consumers'.[572] However, there is a difference between price discrimination where suppliers supply their products to buyers for a different wholesale price and a situation where the final consumers receive no benefit from price competition because the intrabrand prices of hotel rooms are the same due to their fixed rate.

Indeed, the hotel chains admitted that they wanted to control prices in general. The court acknowledged this and stated that it was their right to control online pricing for their rooms.[573] As the court observed, the interest was obvious, the agencies simply wanted to avoid the situation of other agencies – their competitors – selling for less than the published rate. Therefore, obtaining assurances of minimum price was in their individual interests. This does not mean that without the existence of horizontal conspiracy, this would go against defendants' business interests and it does not constitute 'a common motive to eliminate price competition'.[574]

Therefore, although the effect on competition was such that intrabrand price competition was restricted across the industry because the defendants charged the same prices for the same hotel room, a link between the restriction of competition and the alleged conspiracy and even the conspiracy[575] itself was not established. The court did not ask whether parallel pricing would have existed even without the existence of 'plus factors' presented by the plaintiffs based on circumstantial evidence. By applying the case of *Twombly*, the court dismissed the presented factors, referred to as 'further factual enhancements'. It evaluated whether this situation could have been explained by parallel conduct or generally unilateral actions and whether unilateral minimum pricing would be

---

[571] Ibid., 8.
[572] Ibid. The court was quoting Posner J in In re *Brand Name Prescription Drugs Antitrust Litigation*, 288 F.3d 1028 (7th Circuit 2002) 1030–31.
[573] Ibid., 8.
[574] Ibid., 9.
[575] Horizontal conspiracy.

against the interest of defendants. Although vertical 'agreements' restricting competition are not necessarily in the interest of all parties involved and can be forced by one party or a group of entities upon others, horizontal collusion is generally in the interest of its participants. Indeed, both parallel conduct and horizontal collusion fixing prices will be in the interest of its parties. Thus, it is questionable whether the standards set in *Twombly* as applied in this case capture all forms of collusion beyond parallel conduct, including tacit agreements.

VII. APPLICATION AND ENFORCEMENT

US antitrust cases can be both public and private, where private cases also include class actions. Private actions have two functions: first, to compensate the injured party and, second, to deter wrongdoers.[576] The public cases do not compensate the injured parties but Subsection 5(a) of the Clayton Act allows for private plaintiffs to use public-case judgments or decrees as prima facie evidence against defendants.

From the cases discussed above, it is obvious that a significant majority of cases on RPM and VTR, which include *Dr. Miles*, *Sylvania*, *Monsanto*, *Business Electronics*, *Khan* and *Leegin*,[577] are private cases. Private treble damages suits, including class actions, can be brought under Section 4 of the Clayton Act if the plaintiff shows that it has suffered injury to his/her 'business or property' due to a violation of antitrust law.[578] (This is on top of proving a violation of the Sherman Act, which must be proved in both private and public cases.) Private parties can also sue for injunctions under Section 16 of the Clayton Act. The individual injury under Sections 4 and 16 of the Clayton Act must be a result of a restrictive agreement, which violates Section 1 of the Sherman Act. Indeed, there must be a causal link between the individual injury and the anticompetitive violation in question. For example, if the subject matter is an RPM agreement, the plaintiffs can show that consumers would have paid less without the existence of the RPM agreement.

Both RPM and VTR have been judged under Section 1 of the Sherman Act. To prove violation of Section 1, the plaintiffs, in both private and

---

[576] See, e.g., Note 153, *Simpson*.
[577] Note 3, *Colgate* is a public case.
[578] See, e.g., *Brunswick Corp. v. Pueblo Bowl-O-Mat, Inc.*, 429 U.S. 477 (1977).

public procedures, must show three elements: 1) restriction of competition;[579] 2) in the form of an agreement;[580] 3) concluded between independent entities. The last element simply means that Section 1 applies to collusion between independent economic entities and not to a vertically integrated entity or to a relationship based on an agent agreement – an agreement between a manufacturer and his agent.[581] Although the Sherman Act refers to a 'person', for the purposes of the Act the term 'person' is not understood as a legal person but instead as an economic entity.[582]

The second element requires the plaintiff to prove the existence of an agreement (in the form of a contract, combination or conspiracy). The term agreement is broad as it also includes tacit agreements; however, it does not include parallel conduct or any other independent conduct.[583] To prove an agreement, evidence must show activities towards collusion on the part of both parties.[584] The plaintiff must provide direct or circumstantial evidence that excludes the possibility that one or both parties, the supplier and her buyer, were simultaneously acting independently, for example, in the form of conscious parallelism.[585] If the presented evidence points to the possibility of unilateral conduct, including mere parallel conduct because the actions of parties could be explained by

---

[579] Sherman Act refers to the restriction of 'trade or commerce'.

[580] Sherman Act, Section 1: 'contract', 'combination' or 'conspiracy'.

[581] For example, a parent company and its owned subsidiary creates one economic entity and thus an agreement between them fixing prices would not violate Section 1 because there would only be one 'person' (economic entity) and thus no collusion between persons (between independent economic entities). See Note 153, *Simpson*; Note 80, *General Electric*; *Ozark Heartland Electronics Inc. v. Radio Shack*, 278 F.3d 759 (8th Circuit 2002); *Hardwick v. Nu-Way Oil Co.*, 589 F.2d 806 (5th Circuit 1979) 808; *Call Carl, Inc. v. BP Oil Corp.*, 554 F.2d 623 (4th Circuit 1977) 627–8.

[582] See *Copperweld Corp. v. Independence Tube Corp.*, 467 U.S. 752 (1984); *Guzowski v. Hartman*, 969 F.2d 211 (6th Circuit 1992) 214, *cert. denied*, 506 U.S. 1053 (1993); *Century Oil Tool Inc. v. Production Specialities, Inc.*, 737 F.2d 1316 (5th Circuit 1984); *Bell Atlantic Business System Services v. Hitachi Data Systems Corp.*, 849 F.Supp 702 (N.D.Cal. 1994); *Fibreglass Insulators, Inc. v. Dupuy*, 856 F.2d 652 (4th Circuit 1988); *Rio Vista Oil, Ltd. V. Southland Corp.*, 667 F.Supp 757 (D.Utah 1987) 761.

[583] See, e.g., *Brooke Group Ltd. V. Brown & Williamson Tobacco Corp.*, 509 U.S. 209 (1993) 227; *Theatre Enterprises, Inc. v. Paramount Film Distributing Corp.*, 346 U.S. 537 (1954).

[584] Note 279, *Monsanto*, 764.

[585] Note 540, *Twombly*, 556–7, 565; Note 279, *Monsanto*, 757, 764, 768; see also Note 542, *Online Travel Company Hotel Booking*, 4–7.

their own interests based on 'rational profit-maximizing behaviour', this evidence would not be enough to prove an agreement under Section 1.[586] For example, even evidence of pricing strategy discussions and the existence of parallel conduct without providing further evidence do not constitute an agreement, as this shows the existence of 'an opportunity to conspire' but not that the firms in question conspired beyond conscious parallelism.[587]

In relation to RPM, conduct based on a simple announcement of price policy and its enforcement by the manufacturer in the form of a refusal to sell is unilateral conduct and is, according to *Colgate*, legal.[588] Later, in 1988, *Business Electronics* explained that cancelling supply to a price cutter based on an agreement between the manufacturer and his second distributor without the existence of an agreement on price or minimum price is not a vertical price restriction but is a non-price vertical restriction. Such a case would probably not be sufficient to demonstrate a restriction of competition under the rule of reason.[589]

In *Monsanto*, the Supreme Court explained that the disclosure of a manufacturer's intention to set retail prices and discussion on marketing strategy did not prove the existence of collusion as it was based on legitimate intentions.[590] Manufacturers and their distributors need to discuss prices and marketing strategies in order to ensure that the products reach the final consumers 'persuasively and efficiently'; particularly, if they wish to avoid free riding and ensure the existence of services.[591] However, what is required is that 'a conscious commitment to a common scheme designed to achieve an unlawful objective'[592] is proven through evidence showing activities towards collusion by both parties.[593]

The first and most complex element under the current approaches to RPM and VTR agreements is proving anticompetitive effect, in other words, the restriction of competition. Generally, the courts state that only

---

[586] Note 424, *Tempur-Pedic*, 1342; Note 542, *Online Travel Company Hotel Booking*, 4–7.
[587] Note 542, *Online Travel Company Hotel Booking*, 11.
[588] Note 3, *Colgate*, 305–7; further clarified in Note 134, *Bausch & Lomb*, Note 136, *Parke, Davis*, and Note 135, *Beech-Nut*.
[589] Note 4, *Business Electronics*, 726–7; see also Note 408, *Euromodas*.
[590] Note 279, *Monsanto*, 762.
[591] Ibid., 762–4.
[592] Ibid., 764. The Supreme Court was quoting *Edward J Sweeney & Sons v. Texaco, Inc.*, 637 F.2d 105 (3d Circuit 1980) 111.
[593] Ibid., 764.

unreasonable restriction violates Section 1 of the Sherman Act[594] and such restriction must be appreciable.[595] Such restriction can be proved by applying the per se rule, which only requires proving a certain form of restriction, or the rule of reason. RPM agreements used to be anticompetitive per se from 1911 to 2007, until *Leegin* changed the approach to the rule of reason. VTR agreements have been evaluated based on the rule of reason since the judgment in *Sylvania* was delivered in 1977.

Any horizontal price or market allocation restriction, including intrabrand restrictions, in the form of an agreement are decided under the per se rule and not the rule of reason.[596] Agreements on price restrictions or territorial/market allocation restrictions between a manufacturer with a dual distribution system who is partly vertically integrated and also operates as a retailer (or a distributor) and his retailers will most likely constitute vertical restriction in the form of RPM and VTR and, thus, the rule of reason will apply.[597]

The way the rule of reason operates in cases on agreements in VTR and RPM is similar. To prove either RPM or VTR, the court requires proof of an anticompetitive impact on interbrand competition. The courts have held on numerous occasions that interbrand competition is of primary concern under the Sherman Act.[598] Both *Leegin* and *Sylvania* stated that RPM or VTR could reduce intrabrand competition and simultaneously stimulate interbrand competition, especially if the market is competitive.[599] Thus, proving the restriction of interbrand competition is essential (except for proving significant market power in RPM cases, as discussed below) in order to disprove this presumption in particular cases and thus prove the violation of Section 1 of the Sherman Act.

---

[594] Note 29, *Standard Oil*, 3–4.

[595] See Note 27, *Chicago Board of Trade*.

[596] RPM: Note 6, *Leegin*, 893; Note 418, *Mack Trucks*, 221. VTR: Note 290, *Boyd*.

[597] RPM: Note 420, *Leegin 2*; Note 424, *Tempur-Pedic*, 1340; VTR: Note 290, *Abadir*, 427. The Court found horizontal restrictions in dual distribution systems only in a few minor cases: Note 549, *Hobart Bros*, 899; Note 549, *United States v. McKesson*, 313. Other cases on dual distribution which were found to be vertical in nature: Note 549, *Hesco Parts*, 4–5; Note 549, *Midwestern Waffles*, 720; Note 302, *Red Diamond*, 1005–7; Note 290, *Abadir*, 427–8; Note 294, *H & B Equipment*, 245. Note, that cases on dual distribution systems, which are vertical in nature, are the most recent ones.

[598] Note 6, *Leegin*; Note 420, *Leegin 2*; Note 428, *McDonough v. Toys 'R' Us*.

[599] Note 7, *Sylvania* 51–2; see, also Note 290, *Business Cards Tomorrow*, 1205.

How much or how little intrabrand competition matters under this rule of reason approach is questionable. Some cases stated that it is only interbrand competition that is protected under the Sherman Act.[600] A few maintained that intrabrand competition matters and its restriction in the form of collusion could violate Section 1 of the Sherman Act. The Second Circuit in the VTR case of *Eiberger v. Sony* in 1980 ruled that the restriction of intrabrand competition is prohibited under the Sherman Act unless the conduct in question could be justified or it could be proved that VTR increased interbrand competition.[601] However, other cases on VTR since *Sylvania* have followed the strict rule of reason, where the restriction of interbrand competition must be proved. Therefore, *Eiberger v. Sony* was rather an exception, as it is interbrand and not intrabrand competition that matters in VTR cases.

In RPM cases, the courts have stated that competition is also restricted in a situation where it is restricted by a retailer (or a manufacturer) with market power,[602] where *Mack Trucks* referred to both the supplier and the buyer with regard to proving market power as an alternative to proving a restriction of competition. However, *Leegin 2* referred to a buyer with significant market power, as 'only' the buyer can have anticompetitive reasons for introducing RPM. Indeed, the current approach to RPM cases requires evidence of the restriction of interbrand competition unless it can be proved that the retailer (buyer), or perhaps also the manufacturer (supplier), who initiated RPM, had significant market power.[603] How significant the market power must be is questionable, however, it is clear that monopolistic power is significant enough.[604] To prove significant market power or a restriction of interbrand competition, the plaintiff must first correctly determine the relevant market.

It seems that significant market power also plays a role in non-price vertical restrictions, in particular VTR. For example, in *Business Cards Tomorrow*, the court held that this intensive interbrand competition meant

---

[600] Note 290, *Business Cards Tomorrow*, 1205; Note 293, *Crane & Shovel*, 810.

[601] Note 291, *Eiberger v. Sony*, 1075–81.

[602] Note 6, *Leegin*; Note 420, *Leegin 2*; Note 418, *Mack Trucks*, Note 532, *Babyage.Com v. Toys 'R' Us*.

[603] Note 6, *Leegin*, 885, 893–4, 898; Note 418, *Mack Trucks*, 225; Note 420, *Leegin 2*, 419. The differentiation between powers of the supplier and buyer is linked with the differentiation between the motivations for introducing RPM of buyers and suppliers as outlined in Note 6, *Leegin*, and explained below.

[604] Note 6, *Leegin*, 898.

there was no significant restriction on competition.[605] The plaintiff had to prove significant market power, because it is an indication of the potential of an anticompetitive effect.[606] Again, there are question marks surrounding exactly what constitutes 'significant market power'. For example, in *McDaniel*,[607] 43 percent of the market share was deemed insufficient market power because the market was highly competitive. The approach appears to be so strict that the point of whether the plaintiff has any real chance to prove illegality of VTR is moot. Indeed, if in RPM cases significant market power is combined with proving the restriction of interbrand competition,[608] a restriction in the form of RPM under the rule of reason approach would be even harder to prove.

In relation to RPM cases, the Supreme Court in *Leegin* identified another element which could assist with proving restriction of competition: the reasons for introducing RPM. The Supreme Court held that manufacturers (suppliers) would most likely use RPM to increase services, unlike retailers (buyers). If the initiator is a powerful retailer or a group of retailers, this could constitute evidence of an abuse of a dominant position or the facilitation of a retailer cartel.[609]

Hence, it is not surprising that in *Leegin 2*, the Court of Appeals affirmed that the court would be satisfied with the restriction of competition in situations where it is proved that the initiator was a powerful retailer. This interpretation of *Leegin*, especially both elements, market power and motivations of manufacturers and retailers to introduce RPM intentions, in mutual connections, could lead to the conclusion that the only alternative for proving anticompetitive effect on competition other than proving a restriction of competition is the significant market power of a retailer initiating RPM (but not the manufacturer). Alternatively, if there is a horizontal agreement between retailers to maintain prices, the per se rule will apply and Section 1 of the Sherman Act will thus be violated.

The Supreme Court's emphasis on the intentions of the initiators also indicates that, under this new approach based on the rule of reason, not only is the effect on competition important (an objective test) but the Court will also consider the intentions of the parties (supported by a

---

[605] Ibid., 1205.
[606] Note 294, *Jayco*; Note 297, *Valley Liquors*; see Note 165, Areeda and Hovenkamp, 402–6.
[607] *McDaniel v. Greensboro News Co.*, 679 F.2d 883 (4th Circuit 1983).
[608] Currently, it appears that these two elements are applied as alternatives in RPM.
[609] Note 6, *Leegin*, 898; see also Note 418, *Mack Trucks*, 225.

subjective test), as they could assist with establishing the whole picture of the effects on competition.[610]

If it is proved that RPM or VTR restricted interbrand competition or, alternatively, in RPM cases, that the buyer (or maybe also supplier) had significant market power and restricted competition in the form of a reduction of output, a raising of prices or a reduction of quality in a relevant product and geographic market,[611] it does not mean that the plaintiff persuaded the court. The court would also consider any presented justifications by balancing proven anticompetitive effects against procompetitive effects caused by the RPM or VTR.[612] Thus, if the defendant proves procompetitive effects of the conduct in question that outweigh any anticompetitive restrictions, the plaintiff will lose his/her case. Because of the presumption in *Leegin* and *Sylvania* that RPM or VTR could reduce intrabrand competition and simultaneously stimulate interbrand competition, if proof of an RPM or VTR agreement is provided without proving the restriction of interbrand competition but the defendant presents procompetitive justifications, there will be no restriction of competition that would violate the Sherman Act.

This enforcement procedure under the rule of reason in RPM and especially VTR cases indicates a very heavy burden of proof for the plaintiff. In 1981, Judge Posner already predicted that, for VTR cases, such an application of the rule of reason would lead to the de facto legality of VTR in the US due to an unfeasibility for plaintiffs to win their cases.[613] Reality confirms this. Additionally, RPM cases are in danger of not succeeding in proving a violation of Section 1 of the Sherman Act. Therefore, it is not surprising that after *Leegin*, the intensity of the scholarly debate on the right approach to RPM increased, with a number of suggestions being made regarding a structured rule of reason.[614]

---

[610] Also in VTR, in Note 290, *Business Cards Tomorrow*, 1205 the Court of Appeals stated that the restriction must be based on an anticompetitive intention.
[611] See, e.g., Note 418, *Mack Trucks*, 226.
[612] Note 6, *Leegin*, 895–6.
[613] Note 319, Posner.
[614] For instance, a compromise between the per se rule and the rule of reason (applying one or the other depending on the market power): Note 9, Voorhees; Note 487, Areeda and Hovenkamp, 242; Note 165, Areeda and Hovenkamp, 330–39; different forms of a structured rule of reason: Sandra M Colino, *Vertical Agreements and Competition Law: A Comparative Study of the EU and US Regimes* (Hart Publishing 2010) 153–81; Marina Lao, 'Resale Price Maintenance: The Internet Phenomenon and Free Rider Issues' (2010) 55 *Antitrust Bulletin* 473, 511; John B Kirkwood, 'Rethinking Antitrust Policy toward RPM'

A number of US antitrust cases have indeed applied a structured rather than full rule of reason.[615] However, the Court of Appeals is reluctant to officially confirm such a rule, claiming instead that it is still the same rule of reason.[616] In VTR cases after *Sylvania* and RPM cases after *Leegin*, three cases applied a more lenient, 'soft', approach to the rule of reason: *Mack Trucks*, *McDonough v. Toys 'R' Us* and *Eiberger v. Sony*.

First, in the price restriction case of *Mack Trucks*, the Third Circuit acknowledged that proving the restriction of competition under the rule of reason is extremely difficult and stated that the existence of sufficient market power of the defendant (either a buyer or a supplier) could be enough to prove anticompetitive effects on competition. Judge Brody in *McDonough v. Toys 'R' Us* referred directly to the rule of reason approach applied in *Brown University* stating that '[f]or the rule of reason, the Third Circuit employs a burden-shifting analysis'.[617] This is implemented if the defendant has sufficient market power. First, the plaintiff has to prove that the alleged RPM collusion resulted in anti-competitive effects in the form of reduced output, quality or increased prices within the relevant market, or alternatively it would be enough to prove that the plaintiff had the ability to introduce monopolistic prices. If the plaintiff succeeds in showing the sufficient market power of the defendant, the burden of proof shifts to the defendant who, in order to justify his/her conduct, must show that the conduct in question promoted competition. The plaintiff would then have to demonstrate that the restriction was not reasonably necessary to achieve the proven pro-competitive objective in order to succeed with his/her claim.[618]

(2010) 55(2) *Antitrust Bulletin* 423, 423–72; Note 59, Steiner, 56–8; Thomas A Lambert, 'A Decision-Theoretic Rule of Reason for Minimum Resale Price Maintenance' (2010) 55(1) *Antitrust Bulletin* 167, 214–24; Christine A Varney, 'A Post-*Leegin* Approach to Resale Price Maintenance Using a Structured Rule of Reason' (2010) 24 *Antitrust* 22; Patrick Rey and Joseph Stiglitz, 'The Role of Exclusive Territories in Manufacturers' Competition' (1995) 26 *Rand Journal of Economics* 431, 446.

[615] See, e.g., *Polygram Holding, Inc. v. Federal Trade Commission*, 416 F.3d 29 (D.C.Cir. 2005) ('*Polygram*'); see also In re *Matter of Realcomp II Ltd.*, File No 061-0088, (FTC 2009) Docket No 9320; *California Dental Association v. FTC*, 526 U.S. 756 (1999); Note 513, *Brown University*; *NCAA v. Board of Regents*, 468 U.S. 85, 100, 104 S.Ct 2948, 82 LE.d2d 70 (1984).

[616] Note 615, *Polygram*, 35.

[617] Note 428, *McDonough v. Toys 'R' Us* quoted Note 513, *Brown University*, 668.

[618] Ibid., quoted Note 513, *Brown University*, 668.

Both cases show a more lenient approach to RPM collusion in situations when the defendant holds market power or, as explained in *Leegin 2*, when the defendant (buyer) has significant market power, perhaps monopolistic power as suggested by *Leegin*, and is even reflected in the burden-shifting approach in *Brown University* under which proving that the plaintiff had the ability to introduce monopolistic prices would be sufficient. This would mean that, for remaining RPM cases, the full rule of reason would apply, where the plaintiff would hold a heavy burden of proof to show restrictions of interbrand competition. Such a rule of reason has been applied to VTR cases, with the exception of *Eiberger v. Sony*, which stands on protecting both intrabrand and interbrand competition, thereby suggesting a different approach. In this case, the Second Circuit was of the opinion that the Sherman Act also protects intrabrand competition, thus recognizing that VTR primarily restricts intrabrand competition. In agreement with this ideology, the court shifted the burden of proof to the defendant to prove the promotion of interbrand competition rather than for the plaintiff to prove a restriction of interbrand competition. Thus, once the intrabrand competition restriction is proven in the form of collusion, the defendant can provide objective pro-competitive justifications and/or he/she can prove that his/her conduct increased interbrand competition.

This approach is different to the approach applied by the courts to VTR cases after *Sylvania* and recent RPM cases, which have focused on the protection of interbrand competition and thus required that interbrand competition be restricted in order to prove a violation of the Sherman Act. The approach in *Eiberger v. Sony*, which protected both intrabrand and interbrand competition, would significantly simplify the current rule of reason and would allow for the burden of proof to be spread between the plaintiff and the defendant. However, it would also mean that the ideology on which the current approach stands would have to be changed and thus protect both intrabrand and interbrand competition, with proof of a restriction of intrabrand competition being sufficient in order to prove a violation of the Sherman Act.

VIII. CONCLUSION

The US law on vertical territorial and price restraints, particularly with regards to RPM, has changed significantly since the *Dr. Miles* judgment in 1911, which introduced the per se rule to RPM cases. In that case, the

Court was satisfied that intrabrand competition was restricted,[619] labeling the manufacturer an initiator of collusion on RPM. In 1977, *Sylvania* introduced the rule of reason to VTR cases and in 2007, *Leegin* to RPM cases. Both cases held that interbrand competition was of primary concern to US antitrust law, establishing the rule of reason to vertical collusion with the aim of proving restriction of interbrand competition. Or, alternatively, in RPM cases, proving significant market power of the defendant if a buyer with market power was the initiator of RPM collusion.[620] Generally, this rule of reason is very difficult to prove, which has led to the de facto legalization of VTR, and potentially RPM as the future development of the approach to RPM will determine.

The current approach to RPM and VTR contains two elements: the protection of interbrand and horizontal competition and the presumption of competitive reasons when RPM or VTR is introduced by a supplier. In connection with this presumption, Ghosh observed that, under this approach to vertical collusion on RPM (this could also apply to VTR), it is the manufacturer who has the right to determine the retail prices, a concept that arises from contractual freedom, which is preferred over intrabrand price competition.[621] This goes against *Dr. Miles*, where the Court protected the ownership of the buyer and thus held that it was the owner who could determine his/her prices.

The concept of the presumption of competitive reasons when RPM or VTR is introduced by a supplier is governed by the neoliberal idea of the Coase Theorem and its information problem, as advocated in free riding theory based on services. The Coase Theorem presumes that the manufacturer is better placed to determine what services should be offered with the product. Thus, in this situation, granting the right to the manufacturer to impose vertical restrictions such as RPM resolves the information problem based on free riding.[622]

Aside from the promotion of interbrand competition, the courts highlighted that US antitrust law protects the market from restrictions of horizontal competition and restrictions facilitated by a buyer with significant, perhaps monopolistic, power. The second form of protection leads

---

[619] Note that, at that time, the Court did not differentiate between interbrand and intrabrand competition.

[620] See the discussion above; there are a number of unanswered questions, especially in the approach to RPM.

[621] Shubha Ghosh, 'Vertical Restraints, Competition and the Rule of Reason' in Keith Hylton (ed.), *Antitrust Law and Economics* (Edward Elgar Publishing 2010) 223–4.

[622] Ibid., 223.

to the question as to whether such a form of RPM restriction should not have been determined under Section 2 of the Sherman Act, which deals with the monopolization of markets rather than Section 1, which focuses on collusion.

On the other hand, the first form of protection, the protection of horizontal competition, is aimed at collusion and thus Section 1 is well suited. The courts, in this situation, apply the per se rule, notwithstanding whether such collusion restricted interbrand competition or only intrabrand competition. Thus, this approach leads to double standards with regards to intrabrand competition, where, if it is restricted vertically, the rule of reason applies with the focus on proving the restriction of interbrand competition. However, if intrabrand competition is restricted horizontally by an agreement between buyers, it is prohibited per se. The effect of restricting intrabrand competition is still the same notwithstanding whether it is a form of horizontal or vertical collusion.[623] This emphasis on interbrand and horizontal competition is close to the first economic-policy model, explained in Chapter 2,[624] and is influenced by the Chicago and the Post-Chicago Schools. This influence is present in many aspects of the approach to VTR and RPM. It is further evidenced by, for example, the treatment of RPM and VTR in dual distribution systems as vertical restrictions and not horizontal restrictions, and the reasoning behind it.

---

[623] In both situations, from the economic standpoint of the effect on overall competition, additional questions arise as to whether there were any procompetitive effects and/or the reasons, and whether it had a positive or negative effect on interbrand competition, which is analyzed under the rule of reason but not under the per se rule. As dissenting Justice Harlan correctly argued in Note 156, *Albrecht*, 157, the form is not important when determining the effect of the conduct on competition.

[624] However, the first model would not be concerned with horizontal intrabrand competition if it does not affect interbrand competition.

4. EU development, case studies and summaries

I. INTRODUCTION

EU competition law, in particular the law of vertical restraints, has many similarities but also some differences from US antitrust law. One of the most significant differences is that EU competition law is based on two primary goals, where the second is particular to EU law in that it reflects the purpose of the EU. Thus, besides the traditional objective of protecting competition, in particular protecting free and fair competition, EU competition law also assists with the establishment and maintenance of an integrated market. In other words, economic integration, in particular the free movement of goods and services, plays an essential role. Another difference lies in the field of the economic approach. Although both current regimes utilize an economic approach, their application differs. Despite the economic approach accommodated by the current Commission policy and its focus on consumer welfare, the EU approach protects both intrabrand and interbrand competition.

Both differences are well-reflected in the EU cases, which find RPM and VTR restricting intrabrand competition anticompetitive unless justified under relevant provisions; and, at the EU level, there are more VTR cases than RPM cases[1] because VTR restricts parallel imports and exports by dividing the territories between Member States. Any restriction of free trade between Member States, including anticompetitive restrictions, is at the center of the focus of the enforcement of EU law, including EU competition law.

Although EU competition law and its policies have created a very stable competition law regime, it has seen a number of changes since its introduction in the 1950s. These changes are related to changes of the EU, previously the European Community (EC) and originally the European Economic Community (EEC), which reflect the social, economic and political situations in Europe. Thus, this chapter is divided into eras

---

[1] This chapter does not deal with national cases.

accordingly, reflecting these changes and especially changes in EU competition policy as initiated by the European Commission and marked out by the EU courts when interpreting EU competition law. Every era involves significant cases on VTR and/or RPM, which provide a good picture of the policy development, any changes in approach and changes of the application of the law of VTR and RPM in practice. The enforcement and application of VTR and RPM cases are summarized and further explained at the end of this chapter, reflecting the interpretation of EU law by the courts as incorporated in the cases. Finally, some differences between the US and EU regimes are pointed out. In particular, the Conclusion includes a brief comparison to the previous chapter on the US regime.

II. THE ORIGIN OF COMPETITION LAW AND THE TREATY FRAMEWORK

European Union competition law and the existence of the EU itself arose as a consequence of World War Two (WW2). The period after WW2 was dominated by ideas of preventing wars and conflicts in Europe and creating an economically strong and unified Europe. Although these ideas were not being discussed for the first time, they appeared more significant at the end of the war.[2] Indeed, the reasons for establishing a soundly based competition law regime in Europe included not only an economically unified Europe but also a Europe without military conflicts. The country leaders recognized after WW2 that the concentrated and heavily cartelized pre-war German industry assisted with consolidating military power throughout the war.[3]

Germany was one of the first European countries to introduce competition law; however, its competition law statute, enacted in 1923 after

---

[2] Treaty Establishing the European Economic Community (adopted 25 March 1957, entered into force 1 January 1958) 298 UNTS 11 (The Treaty of Rome) Preamble, 14; Nicholas Green and others, *The Legal Foundations of the Single European Market* (1st edn, Oxford University Press 1991), 199, 334, 343; Joanna Goyder and Albertina Albors-Llorens, *Goyder's EC Competition Law* (5th edn, Oxford University Press 2009) 24–5; Damian Chalmers, Gareth Davies, and Giorgio Monti, *European Union Law: Cases and Materials* (2nd edn, Cambridge University Press 2010) 7–9.

[3] David J Gerber, *Law and Competition in Twentieth Century Europe: Protecting Prometheus* (Clarendon Press 1998) 7–8; Herbert Hovenkamp, *Federal Antitrust Policy, The Law of Competition and Its Practice* (4th edn, Thomson Reuters 2011) 67.

World War I, was aimed at avoiding a deepening economic crisis in post-war Germany through increased concentrated industrial production as a key element to military success. Cartelization was recognized as a positive process because the government found this easier to control than small firms. This centralized approach was later intensified and abused by the Nazi ideology, which changed the German competition law statute in order for the competition law regime to serve as a tool for its ideology and military aims.[4]

Therefore, it is not surprising that, after WW2, this regime changed and a new German competition law regime was introduced with its new statute coming into force in the 1950s. This new regime was based on the ideas of ordoliberalism and was required by the US, as one of the conditions for German sovereignty, thus reflecting that competition affects not just the economy, but also other socio-political aspects including the facilitation of concentrated military power.

The US not only influenced the introduction of the new German competition law but also had an impact on the formulation of the new EU competition law and policy. After WW2, the relationship between Western Europe and the US deepened due to the US's involvement in the recovery of post-war Europe.[5] At the time, the US already had a well-established antitrust law regime based on the Sherman Act. The influence of the US was arguably at its strongest at the outset of the EU (at that time, EEC), when the originators needed to establish a new European competition law regime and were thus inspired by the US antitrust experience. When the Rome Treaty was signed in 1957, enacting, among other things, competition law, the US antitrust policy was focused on protecting small businesses, with the Harvard School and its suspicion of non-competitive markets being an influential stream.

However, US antitrust law and policy was not the only influential factor. The origin of EU competition law was also affected by European states and their competition theories, legislations and policies, including the new German competition law regime. One of the first ideas based on the free market concept was the French *laissez-faire*, which became an integrated part of European classical liberalism.[6] Despite this movement, the economy in Europe was rather centralized. For example, the period

---

[4] Note 3, Gerber, 7–8, 115–64.

[5] For example, the US assisted European countries by providing loans, primarily the Marshall Plan, in 1948; Note 2, Goyder and others, 24–5; Note 3, Gerber, 166–8.

[6] David Hutchison MacGregor, *Economic Thought and Policy* (1st edn, Oxford University Press 1949) 54–67.

from the French Revolution to the mid-1870s was characterized by the ideas of government restraints on economic actors, which ensured economic wealth and growth. At the end of the nineteenth century, Austrian scholars, Carl Menger and Eugen Bohm-Bawerk, recognized the benefits of competitive markets and promoted that the competitive process be protected by law. Although such law was not put into practice in Austria at the time, it provided some ideological basis for German ordoliberalism.[7] These ideas of European liberalism and neoliberalism, and particularly ordoliberalism, influenced the formation of EU competition law.

Classical liberalism based on freedoms and social liberalism, together with ideas of social security and social justice, created the essential basis for German ordoliberalism. Ordoliberalism, centered in the so-called 'Freiburg School' in Germany with its founders, economist Walter Eucken and lawyers Franz Böhm and Hanns Grossmann-Doerth, was framed from the 1930s to the 1950s. Despite their existence during WW2, ordoliberalists resisted the Nazi ideology as well as state socialism. Instead they focused on economic freedom, recognizing two threats to this freedom: government power and private, powerful, economic individuals and groups such as cartels and monopolies.[8]

Ordoliberalism advocated a so-called 'transaction economy', where economic decision-making is undertaken primarily by private entities and thus competition is its key mechanism.[9] More competition then results in

---

[7] Massimiliano Vatiero, 'The Ordoliberal Notion of Market Power: An Institutionalist Reassessment' (2010) 6 *European Competition Journal* 689, 689–91; David J Gerber, 'Europe and the Globalization of Antitrust Law' (1999) 14 *Connecticut Journal of International Law* 15, 26; Note 3, Gerber, 6, 16, 43–4.

[8] See, e.g., Walter Eucken, 'What Kind of Economic and Social System?' in Alan Peacock and Hans Willgerodt (eds), *German Neo-Liberals and the Social Market Economy* (Palgrave Macmillan 1989) 34–7 ('*German Neo-Liberals*'); Franz Böhm, Walter Eucken and Hans Grossmann-Doerth, 'The Ordo Manifesto of 1936' in Alan Peacock and Hans Willgerodt (eds), *Germany's Social Market Economy: Origins and Evolution* (Palgrave Macmillan 1989) 17–18 ('*Germany's Social Market Economy*'); David J Gerber, 'Constitutionalizing the Economy: German Neo-Liberalism, Competition Law and the "New" Europe' (1994) 42 *American Journal of Comparative Law* 25, 37; Jan Tumlir, 'Franz Böhm and Economic-Constitutional Analysis' in Peacock and Willgerodt, *German Neo-Liberals*; Hans Willgerodt and Alan Peacock, 'German Liberalism and Economic Revival' in *Germany's Social Market Economy*, 6; Walter Eucken, *The Foundations of Economics* (Terence Wilmot Hutchison (tr), William Hodge 1950), 263–73.

[9] Note 8, Eucken, *The Foundations of Economics*, 152–6.

increased efficiency and greater overall welfare and thus social stability.[10] The function of competition law is to protect the competitive process and ensure that no private group or individual has the economic power to dominate their competitors in the market.[11] However, ordoliberalism does not necessarily prevent competitors from becoming dominant in the market due to their better competing abilities arising from the competitive process, but it requires that competition law make these dominant firms act as if they did not have such power and that the market is competitive.[12]

Finally, ordoliberalism strives for social justice in competition in the form of fairness by ensuring that competitors in the market have equal opportunities.[13] This is reached by competition law, which prohibits anticompetitive private economic power, such as cartels, from interfering with the competitive functioning of the market.[14]

Ordoliberalism is one of the most influential ideologies of EU competition law and policy. It did not only assist with framing both the German and EU competition law regimes, but it continues to influence the German economy and some individual Member States and via them also the current policy of the EU.[15]

Treaties: From Common Market to Internal Market

The first treaty, which set the basis for the later EU, was the Treaty of Rome of 1957. However, before the Treaty of Rome was concluded, France, Germany, Italy, Belgium, the Netherlands and Luxembourg signed the Treaty Establishing the European Coal and Steel Community (the ECSC Treaty) in 1951, with economic integration in the relevant sectors as its main objective. Already the ECSC Treaty recognized and highlighted rivalry, a large part of the competitive process, as necessary

---

[10] See, e.g., Note 8, Eucken, 'What Kind of Social System?' 41–3.
[11] Note 8, Eucken, *The Foundations of Economics*, 269–70; Note 8, Gerber, 43, 49–50.
[12] Note 8, Gerber, 52.
[13] Franz Böhm, 'Rule of Law in a Market Economy' in *Germany's Social Market Economy*, 51–4; Note 8, Gerber, 38.
[14] Note 8, Gerber, 37–8.
[15] See, Sebastian Dullien and Ulrike Guérot, 'The long shadow of ordoliberalism: Germany's approach to the euro crisis' (European Council on Foreign Relations, 2012) <http://www.ecfr.eu/page/-/ECFR49_GERMANY_BRIEF.pdf> accessed 18 June 2015.

for a strong European economy[16] and set competition rules in Articles 65–66. The Treaty expired in 2002.

The Treaty of Rome from 1957 constituted the EEC.[17] The main objective of the EEC was to establish a common market, which required a supranational, decision-making framework. The creation of the common market by the EEC contained a number of elements. The basic element consisted of establishing a customs union with a common external tariff. Other elements were the free movement of goods, persons, services and capital, including the harmonizing of relevant national laws; competition law and policy; the regulation of state intervention in the economy, such as state aids; and others.[18]

The existence of the EEC, therefore, was based on economic integration and possessed the main objective of establishing a common market with undistorted competition and an efficient use of resources.[19] Integration not only had an economic dimension based on free trade, but also a political dimension that meant Member States made decisions collectively. This is confirmed by the principles of supremacy and the direct effect of EEC law, and by provisions on common rules and policies.[20]

Competition law then was an essential element for economic integration, assisting the EEC with establishing and maintaining a common market. The integration of the EEC, later the EC and the EU, is absolutely the essential objective of EU competition law that distinguishes the EU competition law regime from other regimes, including the US antitrust law regime.

---

[16] Treaty Establishing the European Coal and Steel Community (adopted 18 April 1951, entered into force 23 July 1952) 261 UNTS 140 (The ECSC Treaty) Preamble; Note 2, Goyder and others, 28–30.

[17] See Treaty of Rome art. 2.

[18] See Treaty of Rome arts 2, 3; for further discussion see Note 2, Chalmers and others, 12–13.

[19] See Treaty of Rome arts 2, 8; Valentine Korah, *Guide to Competition* (9th edn, Hart Publishing 2007) 2; Alison Jones and Brenda Sufrin, *EU Competition Law: Text, Cases, and Materials*, (5th edn, Oxford University Press 2014) 1–18; Dimitri Barounos, David F Hall and James J Rayner, *EEC Antitrust Law, Principles and Practice* (Butterworths 1975) 1.

[20] See Case 26/62 *Van Gend en Loos v. Nederlandse Administratie der Belastingen* [1963] ECR 95 ('*Van Gend*') (see 'II – the first question'); Case 6/64 *Costa v. ENEL* [1964] ECR 585; Note 3, Gerber, 347–8; Rosita B. Bouterse, *Competition and Integration – What Goals Count?: EEC Competition Law and Goals of Industrial, Monetary, and Cultural Policy* (Kluwer Law and Taxation Publishers 1994) 3–4.

The Preamble of the Treaty of Rome stresses the importance of 'steady expansion, balanced trade and fair competition'. The Community policies were set out in Articles 2, 3, 4 of the Treaty of Rome, which also referred to the principle of free competition. Both EEC concepts of free and fair competition play an important role in the ideology stream of ordoliberalism.

The Treaty of Rome introduced stable provisions on competition law, with the substantive law being enacted in Articles 85 and 86. The rules on EEC competition law started being enforced later, in 1962, when the Commission was empowered as the central executive enforcer of the EEC competition rules.[21] The European Court of Justice, later (in the Lisbon Treaty) renamed the Court of Justice of the European Union (CJEU)[22] was already established in the ECSC Treaty in Paris in 1951 and since the Treaty of Rome has become part of the judicial system of the EEC as, among others, a judicial-review body for competition law.[23]

In the second half of the 1980s, the Community shifted its focus from market integration to policy integration. This new process began with the 'White Paper Completing the Internal Market' in 1985.[24] The White Paper was a tool for establishing an internal market and was followed by the Single European Act in 1986,[25] which identified its main aim in Article 13 as the establishment of the internal market by the end of 1992. The internal market is defined in Article 13 as an area without boundaries that includes the free movement of goods.[26] The aim included a reformation of EEC institutions as well as the establishment of a legal basis for other policies.[27]

The aims of the Single European Act resulted in the Treaty on European Union, ratified in 1993.[28] The Treaty established the European Union, with the new Community's competencies including education, environment, consumer protection, public health, industry and culture. The previous name, 'the European Economic Community', changed to

---

[21] Council Regulation (EEC) 17/62 implementing Articles 85 and 86 of the Treaty [1959] OJ Spec Ed 87.
[22] Originally, 'The European Court of Justice'.
[23] Treaty of Rome art. 164.
[24] Commission, 'White Paper on completing the internal market from the Commission to the European Council', COM (85) 310 final; see Note 20, Bouterse, 8.
[25] Single European Act [1987] OJ L169/29.
[26] Treaty of Rome (consolidated) art. 8a.
[27] See the provisions of Note 25, Single European Act.
[28] Treaty on the European Union – Final Act [1992] OJ C191/29.

'the European Community'.[29] Four years later, in 1997, the Treaty of Amsterdam[30] followed. Besides the aim of the establishment of the single market, this treaty had two additional main objectives: establishing an economic and monetary union and implementing common policies or activities. While the objective of a harmonious, balanced and sustained development of economic activities remained,[31] the objectives of a continuous and balanced expansion and an increase in stability were shifted to a high level of employment and social protection, equality between the sexes, sustainable and non-inflationary growth, a convergence of economic performance and, most importantly for the purposes of this book, a high degree of competitiveness.[32]

In 2000, the European Parliament, the Council and the Commission proclaimed the Charter of Fundamental Rights of the European Union.[33] The Charter included the right to a fair trial and the right of defence on matters of privacy, which were also applicable to competition law;[34] however, it had no legal power. In 2001, the Nice Treaty,[35] amending the founding treaties, was introduced, and, finally, in December 2009, the Treaty of Lisbon[36] came into force. The Lisbon Treaty merged the European Community and its pillars into the European Union and recast the existing treaties into two treaties, the Treaty on the European Union (TEU) and the Treaty on the Functioning of the European Union (TFEU). The Lisbon Treaty proclaimed the Charter of Fundamental Rights of the

---

[29] Further see: Consolidated version of the Treaty on European Union (Maastricht Treaty) [2012] OJ C326/13; Note 2, Chalmers and others, 23–5; Note 19, Korah, 2–3; Vivien Rose and David Bailey (eds), *Bellamy and Child: European Union Law of Competition* (7th edn, Oxford University Press 2013) 4–5; Note 20, Bouterse, 9–10.

[30] Treaty of Amsterdam amending the Treaty on European Union, the Treaties establishing the European Communities and certain related acts [1997] OJ C340/01.

[31] Ibid., arts 1.5, 2.2.

[32] Ibid., arts 1.5, 2.2, 2.3, 2.19, 2.22; Also see other objectives as introduced in arts 1.2, 1.10, 2.2, 2.4, 2.17, 2.22, 2.34.

[33] Charter of Fundamental Rights of the European Union [2000] OJ C364/1; currently [2012] OJ C 326/391, as of June 2015.

[34] Ibid., arts 47–48.

[35] Treaty of Nice amending the Treaty on European Union, the Treaties establishing the European Communities and certain related acts, [2001] OJ C80/1.

[36] Treaty of Lisbon amending the Treaty on European Union and the Treaty Establishing the European Community [2007] OJ C306/1.

European Union legally binding in Article 1 of the Treaty on the European Union.

With the Lisbon Treaty, the initial process of creating an internal market was finalized. The existence of the internal market reflects that the EU market had become even more integrated involving further objectives of the EU, including a common international relations policy.[37] The characteristics of the EU internal market are reflected in Article 3 of the TEU, which set out the objectives of the EU. It provides in Article 3(3) that the EU should establish an internal market, which, among other aims, should be based on 'a highly competitive social market economy'. Its Protocol No 27 on the internal market and competition further elaborates this part of Article 3(3) stating 'that the internal market as set out in Article 3 of the Treaty on European Union includes a system ensuring that competition is not distorted'. Regulation No 1/2003[38] is the main instrument on the enforcement of EU competition law and it thus serves the purpose of ensuring that competition is not distorted.

Also, the TFEU sets the objectives for EU competition law in accordance with the internal market. Article 3(1)(b) TFEU ensures the exclusive competence of the EU to establish competition rules necessary for the functioning of the internal market and Article 120 TFEU requires that the EU and Member States act in accordance with the 'principle of an open market economy with free competition'.

Articles on Competition Law after the Lisbon Treaty

Like the Sherman Act in the US, articles dealing with EU competition law are brief and its substantive law is divided into two major provisions. The substantive EU competition–antitrust rules can be found, as of 2011,

---

[37] Article 3 of the Treaty of the European Union, which repealed art. 2 of the Treaty Establishing the European Union, discussed the objectives of the EU. It is obvious that the TFEU broadened its policies as it included six paragraphs where the old Article had only one. Additionally, in its opening paragraph it states that '[t]he Union's aim is to promote peace, its values and the well-being of its peoples'. Among others, it also includes an international relations policy in Para 5, art. 3(2) and protects cultural and linguistic diversity, as discussed in art. 3(3); art. 4(2), Consolidated version of the Treaty on the Functioning of the European Union [2012] OJ C326/47 (TFEU).

[38] Council Regulation (EC) 1/2003 of 16 December 2002 on the implementation of the rules on competition laid down in Articles 81 and 82 of the Treaty [2003] OJ L1/1.

in Articles 101 and 102 TFEU.[39] These articles were first enacted as Articles 85 and 86 of the Treaty of Rome in 1957, and then recast as Articles 81 and 82 in the Treaty Establishing the European Community as renumbered by the Treaty of Amsterdam.[40] For the sake of simplicity and consistency, I employ the current terminology as applied in the TFEU and the TEU throughout the rest of this book.

Article 101 is the principal provision dealing with RPM and VTR. It prohibits forms of multilateral/bilateral practices in the form of 'agreements', 'concerted practices' and 'decisions by associations of undertakings', which by their effect or object restrict competition in the EU market. As in the US, EU courts do not always differentiate between agreements and concerted practices but instead refer to agreements.[41]

Article 101 is divided into three parts. The first part, Article 101(1), sets the conditions for prohibition. The second part, Article 101(2), states that such practices are void. The third part, Article 101(3), provides an exemption from the prohibition in the form of competitive benefits which overweigh the anticompetitive restriction of the practices prohibited under Article 101(1).

Therefore, RPM and VTR, as for any other prohibited multilateral/bilateral conduct, are subject to two steps of examination under Article 101 TFEU. First, it must be decided whether a particular vertical restriction takes the form of a multilateral conduct (an agreement, concerted practice or decision of an association), and has as its object or effect the prevention, restriction or distortion of competition within the EU, thus affecting trade between Member States. If the answer is yes, then it must be decided whether this restriction might benefit from an exemption under Article 101(3).

Article 102 is a brief provision which includes primarily unilateral but also multilateral restrictions in the form of an abuse of a dominant position which affects the EU market. Both forms of anticompetitive practices, as set out in Articles 101 and 102, may influence the behavior of suppliers and distributors. For instance, a dominant undertaking can abuse its position towards the distributors, exemplified by the action of

---

[39] Other provisions are arts 103–109, which include provisions on state aid and procedural provisions.

[40] The term 'the common market' was replaced with the term 'the internal market' in arts 101 and 102 of Note 37, TFEU.

[41] See, e.g., Joined Cases C-2/01 P and C-3/01 P *Bundesverband der Arzneimittel-Importeure EC and Commission v. Bayer AG* [2004] ECR I-00023 ('*Bayer* appeal'); Case T-41/96, *Bayer v. Commission* [2000] ECR II-3383 ('*Bayer*').

tying. Although Article 102 has never been used with respect to RPM and VTR by the European Commission, theoretically, it is possible in situations when such restraints are forced upon the other party by an undertaking with a dominant position in the market.

III. ECONOMIC INTEGRATION (1950s–BEGINNING OF 1970s)

The economies of Member States were under reconstruction at the beginning of the existence of the EU (originally, EEC) in the era after WW2. Their aim was to secure political and economic stability and economic growth.[42] Indeed, the period of European integration in the form of the European Coal and Steel Community and later, since 1957, the EEC, assisted Europe and European firms to become stronger and more competitive with a better perspective to increase European productivity and, thus, stability.[43]

Therefore, even the goals of the EEC reflected this. In that respect, EU competition law (at that time, EEC competition law) was aimed at two EEC objectives. The first goal was to ensure competitiveness in the EEC market. This was based on the idea that the protection of competition positively interferes with free trade, including economic integration, and assists in providing a self-regulating economic system, ensuring the most efficient use of resources. The second goal of EEC competition law was to aid in the creation and maintenance of the common market to ensure that undertakings did not undermine the prohibitions on state barriers by setting private market barriers, such as VTR. Therefore, both free movement and competition law created the essential bases for the economic integration of the EEC (later, EU). Vice versa, the creation and existence of the common market were essential for the creation of fair and efficient competition and its competition law provisions.[44] The objective of the creation of the common market prevailed from the beginning. For example, the vertical restraint case of *Consten and Grundig*[45] in 1966

---

[42] Note 3, Gerber, 168.
[43] Note 2, Goyder and others, 31–2.
[44] Ibid., 34–5; Note 20, Bouterse, 5; Note 3, Gerber, 334–5; Note 19, Barounos, 2–3.
[45] Joined Cases 56/64 and 58/64 *Établissements Consten S.à.R.L. and Grundig-Verkaufs-GmbH v. Commission of the European Economic Community*, [1966] ECR 299 ('*Consten and Grundig*').

highlighted that the objective of EEC competition law was single/common market integration.[46]

At the beginning of the existence of the EEC, Member States had to deal with the question of the enforceability of the competition law provisions of the Rome Treaty. On one hand, there was the ideology of German ordoliberalism, with a strict legal form of competition law supported by the Netherlands. On the other hand, the French administrative-political approach supported by Italy had a tendency to interpret EEC competition law, Articles 101 and 102 TFEU, as political and policy terms rather than enforceable law. In the end, the legal approach voice was stronger than the administrative-political one and thus competition law became an essential and enforceable part of the EEC and European integration.[47]

At the beginning of the EEC competition law's existence, both the EU (originally, EEC) and national authorities applied the EEC competition rules. However, the CJEU played a centralized judicial role, minimizing the different influences of Member States.[48] This enforcement procedure changed with the creation of Regulation 17 in the 1960s,[49] which introduced a notification system with centralized enforcement and put the policy-making power in the hands of the European Commission. The notification system meant that agreements infringing Article 101(1) could be exempted under Article 101(3) if they were notified. To obtain an exemption, undertakings could either follow the provisions of a particular block exemption regulation, a system that is still available for undertakings, or, undertakings could notify the Commission and that way apply for an individual exemption. This second option was abolished by Council Regulation 1/2003,[50] effective 1 May 2004.

The notification system overburdened undertakings, as well as the Commission and the process was criticized with respect to vertical

---

[46] Ibid., 340.

[47] See, e.g., Note 20, *Van Gend*; Note 3, Gerber, 343–7.

[48] Treaty of Rome arts 87, 88, 89; for further discussion see Note 3, Gerber, 349–53.

[49] Note 21, Council Regulation (EEC) 17/62.

[50] Note 38; also other regulations characterized by the modernization process and the economic approach were adopted in this era. For instance, Commission Regulation (EC) 772/2004 of 27 April 2004 on the application of Article 81(3) of the Treaty to categories of technology transfer agreements [2004] OJ L123/11; Commission Regulation (EC) 2658/2000 of 29 November 2000 on the application of Article 81(3) of the Treaty to categories of specialisation agreements [2000] OJ L304/3; Commission Regulation (EC) 2659/2000 of 29 November 2000 on the application of Article 81(3) of the Treaty to

agreements, among others.[51] For instance, Hawk pointed out that the notification system was inconsistent with the CJEU's judgments and Article 101(1) was overly and broadly applied. It brought about and maintained legal uncertainty, legal formalism and analysis by categories rather than an economic approach.[52]

Due to the objective of the integration of Europe, EEC competition law emphasized vertical relationships in comparison with the traditional horizontal agreement focus. Indeed, some of the first cases, *Grosfillex*,[53] *Consten and Grundig* and *Minière v. Maschinenbau*,[54] dealt with the restriction of parallel imports and exports in the form of VTR. This was due to the fact that vertical restraints were the most obvious relationships in trans-border trade used between manufacturers and their distributors to separate and protect national markets from parallel imports and to create other boundaries which hindered the main objective of the Community: the creation of a single market.[55]

In the first vertical restraint case of *Grosfillex*, the Commission found that an agreement, where a distributor had obtained an exclusive territory outside the common market, did not violate EEC competition law as the product had been re-exported to the common market. In the first CJEU case on vertical restraints, *Consten and Grundig*, the Court applied the objective of market integration. This case provided a sound basis for future policy in this area of competition law focusing on the maximum protection of a single market.[56]

---

categories of research and development agreements [2000] OJ L304/7; Commission Notice (EC) 2001/C3/02 Guidelines on research and development agreements [2001] OJ C3/2.

[51] David Deacon, 'Vertical Restraints under EC Competition Law: New Directions' [1995] *Fordham Corporate Law Institute* 307; Barry E Hawk, 'System Failure: Vertical Restraints and EC Competition Law' [1995] 32 CMLR 973.

[52] Ibid., Hawk, 974–86; also see Alison Jones, 'Completion of the Revolution in Antitrust Doctrine on Restricted Distribution: *Leegin* and Its Implications for EC Competition Law' (2008) 53(4) *Antitrust Bulletin* 903, 935–7.

[53] *Grosfillex Sàrl (Re the agreement of)* (Case (IV/A.00061) Commission Decision 64/233/CEE, [1964] OJ L64/915.

[54] Case 56/65 *Société La Technique Minière v. Maschinenbau Ulm GmbH* [1966] ECR 235 ('*Minière*').

[55] Note 45, *Consten and Grundig* 343, 349; Commission, 'Green Paper on Vertical Restraints in EC Competition Policy' COM (1996) 721 final, i; Note 52, Jones, 936; Note 3, Gerber, 354–5.

[56] See also Note 2, Goyder and others, 55.

Consten and Grundig dealt with exclusive territories as part of exclusive distribution based on trademarks. The CJEU agreed that maintaining the exclusive territory and preventing parallel imports of the product protected by its trademark had infringed Article 101 TFEU. This case was the first one that assisted the Commission in establishing a policy on vertical restraints.[57] Furthermore, not just trademarks but also the use of patents to protect national markets and prevent parallel imports were found to be inconsistent with the Treaty of Rome by the Commission and this was confirmed by the CJEU in the case of *Parke-Davis v. Probel*.[58] However, the case of *Minière* held that an exclusive distribution agreement was not prohibited if it had been necessary for penetrating a new territory. This case also discussed a number of elements of Article 101 and introduced a test for the effect on EU trade (at that time, EEC trade) and the evaluation of restriction by object and effect.

Exclusive distribution systems were common in Europe[59] and cases involving exclusive distribution were typical for this era. Therefore, the Commission decided to introduce a block-exemption regulation on exclusive distribution in 1967.[60] An updated version was published in 1983.[61] This exemption regulation confirmed that exclusive distributions could have a positive impact on the market in the form of distribution improvements, international trade, promotion of products, stimulation of interbrand competition and effectiveness.[62] The concept of stimulating interbrand competition was, most likely, inspired by the Chicago and Post-Chicago Schools and the US antitrust policy of that time, which included an assumption that non-price vertical restraints enhanced interbrand competition.[63]

---

[57] Ibid., 55–6.

[58] See Case 24/67 *Parke-Davis v. Probel* [1968] ECR 55; Case 40/70, *Sirena v. Eda* [1971] ECR 69.

[59] Note 2, Green and others, 241.

[60] Commission Regulation (EEC) 67/67 of 22 March 1967 on the application of Article 85(3) of the Treaty to certain categories of exclusive dealing agreements [1967] OJ 57/849.

[61] Commission Regulation (EEC) 1983/83 of 22 June 1983 on the application of Article 85(3) of the Treaty to categories of exclusive distribution agreements [1983] OJ L173/1; Commission Regulation (EEC) 1984/83 of 22 June 1983 applying Article 85(3) to exclusive purchasing agreements [1983] OJ L173/7.

[62] Note 61, Commission Regulation 1983/83, [5], [6].

[63] See Chapter 3.

VTR: *Consten and Grundig*:[64] Absolute Territorial Protection

In this case, the CJEU clarified the application of Article 101 to vertical agreements. It held that neither Article 101 TFEU nor Article 102 TFEU excluded infringements in the form of vertical conduct as the Treaty did not make any distinction between horizontal and vertical conduct. Therefore, similarly, the Court or any other body applying the Treaty, could not make a distinction and exclude conduct which is not excluded in the Treaty.[65] However, Article 101 TFEU does not apply to conduct of one undertaking.[66]

The facts of the case involved Grundig, a German manufacturer of radios, tape recorders, dictaphones and televisions, who protected their products with a trademark. Grundig appointed Consten as an exclusive distributor for France. They agreed, among other things, that Consten would be the exclusive distributor for France, selling only Grundig products, and that Grundig would not sell their products in France and would prevent their other distributors from distributing there also. The Commission found that the applicants had created absolute territorial protection which had restricted trade between the Member States and infringed Article 101.[67] The CJEU confirmed that it was obvious from the agreement that the aim of some of the clauses was to create absolute territorial protection.[68]

This situation would qualify under US terminology as both exclusive dealership and exclusive dealing and thus it restricted both intrabrand and interbrand competition. Interbrand competition was restricted because Consten was not allowed to distribute products other than the ones from Grundig. Such a form of restriction creates an absolute vertical territorial restriction limiting both parallel imports and exports.

In its judgment, the CJEU evaluated the application of all parts of Article 101: 101(1), 101(2) and 101(3).

Article 101(1): restriction
The Commission found the parts of the agreement between Consten and Grundig which established the absolute vertical territorial restriction to be in violation of Article 101. The Court agreed with the Commission and stated that it was obvious from the agreement that the aim of some of

---

[64] Note 45, Consten and Grundig.
[65] Ibid., 339.
[66] Ibid., 340.
[67] Ibid., 346.
[68] Ibid., 344.

the clauses was to create absolute territorial protection, which was thus an infringement of Article 101 TFEU.[69]

The applicants, Grundig and Consten, supported by the German government, presented three arguments. First, that it was not proven that trade would have been greater without the existence of the agreement in question. Second, that Article 101 was aimed at interbrand and not intrabrand competition. Third, that the exclusive distribution arose from the protection of a trademark.

In connection with the applicants' first argument, that the Commission had not proven that trade would have been greater without the existence of the agreement concerned, the Commission indicated that trade could have been greater immediately after Consten started to distribute new products, Grundig products, in France. However, the Commission argued that once trade had been established in France, the agreement had restricted trade between the Member States primarily because it had restricted parallel exports from and imports into France. The Commission explained that the test was based on the constitution of 'a threat, direct or indirect, actual or potential, to freedom of trade between the Member States in a manner which might harm the attainment of the objectives of a single market between the states'.[70]

The CJEU agreed with the Commission, maintaining that it did not matter whether the agreement increased trade as long as the threat to restrict trade or its actual restriction existed. In this case, trade was restricted by prohibiting Consten from exporting and by establishing Consten as the only distributor for the French market.[71]

The Court also refused the applicants' second claim, that the test should have been aimed at interbrand competition and that the agreement had increased interbrand competition. The Court's ruling established that Article 101 protected both intrabrand and interbrand competition without prioritizing one form of competition over the other. The CJEU explained that if intrabrand competition was restricted, the effect on interbrand competition did not have to be examined. It also stated that if the restrictive object was proven, the effect did not have to be analyzed.[72]

By ruling that it was enough to prove a threat to or object in the restriction of competition under Article 101(1) and that restrictions of intrabrand competition were also not allowed, the Court sent a clear message that trade between Member States must be free from any

---

[69] Ibid.
[70] Ibid., 341.
[71] Ibid.
[72] Ibid., 342.

anticompetitive restrictions. Indeed, in its judgment, the Court applied the main objective of the Treaty of Rome, creating common trade without barriers, explaining that the Treaty could not allow certain undertakings to create barriers to trade between Member States.[73]

With regard to the applicants' claim based on the protection of the trademark, the Court stated that it was obvious from the agreement that the aim of some of the clauses was to create absolute territorial protection[74] (and not to prevent an infringement of the trademark). The Court then explained that it was not the trademark itself but the agreement with Grundig that had affected trade.[75] Therefore, it was the agreement, or clauses of the agreement, and not the trademark that restricted competition.

This issue was also discussed and the boundaries between IP rights and illegal vertical restraints were established in the first US cases on RPM, which involved an assessment based on the common law and the right of ownership. The Supreme Court strictly differentiated between statutory IP rights, such as patents and copyrights, where the manufacturer, the owner of the IP rights, was free to set the conditions for retail sales. This was in contrast to non-statutory IP rights, such as trade secrets, where the manufacturer was not excepted and could not restrict trade.[76] Similar to the case of *Consten and Grundig*, where the Court stated that the trademark did not entitle the parties to restrict competition in certain forms, such as absolute territorial restriction, the US Supreme Court explained that the existence of a trade secret did not restrict trade as such, but it allowed for the protection of the secret manufacturing process.[77]

Article 101(2)

The Court of Justice confirmed that Article 101(2) applied only to the parts of the agreement which restricted competition if they were able to be separated from the agreement itself. In this case, only the restrictive clauses of the agreement should have been annulled under Article 101(2).[78]

---

[73] Ibid., 340.
[74] Ibid., 344.
[75] Ibid., 345.
[76] *Dr. Miles Medical Co. v. John D. Park and Sons* 220 U.S. 373 (1911) 401–2 ('*Dr. Miles*'); *John D. Park & Sons Company v. Samuel B. Hartman*, 153 Fed. Rep. 24 (6th Circuit 1907), at 39 ('*Park & Sons*').
[77] Ibid., *Dr. Miles*, 400–403; *Park & Sons*, 29
[78] Note 45, *Consten and Grundig*, 344.

Article 101(3): balancing test

In *Consten and Grundig*, the CJEU introduced an essential test for Article 101(3), which, with some later modifications, still applies. The test has two parts. It states that first, the procompetitive improvements introduced by the restriction in question must show *appreciable objective advantages* which sufficiently compensate for any anticompetitive effects caused by the restriction.[79] Second, the restriction concerned must be *necessary* for such procompetitive improvements in the production and distribution of the goods by evaluating the effectiveness of any possible justifications in order to grant an exemption based on Article 101(3).[80]

The Court explained that, although the applicants were responsible for introducing the arguments for the application of the exemption under Article 101(3), the Commission must evaluate 'economic matters'[81] and is obliged under the wording of Article 101(3) to examine the available evidence in order to consider the fulfilment of Article 101(3). The applicants introduced three forms of justifications, all of which were refused by the Commission and the CJEU.

First, the applicant claimed that absolute territorial protection assisted Consten's *ability to plan her business in advance*. The Court stated that risks, including parallel imports, were commonplace in competition and in all commercial activities and, therefore, this was not a reasonable justification under Article 101(3).[82]

Second, the applicant complained that the Commission had not considered whether it would have been possible to provide guarantees, such as the protection of the Grundig name and after-sales services, without introducing absolute territories in the market. They claimed that Consten would have had to refuse to provide after-sales services, in particular the repair of the machines which would have been imported by Consten's competitors, if parallel imports had existed. This would be against consumer interests.[83] However, the Court disagreed, stating that consumers could only demand the aforementioned services from the company from which they purchased their products. Moreover, the Court found that the main competitor of Consten also offered after-sale

---

[79] Ibid., 348.
[80] Ibid.
[81] Ibid., 347.
[82] Ibid., 348. This offers an explanation for a motivation of the manufacturer to introduce VTR, and potentially RPM, as further elaborated in Chapter 5.
[83] Note 45, *Consten and Grundig*, 349.

services; therefore, the non-existence of absolute territorial restraints would not have led to such a situation.[84]

Finally, the applicants claimed that the Commission had not considered the necessity of the absolute territorial protection to penetrate the market, including bearing the risks of penetrating a market. The Court found this justification unfounded because this statement was not disputed by the defendant.[85] Although the Court did not examine this justification, the judgment indicated that the Commission considered the penetrating argument, as the Commission claimed that the practice in question had been illegal only after trade had been established in France.[86]

VTR: *Minière v. Maschinenbau*:[87] Object or Effect

Like *Consten and Grundig*, this preliminary ruling case concerned a vertical agreement between a German manufacturer and a French distributor, which granted an exclusive right of sale for France. However, unlike in *Consten and Grundig*, the agreement allowed the distributor to freely re-export the goods and distributors from other Member States, who were free to sell to the market concerned: the French market. Dealers and consumers were allowed to buy from wherever and whomever they wished, including parallel importers. Moreover, if the manufacturer had agreed, the distributor concerned would have been allowed to distribute the products of the manufacturer's competitor.[88] Thus, this agreement did not create an absolute vertical territorial restriction and did not absolutely restrict imports and exports.

The CJEU interpreted Article 101 in order to answer the preliminary questions on the prohibition of this conduct, especially in the form of the restriction in effect, and the potential for justification under Article 101(3) of such conduct. In particular, the CJEU discussed a number of important elements of Article 101, including a potential justification under Article 101(3) in the form of penetrating the market and an annulment of the agreement under Article 101(2). Significantly, this case discussed the restriction of object or effect and the effects on trade between Member States under Article 101(1), introducing the first and still applicable tests for both of these elements.

---

[84] Ibid.
[85] Ibid.
[86] Ibid., 341.
[87] Note 54, *Minière*.
[88] Ibid.

With regard to Article 101(2), the Court confirmed the ruling in *Grundig & Consten* when it stated that only the clauses which are illegal under Article 101(1) are nullified. In the situation where these clauses are not separable from the agreement itself, the entire agreement is nullified.[89]

In contrast to *Consten and Grundig*, where the CJEU found the applicants' justification of penetrating the market unfounded and thus did not examine this claim, in *Minière*, the Court discussed penetrating the market under Article 101(3) as a possible justification. It went as far as to state that competition was not restricted if the agreement was necessary to penetrate the market.[90]

In connection with Article 101(1), the CJEU discussed two essential elements of this provision: the effects on trade between Member States and the restriction of competition in object or effect, setting tests for each of these elements. First, in response to the preliminary question of this case, the Court held that the agreement in question on VTR 'granting an exclusive right of sale' could satisfy the conditions of notification and could possibly be prohibited under Article 101.[91]

The CJEU evaluated the meaning of the connotation of Article 101(1) of the effects on trade between Member States. It explained that this meant that only the agreements, which were 'incompatible with the common market',[92] were subject to Article 101 and it introduced a test under which it should be determined whether this condition of Article 101(1) was fulfilled. The test interprets the meaning broadly covering any direct or indirect, actual or potential effect and is as follows:

> [I]t must be possible to foresee with a sufficient degree of probability on the basis of a set objective factors of law or of fact that the agreement in question may have an influence, direct or indirect, actual or potential, on the pattern of trade between the Member States.[93]

The Court then discussed the connotation of Article 101(1) 'object or effect the prevention, restriction or distortion of competition within the common market' and held that it involves alternative and not cumulative

---

[89] Ibid., 250.
[90] Ibid., 250.
[91] Ibid., 248.
[92] Ibid., 249.
[93] Ibid.

requirements. The Court listed aspects which should be considered in deciding whether the agreement restricted competition either in object or in effect:

> the nature and quantity, limited or otherwise, of the products covered by the agreement, the position and importance of the grantor and the concessionaire on the market for the product concerned, the isolated nature of the disputed agreement or, alternatively, the position in the series of agreements, the severity of the clauses intended to protect the exclusive dealership or, alternatively, the opportunities allowed for other commercial competitors in the same products by way of parallel re-exportation and importation.[94]

Then, the CJEU explained how to determine the restrictive effect, dividing this analysis into two steps. First, the purpose of the agreement and/or some clauses in the agreement must be analyzed 'in the economic context'.[95] If this does not reveal the effect, the consequences of these clauses must then be considered. It must be shown that 'the competition has in fact been prevented or restricted or distorted to an appreciable extent'.[96]

IV. OVERCOMING CRISIS AND FURTHER INTEGRATION (1970s–1980s)

This era started with an international economic crisis, which began after the first oil shock in 1973. The crisis led to widespread inflation and unemployment. Economic growth in Europe stopped for the first time since the end of WW2. The slow economic growth was further exacerbated by imports from Japan. Indeed, Japanese firms began to emerge as major competitors. The European economic policy of the time reflected this situation. The response to the crisis was to strengthen and move forward with the integration process.[97] This appeared to be even more essential as, at the beginning of the 1980s, there was almost no positive news regarding the achievement of Community goals.[98] The Community thus focused on market integration with the view of shifting this further, including policy integration. This is reflected in the 'White Paper

---

[94] Ibid., 250.
[95] Ibid., 249.
[96] Ibid.
[97] Note 2, Chalmers and others, 18–19; Note 3, Gerber, 168–9, 359.
[98] Ibid., Chalmers and others, 19–20; Ibid., Gerber, 359.

Completing the Internal Market' in 1985,[99] which was followed by the Single European Act in 1986.[100]

At the end of the 1980s, the Community established a new court, the General Court (originally, the Court of First Instance),[101] to judge cases on competition and employment. This Court began operation in 1989, and, since then, in competition law, it has operated as a court of first instance, with the CJEU being the court of appeal (second instance).

In agreement with the integration focus of the Community, the CJEU also continued to emphasize the importance of the common market in EU competition law (at that time, EEC competition law) in the cases of *Metro v. Commission*[102] and *Polydor Ltd et al. v. Harlequin Record Shops Ltd et al.*,[103] where the CJEU repeated that one of the objectives of the Treaty of Rome was the creation of a single market with similar conditions to a unified domestic market. The significance of this objective is also obvious in the vertical restraint case of *Nungesser & Eisele*.[104]

To overcome the economic crisis, the CJEU maintained its objective of 'the momentum of integration' relying primarily on strengthening its power and its competition law regime. This took a number of forms. For instance, it began to apply Article 102 TFEU to mergers. It also started to demand more sufficient evidence. Similarly, the Commission became more active in competition law and policy in order to protect European national economies, primarily by strengthening the competitiveness of European undertakings. In the 1980s, the Commission began to focus on the efficiency of competition. Vertical restraints remained at the center of competition policy; however, at the end of the 1980s, the Commission increased its focus on horizontal agreements.[105]

In this era, the Commission and the CJEU broadened their vertical cases to include other forms of vertical restraints and distribution, such as RPM, franchising systems and selective distribution systems. In the

---

[99] Note 24, Commission, 'internal market'; Note 20, Bouterse, 8.

[100] Note 25, Single European Act.

[101] Council Decision 88/591/ECSC/EEC of 24 October 1988 establishing a Court of First Instance of the European Communities [1988] OJ L319/1.

[102] Case 26/76 *Metro SB-Großmärkte GmbH & Co. KG v. Commission of the EC* [1977] ECR 1875, [1978] 2 CMLR 1 ('*Metro SB*') [20].

[103] Case 270/80 *Polydor Ltd et al. v. Harlequin Record Shops Ltd et al.* [1982] ECR 329, [16].

[104] Case 258/78 *LC Nungesser KG and Kurt Eisele v. Commission of the European Communities* [1982] ECR 2015 ('*LC Nungesser*') [47]–[58].

[105] Note 2, Green and others, 203–4; Note 3, Gerber, 364–8, 384; compare with Chapter 4 'Development of the US Law of Vertical Territorial and Price Restraints'.

1980s, based on these vertical cases, the Commission issued new regulations, including three vertical restraint block exemptions: Regulation on Exclusive Distribution Agreements 1983/83,[106] Regulation on Exclusive Purchasing Agreements 1984/83[107] (including special provisions on beer supply and petrol agreements) and Regulation on Franchising Agreements 4087/88.[108] The regulations included elements of economic arguments influenced by the US Chicago and Post-Chicago Schools. For instance, the Regulation on exclusive distribution referred to the positive impacts of exclusive distribution on the market, including reference to the stimulation of interbrand competition and its effectiveness.[109]

Forms of vertical restrictions and distribution systems analyzed by the CJEU for the first time include RPM, selective distribution systems and franchising. Franchising was introduced into Europe in the 1960s after a long existence in the US.[110] The case of *Pronuptia*[111] set the rules for franchising systems. Unlike US cases on vertical restraints in antitrust law, where the Federal Courts applied the term 'franchising' without defining its meaning and without strict differentiation between franchising and non-franchising systems,[112] the CJEU clearly explained the term 'franchising', which was a justified distribution method under EU competition law.[113]

In the distribution franchising system, a franchisee does not have to invest her own capital in an already-existing successful business name and business method.[114] On one hand, the franchisor must disclose his know-how to the franchisee and provide assistance so that the franchisee can start and maintain her business and bear any risks associated with the business. On the other hand, any provision which *necessarily* controls the maintenance of the identity and reputation of the franchisor's business

---

[106]   [1988] OJ L173/1.
[107]   [1983] OJ L173/5.
[108]   [1988] OJ L359/46.
[109]   Note 61, Commission Regulation 1983/83, [5], [6].
[110]   Note 19, Korah, 318.
[111]   Case 161/84 *Pronuptia de Paris GmbH v. Pronuptia de Paris Ismgard Schillgalis* [1986] ECR 353; [1986] 1 CMLR 414 ('*Pronuptia*').
[112]   See *Murphy v. Business Cards Tomorrow, Inc*, 854 F.2d 1202, 1204 (9th Circuit 1986) ('*Business Cards Tomorrow*'); *Continental TV Inc v. GTE Sylvania Inc*, 433 U.S. 36, 49 (1977) ('*Sylvania*'); *United States v. Arnold, Schwinn & Co* 388 U.S. 365 (1967).
[113]   Also see Commission Notice (EC) 2010/C 130/01 Guidelines on Vertical Restraints [2010] OJ C130/1 ('Guidelines 2010'), [189]–[191].
[114]   Note 111, *Pronuptia*, [15].

and network, including the restriction on the transfer of a franchisee business to another person, decorating the shop according to franchisor's instructions and other promotional conditions, does not infringe Article 101(1).[115]

In *Pronuptia*, the CJEU confirmed that franchising systems did not generally restrict competition, with the exception of arrangements on restrictions of RPM and VTR, because RPM and VTR do not serve the purpose of protecting know-how and thus go beyond what is necessary.[116] However, this does not mean that RPM and VTR in a franchising system cannot be justified under Article 101(3), for instance, in a situation where it assists with penetrating the market.[117] Nevertheless, a franchisor or other suppliers are able to provide their distributors with price guidelines as this practice was generally allowed, unless it constituted RPM.[118]

Another case, *Metro*,[119] addressed agreements on selective distribution systems. The CJEU held that distributors should not be chosen according to the quantitative restrictions of distributors, rather they should be chosen according to 'objective non-discriminatory, qualitative criteria relating to the technical qualifications and the suitability of trading premises'.[120] As in the ruling in *Pronuptia*, the CJEU highlighted that price competition, in particular in the form of RPM, should never be eliminated. At the same time, it emphasized that price competition was not the only form of competition.[121]

In the case of *Schmidt*,[122] the CJEU further ruled that a manufacturer had no duty to supply all distributors who fulfil the objective criteria.[123] In the case of *AEG Telefunken*[124] in 1985, the CJEU confirmed that the

---

[115] Ibid., [16]–[18].
[116] Ibid., [23]–[24], [27].
[117] Ibid., [24].
[118] See Case 243/85 *SA Binon & Cie v. SA Agence et Messageries de la Presse* [1985] ECR 2015, [1985] 3 CMLR 800 ('*Binon*'); Note 111, *Pronuptia*; Note 102, *Metro SB*.
[119] Note 102, *Metro SB*.
[120] Ibid., [20].
[121] Ibid., [21]; see also Case 107/82, *AEG – Allgemeine Elektricitäts – Gesellschaft AEG – Telefunken AG v. Commission* [1983] ECR 3151, [1984] 3 CMLR 325, CMR 14018 ('*AEG*') [33].
[122] Case 210/81 *Demo-Studio Schmidt v. Commission*, [1983] ECR 3045, 3056, [1984] 1 CMLR 63, CMR 14009.
[123] Ibid.; Note 102, *Metro SB*, [12].
[124] Note 121, *AEG*.

system of selective distribution was legal if it was required for specialized handling and/or sophisticated products.[125]

The preliminary-ruling case of *Binon* dealt,[126] among other things, with vertical price restrictions. The CJEU maintained that any price fixing, including the fixing of newspaper and periodical prices, infringed Article 101(1) highlighting that Article 101(1) expressly prohibits price fixing.[127] However, taking into consideration the specific nature of the sale of newspapers and other periodicals, such a practice could be exempted under Article 101(3).[128]

In the case of *Nungesser and Eisele*,[129] the CJEU confirmed that absolute territorial protection was prohibited. At the same time, the CJEU discussed the justification under Article 101(3), confirming what had already been stated in *Minière* that exclusive licences were justifiable on the basis that investment was necessary to penetrate the market. Also, the case of single branding in *Delimitis*[130] clarified that vertical restrictions were allowed if difficulties in penetrating a new market existed.[131] In the case of *Remia*,[132] the CJEU ruled that territorial restrictions protecting goodwill did not infringe Article 101(1).

The Commission and CJEU started to face situations where restrictive conduct among parties was not part of explicit agreements. The decisions and judgments on this issue prompted the development of a doctrine which differentiated between, under Article 101(1), prohibited multilateral conduct and unilateral practices, which did not fulfil the condition of Article 101(1) of the existence of 'agreements', 'concerted practices' and 'decisions by associations of undertakings'.

They confirmed the existence of prohibited agreements in situations where suppliers announced restrictive policies and their distributors

---

[125] Note 121, *AEG*, [34]; also see *IHT Internationale Heiztechnik GmbH and Uwe Danzinger v. Ideal-Standard GmbH and Wabco Standard GmbH* [1994] ECR 2789; *Grohe's distribution system* (Case IV/30.299) Commission Decision 85/44/EEC [1895] OJ L19/17; *IBM Personal Computer* [1984] 2 CMLR 347.

[126] Note 118, *Binon*; Case C-31/80 *L'Oreal v. De Nieuwe AMCK* (1980) ECR 3775 [5], [16].

[127] Note 118, *Binon*, [44].

[128] Ibid., [46]–[47].

[129] Note 104, *LC Nungesser*.

[130] Case C-234/89 *Delimitis (Stergios) v. Henninger Bräu* [1991] ECR I-935, [1992] 5 CMLR 210, [1992] 2 CEC 530 (*'Henninger'*).

[131] Ibid., [13]–[27].

[132] Case 42/84 *Remia BV v. Commission* [1985] ECR 2545; [1987] 1 CMLR 1.

generally, and in various forms, followed.[133] For example, in the case of *Sandoz*,[134] the CJEU confirmed the Commission's decision that a supplier sending invoices with the wording 'export prohibited', which were then followed by non-exporting distributors, constituted an agreement that restricted competition. In another case, *Eco System/Peugeot*,[135] the Commission stated that it was not necessary to prove that written instructions sent by a manufacturer had been accepted by its distributors, as such instructions created an agreement within the meaning of Article 101 if acted upon.[136] However, later, at the beginning of the 1990s, the newly established General Court started to change this broad approach to the meaning of 'the agreement', requiring further evidence of an offer and an acceptance.[137]

VTR: *Nungesser and Eisele*:[138] The Principle of Proportionality and IP Rights

This case concerned exclusive dealership in the Federal Republic of Germany for the breeding of a new plant variety regulated by national

---

[133] CJEU cases: Case C-277/87 *Sandoz prodotti faraceuttici SpA v. Commission of the European Communities* [1990] ECR I-45; Case C-25-26/84 *Ford Werke AG v. Commission of the European Communities* [1985] 3 CMLR 528; Note 121, *AEG*; Case C-32/11 *Allianz Hungária Biztosíto and others v Gazdasági Versenyhivatal* [2013] ECR 1 ('*Allianz Hungária*') 36; Joined Cases 32/78, 36/78–82/78 *BMW Belgium SA v Commission of the European Communities* [1979] ECR 2435; Commission decisions: *Eco System / Peugeot* (Case IV/33.157) Commission Decision 92/154/EEC [1992] OJ L66/1; *Bayo-n-ox* (Case IV/32.026) Commission Decision 90/38/EEC [1990] OJ L21/71; *Konica* (Case IV/31.503) Commission Decision 88/172/EEC [1988] OJ L78/34; see Barbora Jedlickova, 'Boundaries between Unilateral and Multilateral Conducts in Vertical Restraints' (2008) 10 *ECLR* 600; Urs Wickihalder, 'The Distinction between an "Agreement" within the Meaning of Article 81(1) of the EC Treaty and Unilateral Conduct' [2006] 1 *European Competition Journal* 91; Peter Stig Jakobsen and Morten Broberg, 'The Concept of Agreement in Article 81 EC: On the Manufacturers' Right to Prevent Parallel Trade within the European Community' [2002] 23(3) *ECLR* 130.
[134] Ibid., *Sandoz*.
[135] [1992] OJ L66/1.
[136] Note 133, *Eco System / Peugeot*, [23].
[137] See next subchapter. For instance, Case T-43/92 *Dunlop Slazenger International Ltd v Commission of the European Communities* [1994] ECR II-441 [60]; for other cases, see below.
[138] Note 104, *LC Nungesser*.

law, which required its registration.[139] A French company assigned its breeders the rights to its new plant variety to be registered under its exclusive distributor in Germany.[140] Under the arrangement in question the only entity allowed to enter the German market was the exclusive distributor and the French manufacturer but only on the proviso that it did not cover more than one-third of German consumer demand.[141] Therefore, the German distributor was almost absolutely protected from territorial intervention. First, the CJEU evaluated whether this conduct could infringe Article 101(1) and second, if yes, whether it could be justified under Article 101(3) by applying the principle of proportionality when evaluating justifications under Article 101(3) and the anti-competitive restriction under Article 101(1).

This case discussed vertical territorial protection in the form of exclusive dealership in connection with IP rights. The CJEU analyzed whether IP protection, in particular the relevant German legislation, required and/or allowed for territorial restrictions to protect the new plant variety or whether the restriction had resulted from the agreement between the manufacturer and the distributor.[142] The Court observed that the legislation in question did not require exclusive production; thus, as in *Consten and Grundig*, the applied territorial restriction was merely based on contractual arrangements between the French manufacturers and the German distributor.[143] The Court therefore concluded that absolute territorial protection that did not allow parallel imports, which could not be assigned to requirements of IP law, could infringe Article 101 if it could not be justified under Article 101(3).[144]

When interpreting Article 101(3), the CJEU applied the principle of proportionality. It held that if there were any procompetitive reasons for introducing the restriction in question resulting in procompetitive effects, the restriction under Article 101(1) could not go beyond what was necessary for these procompetitive effects to be realized.[145] It explained that the procompetitive justifications under Article 101(3) could take the form of improved production or distribution of goods or promotion of technical progress.[146]

---

[139] Ibid., [2]–[3], [15].
[140] Ibid., [10]–[11], [31].
[141] Ibid., [32].
[142] Ibid., [23]–[25].
[143] Ibid., [37]–[42].
[144] Ibid., [29].
[145] Ibid., [76].
[146] Ibid., [33], [77].

In *Nungesser and Eisele*, the applicants presented a justification under Article 101(3), which had already occurred in previous EU cases. They argued that the Commission should have granted them an exemption based on the fact that the agreements concerned, including VTR, assisted in penetrating a new market and launching new products in that market. They argued that the purpose of the agreement was to penetrate a new market and thus the granted exclusivity did not go beyond what was necessary for this purpose, which involved the improvement of the production and distribution of goods.[147]

The CJEU held that the conduct in question could not have been exempted under Article 101(3) on this basis. It found that the agreement that constituted the exclusive distribution was signed because the French manufacturer did not have the capacity to distribute to a new market herself.[148] However, the agreement in question constituted an absolute territorial protection including a ban on parallel imports from third parties.[149] Following older cases and applying the principle of proportionality, the Court concluded that it would have been reasonable if the seeds in question, with their technological and innovative aspects, were protected with 'an open exclusive licence' without a ban on parallel imports.[150] Furthermore, the Court highlighted several times that the prohibition of parallel imports by any kind of licensee would be contrary to the objectives of the Treaty.[151]

Selective Distribution System and RPM: *AEG-Telefunken*[152]

In this case, the applicant, AEG, was a German manufacturer and distributor of electronic products, selling his products through his branches and subsidiaries in Europe.[153] He introduced a selective distribution system, called the 'Five-Point Programme', which was notified to the Commission.[154] However, the Commission suspected that the selective distribution system had not been applied according to the scheme outlined to the Commission but that, in reality, it had involved RPM and other non-notified, non-written selective criteria. It found evidence that

---

[147] Ibid., [44], [68].
[148] Ibid., [47].
[149] Ibid., [53].
[150] Ibid., [54]–[58].
[151] Ibid., [54]–[58].
[152] Note 121, AEG.
[153] Ibid., [2].
[154] Ibid., [3].

confirmed this suspicion and imposed a fine, finding them illegal under Article 101.[155]

The Commission's inspections of the applicant's premises showed that the applicant, the manufacturer, had deliberately maintained a high profit margin in order to provide 'the very expensive services associated with the specialist trade'.[156] (In some cases, AEG also used vertical territorial protection to motivate his distributors to join the network.[157]) For example, the Commission found that in the Federal Republic of Germany, the applicant did not accept a German undertaking to sell his products because it was a discount store.[158] Another distributor refused to guarantee that it would not supply to discount stores and would not export to other Member States, and for these reasons the applicant banned her from his distribution network.[159] One distributor promised not to sell under the lowest price on the market but to sell somewhere between the average retail prices.[160]

In France, the applicant issued a memorandum promoting fixed prices and the requirement of an assurance of compliance with the price policy.[161] The applicant asked one of his distributors to increase her prices for the applicant's products in her promotional catalogue.[162] Two distributors asked the applicant to indicate minimum retail prices.[163] Another distributor promised the appellant that they would not use an obtained promotional discount to decrease their retail prices.[164]

The Court agreed with the Commission that two evidenced aspects of the case proved the existence of RPM: first, systematic refusals to accept distributors who fulfilled the objective qualitative criteria but did not wish to follow the price policy. Second, the fact that the distributors concerned had not taken excessive risks by maintaining high prices because they had known about the price policy and had been willing to follow it.[165] It then confirmed that the aforementioned examples, as well

---

[155] Ibid., [4], [67].
[156] Ibid., [71].
[157] Ibid., [98]–[106].
[158] Ibid., [79]–[83].
[159] Ibid., [84]–[86].
[160] Ibid., [107].
[161] Ibid., [92]–[94].
[162] Ibid., [116].
[163] Ibid., [117]–[118].
[164] Ibid., [120].
[165] Ibid., [17], [39], [68].

as other practices, proved the improper application of the selective distribution system, which infringed Article 101.[166]

The judgment of the CJEU focused primarily on two issues. The first was a dispute about the existence of unilateral conduct rather than a prohibited multilateral one. The second question was whether RPM could be justified merely on the basis of the existence of the selective system and/or due to the presented justification claims under Article 101(3).

With regard to the existence of unilateral conduct, the applicant, AEG, claimed that influencing and setting retail prices constituted unilateral conduct.[167] The Commission disagreed and the CJEU affirmed the Commission's decision. The Commission argued that this practice went beyond the existence of unilateral conduct. It observed that the willingness of a great majority of distributors, who followed the policy and thus opposed low prices, assisted the manufacturer in maintaining prices and threatening others who were against the policy.[168]

The CJEU explained that a situation where it is advisable for distributors to engage in certain conduct does not in itself prove the existence of multilateral conduct prohibited under Article 101. However, the Court held that the RPM in question did not constitute the manufacturer's unilateral conduct but was based on a contractual relationship between the manufacturer and his distributors because distributor approvals, which can be tacit or expressed, were required by the manufacturer as a condition of joining the selective distribution system.[169]

In connection with a potential justification for RPM in a selective distribution system and a selective distribution system itself, the CJEU first confirmed that although a selective distribution system affects competition in the common market, it is legal in some situations, such as where it is necessary to provide specific services regarding high-quality and high-technology products. The CJEU referred to the case of *Metro*, where it stated that a selective distribution system is permissible if the distributors are chosen based on objective qualitative criteria that do not discriminate against any other distributors. Any other criteria infringe Article 101(1). Therefore, RPM as part of a selective distribution system would infringe Article 101(1).[170]

The CJEU observed that a selective distribution system based on qualitative criteria to provide specific services for high-quality and

---

[166] Ibid., [72], [76], [135]–[138].
[167] Ibid., [31].
[168] Ibid., [45].
[169] Ibid., [38].
[170] Ibid., [35].

high-technology products could even justify a reduction in price competition in so far as it improved non-price competition.[171] Such a limitation is only acceptable if the selective distribution leads to an improvement of competition and if it resulted from the product and the selective objective criteria ensuring services and not from the existence of RPM.[172] (Note that the CJEU thus recognized that non-price vertical restrictions could have an impact on price competition and could lead to higher prices.)

The applicant claimed that the higher prices were justified by the higher cost of the specialized trade which increased prices. A distribution system should offer distributors an assurance of the enjoyment of a minimum margin. Furthermore, it claimed that the system was beneficial for consumers as it preserved continuity in the distribution channel, which was in accordance with both Articles 101(1) and 101(3).[173]

The Court explained that, contrary to *Metro*, which had not included direct price restriction but the system had influenced price competition only indirectly, this case included RPM. It stated that RPM could be justified only up to a certain level and only in some circumstances, such as obtaining an appropriate profit margin to ensure the quality of services. This is lawful only if the system in question performs the functions assigned to it by the Treaty. Therefore, the system must improve competition.[174]

However, RPM in the selective distribution system was generally unjustified because it did not motivate distributors to keep fulfilling objective qualitative criteria to remain in the network but created a reason to stop supplying to distributors who did not want, or were not able, to maintain the prices. Therefore, RPM in this selective distribution system restricted competition and thus infringed Article 101.[175] This, nevertheless, does not eliminate the manufacturer's right to observe whether discounting distributors were capable of providing the required services based on the selective distribution system.[176]

---

[171] Ibid., [33].
[172] Ibid., [34].
[173] Ibid., [40].
[174] Ibid., [41], [42].
[175] Ibid., [43].
[176] Ibid., [75].

V. STABILITY AND VERTICAL RESTRAINT REGULATION (1990s–2005)

This era is characterized by the movement of Commission competition policy towards an economic approach based on efficiency and consumer welfare[177] and the reformation of the enforcement of EU (at that time, EC) competition law. With the increased number of Member States and further integration, the Commission's notification process, already criticized in the previous era, became unsustainable for the existence of effective enforcement. Therefore, the Community focused on the reformation of competition law, in particular, its enforcement. In that regard, the Commission issued its White Paper in 1999,[178] where it proclaimed a wish to modernize competition law. This process resulted in Council Regulation 1/2003,[179] which became effective in May 2004. The Regulation abolished the notification procedure and instead enacted the direct applicability of Article 101(3). It strengthened the Commission's power to investigate possible infringements more effectively.[180] At the same time, it decentralized the Commission's power by empowering both national competition authorities (NCAs) and national courts to apply the EU antitrust rules (at that time, EC antitrust rules) directly and in an effective manner. A cooperative competition network with NCAs, the European Competition Network, was created to coordinate the cooperation between the Commission and the NCAs with the focus on informing each other about their cases and other issues.

---

[177] See, e.g., Commission Notice (EC) 2004/C 101/08 Guidelines on the application of Article 81(3) of the Treaty [2004] OJ C101/97, [13]; Note 113, Guidelines 2010, [7]; Ken Heyer, 'A World of Uncertainty: Economics and the Globalization of Antitrust' (2005) 72 *Antitrust Law Journal* 375, 403.

[178] Commission, 'White Paper on modernisation of the rules implementing Articles 81 and 82 of the EC Treaty (formerly Articles 85 and 86 of the EC Treaty)' [1999] OJ C132/1.

[179] Note 38, Council Regulation (EC) 1/2003. Also other regulations characterized by the modernization process and the economic approach were adopted in this era, see Note 50.

[180] The Commission used the new tools in, for instance, Repsol's motor fuel distribution practices; Commission Notice (EC) of 20 October 2004 pursuant to Article 27, [4] of Regulation (EC) No 1/2003, concerning Case COMP/B-1/38348 [2004] OJ C258/7; See regarding art. 9 commitments 'MEMO/04/217 Commitment decisions (Article 9 of Council Regulation 1/2003 providing for a modernised framework for antitrust scrutiny of company behaviour)' (2004) <http://europa.eu/rapid/press-release_MEMO-04-217_en.htm> accessed 27 June 2015.

Competition and its policies have strengthened since their inception.[181] This is further reflected in the Maastricht Treaty, which states that Member States should create economic policy based on the principle of an open-market economy with free competition.[182] Besides modernization and the reformation of competition law, an economic approach including economic efficiency, consumer welfare and an economic assessment began to be central to the Commission's decisions and policies.

The 1980s had already indicated the application of economic theories; however, the 1990s deepened this economic approach further, particularly when economist Mario Monti became the Commissioner for Competition in 1999. (He remained in this position until 2004.) The beginning of the new millennium brought another personnel change in Brussels, which strengthened the economic influence: the economist, Philip Lowe, became the Director-General of Competition in September 2002 and served in this function until February 2010.

The General Court was in favor of the economic approach, acknowledging in *Van den Bergh Foods Ltd.*[183] that economic understanding and market analysis were essential in competition cases.[184] Competition law and policy continued to play an essential role in the economic integration of the Community as stressed by the CJEU in *Eco Swiss China Time*,[185] with the single market remaining the fundamental political objective.[186]

Despite the economic approach in the Community, which was already present in the US at that time, the two jurisdictions, the EU and the US,

---

[181] Commission, 'White Paper on Growth, Competitiveness and Employment: the Challenges and Ways Forward into the 21st Century' (The Delors White Paper) COM (93)700.

[182] Article G of the Treaty on the European Union which amends the Treaty of Rome (the EC Treaty): Articles 3(a), 102(a), 105 of the consolidated version of the Treaty of Rome (1992) – the Treaty Establishing the European Community.

[183] *Van den Bergh Foods Ltd* (Cases IV/34.073, IV/34.395 and IV/35.436) Commission Decision 98/531/EC [1998] OJ L246/1; See also the appeal decision; Case T-65/98 *Van den Bergh Foods Ltd v. Commission of the European Communities* [2003] ECR II-4653, [2004] 4 CMLR 14 ('*Van den Bergh* appeal').

[184] Note 183, *Van den Bergh* appeal, [84].

[185] See, e.g., Case C-126/97, *Eco Swiss China Time Ltd v. Benetton International NV* [1999] ECR I-3055, [2000] 5 CMLR 816, [36]; see also Case C-415/93 *Union Royal Belge des Société de Football Association ASBL & others v. Jean-Marc Bosman* [1995] ECR I-4921, [1996] 1 CMLR 645; Note 19, Jones and Sufrin, 38–9; Note 20, Bouterse.

[186] Note 55, Commission, 'Green Paper on Vertical Restraints', [1].

did not always come to the same conclusion on anticompetitive harm and prohibition of certain conduct.[187] This was not due to a lack of economic evaluation in particular cases but due more to different antitrust/ competition-law goals, rules, perspectives and even, and significantly, economic conclusions based on thorough economic analysis.[188] This indicates that despite the economic approach in both jurisdictions, the laws of RPM and VTR and its application are not necessarily the same.

The importance of an economic approach to vertical restraints became obvious with the discussion on the introduction of guidelines for vertical restraints. This discussion was reflected in, and further intensified by, the Green Paper on vertical restraints in 1996.[189] The Green Paper observed that the previous system was criticized, most notably, for a lack of analysis of economic impacts, a lack of flexibility resulting in a straitjacket effect, over-regulation and discrimination against the plurality of distribution systems.[190] By acknowledging these drawbacks of the previous approach to vertical restraints, the Green Paper stated that vertical restraints could promote objective efficiencies and proclaimed that *efficiency* and *fairness* of competition were the primary objectives of EU (at that time, EC) competition law.[191] In connection with this era, the Green Paper addressed a number of issues and objectives. For example, distinguishing between the procompetitive and anticompetitive effects of restrictions, facilitating market integration, permitting new and innovative distribution systems, consumer welfare and market share thresholds, legal certainty, decentralization and a possible need for substantive legal changes, to name a few.[192]

---

[187] For example, this is obvious in international mergers. In July 2001, the European Commission prohibited the proposed merger between Honeywell Inc. and General Electric. The Commission's stance was different to that adopted by the US Department of Justice, which had cleared the merger. See Commission press release, 'IP/01/939 The Commission prohibits GE's acquisition of Honeywell' (3 July 2001) <http://europa.eu/rapid/press-release_IP-01-939_en.htm> accessed 27 July 2015. See also, Note 177, Heyer, 403–8.

[188] See Note 177, Heyer.

[189] Note 55, Commission, 'Green Paper on Vertical Restraints'.

[190] Ibid., [37] ('Current Rules').

[191] Ibid., [10]–[13], [25]; Note 52, Jones, 940; Sandra Marco Colino, *Vertical Agreements and Competition Law, a Comparative Study of the EU and US Regimes* (Hart Publishing, Oxford and Portland 2010) 98; Note 2, Green and others, 200.

[192] See Note 55, Commission, 'Green Paper on Vertical Restraints' [46] ('Current Rules').

With regard to an economic approach, the Green Paper determined that it was the impact on the market and not the form of conduct that was essential for its approach to vertical restraints. It analyzed the relationship between, and the importance of, intrabrand and interbrand competition, the market structure and the structure of distribution and recognized a number of procompetitive effects of vertical restraints.[193] For instance, they can be allowed for a certain period when they are used to expand or penetrate the market.[194]

The Green Paper also reflected the development in distribution strategies. It acknowledged that distribution had been changing due to developments in information technology and new distribution systems, which had resulted in ongoing greater concentration and integration, and the decline of traditional distribution channels (manufacturers-wholesalers-retailers).[195]

The Green Paper did not exclude a discussion of economic integration and the objective of the single market in connection with vertical restraints. It stressed the integration of the different economic systems of the Member States and the creation of a single market as the main objective of EU competition policy (at that time, EC competition policy), placing singular importance on market penetration without the barriers that could be created by vertical agreements.[196] Moreover, it highlighted the importance of the existence and protection of parallel trade in the Community market.[197] However, at the same time, it recognized that the single market legislation was largely in place. Therefore, it instead promoted a review of the approach to vertical restraints in accordance with the economic approach and changes in the methods of distribution.[198]

The Green Paper resulted in the adoption of a new block exemption on vertical restraints, Regulation 2790/99 (Regulation 1999)[199] and

---

[193] Ibid., [10], [12]–[13] ('Economic Analysis').

[194] Ibid., [12] ('Economic Analysis'), [25] ('Current Rules').

[195] Ibid., [20], [40]–[41], [44] ('Introduction to Green Paper and Invitation to Third Parties to Comment').

[196] Ibid., [1]–[2] ('Executive Summary'), [1]–[2] ('Introduction to Green Paper and Invitation to Third Parties to Comment').

[197] Ibid., [9] ('Executive Summary'), [39] ('Introduction to Green Paper and Invitation to Third Parties to Comment').

[198] Ibid., [3] ('Introduction to Green Paper and Invitation to Third Parties to Comment').

[199] Commission Regulation (EC) 2790/1999 of 22 December 1999 on the application of Article 81(3) of the Treaty to categories of vertical agreements and concerted practices [1999] OJ L336/21.

guidelines on vertical restraints (Guidelines 1999) in December 1999.[200] In agreement with the Green Paper, they recognized the possible benefits of vertical restraints and heralded a more economic approach to vertical restraints.[201]

Generally, Regulation 1999 lightened the burden of individual exemptions on vertical agreements by introducing a system where parties were responsible for determining whether their vertical agreements and arrangements fulfilled the conditions of the block exemption.[202] Both documents covered all forms of vertical restraints for products and services and were applied to vertical restraints in general for the first time. The block exemption applied only if the supplier's market share was below 30 percent.

Regulation 1999 reflects the fact that the Commission had to merge different interests and goals. One of the Commission's main concerns was that territorial restrictions imposed on distributors contradicted the single market objective.[203] On the other hand, the Commission reflected in Guidelines 1999 the previous cases that highlighted the benefits of territorial restrictions when making investments to launch new products or penetrate new markets.[204]

Some cases of this era also reflect the economic arguments. For instance, the case of *Leclerc*[205] discussed the position of a selective distribution system based on luxury criteria. In particular, if a manufacturer selected only those resellers who provided luxury goods or services, this was considered to be legal as far as the criteria were necessary and also included hypermarkets.[206] Despite these changes driven by an economic approach, the Commission applied a strict approach to RPM and VTR, protecting intrabrand competition and freedom of buyers to determine their own business, as follows from the Commission's decision in *Novalliance/Systemform*.[207]

---

[200] Commission Notice (EC) (2000/C 291/01) Guidelines on vertical restraints [2000] OJ C291/1.
[201] See, e.g., ibid., [6] and [115].
[202] Note 19, Jones and Sufrin, 784–6.
[203] See Note 200, Guidelines 1999, [103]; Note 55, Commission, 'Green Paper on Vertical Restraints' [26] ('Current Rules') [70], [78]; Note 51, Hawk.
[204] Note 55, Commission, 'Green Paper on Vertical Restraints' para. 12; Note 200, Guidelines 1999, [119].
[205] Case T-88/92 *Leclerc (Association des Centres Distributeurs Edouard) v Commission*, [1996] ECR II 1961.
[206] Ibid., [109]–[115].
[207] *Novalliance/Systemform* (Case IV/35.679) Commission Decision 97/123/EC [1997] OJ L47/11, [1997] 4 CMLR 876 ('*Novalliance*').

The Commission also applied a strict approach to the determination of the existence of prohibited multilateral/bilateral conduct (an agreement or concerted practice). The EU courts, particularly the General Court, eased this approach by setting boundaries between unilateral and prohibited multilateral/bilateral conduct in vertical restraints in the cases of *Bayer*[208] and *Volkswagen II*.[209]

Bayer clarified that the mere application of anticompetitive policy on distributors was unilateral conduct, unless the distributors had known about the policy through the manufacturer and had decided to follow the policy. The General Court's judgment on RPM in *Volkswagen II*[210] introduced another positive change, stating that distributors 'agreeing' with a supplier's unspecified future policy, namely when this policy infringed competition law, did not constitute a prohibited agreement under Article 101(1).[211] On appeal,[212] the CJEU upheld the General Court's judgment stating that these clauses on future policy have to be specific enough to constitute a concurrence of wills.[213]

The importance of the single market is reflected in the case of *Nintendo*,[214] where the Commission made it clear that absolute vertical territorial restriction in the form of absolute elimination of parallel imports, including restriction of both passive and active sales, constitutes restriction by object under Article 101(1). In this case, the Commission imposed the largest fine of €167.8 million in a vertical restriction case under Article 101.

Due to the existence of an illegal object, the Commission stated in *Nintendo* that the effects upon competition did not have to be determined.[215] Nevertheless, the Commission listed examples where anti-competitive effects occurred in the form of hindering parallel trade.[216] At the same time, when evaluating Article 101(3), the Commission noted that Nintendo did not apply for individual exemption under its old

---

[208] Note 41, *Bayer*; Note 41, *Bayer* appeal.
[209] Case T-208/01 *Volkswagen AG v Commission* [2003] ECR II-5141 ('*Volkswagen*').
[210] Ibid.
[211] Ibid., [39], [43].
[212] Case C-74/04 P, *Commission v Volkswagen* [2006] ECR I-6585 ('*Volkswagen appeal*').
[213] Ibid., [45], [48].
[214] *PO Video Games, Nintendo Distribution, and Omega-Nintendo* (Cases COMP/35.587 PO, COMP/35.706 PO, COMP/36.321) Commission Decision 2003/675/EC [2003] OJ L255/33 ('*Nintendo*').
[215] Ibid., [331]–[332].
[216] Ibid., [333].

notification system. It stated that even if the manufacturer had applied, the actions in question would not have qualified for an exemption because exclusive territorial protection constitutes a hard-core restriction and the actions did not improve the distribution of the products, nor did consumers benefit from them.[217] The lack of analysis of potential anticompetitive and procompetitive effects in this decision is not in agreement with the proclaimed economic approach. Nevertheless, the period following this era further facilitated the economic approach in cases on vertical restraints, with the case of *GSK*[218] requiring a more thorough analysis of procompetitive and anticompetitive effects even in situations where competition was restricted by its object.[219]

VTR and RPM: *Novalliance/Systemform*:[220] Intrabrand Competition and Freedom to Conduct Business

This decision by the Commission involved a number of vertical arrangements in the forms of VTR and RPM between Systemform, a German manufacturer of equipment for processing computer printouts, and her exclusive distributors. Novalliance, the complainant, was a French dealer who sold office equipment, primarily in computer-printing and post-handling systems. Novapost distributed for Systemform in Greece. Both Novalliance and Novapost formed one economic entity with Eurinvest.[221]

In this case, VTR took two general forms: explicit clauses in distribution agreements and further arrangements in the form of a ban on exports. First, Systemform concluded agreements with exclusive distributors outside Germany and with several distributors inside Germany.[222] Both the exclusive and German distribution systems included territorial restrictions,[223] in that the distributors agreed not to sell to any undertaking passively or actively outside their own territories.[224] Moreover, some agreements also included a prohibition on selling to undertakings

---

[217] Ibid., [341].
[218] Case T-168/01 *GlaxoSmithKline v Commission* [2006] ECR II-2969 ('*GSK*'); appealed in Cases C-501/06 P, C-513/06 P, C-515/06 P, and C-519/06 P *GlaxoSmithKline Services Unlimited v Commission of the EC* [2009] 4 CMLR 2 ('*GSK* appeal').
[219] See below.
[220] Note 207, *Novalliance*.
[221] Ibid., [5]–[7].
[222] Ibid., [14].
[223] Ibid., [15].
[224] Ibid., [16]–[29], [60].

inside the territory if they intended to export the products.[225] Novalliance also alleged that, in practice, Systemform delayed supplies in order to prevent exports by her distributors.[226] The Commission argued that the territorial restrictions prohibiting selling to any undertaking with an office outside the contractual territory constituted an export ban. The Commission qualified this as an infringement of Article 101(1) in the form of VTR. The Commission also highlighted that these practices restricted the freedom of distributors to choose their own customers.[227]

With regard to RPM, the Commission found that the agreements included vertical price restrictions. Systemform fixed retail prices for the territory concerned, with each of her distributors. Some distributors agreed to inform Systemform if prices changed.[228] Systemform claimed that those clauses fixing prices were not enforced.[229] Nevertheless, the Commission found these practices prohibited under Article 101. It explained that both VTR and RPM had their effect in restricting competition in the cases where Systemform did not enforce these restrictions. When they were enforced, competition was restricted by object.[230] The Commission also held that the agreements restricted the freedom of distributors to determine their own resale prices.[231]

The Commission based its decision on two values: the freedom of buyers (distributors) to conduct their own business and the protection of intrabrand competition. The Commission highlighted that distributors should have the freedom to conduct their business, which includes freedom of choice of their own price and customers. The Commission also made it clear that proving the restriction of intrabrand competition was enough to infringe Article 101(1). Although the Commission discussed the possibility of the effect on interbrand competition, it simply stated that interbrand competition was likely not to be affected because Systemform did not have a sufficient market share.[232] By finding that the practices in question infringed Article 101(1), although they did not restrict interbrand competition, it implied that not only interbrand competition but also intrabrand competition played an important role in EU (at that time, EC) competition law.

---

[225] Ibid., [56]–[59].
[226] Ibid., [45].
[227] Ibid., [60].
[228] Ibid., [30]–[42].
[229] Ibid., [43].
[230] Ibid., [60]–[61].
[231] Ibid., [61].
[232] Ibid., [76].

These two values are in agreement with *Dr. Miles* and other older US cases; however, they contradict the US VTR case of *Sylvania*. Indeed, *Novalliance/Systemform* does not reflect the US approach to vertical restraints of that time. Although the RPM approach in this era was based on the per se rule, it was made more lenient by *Monsanto* and *Business Electronics* emphasizing the primary role of interbrand competition in US antitrust law. At the same time, the VTR approach accommodating the rule of reason required proving the restriction of interbrand competition and assumed that suppliers would have procompetitive rather than anticompetitive reasons to initiate VTR. Therefore, unlike the Commission's decision in *Novalliance/Systemform*, the US approach to VTR did not protect the 'rights' of buyers to conduct their own business and their freedom to decide where they will sell. This shows that the economic approach as proclaimed by the Commission in the Green Paper was not the same as the approach in the US, with the EU approach of that era standing on other values than the Chicagonist approach to efficiency.

Export Ban: *Bayer*:[233] Multilateral v Unilateral Conduct

The EU courts in the case of *Bayer* followed by *Volkswagen* set boundaries and provided clarification for proving the requirement of Article 101(1) of showing 'an agreement' or 'concerted practice' in cases on vertical restraints. Both cases illustrate that the Commission accommodated a rather broad and flexible approach to this requirement which was limited and narrowed by the courts.

The case of *Bayer* involved the applicant, Bayer AG, a pharmaceutical company selling a product called 'Adalat'. Bayer AG sold Adalat to all Member States via subsidiaries who sold the product to wholesalers. The price of pharmaceutical products, including Adalat, was directly or indirectly fixed by the national health authorities in many Member States, which led to different prices. The price of Adalat was 40 percent more expensive in the UK than in Spain and France between 1989 and 1993. Potential profits from sales to the UK was likely the reason that French and Spanish wholesalers re-exported the product to the UK. Bayer AG, losing profits from UK sales, introduced its new policy based on quotas in order to stop the re-exporting of Adalat. This policy meant that Bayer AG supplied its distributors with Adalat in amounts that did not exceed

---

[233] Note 41, *Bayer*; Note 41, *Bayer* appeal.

the demand in domestic markets, thus de facto restricting parallel exports of Adalat. Prior to this policy, Bayer had supplied distributors at their request.[234]

The Commission found Bayer's new policy to be in violation of Article 101(1) in the form of an export ban. The issue of whether this practice constituted an agreement or concerted practice under Article 101(1) was the subject matter for the appeal to the General Court and then the CJEU. When determining the requirement of an agreement, the General Court found two issues in the Commission's decision which, according to the General Court, led to a lack of evidence of the existence of an agreement. The Commission did not prove that, first, an export ban was imposed and, second, that there was the existence of a meeting of the minds.

The General Court claimed that the alleged intention of Bayer to impose an export ban had not been proved by the Commission due to the absence of a monitoring system and a non-demonstration of threats and penalties.[235] The CJEU agreed with these findings[236] stating that a tacit acceptance of the ban on exports had not been proven, as the Commission had not sufficiently established in law that such a ban was imposed or that the medicines were supplied only with the condition of not exporting them.[237]

Second, the General Court evaluated the intentions of Bayer's distributors in order to determine the parties' 'common intention to conduct themselves on the market in a specific way'.[238] In that respect, the General Court noted, from the documents provided by the Commission, that certain wholesalers had pretended that the demand for Adalat destined for the national market had increased in order to obtain more Adalat than was necessary for their home market. By examining the intention of the wholesalers, the General Court concluded that Bayer's new policy could not have constituted an agreement because it did not correspond with the ban on parallel export.[239]

The CJEU agreed with the General Court that this contradicted the Commission's claim that these wholesalers had acquiesced with Bayer's policy.[240] The CJEU explained that after the existence of the ban was not

---

[234] Note 41, *Bayer* appeal, [2]–[4].
[235] Note 41, *Bayer*, [126]–[129], [148], [183].
[236] Note 41, *Bayer* appeal [83], [89]; *Bayer*, [108]–[109], [119], [126]–[129], [148], [183].
[237] Note 41, *Bayer* appeal [119].
[238] Ibid., [97].
[239] Note 41, *Bayer* [126]–[129], [148], [183].
[240] Note 41, *Bayer* appeal [54]–[56].

proved, it was right that the General Court examined whether the parties had intended to prevent parallel trade. Thus, the General Court was correct in determining the genuine wishes of the parties.[241] The CJEU held that the strategy of the wholesalers who pretended that they needed a larger supply for their national market to turn Bayer's policy to their advantage confirms that there was no existence of a meeting of the minds.[242]

However, the CJEU also held that it was not necessary for the interests of the parties to correspond in order to prove an agreement under Article 101(1). It said that: 'an agreement exists within the meaning of Article [101(1)] of the Treaty, even if one of the parties to that agreement is forced to conclude it against its own wishes'.[243]

It explained that, notwithstanding this, proving the intentions of wholesalers was right in this case because the existence of an export ban was not proved from the conduct of the manufacturer due to the lack of a monitoring system, threats and penalties on the side of the manufacturer. The CJEU then clarified that this does not mean that for an agreement to exist under Article 101(1) the intention of both parties must always correspond. On the contrary, an agreement can exist even in situations where one party forces the other party to implement an agreement that goes against the other party's wishes.

This part of the judgment involves two interesting points: the free will of parties to collude under Article 101(1) and a dissimilarity between the EU and US approaches. First, the judgment made it clear that the absolute free will of both parties is not a requirement for an agreement to exist under Article 101(1). Therefore, any 'economic duress' when one party with bargaining power threatens a weaker party is not a justification, nor does it prove that there was no agreement between parties.[244] Assume that a Spanish wholesaler is an exclusive distributor for Bayer. Not complying with the Bayer policy would mean a loss of business for her and the likelihood of bankruptcy if she did not find another supplier

---

[241] Ibid., [121].
[242] Ibid., [123].
[243] Ibid., [114].
[244] For instance, the UK recognizes the doctrine of economic duress in other areas of the law than competition law. This doctrine is relatively new and is still developing. It is based on the idea of the unfairness of one-sided arrangements on the side of an economically weaker party. For example, see *Universe Tankships Inc of Monrovia v International Transport Workers Federation* (*The Universe Sentinel*), [1983] 1 AC 366; also see *UNIDROIT Principles* of 2010, art 3.2.6 ('Threat') and art 3.2.7 ('Gross Disparity').

she could sell for. Therefore, she would comply with this policy in order to keep the supply going from Bayer despite the fact that profit-wise she is worse off under this new policy because she cannot re-export Bayer's products. The under-duress doctrine was expressly refused by the General Court in *Tréfileurope*[245] and thus does not play any role for the purposes of Article 101.

For the comparison with the US approach, it is important to note that the CJEU does not differentiate between the motivations of suppliers and buyers for introducing a vertical restriction (in this situation, a non-price vertical restriction). However, in the case of *Bayer*, the manufacturer was not motivated by any procompetitive reasons, such as the introduction of services. Instead, Bayer was competing with his wholesalers for sales in the UK and was thus interested in stopping the parallel exports in order to maintain better profit for himself.

RPM: *Volkswagen*:[246] Future Policy and Concurrence of Wills

In the case of *Volkswagen*, the CJEU and the General Court discussed whether a clause in a dealership agreement that allowed a manufacturer to set a new policy in the future, and her dealers agreeing to comply with such future policy, would constitute an agreement under Article 101(1). Both courts clarified that only a clause in the main agreement which includes a foreseeable future policy could constitute an illegal agreement if applied for illegal restriction.[247]

In this case, Volkswagen, a manufacturer of motor vehicles, sold its products through a selective, exclusive distribution system on the basis of dealership agreements with its dealers, where the dealers agreed to comply with Volkswagen's future instructions on recommended retail prices and discounts.[248] Later, Volkswagen made calls and sent letters to its German dealers announcing fixed resale prices for the Volkswagen Passat model.

The Commission claimed that the calls and letters from Volkswagen to its German distributors announcing the fixed resale prices formed part of the above-described dealership agreement. According to the Commission, the distributors agreed with the new Volkswagen policy to fix the price in

---

[245] Case T-141/89 *Tréfileurope v Commission* [1995] ECR II-791 [58].
[246] Note 209, *Volkswagen*, Note 212, *Volkswagen* appeal.
[247] This is also expressed in the current Guidelines, Note 113; [25(a)] where the Commission used the wording 'a specific unilateral policy'.
[248] Note 212, *Volkswagen* appeal, [3]–[4].

advance of signing the dealership agreement.[249] Thus, the Commission found that Volkswagen had infringed Article 101(1) by setting retail prices of the VW Passat.[250] The Commission's decision was annulled by the General Court. The CJEU affirmed the General Court's decision in its main finding of the non-existence of a concurrence of wills.

Both courts ruled that the Commission had not sufficiently established the existence of a concurrence of wills, one of the important requirements of Article 101(1), highlighting the lack of knowledge of an offer as an important element of a concurrence of wills. The General Court held that the existence of an agreement, its concurrence of wills, required knowledge of the conduct at the time the agreement was concluded.[251] The Court said that the dealers could not sign in advance a variation that they could not foresee or which they could not refuse; the illegal act could not be foreseen by dealers and therefore they could not agree to it in advance.[252]

The General Court explained that an unlawful contractual variation could not be lawfully accepted in advance in a distribution agreement.[253] Therefore, the mere fact that the distributors signed distribution agreements agreeing with the manufacturer's unspecified future policy does not constitute a concurrence of wills with regard to anticompetitive agreements under Article 101(1).[254] The concurrence of wills can only be based on conduct known to the parties when they accept it because,[255] as the General Court citing its judgment in *Bayer* explained, the Commission must prove the existence of a concurrence of wills between at least two parties based on a 'faithful expression of the parties' intention'.[256] If there is no faithful expression of intention, the concurrence of wills is not constituted. Instead, this creates unilateral conduct.[257]

The Commission argued that, according to judgments in previous cases, the parties concerned had indeed concluded agreements.[258] It

---

[249] Ibid., [16].
[250] Note 209, *Volkswagen*, [10].
[251] Ibid., [36].
[252] Note 212, *Volkswagen* appeal, [17]–[18]; Note 209, *Volkswagen*, [39], [43].
[253] Ibid., *Volkswagen* appeal, [18]; Ibid., *Volkswagen*, [45].
[254] Ibid., *Volkswagen* appeal, [20].
[255] Ibid., [21].
[256] Ibid., [12].
[257] Ibid., [14].
[258] Ibid., [28]–[30]. (The Commission refers to the cases: Note 121, *AEG*, [38]; Note 133, *Ford Werke AG* [21]; Note 41, *Bayer* appeal, [144]; Case C-338/00 P *Volkswagen v Commission* [2003] ECR I9189 [60].)

claimed that the concurrence of wills existed merely because of the existence of the clauses in question.[259] The CJEU stated that this was not sufficient because there must be another aspect to claim that the dealers agreed with the specific conduct in question.[260]

The CJEU first confirmed the necessity of proving the concurrence of wills of at least two parties in order to prove an agreement under Article 101(1).[261] This requirement of Article 101(1) can take the form of a clause of an agreement. It also includes other practices of parties, for instance, tacit acquiescence by a distributor during a telephone call.[262]

The CJEU then turned to the facts of the case, looking at the content of the agreement in question and highlighting that it was not in its jurisdiction to find and assess facts but merely to review legal characterization and the conclusions of those facts under Article 256 TFEU.[263] Therefore, without analyzing the accuracy of the facts, the CJEU referred to the General Court the finding that the clauses of the agreement in question could not have authorized Volkswagen to maintain retail prices. The CJEU explained that because the provisions of the agreement in question did not specify sufficiently the manufacturer's future policy on RPM but were instead drafted in neutral terms, the requirement of Article 101(1) on the existence of an anticompetitive agreement was not constituted by these provisions of the dealership agreement.[264]

Although the CJEU confirmed the conclusion of the General Court, it disagreed with the General Court on its ruling that the agreement in question did not authorize calls on RPM. Nevertheless, the Court stated that such an error of law did not affect the rightness of the conclusion that the contested decision should be annulled because a concurrence of wills was not established.[265]

VI. ECONOMIC CRISIS AND NEW VERTICAL RESTRAINT REGULATION

This era is characterized by the commencement of an economic crisis in the EU, a deepening of the integration of the EU embodied in the Treaty

---

[259] Note 212, *Volkswagen* appeal, [40].
[260] Ibid., [47]; Note 209, *Volkswagen* [62]–[68].
[261] Ibid., [37].
[262] Ibid., [39].
[263] Ibid., [49].
[264] Ibid., [52]–[53].
[265] Ibid., [53]–[55].

of Lisbon, further facilitation of the economic approach, publishing of new regulations and guidelines on vertical restraints issued in 2010 (Regulation 2010 and Guidelines 2010)[266] and a decrease in interest in the enforcement of vertical restraints by the Commission, which ended in the stagnation of enforcement of RPM and VTR cases after Council Regulation 1/2003 came into force.

The Treaty of Lisbon, an important treaty of this era, entered into force in December 2009. It merged the policy of the Community into the EU. It transformed, among other things, the principal objective of EU competition law. Under the previous EC Treaty, one of the objectives of the Community was to establish a 'system ensuring that competition in the internal market is not distorted' as stated in Article 3(1)(g). The Treaty of Lisbon repealed this Article and replaced it with Protocol 27, which linked the system of undistorted competition with establishing a fully effective internal market. Indeed, Article 3(1)(b) TFEU ensured the exclusive competence of the EU to establish competition rules necessary for the functioning of the internal market. Articles 101 and 102 were amended to refer to the protection of competition in the *internal market*.

This shows that the process of integration was not only deepened in the Treaty of Lisbon but that it remained an essential principle for EU competition law, even during the time of economic crisis. For instance, the Commissioner, Margrethe Vestager, stated that if the EU is 'serious about boosting growth in Europe, [it] must rely on the Single Market'.[267]

At the same time, the economic approach with an emphasis on consumer welfare played an even more central role than in the previous era.[268] For instance, Commissioner Joaquín Almunia stated that consumer welfare 'is the cornerstone, the guiding principle of EU competition

---

[266] Commission Regulation (EU) 330/2010 of 20 April 2010 on the application of Article 101(3) of the Treaty on the Functioning of the European Union to categories of vertical agreements and concerted practices [2010] OJ L102/1 ('Regulation 2010'); Note 113, Guidelines 2010.

[267] Margrethe Vestager, 'Competition policy in the EU: Outlook and recent developments in antitrust' (Speech delivered at Peterson Institute for International Economics, Washington DC, 16 April 2015), available at <http://ec.europa.eu/commission/2014-2019/vestager/announcements/competition-policy-eu-outlook-and-recent-developments-antitrust_en> accessed on 14 May 2015.

[268] For example, this economic approach is obvious in the case of T-286/09 *Intel v. European Commission* [2014] ECR 0, [140]–[166]; and appeal by Intel in Case C-413/14 P *Intel v European Commission* [2014] OJ C395/25.

policy'.[269] The current Commissioner, Margrethe Vestager, also highlighted that the task of competition enforcement is 'to keep the Single Market open and efficient'.[270] Indeed, Article 120 TFEU required EU and Member States to act in accordance with the 'principle of an open market economy with free competition'. Vestager also added that competition enforcement must ensure that the game for competitors is *fair*,[271] which is another goal besides the economic approach goal that centers on consumer welfare and efficiency. Fairness together with economic integration has been present in EU competition law since the beginning, as discussed in previous sections.

Consumer welfare has been projected in Commission regulations and also in its soft law.[272] This objective is also reflected in the new Regulation 2010 and the Guidelines 2010 on vertical restraints.[273] Naturally, this shift was welcomed by consumers and their associations.[274] However, the CJEU does not necessarily support consumer welfare as the primary standpoint for EU competition law and policy. For instance, in *GSK*, the CJEU highlighted that the objective of EU competition law involved more than just the protection of consumers and

---

[269] Joaquín Almunia, 'Competition – what's in it for consumers?' (Speech delivered at European Competition and Consumer Day, Poznan, 24 November 2011), available at <http://europa.eu/rapid/press-release_SPEECH-11-803_en.htm?locale=en> accessed on 14 May 2015.

[270] Note 267, Vestager.

[271] Ibid.

[272] For instance, Commission Notice 2008/C 265/07 Guidelines on the assessment of non-horizontal mergers under the Council Regulation on the control of concentrations between undertakings [2008] OJ C265/7, [10]; Commission Notice 2004/C 101/97 Guidelines on the application of Article 81(3) (Article 101(3) TFEU) [2004] OJ C101/08, [13]; Commission Notice 2004/C 31/03 Guidelines on the assessment of horizontal mergers under the Council Regulation on the control of concentrations between undertakings [2004] OJ C31/03 [8]; Commission Notice 2009/C45/02 Guidance on the Commission's enforcement priorities in applying Article 82 of the EC Treaty to abusive exclusionary conduct by dominant undertakings [2009] OJ C45/7 ('Guidance on Article 82'); Commission (EC) 'Green Paper – Damages actions for breach of the EC antitrust rules' COM(2005) 672 final ('Green Paper – Damages'); See also, Consumer Focus 'Consumer Focus Response to Vertical Restraints Block Exemption Regulation' (Discussion Paper, Consumer Focus Group, London, 2009) ('Consumer Focus') 15.

[273] Note 266, Regulation 2010, Preamble 10, [7], [101]–[102], [122].

[274] Note 272, 'Consumer Focus' 6.

their welfare,[275] while in an older case of *Lelos*, the CJEU said that it aims for the protection of 'consumers by means of undistorted competition and the integration of national markets'.[276]

The importance of consumer welfare in EU competition policy is also projected in enforcement. One of the Commission's priorities in this era was to promote private enforcement in the form of recovering damages for consumers who suffered from infringements of competition law. This is in agreement with consumer welfare as such private enforcement is aimed at compensation for detriment to consumers.[277]

The economic approach is further reflected in the Commission's enforcement priorities during this era.[278] At the center of the economic approach is the determination of economic harm. Economic harm plays a significant role in prioritizing and rejecting complaints and cases by the Commission as it determines the economic importance of potential cases.[279] In that respect, this era followed the development of the previous era in the way that the Commission has focused on other forms of restrictions than vertical restrictions. Aside from mergers and the abuse of dominant positions, state aid has been at the center of attention due to the economic crisis and, most importantly, the Commission has

---

[275] Note 218, *GSK* appeal, [63], citing Case C-8/08 *T-Mobile Netherlands BV v. Road van bestuur van de Nederlandse Mededingingsautoriteit* [2009] 5 CMLR 11 (*'T-Mobile Netherlands'*) [38]–[39].

[276] Joined Cases C-468–478/06 *Sot. Lelos kai Sia EE and others v GlaxoSmithKline AEVE Farmakeftikon Proionton* [2008] ECR I-7139 (*'Lelos kai'*) [68].

[277] In June 12013, the Commission presented two important documents in this matter which were based on Note 272, Commission, 'Green Paper – Damages' and 'MEMO/05/489 European Commission Green Paper on damages actions for breach of EC Treaty anti-trust rules' (20 December 2005) <http://europa.eu/rapid/press-release_MEMO-05-489_en.htm?locale=en> accessed 27 June 2015. These documents are: Commission, 'Proposal for a Directive of the European Parliament and of the Council on certain rules governing actions for damages under national law for infringements of the competition law provisions of the Member States and of the European Union' COM(2013) 404 final, and; Commission Recommendation 2013/396/EU of 11 June 2013 on common principles for injunctive and compensatory collective redress mechanisms in the Member States concerning violations of rights granted under Union Law [2013] OJ L201/60.

[278] See, e.g., in connection with Article 102; Note 272, Guidance on Article 82, [2]–[3].

[279] See Case T-427/08 *Confédération Européenne des associations d'horlogers-réparateurs (CEAHR) v. European Commission* [2010] ECR II-5865 (*'CEAHR'*) [22], [26]–[29].

focused primarily on cartels, including related issues such as the criminalization of cartels, leniency policy and private enforcement.[280]

The decreased interest in vertical restrictions has economic as well as legal and enforcement reasons. With regard to the economic reasons, the European Commission's recent position could be explained by the significant difference in harm between cartels and vertical restrictions. This economic approach accommodated by policies of both the European Commission and US antitrust agencies as discussed in the previous chapter, involves difficulties for dealing with vertical restraints arising from the existence of a number of procompetitive economic theories (further discussed in Chapter 5) and the central focus on interbrand competition. The position is more or less uniform in terms of the prohibition of cartels being economically justified on the basis of obvious economic harm, while in the case of vertical restrictions, the mere restriction of intrabrand competition and the unresolved impact on interbrand competition has played an important role in the law enforcement of RPM and VTR in both jurisdictions. This can also facilitate legal and enforcement issues. In general, the issue remains how to prove a restriction of competition, in particular economic harm on competition, when the knowledge of different procompetitive theories is considered.

The enforcement reason can be traced to the introduction of Regulation 1/2003. Since it came into force in May 2014, the Commission has not dealt with any cases on VTR and RPM except for cases it had started to investigate prior to May 2004.[281] (However, the NCAs have been active in that regard.[282]) Regulation 1/2003 changed the enforcement of EU (at that time, EC) competition law by abolishing the notification and centralized enforcement system. Since then, the NCAs have been

---

[280] See Commission, 'Ten Years of Antitrust Enforcement under Regulation 1/2003: Achievements and Future Perspectives' Communication from the Commission to the European Parliament and the Council, COM(2014) 453 available at <http://ec.europa.eu/competition/antitrust/legislation/antitrust_enforcement_10_years_en.pdf> accessed 19 May 2015 ('Ten Years'). At p. 5, the Commission stated that since Regulation 1/2003 came into force, 48 percent of its cases were cartel cases, while only 9 percent were vertical agreements cases specifically aimed at the car industry. NCAs had 27 percent of cartel cases and 18 percent of vertical agreements cases where the vertical cases included RPM and VTR.

[281] One of the latest Commission decisions is a decision on the restriction of parallel imports: *Souris-Topps* (Case COMP/37.980) Commission Decision 2006/895/EC [2006] OJ L353/5 ('*Souris-Topps*'). See also *SEP and others/ Automobiles Peugeot* (Cases COMP/36.623, 36.820, and 37.275) Commission Decision 2006/431/EC [2005] OJ L173/20.

[282] See Note 280, Commission, 'Ten Years' 5.

empowered to enforce EU competition law. Therefore, the Commission prioritizes cases, focusing on complaints which, according to the Commission, have Community interest. By applying the economic approach, it selects the cases with potential significant economic harm for the EU, such as cartels and significant abuse of dominant position but not vertical restraints including VTR and RPM. It leaves these cases up to the NCAs to decide despite the fact that the General Court stated in *CEAHR*[283] that allegations of vertical restrictions concerning several Member States should primarily be investigated by the European Commission and not by Member States themselves. The General Court also urged the Commission to satisfactorily assess the existence of sufficient Community interest without making mere assumptions but by evaluating all the relevant and available factors when it receives an official complaint.

The case of *CEAHR* involved an alleged vertical restriction in the form of a refusal to supply by the CEAHR, the European confederation for watch repairers association. The CEAHR successfully applied to the General Court for the annulment of the Commission decision rejecting the confederation's complaint that the manufacturers of Swiss watches infringed Articles 101 and/or 102 by refusing to supply to independent watch repairers within their 'selective distribution system'.[284]

The General Court explained that the Commission's prioritizing process is based on sufficient community interest, which is determined through a balancing test;[285] and, in this case, had three elements:

- The impact on the functioning of the common market, including the economic importance of the allegation in question;[286]
- The complexity of potential investigation;
- The likelihood of proving infringements.[287]

The General Court found that the Commission did not sufficiently determine CEAHR's arguments on the relevant market and thus made a manifest error by assessing it.[288] Nevertheless, after dealing with this complaint again based on the judgment in *CEAHR*, the Commission

---

[283] Note 279, *CEAHR*.
[284] They also alleged that the manufacturers colluded and thus created a cartel but the Court confirmed the Commission's prejudgment that there was no evidence leading to such a conclusion. See ibid., [130]–[132].
[285] Ibid., [156].
[286] Ibid., [22], [33], [153].
[287] Ibid., [153], [158].
[288] Ibid., [50]–[121].

closed its new investigation in July 2014.[289] This illustrated the Commission's current approach, which is a refusal to deal with vertical restraint cases thus supporting its approach to its enforcement priorities.[290]

Despite the Commission's decreased interest in vertical restriction case enforcement, it issued new vertical Regulation and Guidelines 2010, which did not contain any significant changes from the previous Regulation 1999 and Guidelines 1999. Indeed, forms of passive sale, minimum resale maintenance and retail price fixing remained the hard-core restrictions. Although the revised Regulation and Guidelines 2010 did not differ much from Regulation 1999 and Guidelines 1999, they highlighted that Article 101(3) also applies to hard-core restrictions[291] and that the list of hard-core restrictions is exhaustive.[292] Thus, they eliminated any doubts in that sense and arguments that a similar approach to the US per se rule applied to hard-core restrictions.[293]

In 2009, prior the introduction of Regulation and Guidelines 2010, the Commission published a draft of the new regulations and guidelines on vertical restraints and invited the public to take part in discussions on the matter. The discussion around the new guidelines and regulation shows different opinions on vertical restraints reflected in different interests of different stakeholders. Logically, consumers appealed to the Commission to keep the protective approach and to take it even further.[294] Consumers agreed with the Commission's view on keeping the hard-core approach to

---

[289] Commission Decision rejecting the complaints, Case AT.39097 (29 July 2015), Rejection Decision published on 13 May 2015.

[290] Although the Commission has to investigate official complaints sufficiently, it does not have a duty to proceed and deliver a final decision. If it does not, it has to make a formal rejection of the complaint.

[291] Note 266, Regulation 2010, Preamble, [7]; Note 113, Guidelines 2010, [6], [23], [97], [99], [106], [110]–[111].

[292] Note 266, Regulation 2010, art. 4; Note 113, Guidelines 2010, [47]–[64].

[293] For previous criticism in this matter in connection with the Guidelines 1999 (See Note 200) and the Regulation 1999 (see Note 199), see, Frances Dethmers and Pier Posthuma de Boer, 'Ten Years On: Vertical Agreements under Article 81' [2009] 30(9) *European Competition Law Review* 424, 427; Derek Ridyard and Simon Bishop, 'E.C. Vertical Restraints Guidelines: Effects Based on Per Se Policy?' [2002] 23(1) *European Competition Law Review* 34, 35–8.

[294] For example, they believed there was no justification for the suggested two-year protection of new products to penetrate the market. Note 272, 'Consumer Focus' 5, 12–14; On the other hand, businesses represented by law firms welcomed this period for starting a new distribution and/or penetrating a new market. LAWIN, 'Review of the Competition Rules Applicable to Vertical Agreements: Response to Consultation' (Response to Draft Commission Regulation, 2009) ('LAWIN Review') 2.

RPM in the EU.[295] They explained that free riding is of benefit to society and consumers as it decreases prices, improves innovation and adapts to consumer demand. The message was very strong urging the Commission to protect free riding and freedom of choice.[296]

Consumers also welcomed the protection of the freedom of distributors' Internet advertising, asking for even more freedom for distributors with regard to, among other things, exclusive distribution systems.[297] On the other hand, businesses and the ICC welcomed a weakening of further limitations to the hard-core restrictions, for instance, paragraph 225 of the Guidelines allows franchisors to fix resale prices, to organize a coordinated short-term low price campaign for a duration of up to six weeks, and recognizes other efficiencies of RPM.[298]

Regulation and Guidelines 2010 came into force in June 2010 and will be valid until 2022. With respect to RPM and VTR, the main policy remained the same. The only significant change was that the Guidelines added further exemptions to the main hard-core rule and explanations, reflected in the difference between active and passive sales, Internet sales, promotion and advertising.[299] The most significant change was the introduction of a 30 percent threshold of market power of buyers involved,[300] which had already been changed in the technology transfer block exemption in 2004.[301] This change sends the message that the Commission is not only concerned with upstream level market power, but it also takes into consideration downstream level market power.

The economic approach typified for this era is well reflected in court judgments, in particular the cases of the General Court. In *GSK*,[302] which dealt with the Commission decision from the previous era, the General Court promoted proper economic examination explaining, amongst other things, that even the existence of restriction by object must be proved by

---

[295] Note 272, 'Consumer Focus' 14.
[296] Ibid., 5, 11–13.
[297] Ibid., 9–10.
[298] Note 294, 'LAWIN Review'; American Chamber of Commerce to the European Union 'AmCham EU Response to the European Commission's Consultation on the Review of the Vertical Restraints Block Exemption Regulation and Guidelines' (Response to Draft Commission Regulation, 2009) ('Amcham EU Response') 4.
[299] Note 113, Guidelines 2010, [51]–[54].
[300] Note 266, Regulation 2010, arts 3, 7(g).
[301] Note 50, Commission Regulation (EC) 772/2004, art. 3(2).
[302] Note 218, *GSK*, and *GSK* appeal.

analysis. The General Court differentiated between intrabrand and interbrand competition, explaining that conduct restricting intrabrand competition can only restrict and not eliminate competition if there are other companies competing in the market. Furthermore, *GSK* incorporated the principle of proportionality in order to determine whether conduct can be exempted under Article 101(3). It explained that it is enough if the alleged infringer shows the likelihood of the existence of appreciable objective advantages, which also includes increased profit from restrictive conduct, if it leads to increased innovation. If the alleged infringer shows this, then the Commission must make a proper economic evaluation of such advantages in connection with the restrictive impact of the practice in question with an emphasis on economic efficiency.

In *GSK*, the CJEU refused to accept that the only goal of Article 101 is consumer welfare. Instead, it held that the objective is broader as it protects competition. It also made it clear that the restriction of parallel trade constitutes the restriction of competition in its object. Another restriction by object proclaimed by the CJEU in *Pierre Fabre* is absolute restriction of online sales or another 'area of activity'.[303] The CJEU ruled in this case that even qualitative conditions of selective distribution systems could infringe Article 101(1) if such conditions were aimed at eliminating online sales. By applying the principle of proportionality, the CJEU explained that if such elimination is absolute and does not have a proportionate objective justification, in other words, an object that does not go beyond what is necessary, it constitutes restriction of competition in object.

In the case of *Peugeot Nederland*,[304] the General Court confirmed that the restrictions of passive sales and parallel trade of the agreements in question constituted an infringement by object under Article 101(1) TFEU. It approved the Commission's ranking of the restrictions of passive sales and parallel trade among very serious infringements of EU competition rules since they, inter alia, contradicted the internal market as one of the most fundamental objectives of the EU (at that time, EC).[305] The Court said that proof of the absence of anticompetitive effects is not

---

[303] Case C-434/09 *Pierre Fabre Dermo-Cosmetique SAS v Président de l'Authorité de la Concurrence, Ministre de l'Èconomie, de l'Industrie et de l'Emploi* [2011] 5 CMLR 31 ('*Pierre Fabre*'); [38].

[304] Case T-450/05 *Automobiles Peugeot SA, Peugeot Nederland NV v. Commission* [2009] OJ C205/32 ('*Peugeot Nederland*').

[305] Ibid., [281]; see also Commission Notice (EC) 98/C 9/03 Guidelines on the method of setting fines imposed pursuant to Article 15 (2) of Regulation No 17 and Article 65 (5) of the ECSC Treaty [1998] C9/3, [1A].

relevant in the rebuttal to the existence of an infringement by object. However, the actual impact of the infringement on the market is relevant, particularly where this could be measured to assess the gravity of that infringement.[306]

The preliminary-ruling case of *Lelos*[307] dealt, for the first time, with the question of whether vertical territorial restriction in the form of preventing parallel exports could infringe Article 102 and thus constitute an abuse of a dominant position. The facts of the case were similar to those in the case of *Bayer*. In *Lelos*, the CJEU discussed whether a refusal to supply wholesalers in one Member State by a pharmaceutical company beyond a certain amount in order to prevent the wholesalers from re-exporting the products to other Member States could constitute an abuse of a dominant position and infringe Article 102. Unlike in *Bayer*, in *Lelos*, it was not disputed whether the manufacturer's practice was aimed at eliminating parallel exports, rather, the question was whether this could constitute an abuse of a dominant position. Notwithstanding the fact that prices of medicine are regulated by Member States, the CJEU found that parallel trade (exports and imports) involves benefits for health insurance funds and also final consumers, as 'parallel trade is liable to exert pressure on prices'.[308]

The CJEU held that a situation where a dominant manufacturer of pharmaceutical products refused to meet 'ordinary orders' in order to prevent parallel exports would infringe Article 102 by abusing his dominant position. The CJEU referred to two objectives of EU competition law. First, competition law ensures that 'competition in the internal market is not distorted'.[309] Second, for the purposes of this situation, an essential objective of EU competition law is 'to achieve the integration of national markets through the establishment of a single market'[310] (currently, internal market), which is the objective of the Treaty. The Court explained that this objective applies to both Articles 101 and 102.[311]

In order to determine whether such conduct abused a dominant position, the Court must examine whether the company refused to meet ordinary orders. In order to do so, they must determine whether refusal to supply a certain amount of products is 'reasonable and in proportion to

---

[306] Note 304, *Peugeot Nederland*, [22], [43]–[141].
[307] Note 276, *Lelos kai*.
[308] Ibid., [56].
[309] Ibid., [66].
[310] Ibid., [65].
[311] Ibid., [65]–[78].

the need to protect [manufacturer's] own commercial interest'[312] such as the company's ability to ensure research and future innovation.[313] Nevertheless, the manufacturer must fulfill his obligation to meet the demands of the pharmaceutical product in question for the national market.[314]

One of the Commission's latest decisions on cases on vertical restraints under Article 101 is *Nintendo*.[315] This decision was decided by the Commission in the previous era; however, its last appeal, *Activision*,[316] was decided in 2011. *Activision* dealt with proving a concurrence of wills under Article 101. In particular, to what extent the behavior of a particular distributor should have been analyzed to determine the existence of a concurrence of wills. In this case, the CJEU found that a participant of an illegal vertical arrangement was interested in both arriving at an agreement with the supplier on conduct prohibited under Article 101(1) and cheating, profiting from both situations.

VTR: *Activision*[317] (*Nintendo* Appeal): Concurrence of Wills

This case involved VTR between Nintendo, a Japanese manufacturer of game consoles, video games and games cartridges, and its exclusive distributors based across the EU. The prices of Nintendo's products differed in different Member States. In its decision from 2002, the Commission found evidence of practices blocking parallel trade from low-priced to high-priced territories or Member States. Exclusive distributions were replaced by absolute territorial protections and all competition was eliminated in each territory. This vertical restriction was further implemented by different methods of monitoring parallel imports and exports.[318] The Commission concluded that all the actions in question were a combination of agreements and concerted practices forming a single and continuous infringement between the manufacturer and its exclusive distributors and others.[319] It found that the object of the agreements and/or concerted practices in question restricted competition

---

[312] Ibid., [69].
[313] Ibid., [69]–[78].
[314] Ibid., [75].
[315] Note 214, *Nintendo*.
[316] C-260/09 *Activision Blizzard Germany GmbH v. European Commission* [2011] ECR 419 ('*Activision*').
[317] Ibid.
[318] Note 214, *Nintendo*, [104]–[106], [116], [119]–[160], [170]–[229], [230]–[236].
[319] Ibid., [261]–[286].

and formed an infringement within the meaning of Article 101(1) as it established absolute territorial protection eliminating even passive sales, resulting in a negative impact on prices.[320]

Two appeals followed the Commission's decision: Nintendo appealed to the General Court regarding just the fine itself, which the Court reduced to a total of €119.2425 million.[321] One distributor, CD-Contact Data GmbH (currently, Activision Blizzard Germany, GmbH), appealed to the General Court and later to the CJEU claiming that the evidence presented was not sufficient to prove that she was involved in the prohibited conduct constituting restrictive agreements and/or concerted practices.[322] The dispute concerned, amongst other things, the existence of a concurrence of wills in the form of an agreement or concerted practice.

This appeal involved the following facts: CD-Contact Data GmbH, later Activision Blizzard Germany, GmbH (CD-Contact), entered the market with Nintendo's product in April 1997 as Nintendo's exclusive distributor for Belgium and Luxembourg.[323] Although the distribution agreement between Nintendo and CD-Contract allowed passive exports,[324] CD-Contact gave written assurance in the form of a fax to Nintendo not to allow the export of Nintendo's products outside her territory of Luxembourg and Belgium in October 1997. However, CD-Contact admitted that she cheated by selling to companies which then exported the products and also by exporting them herself.

CD-Contact also asked Nintendo to 'address' the issue of parallel imports into Luxembourg and Belgium territory in three separate letters in September, November and December 1997.[325] This correspondence, including the fax, proved, according to the Commission, the General Court and the CJEU, the infringement of Article 101(1). The General Court and the CJEU found that CD-Contact was involved in Nintendo's information exchange system with the aim of preventing both active and passive parallel trade and that the object of the correspondence between

---

[320] Ibid., [168], [331]–[332].
[321] Case T-13/03 *Nintendo Co Ltd and Nintendo of Europe GmbH v. Commission of the EC* [2009] ECR II-947 [215].
[322] Case T-18/03, *CD-Contact Data GmbH v. European Commission* [2009] ECR II-1021 ('*CD-Contact*'); appealed to the CJEU: Note 316, *Activision*.
[323] Note 316, *Activision*, [2]–[4].
[324] Ibid., [12].
[325] Ibid., [8]–[9].

CD-Contact and Nintendo 'was to denounce parallel imports of Nintendo products into Belgium'.[326]

CD-Contact claimed in her appeal that the Commission did not prove a concurrence of wills between CD-Contact and Nintendo because CD-Contact de facto exported, in the form of passive sales, Nintendo's products.[327] CD-Contact argued that vertical arrangements differ from that of horizontal in the way that, first, vertical agreements are needed but horizontal agreements are from the status quo suspicious. Unlike horizontal competitors, there is a dependent relationship between distributors and suppliers whereas distributors are 'in a weak position vis-à-vis the supplier'.[328] This makes it difficult for distributors to differentiate (dissociate) themselves from the policy imposed by the supplier and therefore the behavior of a particular distributor should have been analyzed to determine the existence of a concurrence of wills.[329] The CJEU agreed with CD-Contact that the establishing of the existence of a vertical agreement can differ from that of a horizontal agreement because 'a certain measure of contact is lawful' on the vertical chain.[330] However, the CJEU supported the ruling of the General Court stating that the General Court evaluated all evidence presented and found a concurrence of wills between CD-Contact and Nintendo infringing Article 101(1) without making any error in law.[331]

The General Court found that CD-Contact actively participated in an information exchange and that she asked Nintendo to take action to prevent parallel imports to Belgium.[332] The fact that she cheated on this arrangement by allowing and participating in passive parallel exports did not, under these circumstances, mean that Nintendo and CD-Contact had not reached an agreement with the object of limiting parallel imports. It was simply a way for CD-Contact to exploit this arrangement for her own benefit.[333] The CJEU stated that a participant of an illegal vertical arrangement can be interested in both arriving at an agreement with the supplier on conduct prohibited under Article 101(1) and cheating.[334] Indeed, in this situation, CD-Contact profited from the existence of

---

[326] Ibid., [18]; see Note 322, *CD-Contact*, [62].
[327] Note 322, *CD-Contact*, [59], [63]–[64].
[328] Note 316, *Activision*, [65].
[329] Ibid., [65]–[66].
[330] Ibid., [72].
[331] Ibid., [73]–[78].
[332] Note 322, *CD-Contact*, [59]–[66]; Note 316, *Activision*, [80].
[333] Ibid., *CD-Contact*, [67].
[334] Note 316, *Activision*, [82].

absolute territorial protection in her own territory, which she actively protected by demanding that Nintendo ensure that no parallel imports were allowed. At the same time, she increased her sales even more by secretly allowing exports and exporting Nintendo's products from her territory.

Interestingly, the CJEU did not refer to the case of *Bayer*, where it stated that it was not necessary for the interests of the parties to correspond in order to prove an agreement under Article 101(1).[335] This case could have provided an opportunity to comment and perhaps further clarify this statement in *Bayer*. Here, in *Activision*, it was in the interest of CD-Contact that no one either actively or passively sell in her own territory. Therefore, she made sure that Nintendo would not allow anyone to enter her territory. At the same time, it was in her interest to export Nintendo products in order to obtain extra profit from the exports. In *Bayer*, unlike *Activision*, the manufacturer did not facilitate monitoring arrangements, nor did wholesalers from 'cheaper' Member States have to face parallel imports, rather they were interested in parallel exports. Referring to *Bayer* and distinguishing between these two cases by the CJEU and hence explaining whether and under what circumstances the intentions of the parties should be analyzed and should be in agreement and not in contradiction would have served the clarity of law.

VTR: *GSK*:[336] Restriction by Object and Economic Evaluation

This case reflects the importance of economic analysis, including the restriction of interbrand competition, in vertical restraint cases under Article 101. Article 101(1) discusses the existence of a concurrence of wills, restriction by object and the effect and importance of determining the anticompetitive effects either in connection with consumer welfare or the protection of competition. The CJEU refused the Commission's and the General Court's argument that the object of Article 101(1) is pure consumer welfare, stating that Article 101 includes other elements that protect the competitive process in general. This case also explains the application of the principle of proportionality when evaluating procompetitive effects with regards to Article 101(3).

Summary of facts
This case involved pharmaceutical products produced by GlaxoSmithKline Services Unlimited (GSK), one of the world's leading manufacturers

---

[335] Note 41, *Bayer* appeal, [114].
[336] Note 218, *GSK*, *GSK* appeal.

of pharmaceutical products. The prices of pharmaceutical products differed between Member States due to the fact that prices were controlled by individual Member States in a number of different ways. This led to parallel exports of medicine from 'cheaper' Member States to 'expensive' Member States.

Glaxo Wellcome, SA (GW), a Spanish subsidiary of GSK, manufactured, developed and distributed medicines in Spain.[337] It applied for an exemption for a document entitled 'General Sales Conditions of Pharmaceutical Specialities Belonging to [GW] and its Subsidiaries to Authorised Wholesalers' (Conditions). The Conditions concerned 82 medicines intended for sale to wholesalers, who could be interested in exporting primarily to the UK and other Member States. The Conditions provided two different prices for home sales and exports. The wholesalers were required to sign copies of the Conditions and return them to GW as proof of acceptance. Seventy-five wholesalers with sales accounting for more than 90 percent of the total GW sales in Spain signed the Conditions.[338]

The Commission's decision stated that GW's agreement infringed Article 101(1) by charging higher prices if the medicines were exported to other Member States.[339] GSK appealed to the General Court and to the CJEU.

Concurrence of wills to restrict competition

The Commission found that signed copies of the Conditions constituted an agreement between GW and those wholesalers who signed the Conditions.[340] GW disagreed, arguing that this did not constitute an agreement because a concurrence of wills to restrict competition was not present.[341]

The General Court examined the existence of independent will and of a concurrence of wills on the wholesale price of medicines.[342] First, the Court stated that Spanish legislation did not maintain wholesale prices of medicines, thus setting wholesale prices outside the Spanish sickness scheme was within the scope of the undertakings.[343] Second, the General Court found that the case file showed that it was GW who adopted the

---

[337] Note 218, *GSK* appeal, [4]; *GSK*, [8]–[9].
[338] Note 218, *GSK* appeal, [5]–[8]; *GSK*, [8]–[14].
[339] Note 218, *GSK* appeal, [2]; *GSK*, [18]–[20].
[340] Note 218, *GSK*, [60].
[341] Ibid., [61]–[64].
[342] Ibid., [65].
[343] Ibid., [67], [72]–[73].

Conditions as well as a system of setting prices and that 75 of the 89 wholesalers signed copies of the Conditions as requested by GW. In doing so, they accepted the offer and an agreement with GW was formed.[344]

The General Court also observed that some wholesalers who signed the Conditions, 'expressed doubts as to the legality of those conditions';[345] however, they did not withdraw from the agreement. Some wholesalers who signed the Conditions were members of associations who complained to the Commission about the Conditions. However, the General Court stated that this did not prove that all or some of the wholesalers did not intend to collude with GW. Therefore, a concurrence of wills existed.[346]

Economic approach and restriction by object or effect

The General Court referred to both forms of competition, interbrand and intrabrand, when evaluating anticompetitive effect and object. In connection with this case, the General Court observed that, despite the allowed restriction on price competition based on national and EU legislation, there was competition among the manufacturers of medicine, between manufacturers and their distributors and between parallel traders and national distributors. Therefore, GSK had no capability to eliminate competition altogether, but it was able to restrict competition.[347] In other words, the General Court held that conduct restricting interbrand competition can only restrict and not eliminate competition if there are other companies competing in the market.

In this part of the judgment, the General Court, on one hand, differentiated between these two forms of competition unlike in *Consten and Grundig*, where the CJEU simply stated that it was enough to show that intrabrand competition was restricted without evaluating interbrand competition.[348] On the other hand, it made it clear that even the restriction of intrabrand competition can infringe Article 101(1), unlike the current approach in the US, which requires (with some exceptions) proving the restriction of interbrand competition to establish a violation

---

[344] Ibid., [79].
[345] Ibid., [87].
[346] Ibid., [87]–[89].
[347] Ibid., [104]–[108].
[348] Note 45, *Consten and Grundig*, 342.

of Section 1 of the Sherman Act, assuming that the restriction of intrabrand competition can increase interbrand competition.[349]

In the case of *GSK*, the Commission argued that the Conditions had both the effect and the object of restricting competition in the form of limiting parallel trade.[350] The General Court found restrictive effect but disagreed with the Commission that the conduct in question also restricted competition in its object. Both the Commission and the General Court set their analysis on determining the anticompetitive effects on consumer welfare.

Although the General Court confirmed that an action which intended to differentiate prices and restrict parallel trade had a restrictive object,[351] it held that even the existence of illegal object must be proved by analysis.[352] It is not enough to state that the Conditions had a restrictive object, it must be determined whether this restrictive object arose from the Conditions themselves or whether they were a consequence of other circumstances.

The General Court found that the restriction of competition existed as a consequence of other circumstances and not the Conditions themselves. The General Court criticized the Commission for not analyzing the market in detail,[353] and for providing a random economic examination.[354] The General Court referred to consumer welfare in its analysis as the objective of Article 101(1). It stated that for an action to be illegal, it must be proved that the restriction negatively affected final consumers and thus decreased consumer welfare.[355]

Although the Commission stated several times in its decision that the Conditions affected the welfare of consumers in terms of price by restricting parallel trade,[356] the General Court disagreed, concluding that neither the Conditions themselves nor their object decreased the welfare of consumers, and the content of the Conditions did not prove a restriction of competition.

---

[349] *Leegin Creative Leather Products, Inc. v. PSKS, Inc, DBA Kay's Kloset ... Kays' Shoes*, 551 U.S. 877 (2007), 890 ('*Leegin*'); Note 112, *Business Cards Tomorrow*, 1205; Note 112, *Sylvania*, 51–2, 65.

[350] Note 218, *GSK*, [91]–[98].

[351] Ibid., [114]–[116].

[352] Ibid., [117]–[119].

[353] Ibid., [133], [138].

[354] Ibid., [275]–[277].

[355] Ibid., [171]–[172].

[356] Ibid., [118], [121].

The General Court found that Member States controlled the prices of medicines in various ways. This and the exchange rate caused the existence of different medicine prices in different Member States. As the Commission confirmed itself, the geographic market was each Member State as each Member State had different conditions based on its national rules. The General Court argued that different prices applied because different markets already existed and these price differentiations caused parallel imports of medicines.[357] Hence, the Conditions did not restrict competition in object.

However, as the General Court explained, finding no restriction in object does not mean that the welfare of consumers did not decrease in its effect. Indeed, it found that the Conditions reduced the welfare of final consumers as the final consumers could not take advantage of the reduced cost and prices which would follow from unlimited parallel trade.[358] In particular, the Commission found that in some Member States the patients paid for some medicines or they financially contributed in order to purchase them. Thus, the Conditions deprived consumers of advantages that would have existed if parallel exports had not been limited.[359]

The CJEU disagreed with the General Court on its ruling on restrictive object. The CJEU concluded that the case concerned, including the parallel trade, had its object in restricting competition.[360] It criticized the General Court's statement that an agreement can have the object of restricting competition only when the agreement was likely to lead to negative effects for consumers. The CJEU held that the aim of Article 101 TFEU was not just to protect consumers but to protect competition, which includes the protection of market structure.[361] It said that:

> there is nothing in that provision to indicate that only those agreements which deprive consumers of certain advantages may have an anti-competitive object. Secondly, it must be borne in mind that the Court has held that, like other competition rules laid down in the Treaty, Article [101] aims to protect not only the interests of competitors or of consumers, but also the structure of the market and, in so doing, competition as such. Consequently, for a finding that an agreement has an anti-competitive object, it is not necessary that final

---

[357] Ibid., [125]–[129], [178]–[179].
[358] Ibid., [182].
[359] Ibid., [189].
[360] Note 218, *GSK* appeal, [55]–[64].
[361] Ibid., [63], citing Note 275, *T-Mobile Netherlands*, [38]–[39].

consumers be deprived of the advantages of effective competition in terms of supply or price.[362]

The CJEU also explained factors which must be considered in order to decide whether competition was restricted in object. These are: 'the content of the clause, the objectives it sought to attain and the economic and legal context of which it formed a part'.[363]

Despite the General Court's focus on consumer welfare arising from the economic approach, the CJEU made it absolutely clear that it is the protection of competition and not of consumers and their welfare that governs Article 101. It also gave a clear message that a restriction of parallel trade constituted the restriction of competition in its object.

Article 103: justifications and the principle of proportionality

The General Court judgment on Article 101(3), in particular the promotion of interbrand competition, evaluation of potential procompetitive effects and requirement of establishing market power in order to determine the impact on competition, shows an inclination towards the application of an economic approach. The General Court argued that intrabrand loss must be compared with interbrand gain in competition, highlighting the leading role of interbrand competition rather than that of intrabrand competition.[364] It found that competition increased with an increase in GSK's innovation.[365] Hence, the Court disagreed with the Commission's mere rejection of GSK's argument that parallel trade had prevented it from making profits, which were essential for innovation.[366] The Court missed a proper examination of this issue in the Commission's decision, which should have been based on balancing the advantages against the disadvantages of the examined conduct.[367]

The General Court referred to the justifications of GSK. GSK based its argument on improvements in innovation and, thus, on an increase in efficiency.[368] GSK argued that parallel trade would have led to a loss of efficiency in the form of a reduction in innovation.[369] The General Court agreed with GSK, explaining that innovation was paid for by the final

---

[362] Ibid.
[363] Ibid., [55]; Note 303, *Pierre Fabre*, 1159, [34]–[35].
[364] Note 218, *GSK*, [296].
[365] Ibid., [297].
[366] Ibid., [300]–[301].
[367] Ibid., [303]–[304], [306].
[368] Ibid., [258]–[259].
[369] Ibid., [220].

consumers who were prepared to pay more due to different prices in different states.[370] The UK was more profitable for GSK and allowed innovation to be recuperated globally not just locally.[371]

The General Court ruled that it was enough for applicants to prove the likelihood of *appreciable objective advantages* which could compensate for the resulting disadvantages.[372] The relevant test is based on demonstrating with *a sufficient degree of probability* that the possibility of obtaining an appreciable objective advantage existed.[373] By applying this test, the General Court concluded that the Commission could not rule that GSK did not demonstrate the promotion of technical progress under Article 101(3).[374] Furthermore, the Commission could not conclude 'that competition would be eliminated for a substantial part of the relevant products'[375] as confirmed by the Commission, because the real market power of GSK had not been estimated.[376] Thus, the Court annulled the part of the decision that stated that the Conditions did not fulfil the conditions for granting an exemption.[377]

The CJEU endorsed the General Court's ruling on Article 101(3).[378] The Commission disagreed with the General Court's ruling that the advantage of the conduct in question was higher profits which promoted innovation. It stated that there was no causal link between this advantage and the conduct itself, explaining that the conduct must promote technical progress, such as innovation, and not simply increase profits.[379] However, the CJEU rejected this argument and affirmed the General Court's conclusion that the advantage was that the increased profit could be dedicated to incremental innovation.[380] It held that although the applicants had the burden of proof, the Commission did not evaluate the applicant's arguments satisfactorily as the Commission rejected evidence without explanation or justification.[381]

The CJEU thus upheld the test of Article 101(3), as established by the General Court, and summarized it as follows. First, it must be shown that

---

[370] Ibid., [271].
[371] Ibid., [272].
[372] Note 218, *GSK* appeal, [92]–[95].
[373] Ibid., [95].
[374] Ibid., [308], [310].
[375] Ibid., [313].
[376] Ibid., [312].
[377] Note 218, *GSK*, [316]–[317].
[378] Note 218, See *GSK* appeal, [69]–[168].
[379] Ibid., [112].
[380] Ibid., [118]–[119].
[381] Note 218, *GSK* appeal, [81]–[83].

there was an appreciable objective advantage. Second, the Commission must analyze whether the conduct in question decreased efficiency. Third, if efficiency was reduced, the Commission must analyze the extent to which it was reduced. And, last, the gain in efficiency must be analyzed.[382] The CJEU agreed with the General Court that the Commission erred when it did not consider the gain in efficiency of the conduct in question.[383]

The applied test of proportionality is undoubtedly the right assessment under Article 101(3) as the wording of Article 101(3) requires the balancing and evaluating of both anticompetitive and procompetitive effects. Nevertheless, it would be useful to further clarify in future judgments the Courts' agreement with the GSK justification that increased profit increases innovation. In general, any potential infringer, including cartel participants and dominant position holders, could argue that the profit they have generated by their restrictive conduct will be used for innovation. It is primarily competition which is an essential incentive for innovation and not conduct that restricts competition. If the market is competitive, as it was in this case, competitors are motivated to innovate and introduce new and/or better products. If, as stated by the CJEU, the objective of Article 101 is to protect competition, it is essential that this form of justification is further clarified. In particular, the Commission's argument requiring proof of a causal link between increased profits and the claim that this leads to increased innovation appears to be well placed.

Pierre Fabre:[384] Restriction in Object in the Form of Absolute Restriction of Online Sale

Despite the fact that this preliminary ruling case deals with a form of customer restriction as part of a selective distribution system and includes VTR only partially, it is important for the approach to VTR and RPM as it clarifies the CJEU standpoint on the conditions that must be fulfilled in order to find a restriction by object under Article 101(1).

Facts

In this preliminary-ruling case, the cour d'appel de Paris asked the CJEU under Article 267 TFEU to answer whether a de facto absolute

---

[382] Note 218, *GSK*, [263]–[303]; *GSK* appeal, [128].
[383] Note 218, *GSK*, [261]–[262]; *GSK* appeal, [118], [131], [133], [156].
[384] Note 303, *Pierre Fabre*.

restriction of online sales constituted a hard-core restriction of competition by object for the purposes of Article 101(1) TFEU and whether the previous block exemption regulation, Regulation 1999, and/or the individual exemption under section 101(3) applied to this situation.[385]

Pierre Fabre, a French manufacturer of cosmetic products and personal care products, operated a selective distribution system in the European market, including the French market. The selective distribution arrangements required retailers to sell the cosmetics only where a qualified pharmacist was present.[386] This meant that Internet sales were de facto excluded.[387] Furthermore, the French competition authority, Conseil de la concurrence, argued, and the CJEU confirmed, that such a customer restriction practice restricted territories, stating that:

> by excluding de facto a method of marketing products that did not require the physical movement of the customer, a contractual clause would considerably reduce the ability of an authorised distributor to sell the contractual products to customers outside its contractual territory or area of activity.[388]

Restriction by object

The CJEU held that although the system in question was a qualitative selective distribution system allowed under previous cases,[389] it differed from the allowed qualitative selective distribution systems. The reason for this is that Pierre Fabre's selective distribution system restricted competition by object because it de facto eliminated online sales and because such an elimination had no objective justification, which would be proportionate; in other words, the object for the qualitative selective system would not go beyond what is necessary.[390] The CJEU presented two requirements which must be fulfilled for a qualitative selective distribution system to constitute restriction by object:

1. Absolute elimination of an 'area of activity' such as online sales or absolute VTR;[391] and

---

[385] Ibid., [31]–[32]. The preliminary questions were asked in 2009. In 2009, the new Regulation 2010 (see Note 266) had not been introduced yet and thus did not apply to this case.
[386] Note 303, *Pierre Fabre*, [9]–[13].
[387] Ibid., [14], [37].
[388] Ibid., [38].
[389] Ibid., [41].
[390] Ibid., [39], [41], [47].
[391] Ibid., [37].

2. 'absence of objective justification',[392] which is justification with no legitimate and proportionate aims; in other words, the purpose of justification would go beyond what is necessary.[393]

By stating that selective distribution systems which de facto eliminate all online sales without 'objective' justification of such a clause/system constitute restrictions by object not exempted under block exemption, the CJEU de facto excluded all or almost all selective distribution systems based purely on face-to-face services if these are not justified. Such face-to-face services restrict online sales absolutely. In other words, any selective distribution system where the supplier requires that his/her distributors or retailers must provide a face-to-face service, such as a technical consultation, will automatically restrict competition by object as it will exclude online sales unless such a restriction is proportionate to its purpose. In the latter situation, the particular clause of a selective system could constitute restriction by effect.

In *Pierre Fabre*, it was not proportionate to argue that the conduct de facto eliminating Internet sales was justified by providing qualified advice by a pharmacist to customers on Pierre Fabre's cosmetic products. The CJEU referred to previous cases where, by applying the principle of freedom of movement, it was stated that such justification was not accepted for non-prescription medicines and contact lenses; however, such justification could apply for the purposes of prescription medicine.[394] It was not also a proportionate objective justification that this conduct served the protection of the reputation of a luxurious/prestigious image of the product in question. The CJEU explained that this was 'not a legitimate aim for restricting competition'.[395] None of these arguments thus constituted proportionate objective justification which would show that this was not a restriction by object under Article 101(1).

It could appear that by applying the interpretation of the restriction by object in *Pierre Fabre*, the restrictions by object cannot be justified under Article 101(3) because the second condition established in *Pierre Fabre* was that there was no objective justification. Such interpretation would not be in agreement with the wording of Articles 101(1) and 101(3) and

---

[392] Ibid., [39], [47].
[393] Ibid., [41], [43].
[394] Ibid., [44]. The CJEU was referring to Case C-322/01, *Deutscher Apothekerverband v. 0800 DocMorris, Jacques Waterval* [2005] 1 CMLR 46, [106]–[107], [112]; and Case C-108/09 *Ker-Optika bt v. ANTSZ del-dunantuli Regionalis Intezete* [2011] 2 CMLR 15, [76].
[395] Note 303, *Pierre Fabre*, [46].

does not reflect the judgment of the CJEU in this case. The CJEU refers to 'objective justification' when it interprets Article 101(1) and not Article 101(3).[396] This objective justification is based on the objective test 'where, following an individual and specific examination of the content and objective of that contractual clause and the legal and economic context of which it forms a part, it is apparent that ... that clause is not objectively justified'.[397] If it was restriction in effect, its object would be justified, in other words legitimate, but its effect would be restrictive. Therefore, this objective justification determines the existence of restriction by object and cannot be mistaken with potential justifications under Article 101(3). Even restriction by object under Article 101(1) could be justified under Article 101(3).

The CJEU also confirmed by referring to *GSK* (in particular, when the CJEU highlighted that the restriction by object or effect were alternative and not cumulative conditions)[398] that once the object is established, it is not necessary to determine the existence of restriction by effect.[399] The restriction by object in this case included the restriction of passive sales. Therefore, the CJEU applied Article 4(c) of Regulation 1999, which states that the block exemption does not apply to selective distribution systems where the object is the restriction of active or passive sales to end users. Such restrictive object can be direct or indirect, in isolation or in combination with other factors. The CJEU stated that the contractual clause in question, which de facto prohibited online sales of Pierre Fabre cosmetic products, constituted a restriction by object also in the form of a restriction of retail passive sales to final customers.[400] Even under current Regulation 2010, such a restriction would not be exempted under the block exemption.[401] Nevertheless, the CJEU confirmed that even for restrictions that constitute restrictions by object and are not exempted under the block exemption regulation, Article 101(3) still applies. Therefore, in this case, the French court could consider whether this conduct could be individually exempted.[402]

---

[396] Ibid., [47].
[397] Ibid.
[398] Note 218, *GSK* appeal, [55].
[399] Note 303, *Pierre Fabre*, [34].
[400] Ibid., [52]–[54].
[401] Note 266, Regulation 2010, art. 4(b); but also see art. 4(c), 4(d) and 4(e); Note 113, Guidelines 2010, [48]–[64].
[402] Note 303, *Pierre Fabre*, [59].

VII. APPLICATION AND ENFORCEMENT

The above-discussed cases show that it is Article 101 TFEU which has been applied to cases on RPM and VTR. However, Article 102 could also apply if RPM or VTR constituted an abuse of a dominant position, as confirmed by the CJEU in the preliminary ruling case of *Lelos* with regard to VTR in the form of a restriction of parallel exports and imports.

In order to determine the correct application of EU competition law to RPM and VTR cases, the enforcement and substance of current EU law needs to be surveyed. The law of RPM and VTR is based on primary sources of law: Articles of TFEU, in particular Article 101; secondary sources of law: the current vertical block exemption regulation, Regulation 2010 and the interpretation of law by EU courts, especially the CJEU, which has to be followed by the Commission, NCAs and national courts. The interpretation by the Commission contained in the Guidelines 2010, which creates so-called 'soft law', is also crucial as it shows how the Commission and most likely NCAs would interpret EU law unless the CJEU states otherwise. Therefore, after briefly outlining the enforcement of EU competition law, I will first determine where RPM and VTR are positioned with regard to Regulation 2010 and then explain the application of Article 101 to RPM and VTR cases.

Enforcement

EU competition law can be enforced by both the European Commission and proceedings in individual Member States. Since Council Regulation 1/2003 came into force, public enforcement has been decentralized, meaning that both the Commission and NCAs can enforce EU competition law. Since then, the majority of cases on EU competition law have been decided by NCAs and not the Commission.[403] With regard to vertical-restraint cases, despite the arguably strict approach to RPM and VTR under Regulation and Guidelines 2010, the Commission has not made any recent decisions on RPM or VTR, while the NCAs have been active in that regard.[404]

Unlike in the US, in the EU, public enforcement prevails over private enforcement in general and with regards to vertical restraints. At the EU level, the enforcement is always public as it is governed by the decisions

---

[403] See Note 280, Commission, 'Ten Years' 4.
[404] Of all NCA cases on EU competition law between May 2004 and December 2013 18 percent were vertical agreements cases which included RPM and VTR; see ibid., 5.

of the European Commission. The Commission investigates and makes procedural and final decisions, finding infringements and imposing fines and behavioral and structural remedies.[405] These decisions can then be reviewed by the General Court, which operates as the court of first instance in those situations, and then appealed on a point of law to the CJEU as the court of last instance. The courts can annul the Commission's decision under Article 263 TFEU and change fines and penalties imposed by the Commission under Article 261 TFEU.

Even enforcement of EU competition law that takes place in individual Member States is predominantly public. Nevertheless, it also includes private enforcement. Articles 101 and 102 TFEU have direct effect which allows for private enforcement to take place in the national courts. EU competition law can also be privately litigated in cases on damages in individual Member States. Although the frequency of damages cases is very low in comparison with the US, a number of experts and the Commission have recently been promoting such enforcement, finding benefits in these cases for addressing both deterrence and compensation.[406] In this respect, the Commission initiated discussion on private enforcement to ensure compensation for consumers and recovering of damages.[407] Although the Commission's initiative was motivated by increasing private enforcement and compensating consumers with regards to cartels, this does not mean that cases on damages cannot exist in connection with vertical restraint cases.

The private enforcement of EU competition law by national courts is governed by national procedural rules due to national procedural autonomy.[408] Also, public litigation procedural rules differ between individual Member States and the Commission. For instance, NCAs have

---

[405] The Commission can also make Commitment Decisions under Article 9 of Regulation 1/2003 (see Note 38) and since 2008 settlements used in respect of cartels.

[406] See, e.g., Wouter P J Wils, 'The Relationship between Public Antitrust Enforcement and Private Actions for Damages' (2009) 32 *World Competition* 3; Renato Nazzini and Ali Nikpay, 'Private Actions in EC Competition Law' (2008) 4(2) *Competition Policy International* 107; Assimakis P Komninos, 'Public and Private Antitrust Enforcement in Europe: Complement? Overlap?' (2006) 3 *Competition Law Review* 1.

[407] This resulted in two documents, see Note 277.

[408] See Case 33/76 *Rewe-Zentralfinanz eG and Rewe-Zentral AG v. Landwirtschaftskammer für das Saarland* [1976] ECR 1989.

different investigative and enforcement powers, although, like the Commission, many NCAs have the power to make the final decision and impose fines.[409]

Despite the differences in enforcement, which can have an impact on the efficiency of enforcement of EU competition law, the EU involves a number of mechanisms to ensure consistent interpretation. This consistent interpretation is crucial for legal clarity and transparency. Both the NCAs and the national courts have to interpret Articles 101 and 102 TFEU in accordance with the interpretation of the CJEU. A national court, when dealing with a case on EU competition law, can refer a preliminary question to the CJEU under Article 267 TFEU and the CJEU will make a judgment on that matter. Preliminary ruling cases are common in vertical restraint matters, including cases such as *Minière*, *Lelos* and *Pierre Fabre*. The Commission is also obliged to assist national courts if required by them[410] and can act as amicus curiae at national court proceedings.[411] Furthermore, the European Competition Network ensures a very effective cooperation and consistent application of EU competition law among the Commission and NCAs.[412]

These, as well as other mechanisms, ensure consistency in interpretation and application of EU competition law. Therefore, although this book does not include NCA decisions and national court judgments, the analysis of EU competition law and EU cases, including CJEU and General Court cases, and Commission decisions provides a detailed overview of the application of EU competition rules to VTR and RPM showing which and how these rules should be applied across the whole of the EU.

Application of Block Exemption Regulation

Article 101(1) TFEU explicitly prohibits forms of price fixing including RPM in point (a) when it states that the prohibited forms of multilateral/bilateral practices (agreements) are illegal if they 'directly or indirectly fix purchase or selling prices or any other trading conditions'. It partly mentions territorial restrictions in point (c), which includes 'share[ing] markets or sources of supply'. When applying the legal positivism approach to this matter and considering the legal power of TFEU, which

---

[409] See Note 280, Commission, 'Ten Years'.
[410] See, e.g., Note 130, *Henninger*, [53].
[411] Note 38, Council Regulation (EC) 1/2003, art. 15.
[412] See European Commission, 'European Competition Network – Overview' <http://ec.europa.eu/competition/ecn/index_en.html> accessed 30 June 2015.

is the primary source of EU law,[413] we can conclude that RPM is prohibited unless the conduct concerned fulfills the terms and conditions of Article 101(3), in which case the conduct can be exempted and is considered to be legal.

The prohibited agreements can be exempted individually under Article 101(3) or by the Commission's block exemption regulations. Regulations form the secondary source of EU law and provide specific applications for Article 101(3). Regulation 2010, which applies to vertical restrictions including RPM and VTR, reflects the content of Article 101 by ranging RPM and some forms of VTR, such as passive sales,[414] which restrict competition in object,[415] among hard-core restrictions under Article 4 of Regulation 2010. Hard-core restrictions are based on the assumption that they have actual or potential negative results to such an extent that fulfilment of the conditions of Article 101(3) TFEU is highly unlikely.[416] However, they can still be exempted in individual cases under Article 101(3), as explicitly explained in Guidelines 2010.[417]

With respect to some forms of customer allocations and territorial restraints, the block exemption does not apply to restrictions of active and passive sales to 'end users by members of a selective distribution system operating at the retailer level of trade'[418] because distributors within their selective distribution system should be free to sell the product concerned and the system cannot be combined with an exclusive distribution system. It also does not apply to 'the restriction of cross-supplies between distributors within a selective distribution system, including distributors operating at different levels of trade'[419] because selective distributors must remain free to purchase the product concerned from another distributor in the selective distribution system and they cannot be obliged to purchase the product from only one manufacturer. Finally, it does not apply to:

---

[413] EU law is based on *lex scripta* (written law); EU courts do not have the power to change the rules of valid EU treaties.

[414] Note 266, Regulation 2010, art. 4(b); but also see art. 4(c), 4(d) and 4(e); Note 113, Guidelines 2010, [48]–[64].

[415] See cases; Note 212, *Volkswagen* appeal; Note 218, *GSK* appeal; Note 214, *Nintendo*; Note 54, *Minière*.

[416] Note 266, Regulation 2010, Preamble, [10]; Guidelines, [47], [223].

[417] Note 113, Guidelines 2010, paras 47, 106–109, 223, 229; cf Alison Jones, 'Left Behind by Modernisations? Restrictions by Object under Article 101(1)' (2010) 6(3) *European Competition Journal* 649 ('Left Behind?').

[418] Note 266, Regulation 2010, art. 4(c), see Note 113, Guidelines 2010, [57].

[419] Ibid., art. 4(d); see Note 113, Guidelines 2010, [58].

the restriction, agreed between a supplier of components and a buyer who incorporates those components, of the supplier's ability to sell the components such as spare parts to end-users or to repairers or other service providers not entrusted by the buyer with the repair or servicing of its goods.[420]

Although the block exemption does not apply to RPM (minimum price fixing and price fixing) or to some forms of VTR,[421] it applies to maximum price setting, price recommendations and some forms of territorial restriction.[422] Listed below are four forms of VTR included in the block exemption. Despite the fact that all four are ranged among territorial restrictions, some forms could be classified as other than VTR forms of vertical restraints, with the last one creating customer allocations rather than territorial restraints:

1. exclusive territory or customer policy, restrictions of active sales which do not include restrictions of customers;[423]
2. restrictions of sales to end users by a buyer operating at the wholesale level of trade to keep the two levels of trade, wholesale and retail, separate;[424]
3. selective distribution systems, restrictions of sales to unauthorized distributors within the territory where the selective distribution system operates;[425] and
4. restrictions which aim to avoid imitations of the same types of goods by potential competitors to avoid selling components to undertakings who would use them to manufacture the same type of goods as those produced by the supplier.[426]

In situations where the block exemption regulation applies, including the above-described forms of VTR, it concerns only prohibited vertical agreements which are within the so-called 'safe harbour'.[427] The safe harbor is determined based on market power which plays an important role in the EU law of vertical restraints.[428] In cases other than hard-core

---

[420] Ibid., art. 4(e); see Note 113, Guidelines 2010, [59].
[421] Ibid., art. 4; Note 113, Guidelines 2010, [47]–[64].
[422] Ibid., art. 4(a), 4(b); Note 113, Guidelines 2010, [4], [50]–[63].
[423] Ibid., art. 4(b)(i); Note 113, Guidelines 2010, [55].
[424] Ibid., art. 4(b)(ii); Note 113, Guidelines 2010, [55].
[425] Ibid., art. 4(b)(iii); Note 113, Guidelines 2010, [55].
[426] Ibid., art. 4(b)(iv); Note 113, Guidelines 2010, [55].
[427] Note 113, Guidelines 2010, [23].
[428] Note 266, Regulation 2010, Preamble, [7]; Note 113, Guidelines 2010, [6], [23], [97], [99], [106], [110]–[111].

restrictions, the block exemption does not apply if the buyers' and sellers' market share of involved sellers and buyers is higher than 30 percent. Block exemptions, and thus only the agreements within the safe harbor, are based on the assumption that the efficiency-enhancing effects of such agreements outweigh any restrictive effects unless the market is not sufficiently competitive.[429] Additionally, the Commission or an NCA can decide that the block exemption does not apply in individual cases if the conditions of Article 101(1) are fulfilled but the conditions of Article 101(3) are not.[430] This follows from the fact that Article 101 is the primary source of EU law, while Regulation 2010 is the secondary source.

Regulation and also Guidelines 2010 appear to be overcomplicated, which does not assist with legal clarity and transparency. Both have been criticized in that regard. For example, Dethmers and Posthuma de Boer criticized the Commission for the Guidelines being too extensive and both the Guidelines and Regulation for being too complicated and theoretical without providing any legal certainty for their practical application.[431] In particular, the differentiated approach to VTR seems to be too complicated and perhaps unnecessary. This could be replaced with a simpler approach, which would reflect the economic integration principle and the court's interpretation. For instance, it would be easier to differentiate between absolute territorial and other territorial restrictions.

The change in Regulation 2010, which added another 30 percent threshold requiring the determination of the market share of buyers, has been criticized. Despite its potential economic justification and acknowledgement that not only the upstream level but also the downstream level plays an important role in vertical restraints, its practical application has been questioned by stakeholders based on the difficulty in estimating the market share regarding the length of time, obtaining and possessing data, the market structure including its concentration and the existence of the same vertical agreements with a number of buyers, or a vertical network.[432]

---

[429] Ibid., arts 3, 7, Preamble, [7]–[9]; Note 113, Guidelines 2010, [23], [87]–[92], [110].

[430] Ibid., Preamble, [13]–[16].

[431] Note 293, Dethmers and others, 'Ten Years on', 425, 439; although this article discusses previous Guidelines 1999 and Regulations 1999, the few changes to the current Regulation and Guidelines mean that the same could be stated regarding the current system.

[432] Note 272, 'Consumer Focus' 6–7; European Federation of Pharmaceutical Industries and Associations, 'The Proposal to Revise the Vertical Restraints

Interpretation and Application of Article 101 to RPM and VTR Cases

The block exemption regulation, Regulation 2010, does not apply to RPM and some forms of VTR, generally in the form of absolute VTR. Nevertheless, even these forms can be exempted under Article 101(3) TFEU. Before applying Article 101(3) or its specified version, Regulation 2010, it must be determined whether the particular practice infringes Article 101(1) TFEU in order to be exempted. Therefore, the whole approach to RPM and VTR, which is based on Article 101 TFEU, has the following five steps:

1. Article 101 applies to multilateral or bilateral conduct in the form of agreements, concerted practices or decisions of associations (generally referred to as 'agreements') among independent entities which do not include agency agreements.
2. It must appreciably affect competition and trade between Member States.
3. There must be a restriction in a) object, or b) effect.
4. If the above three requirements are met, Article 101(1) is infringed and the agreement or the part of the agreement in question is void under Article 101(2).
5. However, such an agreement or part of the agreement can be exempted under Article 101(3) or under block exemption regulations, which are secondary sources of law and interpretations of Article 101(3). The test that applies to Article 101(3) is a balancing test of effects.

First, it must be proved that the restriction in question is formed by multilateral/bilateral conduct not by unilateral conduct,[433] or agency agreements.[434] Some conditions of subcontracting agreements are also exempted.[435] The CJEU and the General Court have clarified when a prohibited agreement exists and when it does not. For example, the CJEU

Block Exemption Regulation' (2009) 2; Note 294, 'LAWIN Review' 1; Note 298, 'Amcham EU Response' 1–2; International Chamber of Commerce Commission on Competition 'Review of EC Competition Rules Applicable to Vertical Agreements" (Document 225/662, 2009) 3.

[433] Note 113, Guidelines 2010, [24]–[30]; see the discussion above regarding Note 212, *Volkswagen* appeal, and Note 41, *Bayer*.

[434] Ibid., [12]–[21].

[435] Ibid., [22]; Commission Notice of 18 December 1978 concerning assessment of certain subcontracting agreements in relation to Article 85(1) of the EEC Treaty [1979] OJ C 1/2.

explained that the prohibited multilateral/bilateral conduct includes tacit agreements which can be determined from the evaluation of parties' intentions. Such an agreement would exist even if one party forces the other to comply.[436] An agreement is also concluded in situations where the other party expresses his/her concern with the legality of such an agreement or clause as long as he/she signs the agreement.[437] Even the existence of cheating does not necessarily mean that an agreement has not been concluded as long as it was the cheat's intention to both reach the agreement and cheat in order to exploit the arrangement for her own benefit.[438]

A prohibited agreement can arise from a clause on future policy set by one party only if such policy is foreseeable, as both parties must have sufficient knowledge of the conduct at the time the agreement is being concluded, in other words, it must be based on 'faithful expression of parties' intention'.[439] If the future policy is not specified but the clause in question is drafted in neutral terms, a prohibited agreement under Article 101(1) is not established.[440]

Second, there must be an appreciable effect on both competition and trade between Member States.[441] In cases of restriction by effect, the Commission is of the opinion that there is no appreciable effect on trade between Member States when the market share of the parties at the vertical level is below de minimis 15 percent threshold.[442] The Commission also presumes that vertical agreements among small- and medium-sized undertakings rarely affect trade between the Member States appreciably.[443] However, none of these apply to restrictions by object.

---

[436] Note 41, *Bayer* appeal, [114], [121]–[123].
[437] Note 218, *GSK* [87]–[89].
[438] Note 316, *Activision*, [82]; Note 322, *CD-Contact*, [67].
[439] Note 212, *Volkswagen* appeal, [12].
[440] Ibid., [17]–[18], [52]–[53]; see also Note 113, Guidelines 2010, [25(a)].
[441] Note 41, *Bayer* appeal, [47], [174]; Note 207, *Novalliance*, [63]–[65]; Note 54, *Minière*, [248]–[249]; Note 113, Guidelines 2010, [2(5)], [8]–[11], [97].
[442] Note 113, Guidelines 2010, [9]; Commission Notice (EC) 2014/C 291/01 on agreements of minor importance which do not appreciably restrict competition under Article 101(1) of the Treaty on the Functioning of the European Union (De Minimis Notice) [2014] OJ C291/1, [8(b)].
[443] Note 113, Guidelines 2010, [11]; see Commission Recommendation (EC) 2003/361/EC of 6 May 2003 concerning the definition of micro, small and medium-sized enterprises [2003] OJ L124/36, Annex.

In *Minière*, the CJEU explained that the wording of Article 101(1) 'may affect trade between Member States' meant that only those agreements that were 'incompatible with the common market'[444] were subject to Article 101. The CJEU introduced a test for determining the existence of the effect on trade between Member States which defined this connotation broadly and which has been applied since.

> [I]t must be possible to foresee with a sufficient degree of probability on the basis of a set of objective factors of law or of fact that the agreement in question may have an influence, direct or indirect, actual or potential, on the pattern of trade between the Member States.[445]

Third, the restriction must restrict competition directly or indirectly[446] either in its object or effect. If the object is established, the effect does not have to be established because these requirements are cumulative.[447]

A particular agreement restricts competition by its object if competition is 'almost' always restricted, irrespective of economic circumstances.[448] In other words, such conduct must 'reveal a sufficient degree of harm to competition' for a restriction by object to be established.[449] Intention is not essential but the objective purpose of the agreement or relevant clauses in the agreement[450] and the objective potential to have a negative impact on competition are.[451] To determine such potential to cause a sufficient degree of harm to competition, the clause and its content must be evaluated in the relevant economic and legal context; in particular, the structure and functioning of the relevant market including its products or services must be examined to determine whether there is a restriction by object.[452]

---

[444] Ibid., 249.
[445] Ibid.
[446] See Note 266, Regulation 2010, arts 4–5.
[447] Note 303, *Pierre Fabre*, [34]; Note 218, *GSK* appeal, [55]; Note 54, *Minière*, 250.
[448] Note 275, *T-Mobile Netherlands*, [20].
[449] Note 133 *Allianz Hungária*, [34].
[450] Note 54, *Minière*, 249.
[451] Note 218, *GSK* appeal, [58]; Note 275, *T-Mobile Netherlands*, [27], [31]; Note 304 *Peugeot Nederland*, [55]–[56]; Craig Callery, 'Should the European Union Embrace or Exorcise *Leegin*'s "Rule of Reason"?' (2011) 32(1) *ECLR* 44.
[452] Note 133 *Allianz Hungária*, [33], [36]; Note 303, *Pierre Fabre*, [35]; Note 218, *GSK* appeal, [58].

In contrast to restrictions by effect, restriction by object is restrictive of the 'normal functioning of competition' *by its very nature*.[453] Previous cases and Regulation 2010 state that such nature is present in agreed and/or enforced RPM, and some forms of VTR, including restriction of parallel imports and exports where even passive sales are restricted.[454] In *Pierre Fabre*, the CJEU held that absolute elimination of an 'area of activity', in particular absolute restriction of online sales, constitutes restriction by object if there is no objective justification. This objective justification means that the agreement or its clause has no legitimate aims or proportionate aims for a restriction by object to be established.[455]

When a restriction by object is present, it is not necessary to analyze the restrictive effect as it is presumed that such a restriction restricts competition.[456] This means that there does not have to be a direct link between the conduct in question and the restrictive consequence, such as an increase in consumer prices.[457]

Both restrictions by effect and object require some form of a restrictive object. However, in restriction by object, the restrictive object is restrictive in its nature. Therefore, it is assumed that restriction by object causes an increase of allocative inefficiency and that it will trigger deadweight loss;[458] in other words, the above-mentioned sufficient degree of harm. The aim of restriction by object is to increase competitive constraints, such as price increases. However, in comparison with the US approach to per se restrictions, the EU restrictions by object are not true per se forms of restraints because they can be exempted individually under Article 101(3).

A restriction by effect, on the other hand, does not necessarily aim to lessen competition; however, it leads to such results by its effect.[459] Therefore, restriction by effect requires further analysis, which will lead to the conclusion of deadweight loss, to prove a restriction of competition.[460] Restriction by effect means that competition has been

---

[453] Note 133 *Allianz Hungária*, [35]; Note 275, *T-Mobile Netherlands*, [29].
[454] Note 207, *Novalliance*, [60]–[61]; parallel import: Note 218, *GSK* appeal, [62]–[64]; see Note 276, *Lelos kai*, [65].
[455] Note 303, *Pierre Fabre*, [39], [41], [43], [47].
[456] See, e.g., Note 113, Guidelines 2010, [21]; Note 417, Jones, 656.
[457] Note 275, *T-Mobile Netherlands*, [43].
[458] Edith Loozen, 'The Application of a More Economic Approach to Restrictions by Object: No Revolution after all (T-Mobile Netherlands (C-8/08))' (2010) 4 *ECLR* 146, 148–9.
[459] Ibid.
[460] Note 54, *Minière*, 249; ibid., Loozen, 149.

restricted or there is a potential for a restriction, which is expected with a reasonable degree of probability and to an appreciable extent.[461] Indeed, the restriction by effect includes evaluation of both actual or likely restrictive effects.[462]

Fourth, the consequence of the infringement of Article 101(1) is the annulment of the restrictive agreement as stated in Article 101(2). *Consten and Grundig* and *Minière* clarified that only the clauses which are illegal under Article 101(1) are nullified, unless these restrictive clauses are not separable from the agreement itself. In that case, the entire agreement is nullified.[463]

Fifth, as mentioned above, the key difference between the EU approach to restriction by object, most notably the hard-core restrictions, and the US approach to per se restrictions lies in the existence of Article 101(3). Although RPM and absolute VTR are hard-core restrictions and restrictions by object, they can be justified on the basis of Article 101(3). Guidelines 2010 provides examples of potential justifications. For instance, VTR can be exempted in situations where a product is penetrating a new market or a new brand is introduced into a new market. In such cases, not only vertical agreements protecting new territories but also RPM are usually allowed for up to two years; in RPM, the period is only two weeks.[464]

Indeed both forms of restrictions in effect and object can be exempted under Article 101(3) and therefore relevant analysis of anticompetitive and procompetitive effects is required. The application of Article 101(3) is based on an economic evaluation of the available evidence, which must determine an improvement of competition in distribution and production and/or whether the conduct in question promotes technical and/or economic progress, showing 'appreciable objective advantages' that outweigh the disadvantages of the restriction concerned.[465] Therefore, the principle of proportionality must apply, meaning that the restriction cannot go beyond what is necessary to use a certain positive effect in the market under Article 101(3).[466] Moreover, for Article 101(3) to apply, the

---

[461] Note 275, *T-Mobile Netherlands*, [28]; Note 113, Guidelines 2010, [97].
[462] Note 54, *Minière*, 249; Note 113, Guidelines 2010, [97].
[463] Note 54, *Minière*, 250; Note 45, *Consten and Grundig*, 344.
[464] Note 113, Guidelines 2010, [61], [107(b)–(c)], [225].
[465] Note 207, *Novalliance*, [70]–[72], [74]–[75]; Note 104, *LC Nungesser*, [76]; Note 121, *AEG*, [41], [42]; Note 45, *Consten and Grundig*, 347–8; Note 113, Guidelines 2010, [125].
[466] Note 104, *LC Nungesser*, [76]–[77].

vertical restriction in question should not eliminate a substantial part of competition.[467]

For the Commission or NCA to analyze potential justifications, it is enough for the alleged infringer to prove the likelihood of 'appreciable objective advantages', which can compensate for the resultant disadvantages.[468] The test should show whether the conduct in question makes it possible to obtain appreciable advantages or not.[469] This must be demonstrated with 'a sufficient degree of probability' that the possibility of obtaining an appreciable objective advantage exists.[470]

To summarize, the balancing test of Article 101(3) contains the following. First, it must be shown that there was an appreciable objective advantage. Secondly, the Commission must analyze whether the conduct in question decreased efficiency. Thirdly, if so, it must decide the extent to which efficiency was decreased. Lastly, the gain in efficiency must be analyzed.[471] If the gain is greater than the loss of efficiency, then the conduct will be justified under Article 101(3).

The Commission will most likely measure the gain and losses from the consumer welfare perspective as it states in its Guidelines on the application of Article 101(3), which says that Article 101(3) applies if the conduct enhances consumer welfare.[472] However, the CJEU held only a few years after the Guidelines had been issued that Article 101 protected competition and not just consumer welfare.[473] Therefore, it is most likely that evaluation based only on consumer welfare will be found insufficient by the CJEU. Indeed, the CJEU requires showing whether competition has been enhanced or restricted. In contrast with US antitrust policy, the Commission (or NCA or the court) must examine both intrabrand and interbrand competition.[474] Usually in vertical restraints, the intrabrand (and any potential interbrand) loss must be compared with interbrand and intrabrand gain, with the interbrand competition taking the leading role rather than intrabrand competition.[475]

---

[467] Note 113, Guidelines 2010, [127].
[468] Note 218, *GSK* appeal, [92]–[95].
[469] Ibid., [94].
[470] Note 218, *GSK* appeal, [95].
[471] Note 218, *GSK*, [263]–[303]; *GSK* appeal, [128].
[472] Guidelines on the application of Article 81(3), [13].
[473] Note 218, *GSK* appeal, [55]–[64]; see discussion in Chapter 3 'Vertical Competition and Structure'.
[474] Note 218, *GSK*, [104]–[108].
[475] Ibid., [296].

VIII. CONCLUSION

EU competition law, including the law on vertical restraints, is based on two principal objectives:

1. A competition law objective: the protection of competition, in particular, protecting free and fair competition and, if we refer to the policy of the Commission, enhancing consumer welfare; and
2. The EU-purpose objective: establishing and maintaining an integrated market.

Thus, the EU approach, unlike the US one, is focused more on the free flow of goods among Member States. This was especially obvious in early vertical restraint cases such as *Consten and Grundig* and *Minière* and is reflected in the fact that absolute VTR, including absolute restriction of parallel exports and imports, constitute restrictions by object under Article 101(1) TFEU.

Both restrictions by object and effect can be exempted and thus justified under Article 101(3) TFEU. In comparison, the US per se rule, which applied to RPM before *Leegin*, was stricter than the EU approach to RPM as the per se rule did not allow any justification. Under the EU approach, the authorities and courts applying EU competition law must take into account any justification. Nevertheless, although Article 101(3) can apply in RPM, under new and also older vertical restraint block exemption regulations and guidelines, the EU Commission assumes that agreements on RPM and some forms of VTR, have 'actual or likely negative effects' with no positive effect,[476] meaning that justification is possible but unlikely. Nevertheless, the current Guidelines 2010 provides examples of potential justifications of RPM and VTR and in *GSK* both EU courts urged the Commission to analyze potential justifications under Article 101(3).[477]

The difference between the US and EU approaches can be explained using, among others, the intrabrand competition standpoint, where the EU approach protects both intrabrand and interbrand competition. As Peeperkorn explains it, any form of competition that is of benefit to

---

[476] Note 113, Guidelines 2010, [223]; Luc Peeperkorn, 'Resale Price Maintenance and Its Alleged Efficiencies' (2008) 1 *European Competition Journal* 201, 202–4.

[477] Note 218, *GSK*, [294]; *GSK* appeal, [69]–[168]; also see Note 281, *Souris-Topps*, [130]; Note 207, *Novalliance*, [70]–[72], [74]–[75]; Note 451, *Callery*, 43.

consumers, including intrabrand competition, should be protected.[478] This is also the ideology of the current EU approach, where both forms of competition are protected, with interbrand competition playing the primary role.

Indeed, restrictions by object under Article 101(1), such as RPM, stand on the presumption that some restrictions always have a restrictive effect. They can still be exempted under Article 101(3) if any potential procompetitive benefits are identified and if they are proportionate and outweigh anticompetitive effects. Therefore, under Article 101(3), the EU approach applies a balancing test and requires that the vertical restriction is proportionate. This proportionality is a very important element. It determines whether there are other and more direct means which would lead to the same procompetitive effect without necessarily restricting competition. Such means could be, for example, direct payments for promotion of products, discounting wholesale price for high street retailers offering services and selective distribution systems based on quality of retailers.

The initial step of the EU balancing test is based on the assumption that RPM and some forms of VTR are anticompetitive unless justified under Article 101(3). The US test is reversed. The application of the rule of reason means that RPM and VTR are legal unless it is proved that they are unreasonable, placing a significant burden of proof on the plaintiff. In RPM, this is true in the situation where the supplier introduces RPM because the Supreme Court expressed its presumption that an agreement on RPM introduced by a supplier is rather for a procompetitive reason.[479] (The court in *Leegin* referred to literature on transaction costs and information problems.) If an RPM agreement is initiated by a buyer with significant market power, such an agreement would likely be found anticompetitive in the US. Market power also plays an important role in the EU approach as reflected in the threshold of market share in Regulation 2010. However, this threshold is not applicable to RPM as it creates hard-core restrictions.

---

[478] Note 476, Peeperkorn, 206–7.
[479] Note 349, *Leegin*, 898.

5. Theories and impacts of RPM and VTR on competition

I. INTRODUCTION

Competition/antitrust law is underlined by economic thinking. Indeed, economic theories proving or disproving economic harm have played an essential role in both US antitrust law and EU competition law. This economic thinking has also influenced the law of vertical restraints and provided, most notably, procompetitive explanations for introducing RPM or VTR.

An anticompetitive practice causes anticompetitive harm if it decreases efficiency and welfare. Economic efficiency includes productive and allocative efficiency; welfare can be total or consumer. The measurement of these elements is illustrated by the Pareto or Kaldor-Hicks efficiency models.[1] At the center of focus for the economic harm theory, as adopted by the US and the European Commission, is consumer welfare. If a particular practice causes economic harm, consumer welfare decreases; however, if it does not, consumer welfare remains the same or is even increased.

Another element that is essential when determining the existence of economic harm is competition. In order to find a certain practice anticompetitive, the practice in question must restrict competition.[2] The

---

[1] Vilfredo FD Pareto, *Manuale d'economia politico* (Milan, 1906); John Hicks, 'The Foundations of Welfare Economics' (1939) 49(196) *Economic Journal* 696, 696–712; Nicholas Kaldor, 'Welfare Propositions in Economics and Interpersonal Comparisons of Utility' (1939) 49(195) *Economic Journal* 549, 549–52.

[2] As seen in Joined Cases C-501/06 P, C-513/06 P, C-515/06 P, C-519/06 P, *GlaxoSmithKline Services Unlimited v. Commission of the EC* [2009] 4 CMLR 2, [63] citing C-8/08 *T-Mobile Netherlands BV v. Road van bestuur van de Nederlandse Mededingingsautoriteit* [2009] 5 CMLR 11, [38]–[39], the CJEU reminded the European Commission that the main focus of EU competition law is on competition itself and not consumer welfare. Therefore, the consumer welfare approach does not apply across the EU regime but is mostly promoted by the Commission.

meaning of competition as used in approaches to RPM and VTR in the US and EU differs and, indeed, there exists a difference as to how competition is perceived in connection with VTR and RPM. Both EU and US regimes place an emphasis on interbrand competition. However, while the EU is satisfied if a particular agreement restricts intrabrand competition in order to find an anticompetitive infringement, the US regime is centered around horizontal and interbrand competition. In order to find a violation of Section 1 of the Sherman Act, the US approach either requires evidence that interbrand competition has been restricted or that there existed horizontal collusion to fix or maintain prices or divide territories. In the case of RPM, it is also satisfactory if most of the horizontal market has been affected by price maintenance which can be proved by significant market power.[3]

The forms of anticompetitive harm based on decreased consumer welfare and restricted competition include increased prices, decreased output, decreased consumer choice and innovation. Thus, the standpoints of any procompetitive or anticompetitive theories, including that which applies to RPM and/or VTR, are focused on these forms of harm with a restriction of output playing the principal role in the US.[4]

In the EU, competition law and economic harm are also perceived from a more general objective: the protection and maintenance of free

---

[3] As I explained in Chapter 3, it is questionable whether this would be enough to prove anticompetitive harm in a VTR case in the US. In the EU, market power plays some role with regards to vertical restrictions. However, it is not so much in RPM and absolute vertical territorial restrictions cases where only cases below 'de minimis' market power (based on market shares) are tolerated by EU competition policy. See, Chapter 4; Commission Notice (EC) 2014/C291/01 on agreements of minor importance which do not appreciably restrict competition under Article 101(1) of the Treaty on the Functioning of the European Union (De Minimis Notice) [2014] OJ C291/1, [8(b)]; Commission Regulation 330/2010, 'The application of Article 101(3) of the Treaty on the Functioning of the European Union to categories of vertical agreements and concerted practices' OJ L1021.

[4] See *Business Electronics Corp. v. Sharp Electronics Corp.*, 485 U.S. 717 (1988) 723, 726–7 (*'Business Electronics'*); Speech by Joshua D Wright, 'The economics of resale price maintenance and implications for competition law and policy' (9 April 2014, British Institute of International and Comparative Law, London) 16; Phillip E Areeda and Herbert Hovenkamp, *2009 Supplement to Antitrust Law: An Analysis of Antitrust Principles and Their Application* (Aspen Publishers, Frederick 2009) 238–9, 243; Timothy J Muris, 'The FTC and the Law of Monopolization' (2000) 68 *Antitrust Law Journal* 325; Frank H Easterbrook, 'Vertical Arrangements and the Rule of Reason' (1984) 53 *Antitrust Law Journal* 135, 163.

trade among Member States. This, together with the influential ideology stream of ordoliberalism emphasizing the economic freedom of individuals, has led to the prevention of free trade obstructions and of suspicion of actions not based on competitive merits. These differences have to be borne in mind when looking at different pro or anticompetitive theories and their applicability to the US and EU regimes.

The traditional economic procompetitive theories which have found their place in the US approach and, to a lesser extent, the EU approach and which are centered around free riding theory are based on traditional economic thinking, and have their roots in the cost transaction theory and the Chicago School. The central argument of the Chicago School was that the free market has the ability to regulate itself and maintain competition[5] and that vertical restraints, including RPM and VTR, have a positive impact on competition, with RPM and VTR acting as strategic tools for manufacturers to create the best conditions for manufacturers, their distributors and consumers.[6]

In contrast, exponents of the Harvard School argued that vertical restraints result in restrictions of competition. The Harvard School theory is based on the relationship between structure, conduct and performance. The market structure influences firms' conduct, which determines market performance, thus explaining how certain markets lead to certain types of conduct and performance. The founder of the Harvard School, Mason, along with others, studied industrial organizations. According to them, profit-making is at the center of organizations and it is the market structure that determines price behavior.[7]

---

[5] Wesley A Cann, 'Vertical Restraints and the "Efficiency" Influence – Does any Room Remain for More Traditional Antitrust Values and More Innovative Antitrust Policies?' 24 *American Business Law Journal* (1986) 483, 487; Richard A Posner, 'The Chicago School of Antitrust' (1979) 127 *University of Pennsylvania Law Review*, 925, 928; see also Herbert Hovenkamp, 'Harvard, Chicago, and Transaction Cost Economics in Antitrust Analysis' (2010) 55(2) *Antitrust Bulletin* 615, 631.

[6] Ibid., Hovenkamp, 617; Nikolaos Vettas, 'Developments in Vertical Agreements' (2010) 55(4) *Antitrust Bulletin* 843, 858; B Durand, 'On the Efficiency of VTR' (May 2000, Boston College Thesis, The Department of Economics, USA) 3–4; Jean W Burns, 'Vertical Restraints, Efficiency, and the Real World' (1993) 62 *Fordham Law Revue* 597, 597–8; Note 4, Easterbrook 135.

[7] See, e.g., Note 5, Hovenkamp, 615–16; Joe S Bain, *Essays on Price Theory and Industrial Organization* (Little, Brown and Company, Boston 1972); H Michael Mann, 'Seller Concentration, Barriers to Entry, and Rates of Return in Thirty Industries, 1950–1960' (1966) 48 *Review of Economics and Statistics* 296.

An economic perspective rooted in transaction costs and represented by, for example, Coase[8] or Williamson,[9] challenges the Harvard School's views. As Williamson points out, the transaction cost aspect is a missing piece in the Harvard approach. He said that 'if transaction cost economies are unimportant, the suspicion that novel business practices are motivated by anticompetitive purposes is easy'.[10]

As explained in Chapter 2, transaction cost theory based on Coase's theorem focuses on solving information problems between the manufacturer and her retailers. It studies independent entities applying vertical restrictions with a vertically integrated entity, which internally determines the final price for consumers. In situations where it is not feasible for a firm to be vertically integrated and at the same time to introduce contracts on explicit services and other procompetitive benefits, the manufacturers can encourage the introduction of services and at the same time stop free riding on such services by imposing RPM or VTR. The Coase theorem presumes that the manufacturer is better placed to determine what services should be offered with the product. Thus, in this situation, granting the right to the manufacturer to impose vertical restrictions, such as RPM or VTR, resolves the information problem of free riding. Both forms of vertical restrictions are based on providing enough return for retailers as an incentive to implement and maintain desirable services.

However, there are other streams that explain the nature of RPM and VTR, such as behavioral economics, which challenge the traditional economic view. Behavioral economics recognizes that the rationality behind introducing RPM or VTR is not always perfect but is bounded, which leads to an underestimation or overestimation of the effects of RPM on profit. Theirs and other arguments and observations from cases can explain why RPM or VTR is introduced in situations where procompetitive theories would not make economic sense or did not apply in practice.

Furthermore, empirical data do not necessarily support the arguments of procompetitive theories. Together with the facts from the cases, they provide a reality check and show that the procompetitive theories are not as common as argued by some proponents of these theories and that

---

[8] Ronald Coase, 'The Problem of Social Cost' (1960) 3 *Journal of Law and Economics* 1; Ronald Coase, 'The Nature of the Firm' (1937) 4(16) *Economica*, 386, 386–405.

[9] Oliver E Williamson, *Antitrust Economics: Mergers, Contracting, and Strategic Behaviour* (Basil Blackwell 1987).

[10] Ibid., 156.

RPM and VTR can have a number of anticompetitive effects. By concentrating on horizontal competition and forms of behavior, the traditional anticompetitive theories provide only two anticompetitive explanations: cartels among suppliers and cartels among buyers. However, I name and explain other anticompetitive explanations in this chapter.

Structure

The procompetitive theories are based on suppliers' procompetitive reasons for introducing RPM or VTR. In the first part of this chapter I describe particular procompetitive theories, based on the suppliers' procompetitive perspectives. In the second part, I look at these theories from the consumer welfare and efficiency angles. These two sections are correlated, representing two sides of the same coin.

At the beginning of this chapter, when surveying procompetitive theories and effects, I provide different points of view with respect to some 'procompetitive' explanations, showing that some of these explanations could have rather anticompetitive effects and/or could be seen as competitively neutral or having anticompetitive explanations. Part V of this chapter then outlines evidence from empirical studies revealing a number of anticompetitive effects associated primarily with RPM and showing that procompetitive theories are perhaps not as common in practice as anticipated by some of their proponents. In that regard, in Part VI, I explain different forms of anticompetitive effects associated with RPM and VTR, and in Parts VII and VIII I discuss the two anticompetitive theories. The final part then surveys different motivations for introducing RPM or VTR, showing that suppliers can have anticompetitive reasons and/or reasons which do not necessarily lead to procompetitive effects and thus it is not accurate to claim that suppliers introduce RPM or VTR for procompetitive reasons only.

II. PROCOMPETITIVE THEORIES OF SERVICES, QUALITY CERTIFICATION AND EXCLUSIVITY: FREE RIDING

In comparison to other forms of vertical restraints, RPM is distinguished by a number of well-developed, economically-rooted procompetitive theories. One of the first procompetitive explanations for the existence of RPM to provide a basis for the currently advocated procompetitive theories was introduced at the beginning of the last century. Taussig in

1916 and Silcock in 1938 expressed the idea that RPM increased consumer services.[11] Already in 1907, the US Court of Appeals stated in one of the oldest US cases on RPM of the Sherman Act era, *Park & Sons*, that in individual cases, RPM could be used to avoid price-cutting and free riding.[12]

Indeed, all theories discussed in this part have one common reasoning: RPM is utilized to prevent *free riding*. A free rider is a buyer, for instance a retailer, who takes advantage of services, which are usually beneficial to consumers, provided by other retailers. The free rider does not invest in such services, unlike the retailers who provide them; thus, the free rider is able to sell her products for less than the retailers providing the services. Consumers can obtain these services for free from those retailers who provide them and then decide to purchase the product for less from the free rider. The free rider thus benefits from the services, while the services providing retailer's efforts are not adequately rewarded. Their supplier, a manufacturer, and the retailers providing services are motivated, for different reasons,[13] to stop the free rider from free riding. One of the ways this can be done is by introducing RPM. RPM provides a minimum retail margin for all retailers and ensures that the free rider cannot sell for less than the retailers providing the services. Another way of addressing this issue is via VTR. Retailers in a VTR distribution system can be encouraged to provide such services while, at the same time, no one can free ride on their efforts as they are given specific territories which are not disturbed by other retailers, including free riders.

The 'services' subject to free riding theories can be divided into three groups: services; quality certification and exclusivity or, in other words, luxurious brands; and incentives to sell and promote.

Theory of Services

The theory of services involves after-sale and pre-sale services, including promotional services. Telser, one of the pioneers of the theory on pre-sale

---

[11] Frank W Taussig, 'Price Maintenance' (1916) 6 *American Economic Review* 170; Thomas H Silcock, 'Some Problems of Price Maintenance' (1938) 48 *Economic Journal* 42.

[12] *John D. Park & Sons Co. v. Samuel B. Hartman*, 153 Fed. Rep. 24 (6th Circuit 1907) 45 ('*Park & Sons*').

[13] The supplier wants to ensure that these services continue their existence, while retailers are primarily interested in maintaining and/or increasing their profits.

services and one of the most cited scholars with regard to the theory of services, justified the existence of RPM for products unfamiliar to consumers, such as new products or products that are purchased infrequently, on the basis of this theory. He referred to these services as promotional services, such as product demonstrations, explaining that RPM encourages retailers to promote manufacturers' products and protects them from free riders who benefit from the promotional services of other retailers while charging low prices. Telser argued that if RPM set the minimum price at such a level that includes the manufacturer's price, retailers' profits and services' expenses, then no retailer could benefit from the services of other retailers while charging lower prices.[14]

Therefore, the benefits of RPM lie in preventing competing retailers from free riding on the promotional services of retailers, such as product demonstrations and consultations.[15] This theory has also been applied to VTR, where VTR can protect a retailer from free riders because only retailers with assigned territories can sell the manufacturer's products.[16]

In order for this theory to apply, the services must be provided before the sale without charging a separate fee for them and consumers must seek these services. If consumers are not interested in the services, RPM or VTR would not serve efficiency and would not increase consumer welfare because consumers would end up paying more for a product with services where they could have paid less if the unwanted services were not encouraged and RPM or VTR did not apply. Hence, as Kneepkens observes, the argument that free riding on promotional and pre-sale services has a potential to be anticompetitive applies only to a limited group of services.[17] And, as already recognized by Telser, the theory of

---

[14] Lester G Telser, 'Why Should Manufacturers Want Fair Trade?' (1960) 6 *Journal of Law & Economics* 86. See also Ward S Bowman, 'The Prerequisites and Effects of Resale Price Maintenance, (1955) 22 *The University of Chicago Law Review* 825.

[15] Rudolph J Peritz, 'A Genealogy of Vertical Restraints Doctrine' (1988–1989) 40 *Hastings Law Journal* 511; Note 4, Easterbrook, 152–3; Robert Pitofsky, 'In Defense of Discounters: The No-Frills Case for a *Per Se* Rule Against Vertical Price Fixing' (1983) 71 *Georgetown Law Journal* 1487, 1494; Note 5, Posner, 926–7; Note 14, Telser, 86, 91.

[16] Howard P Marvel, 'Resale Price Maintenance and Resale Prices: Paying to Support Competition in the Market for Heavy Trucks' (2010) 55(1) *Antitrust Bulletin* 79, 83–4.

[17] Mart Kneepkens, 'Resale Price Maintenance: Economic Call for a More Balanced Approach' (2007) 28(12) *European Competition Law Review* 656, 657; David F Shores, 'Vertical Price-Fixing and the Contract Conundrum: Beyond Monsanto' (1985) 54 *Fordham Law Review* 377, 400–402.

services applies to a specific group of products: new products and products purchased infrequently.

Another group of services included in the theory of services involves after-sale services, a typical example of which is free maintenance. However, after-sale services operate differently to pre-sale services, in that pre-sale services assist customers primarily with their decision-making as to which products to buy, while after-sale services help them decide who to buy the product from. Consumers can decide whether to purchase the product from retailer A, who provides free after-sales maintenance or from retailer B, who sells the product for less. Consumers who want peace of mind that the product will be taken care of if anything goes wrong might opt to purchase it from retailer A, while consumers who are price-driven and at the same time willing to take the risk and pay for maintenance separately will opt to purchase from retailer B. Thus, an unrestricted market, which allows for both options to take place, covers the different needs of different consumers and allows unrestricted, non-price and price, intrabrand competition.

Therefore, after-sale services clearly operate as a form of non-price competition between retailers. They are incorporated in their strategic plan of how their business should be operated. The same applies to pre-sale services. However, in addition, pre-sale services can determine whether the product would be sold in the first place because, without pre-sale services, (some) customers would not know how to use the product or even that the product existed, as explained by Telser.[18]

Indeed, after-sales theory operates on the idea that the manufacturer values such services and wants to encourage the usage of these services by utilizing vertical restraints such as RPM. The reason for wanting such services is not necessarily increased sales, as it is with pre-sale services (where valuing such services by the manufacturers is also important), but that the manufacturer has a certain idea as to how her products should be sold to fit within her image of the product. This leads us to another group of potential benefits aimed at creating the image of a brand.

Quality Certification and Luxurious Brands

Both the theory of quality certification and the protection of a luxurious brand reputation operate on the assumption that discounting retailers free ride on the image of the product in question. The quality certification theory is based on the idea that RPM assists a manufacturer with creating

---

[18] Note 14, Telser.

and maintaining brand image and, hence, differentiates her product from others.[19] Retailers who hold quality certifications and thus have a reputation for being high-quality retailers, sell the most fashionable and highest quality products (or services). If a free rider sells this product or products, he can benefit from the reputation established by those retailers with quality certifications.[20] In other words, the theory of quality certification is based on the assumption that a high-quality certification creates useful and essential information for consumers who will buy this product based on this information, but from a retailer with the lowest price: a free rider.

There are a number of possibilities for preventing free riders from selling these products. The most direct one is to refuse to sell to discounters. Another one involves imposing RPM, which guarantees that dealers receive compensation for the quality certifications.[21] Finally, VTR can be used in that respect, because dividing territories among retailers with quality certifications prevents free riding, as only those retailers within an assigned territory can sell the product.

With regard to image protection, some scholars, most notably the supporters of the Chicago School, argue that RPM can protect retailers and manufacturers from free riders on brand reputation and image. They explain that price gives a signal about the product, arguing that high retail price on its own is of benefit to some consumers and manufacturers because some consumers only want to purchase expensive products. If the product is discounted, these consumers will lose interest in purchasing it. For instance, Orbach explains that some manufacturers are motivated to maintain and initiate high resale prices for their products to create and maintain an image of an exclusive product, which is appealing for some consumers. Therefore, high prices are a product feature that

---

[19] William F Baxter, 'Vertical Practices – Half Slave, Half Free' (1983) 52 *Antitrust Law Journal* 743, 748; see the US case of *Leegin Creative Leather Products, Inc. v. PSKS, Inc, DBA Kay's Kloset ... Kays' Shoes*, 551 U.S. 877 (2007) 882 ('*Leegin*').

[20] Note 17, Kneepkens, 657–8; Phillip E Areeda and Herbert Hovenkamp, *Antitrust Law: An Analysis of Antitrust Principles and Their Application* (Volume VIII, Second Edition, Aspen Publishers 2004) 12–13; Howard P Marvel and Stephen McCafferty, 'Resale Price Maintenance and Quality Certification' (1984) 15(3) *Rand Journal of Economics* 346, 347; see also the US case of *United States v. Bausch & Lomb Optical Co.*, 321 U.S. 707 (1944) 728.

[21] Ibid., Marvel and McCafferty, 348–50.

should be protected by competition policy and, in that respect, RPM should be allowed.[22]

Unlike the quality certification theory where the products sold by the holder of the quality certification are connected with the quality outlets, Orbach sees the benefit for consumers in RPM itself because RPM creates the image of expensive and thus luxurious products. This is perceived on the basis that there are some consumers who only want to purchase expensive products as they create an image of luxury. Luxury is linked with high prices. If free riders lower such prices, the luxury image is devalued as these luxury-product customers would not be interested in buying the same products that others can purchase for less. Thus, free riders can have a negative impact on such a reputation.

Incentive to 'Promote'

RPM has also been perceived as a promotional tool, in that it provides incentives to retailers to promote the manufacturer's product with RPM. As Klein explains it, RPM serves as the manufacturer's tool to resolve the incentive differential. By guaranteeing a margin for retailers, RPM motivates retailers to promote a manufacturer's products.[23] If a customer intends to purchase a product such as a watch, mobile phone or sport shoes, but is not sure which specific product she/he wants, it is likely that a retailer will 'promote', in other words try to sell, a product from which the retailer can get the better margin. RPM ensures a margin for retailers while products without RPM do not as retailers compete on price if the market is competitive. It is likely that the retailer would be motivated to sell the product with RPM with the higher margin and certainty that the customer would not find this product for less from a different retailer. This can go as far as establishing downstream-level exclusivity. In other words, it can motivate retailers to sell only a particular product or

---

[22] Barak Y Orbach, 'The Image Theory: RPM and Allure of High Prices' (2010) 55 *Antitrust Bulletin* 277, 277–307; see also George R Ackert, 'An Argument for Exempting Prestige Goods from the *Per Se* Ban on Resale Price Maintenance' (1995) 73 *Texas Law Review* 1185; Note 11, Taussig, 172.

[23] Benjamin Klein, 'Competitive Resale Price Maintenance in the Absence of Free-Riding' (2009) 76(2) *Antitrust Law Journal* 431, 437; see also Alan J Meese, 'Property Rights and Intrabrand Restraints' (2003) 89 *Cornell Law Review* 553; G Frank Mathewson and Ralph A Winter, 'An Economic Theory of Vertical Restraints' (1984) 15(1) *RAND Journal of Economics* 27.

products with RPM or to display them exclusively.[24] Under this form of incentive to promote, this promotion is merely based on RPM, in other words margin, which is ensured by RPM.

This theory can also apply to some forms of VTR. In particular, absolute VTR in combination with exclusive dealing can motivate retailers to involve different promotional techniques. Absolute VTR, where the retailers sell a range of competing products, can provide similar incentives to RPM because the retailers know that no one can compete with them with regard to the VTR product at the intrabrand level. This means that the retailers can receive a guaranteed margin if they sell the products with VTR because consumers within a certain territory would only purchase these products from them.

It is obvious that under this theory both the manufacturer and the retailers benefit from selling products with RPM. However, what is the benefit for consumers? Consumers, if indecisive, may be persuaded by retailers' selling and promotional techniques to purchase products with RPM rather than alternative products without RPM. RPM products are generally more expensive.[25] The consumers would have paid less if the (minimum) retail price were not fixed. At the same time, the selling techniques used by the retailers in order to sell the products with RPM mean that consumers unaware of which brand they want to purchase could be persuaded to purchase the RPM products despite the fact that cheaper equivalent alternatives which could be of even better quality and/or with better functions exist in the market. Thus, RPM as an incentive to promote RPM products can mislead consumers into thinking that they are buying something better, while in reality there could be other competing products of the same, or even better, quality and functions.

Thus, RPM increases prices. By paying more, the consumers and the economy are worse rather than better off. It is the manufacturer who benefits if RPM increases output, as well as retailers receiving higher profits from products with RPM. Increased output of products with RPM is simply linked to retailers' motivation to sell such products in order to ensure better margins for themselves. This results in the restriction of

---

[24] Ittai Paldor, 'RPM as an Exclusionary Practice' (2010) 55 *Antitrust Bulletin* 309, 309–42.

[25] There is an agreement even among the followers of procompetitive theories that RPM and other vertical restraints lead to higher prices. See Brief for William S Comanor and Frederic M Scherer as Amici Curiae Supporting Neither Party, *Leegin Creative Leather Products, Inc. v. PSKS, Inc, DBA Kay's Kloset ... Kays' Shoes*, 551 U.S. 877 (2007), No 06-480.

intrabrand competition without any procompetitive benefits or increased consumer welfare.

With regard to the US regime (and partly the EU regime), another question that must be answered, aside from the impacts on consumer welfare, is whether such conduct positively affects interbrand competition. If the manufacturer with RPM increases his output, his competitors' output will likely decrease because products with RPM, where RPM is successfully used as an incentive to sell, will likely pull potential customers from competing products. Competing manufacturers will need to address this issue if they do not want to lose their profit. They could decrease their wholesale price; however, this is unlikely. Decreasing their prices would not guarantee that retailers would be motivated to promote such products, because, unlike with RPM products, intrabrand price competition is not limited. Furthermore, by decreasing wholesale prices, competing manufacturers face the significant risk that their profit would decrease as this would not necessarily lead to increased output. One of the easiest ways for a manufacturer to compete with a manufacturer with an RPM policy is to introduce RPM as well in order to motivate retailers to sell his products. If everyone in the market implements an RPM strategy, the prices will increase across the interbrand level while the advantage in the form of incentive to promote is lost.

This domino effect or follow-the-leader strategy is illustrated with regards to VTR in the US, where the rule of reason approach to VTR led to the de facto legalization of VTR.[26] There are also examples of RPM being implemented at the interbrand level across one industry. For example, the American Antitrust Institute appealed to the DOJ and FTC

---

[26] For example, exclusive territories became typical practice for all major soft drink manufacturers. See, *First Beverages, Inc. of Las Vegas and Will Norton v. Royal Crown Cola Co. and H & M Sales Co.*, 612 F.2d 1164 (9th Circuit 1980) 1166; In re *Coca Cola Co.*, No. 8855 (F.T.C. 25 April 1978), Trade Reg. Rep. (CCH) Supp. No. 330; In re *PepsiCo, Inc.*, No. 8856 (F.T.C. April, 1978); also the beer industry is typified by VTR. See *Mendelovitz v. Adolph Coors Co.*, 693 F.2d 570 (5th Circuit 1982). See also Stanley I Ornstein and Dominique M Hanssens, 'RPM: Output Increasing or Restricting?' (1987) 36(1) *Journal of Industrial Economics* 1. In the beer industry, this is further implemented due to state legislation that allows VTR and other vertical restrictions. See Tim R Sass and David S Saurman, 'Mandated Exclusive Territories and Economic Efficiency: An Empirical Analysis of the Malt-Beverage Industry' (1993) 36(1) *Journal of Law and Economics* 153, 174.

As I explained in Chapter 3, the rule of reason approach to VTR led to the de facto legalization of VTR in the US. Thus, initiators of VTR do not have to fear successful antitrust litigation.

in October 2014 to investigate the US contact lenses market because of the implementation of RPM. Contact lenses in the US can be purchased only after being prescribed by an ophthalmologist. Many ophthalmologists both prescribe lenses and sell them. Therefore, they are interested in prescribing more expensive, higher-margin lenses over cheaper alternatives. Once lenses are prescribed to a consumer, he/she can purchase them either directly from his/her ophthalmologist or from other retailers, which used to sell them for less until RPM was introduced, saving customers up to around 40 percent of the ophthalmologists' price. This situation began to change in 2013. First, the manufacturer Alcon introduced RPM in 2013 and others followed in 2014 with 40–80 percent of contact lenses being sold under an RPM policy.[27]

In the contact lenses market, RPM can be even more harmful than in other industries due to the fact that the product needs to be prescribed first. Ophthalmologists, for the reasons described above, are motivated to sell the lenses with higher margins ensured by limited price intrabrand competition. The ophthalmologists know that if they prescribe lenses with RPM they will not face price competition. Furthermore, if no one sells below their retail price the chance that their customers will purchase lenses from them is increased. Once a specific brand is prescribed, a customer cannot switch to a different, cheaper brand without a new prescription. Thus, intrabrand price competition is substantial, while interbrand price competition is less significant than in other markets.[28] Similarly, products not purchased on a regular basis can benefit more from RPM than products purchased by consumers regularly.

Free Riding or Discounting?

All the above theories have one common reasoning: the motive for using RPM and VTR (where it applies) is to avoid free riding on benefits. These benefits can be divided into two groups. The first group includes

---

[27] The American Antitrust Institute, 'Action needed to address resale price maintenance in contact lenses – and countless other markets' (letter sent to FTC and DOJ 24 October 2014) <http://www.antitrustinstitute.org/sites/default/files/AAI%20Letter%20on%20RPM%20in%20Contact%20Lenses.pdf> accessed 1 August 2015.

[28] However, this does not mean that a potential US antitrust case would be successful, most notably due to proving an anticompetitive agreement under the Sherman Antitrust Act 15 USC §1. One of the dangers, which could lead to a loss for the plaintiff, is the doctrine in *United States v. Colgate & Co.*, 250 U.S. 300 (1919) ('*Colgate*') which was not explicitly overruled by any of the Supreme Court cases.

benefits for consumers and society in general in the form of increased competition. The second group includes other benefits, which have a form of extra cost associated with running a business and are wanted by both the manufacturer and its retailers due to increased profits, unless there are discounters/free riders who would undermine such profit. However, the second group does not include profound genuine consumer benefit.

In that regard, free riding can be divided between a broad concept and the genuine free riding concept. The genuine free riding concept involves only the first group of benefits while the broad concept includes both groups. The second group of benefits would constitute discounting for the purposes of the genuine free riding concept while it would still be labelled as 'free riding' under the second concept.

Selling below the RPM price is discounting and not free riding unless there is a reason, a benefit for consumers, on which basis free riders free ride. If there are no objective benefits, such as increased pre-sale services, only the subjective benefits of increased profit for retailers and their manufacturer, RPM does not benefit consumers or society. Retailers who discount a product with RPM cannot be labelled as free riders, they are merely discounters.

Although all the above-described theories refer to free riding, not all of them assist with addressing the problem of genuine free riding. For example, we have seen that RPM can serve as a mere incentive to sell and promote products with RPM. This is beneficial for the manufacturer and his retailers but it does not create any specific benefits for the consumer (except for being advised to purchase such products) and thus there is nothing to free ride on.

In addition, creating a luxurious brand image with the assistance of RPM can belong to the broad concept of free riding but not necessarily to the genuine free riding concept. The luxurious brand image theory links RPM with high price itself, claiming that it is the high price which attracts some consumers as it creates the image of a 'luxurious' product.[29] However, there is nothing else, such as quality of the product, which would be linked with RPM and would enhance competition. Although frequent discounting could destroy the image that the manufacturer is aiming for, there is no tangible consumer benefit on which a discounter could free ride, except that the price itself creates the image of luxury. Considering that RPM is not the only way to create a luxury image, the reasons for ranking such a theory among the genuine free

---

[29] See, e.g., Note 22, Orbach.

riding theories is even less justified. For instance, advertising and higher wholesale prices leading to higher final prices can also target consumers purchasing luxury/expensive products without restricting intrabrand price competition.

The differences between the broad concept and the genuine free riding concept are partially reflected in the differences in the US and EU approaches to vertical restraints. The US cases have not absolutely clarified which of these procompetitive theories are accepted as valuable justifications under Section 1 of the Sherman Act in RPM and VTR cases. In the RPM case of *Leegin*, the Supreme Court referred to 'services' when advocating the free riding theory.[30] When explaining the benefits for consumers, the Court said that it can lead to diversity and more choice for consumers, linking the low-price with 'low-service brands' and high-price with 'high-service brands'.[31] It is not clear from this judgment whether the Court meant genuine services or whether the term services also includes promotion in the sense of incentive to sell and a luxurious brand image. The cases on RPM following *Leegin* have also failed to clarify this.

The VTR case of *Sylvania* refers to both services and promotion.[32] Likewise, it is not clear whether the term promotion is linked with services or whether it was referred to in a broader context and thus included incentive to sell. However, by referring to 'promotional activities' it is likely that the Court meant genuine services, as the word 'activity' indicates behavior, such as product demonstrations, which goes beyond the mere incentive to sell. Nevertheless, due to the US emphasis on interbrand competition, showing procompetitive justifications is not usually necessary unless the restriction of interbrand competition is proven or, alternatively, the initiator (most likely a buyer) has significant market power.[33]

In comparison, the EU approach is clearer due to the vertical restriction Guidelines 2010 and recent cases. The older EU cases emphasized

---

[30] Note 19, *Leegin*, 890–92.
[31] Ibid., 890.
[32] *Continental T.V. v. GTE-Sylvania*, 433 U.S. 36 (1977) 55, 56 ('*Sylvania*'); Robert H Bork, 'The Rule of Reason and Per Se Concept: Price Fixing and Market Division' (1966) 75(2) *Yale Law Journal* 373; William S Comanor, 'Vertical Territorial and Customer Restrictions: *White Motor* and Its Aftermath' (1968) 81(7) *Harvard Law Review* 1419; Almarin Phillips, '*Schwinn* Rules and the "New Economics" of Vertical Relations' (1975) 44 *Antitrust Law Journal* 573.

[33] For differences between the approaches to RPM and VTR and their exact application see Chapter 3.

free riding as a legal and procompetitive activity with the aim of protecting (price) competition and the free market.[34] Currently, the European Commission under Guidelines 2010 considers the theory of free riding as a potential justification for applying vertical restrictions. However, EU competition policy implements the genuine free riding concept, and perhaps a concept which is even narrower than that. It recognizes free riding justifications only in the case of pre-sale services, including promotional activities such as product demonstrations to potential customers, without including promotion as an incentive to sell, luxurious image or after-sale services.[35] The justification on the basis of pre-sale services is acceptable only when the product in question is relatively new and/or technically complex and/or where reputation plays an essential role. The product must also have a high value and it must not be practical for the manufacturer or other suppliers to include a requirement for promotional activities and other pre-sale services in the distribution contract with all distributors.[36]

The last condition shows that the Commission considers other alternatives available to the parties involved in RPM (or VTR). This consideration is deeply rooted in the principle of proportionality, which applies in the EU regime to both Articles 101(1) and 101(3). The current CJEU approach is well illustrated in the case of *Pierre Fabre*. In this case, the Court found that vertical restrictions which absolutely eliminate an 'area of activity', such as online sales, constitute a restriction by object under Article 101(1) unless such restriction can be justified based on legitimate and proportionate aims, meaning that the purpose of the justification does not go beyond what is necessary.[37] Creating and maintaining a luxurious

---

[34] See, e.g., Case 56/64, 58/64 *Établissements Consten SàRL and Grundig-Verkaufs-GmbH v. Commission of the European Economic Community* [1966] ECR 299 ('*Consten and Grundig*'); Case 258/78, *LC Nungesser KG and Kurt Eisele v. Commission* [1982] ECR 2015; Case 161/84, *Pronuptia de Paris GmbH v. Pronuptia de Paris Irmgard Schillgallis* [1986] ECR 353.

[35] Perhaps because after-sale services can easily be sold separately, as they do not play the same role as pre-sale services when customers are making their mind up about purchasing certain products. See the discussion above.

[36] Case 107/82 *Allgemeine Elektrizitäts-Gesellschaft AEG-Telefunken AG v. Commission of the EC* [1983] ECR 3151, [33]–[34], [41]–[42], [75]; Guidelines on vertical restraints [2010] OJC 130/1, [107] ('Guidelines 2010').

[37] *Pierre Fabre Dermo-Cosmetique SAS v. Président de l'Autorité de la Concurrence, Ministre de l'Économie, de l'Industrie et de l'Emploi* (Case C-439/09) [2011] 5 CMLR 31, [37], [41], [43].

image is 'not a legitimate aim for restricting competition'[38] and thus does not constitute proportionate objective justification, which shows that the absolute elimination of online sales (or other areas of activity) can most likely be a restriction by object under Article 101(1).

The following two examples illustrate the EU approach and show the difference between the genuine free riding concept and the broad concept: pre-sale service as an example of the genuine free riding concept and creating and maintaining an image of a luxurious product which is not classified as an example of the genuine free riding concept under the EU approach.

Suppose that X is a consumer interested in joining a cycling club. He goes to a high street retail store where he tries different road bikes. The shop assistant provides the pre-sale services of measuring him, recommending the best size of road bike and explaining the advantages and disadvantages of different types of bikes, their materials and components. Based on this pre-sale service, X makes a decision to purchase a particular bike. However, he purchases this bike from an online retailer because the online retailer sells the bike for less than the high street retailer, who has to include additional costs in the final price, including the cost of the pre-sale services. In this situation, the online retailer free rides on the pre-sale services of the high street retailer as she does not offer such services and thus can sell the road bike for less.

In order to stop free riding, the manufacturer of bikes could decide to introduce RPM (or even VTR) or a selective distribution system. Under the EU approach, RPM is a hard-core restriction by object and thus the manufacturer could not rely on the block exemption regulation, Regulation 2010. In this situation, RPM is used to avoid genuine free riding, which complies with conditions of the European Commission's soft law, the Guidelines 2010, because this involves pre-sale and promotional services and a road bike is a technically complex product with a high value. By applying another condition, the principle of proportionality, it is questionable whether RPM would be justified under Article 101(3) as there are other options to stop free riding than RPM, such as a selective distribution system.

Indeed, the second option, the selective distribution system, would tackle the free riding problem directly, rather than indirectly (as RPM would). In *Pierre Fabre*, selective distribution systems are interpreted such that a system which de facto absolutely restricts online sales constitutes a restriction by object under Article 101(1) unless it has a

---

[38] Ibid., [46].

legitimate and/or proportionate justification.[39] Therefore, if the purpose of preventing free riding on pre-sale services goes beyond what is necessary, the restriction by object is constituted. However, both situations could be exempted under an individual exemption of Article 101(3) of the TFEU where the principle of proportionality also applies.

Therefore, suppose that the manufacturer of bikes is considering the introduction of two forms of selective distribution system: A and B. Selective distribution system A is a system where the manufacturer would enter into a contract with retailers who always offer particular pre-sale services to potential customers. This would completely eliminate online sales and, thus, most likely establish a restriction by object under Article 101(1) under the case of *Pierre Fabre*. Despite the fact that this would constitute a restriction by object, the exemption under Article 101(3) still applies. Under Article 101(3), a competition authority and the court would consider whether the absolute restriction of online sales is proportionate to the aim of avoiding free riding on pre-sale services.

Selective distribution system B would include all retailers who can offer particular pre-sale services but only if required by the customers. High street retailers who also sell bikes online would meet such criteria. This would eliminate the absolute restriction of online sales, with online sales being restricted only partially. Thus, selective distribution system B would likely constitute a restriction by effect rather than object, which could be proportionate to the restriction under Article 101(3). Both the block exemption and individual exemption could apply. Furthermore, by taking into consideration previous cases on selective distribution systems, it is likely that system B would be exempted under Article 101(3) either under the block exemption or the individual exemption. Therefore, distribution system B is the safest option for the manufacturer between implementing RPM and selective distribution systems A and B as it has the highest possibility of an exemption under Article 101(3).[40]

Now, compare this situation, the purchase of the bike by customer X, with the sale of 'luxurious' perfumes. If some retailers, including online retailers, discount these 'luxurious' perfumes, the manufacturer could tend to stop discounting if it wants to create and maintain an image of an expensive, luxurious brand, as such a brand needs to be sold for a high price. However, based on Guidelines 2010 and the ruling in *Pierre Fabre*

---

[39] The European Commission standpoint is the same. Note 36, Guidelines 2010, [52] states that '[i]n principle, every distributor must be allowed to use the Internet to sell products' where the absolute restriction of online sale would constitute a hard-core restriction.

[40] See also Note 36, Guidelines 2010, [174]–[188].

on Article 101(1), this does not constitute genuine free riding and thus a legitimate justification under Article 101(1), as well as a justification under Article 101(3) with regards to RPM. There is nothing to free ride on because the free riding element is the high prices creating the image of an expensive, luxurious brand. It is likely that such a justification would not even be accepted for other vertical restraints, as the Commission's standpoint is that brand image is valuable in connection with 'uniformity and quality standardisation' and not necessarily high prices themselves.[41]

Benefits of 'Free Riding'

Based on current consumer behavior, where many consumers utilize information from different distribution channels, especially the Internet, before purchasing products, free riding can be identified as a problem, primarily because it is easy to perceive that many customers find products in the shops and then purchase them online from free riders. On this basis, it is also easy to argue that free riding should have been addressed by manufacturers and retailers in the form of vertical restraints such as RPM and VTR in order to preserve high street stores and the services they can potentially offer to consumers.[42]

RPM can, however, have a negative impact on online sales given that online retailers profit from offering products for a lower price because they have lower overhead costs and thus can offer the same products for less. The online retailers, therefore, profit from discounting and such discounting can be labeled as free riding. If RPM is utilized to tackle free riding, the online sales can suffer having the same prices as other channels of sale. Similarly, VTR where the retailers do not sell online would have a negative impact on online sales.

Therefore, from the perspective that any form of free riding (including discounting) is negative and should be prevented, we could also easily prevent certain forms of sales, such as online sales, and allow RPM and VTR to tackle free riding issues. However, this perspective can be flipped so as to argue that online sales and even free riding or some forms of free riding should be left alone and should even be protected. I will explain this flipped perspective from two angles: the goal angle and the angle of procompetitive effects on competition.

---

[41] Ibid., [107(i)].
[42] Gregory T Gundlach, Kenneth C Manning and Joseph P Cannon, 'Resale Price Maintenance and Free Riding: Insights from Multi-channel Research' (2011) 1 *Academy of Marketing Science Review* 18, 20.

As we have seen in the CJEU case of *Pierre Fabre*, and as is further illustrated in paragraph [52] of Guidelines 2010, which states that '[i]n principle, every distributor must be allowed to use the Internet to sell products', the EU approach to online sales is adamant. This approach for the protection of online sales is rooted in the free trade objective of the EU. Absolute prohibition of free riding under the broad concept (including discounting) would lead to the significant restriction of online sales. Free riding from the broad perspective enhances online trade and this then enhances rather than restricts competition by diminishing trade boundaries between nations. Online sales thus create a trading democracy in practice.[43] Therefore, the restriction of online sales, especially their absolute elimination, does not have a place in the allowed free-riding justification in the EU regime.

Similarly, Pitofsky argues that trying to prevent free riding would go against the US free market ideology and thus against democracy. He also states that a competitive market should not give manufacturers the authority to decide which retailers will stay in the market, whether the retailers are offering services or charging lower prices.[44]

Now, let us explore the angle of procompetitive effects on competition. Free, unrestricted competition leads to innovation, including discovering new channels of sale. Online sales are a part of this process of innovation. Vertical restrictions such as RPM and VTR can hinder the natural process of innovation and stop innovative buyers, distributors and retailers from introducing new methods of sale where certain services would not be possible but which could have other positive effects, such as lower costs. The lenient approach to RPM and VTR in the US can lead to such results, unlike the EU approach which highlights the importance of online sales and has a strict view on RPM and absolute vertical territorial restrictions.[45]

---

[43] The idea of referring to online sales as democracy in practice came across from the discussion with Professor Koen Lenaerts, the Vice President of the Court of Justice of the EU, on 25 September 2014.

[44] Note 15, Pitofsky, 1493. The US Supreme Court stated in its older cases that antitrust law could not accept a defence that competition itself, for instance price competition, is unreasonable: *National Society of Professional Engineers v. United States*, 435 U.S. 679 (1978) ('*Professional Engineers*').

[45] Although the US FTC deals with the Internet and consumers, one of its main current focuses is on the protection of privacy. The FTC does not promote online sales to the extent the European Commission does with regards to vertical restraints and competition.

On the basis of innovation, free choice and free trade, Consumer Futures (previously, Consumer Focus) representing UK consumers completely refuses the free riding justification and provides a different perspective on free riding than the conventional economic view. They argue that free riding should be protected as it reflects consumer demand and the nature of markets. Free riding not only decreases prices, it also increases innovation as suppliers must find different ways to sell their products and fulfil consumer needs.[46] Preventing free riding can thus increase price and restrict consumer choice and the efficiency of distributors and/or retailers.

Therefore, like Pitofsky, Consumer Futures argues that it should be left to free competition and consumer preferences and not the preferences of the manufacturers to decide which sale methods are the most efficient to reach final consumers:

> If [consumers] wish to seek advice from 'official' suppliers and then shop online to get a better price then they are simply expressing their preference for price over information. This choice will then drive change in the marketplace. Existing suppliers will either have to rebalance their offer, lowering prices or offering some other innovation (such as in-house coffee shops in bookstores) or exit the market. This is the normal operation of the marketplace. Every product or service is a combination of item and information. If there is a market for both parts of the offer the suppliers, assuming a degree of efficiency in both elements, will find alternative ways to supply consumer demand.[47]

This freedom of choice for consumers also leads to the expansion of online sales. Marketing and other studies agree with the EU approach to online sales and Consumer Futures on the benefits of undisturbed

---

[46] Consumer Focus (a statutory organization for consumers across England, Wales, Scotland and Northern Ireland) 'Consumer Focus Response to Vertical Restraints Block Exemption Regulation' (September 2009) 11–12; Statement of Daniel J Schuler, *Consumer Protection Against Price Fixing*, hearings on S. 429 before the Subcommission on Antitrust, Monopolies and Business Rights of the Senate Commission on the Judiciary, 102d Cong., 1st Sess., 66 (1991); Retail Competition Enforcement Act, hearing before Senate Commission on the Judiciary, 100th Cong., 1st Sess. 281 (1987); see also Marina Lao, 'Resale Price Maintenance: The Internet Phenomenon and Free Rider Issues' (2010) 55 *Antitrust Bulletin* 473, 473–512; Pamela J Harbour and Laurel A Price, 'RPM and the Rule of Reason: Ready or Not, Here We Come?' (2010) 55(1) *Antitrust Bulletin* 225, 229; Robert L Steiner, 'The *Leegin* Factors – a Mixed Bag' (2010) 55(1) *Antitrust Bulletin* 25, 55.

[47] Note 46, Consumer Focus, 12.

different retailers' channels, including online sales.[48] Marketing studies show that information technology, in particular the Internet, have led to research-shopping by consumers, multichannel selling systems where one product is sold via different selling channels and multichannel competition. Many consumers when research-shopping seek available information and compare not just prices, but also services and quality. This process reflects the diversity of consumer demand leading to enhanced competition.[49] However, this does not mean that, as part of this process, consumers first seek information from high street shops and then purchase a particular product online for less. On the contrary, marketing research shows that the majority of consumers first receive and compare information online and then purchase a particular product from a high street shop and not the other way round.[50] This pattern does not support the traditional free riding view that online retailers free ride on services provided by high street shop retailers.

Marketing research, when analyzing the current phenomenon of research shopping and multiple channel distribution, has discovered two perspectives of manufacturers on so-called free riding, or in other words multiple channel distribution where consumers purchase their products from one channel while utilizing other channels to research and obtain information and services. The first group of manufacturers believe that this phenomenon leads to 'cannibalistic effects', in other words free riding effects. The second group view this phenomenon as having synergistic effects, where using different methods of distribution increases sales and decreases costs as different channels complement each other and lead to attracting more consumers with different preferences.[51]

Contrary to traditional economic thinking, it is more profitable for manufacturers to adopt the synergistic-effect approach and utilize different forms of sale channelling. On the other hand, situations where

---

[48] See, e.g., Note 42, Gundlach, Manning and Cannon, 18; Note 46, Lao, 492–4; see also Sebastian van Baal and Christian Dach 'Free Riding and Customer Retention across Retailers' Channels' (2005) 19(2) *Journal of Interactive Marketing* 75, 76.

[49] Gregory T Gundlach, Joseph P Cannon and Kenneth C Manning, 'Free Riding and Resale Price Maintenance: Insights from Marketing Research and Practice' (2010) 55(2) *The Antitrust Bulletin* 381, 391–401, 403–10, 412–13; Note 46, Harbour and Price, 225–44.

[50] Peter C Verhoef, Scott A Neslin and Björn Vroomen, 'Multichannel Customer Management: Understanding the Research-Shopper Phenomenon (2007) 24 *International Journal of Research in Marketing* 129.

[51] Note 42, Gundlach, Manning and Cannon, 18, 22–5.

manufacturers believe that multichannelling leads to cannibalistic effects that must be addressed, for instance by utilizing RPM or VTR or other vertical restrictions, leads to a paradox. In cases where manufacturers introduce RPM, such conduct tends to increase the cannibalistic effects – the free riding phenomenon – and, aside from a unified price or price range, it also results in the same or similar non-price strategies. Thus, RPM tends to have adverse effects, restricting choice and diversity and encouraging cannibalistic behavior. On the other hand, in situations where a manufacturer encourages the use of different distribution channels, the multichannel distribution results in synergistic (mutually complementing) effects.[52]

Other Options

As we have seen, the EU approach is based significantly on the principle of proportionality with regards to Article 101(3) and to a certain extent to Article 101(1). This principle involves exploring other, less restrictive, options than the vertical restriction in question and at the same time would include the same procompetitive effects, in particular competition enhancements in the form of consumer benefits. In particular, these effects must contribute 'to improving the production or distribution of goods or to promoting technical or economic progress, while allowing consumers a fair share of the resulting benefit'.[53]

These other options also play an essential role in the above-discussed theories. For instance, Grimes points out that the procompetitive theory of promotion does not lead to procompetitive results in practice if there are other, less restrictive options than RPM.[54] One of the most obvious counterarguments to RPM and VTR ensuring services and thus addressing genuine free riding is that the most direct way to deal with free riding and ensure services is through the use of direct financial compensation

---

[52] Ibid 18, 22–6; Note 49, Gundlach, Cannon and Manning, 384, 412–18. There are other ways for retailers to free ride once RPM is introduced. For instance, Klein and Murphy explain that in situations where the price (or the minimum price) of the main product is fixed, free riders can offer accessories at a lower price. That way, potential customers still receive services from retailers offering those services but purchase the product from free riders. Benjamin Klein and Kevin M Murphy, 'Vertical Restraints as Contract Enforcement Mechanisms' (1988) 31 *Journal of Law and Economics* 265, 266.

[53] Article 101(3) Treaty on the Functioning of the European Union.

[54] Warren S Grimes, 'A Dynamic Analysis of Resale Price Maintenance: Inefficient Brand Promotion, Higher Margins, Distorted Choices, and Retarded Retailer Innovation' (2010) 55(1) *Antitrust Bulletin* 101.

for certain services. This approach can ensure the same conditions for retailers who promote products by providing services and free riders who may be advantaged by not carrying promotional costs. This compensation could be reflected in the wholesale price for the distributors or retailers.[55]

However, the proponents of procompetitive theories would argue that RPM or VTR is more efficient or effective than direct compensation primarily because RPM or VTR is cheaper and easier to monitor. For instance, Telser refused the argument of direct compensation from the outset providing an explanation as to why direct compensation and other potential means are more expensive than RPM. He argues that, first, it is difficult to set prices for services because it is difficult to predict how many customers of a particular retailer will be interested in the promotional services. Second, by using the transaction cost theory and knowledge from the cost of contracting, he argues that direct compensation can be very expensive due to the cost of negotiating and concluding specific contracts on direct compensation.[56]

The second argument justifying RPM over direct compensation lies in monitoring prices over monitoring services. For instance, Easterbrook claims that if RPM is imposed, it is easy to observe if services are used because if the price drops then services also drop.[57] RPM is then less costly because monitoring price floors is easier than monitoring the implementation of specific services.[58] However, this depends on the kind of services the manufacturer would like to implement. For example, if it is related to the quality of the selling premises such as a showroom, it is arguably easier to monitor their existence than RPM because this can be done at the outset, while monitoring prices is a continuous process. On the other hand, monitoring whether each customer receives a specific service, such as bicycle fitting, would be more difficult than monitoring RPM.

One of the most significant counterarguments to these procompetitive arguments and their justification on the basis of saved costs is that RPM

---

[55] Note 15, Peritz, 571; William S Comanor, 'Vertical Price-Fixing, Vertical Market Restrictions, and the New Antitrust Policy' (1985) 98(5) *Harvard Law Review* 983, 987.

[56] Note 14, Telser 92–4; see also Pauline M Ippolito, 'RPM Myths that Muddy the Discussion' (2010) 55 *The Antitrust Bulletin* 157–8, 161.

[57] Note 4, Easterbrook, 156; see also Benjamin Klein and Kevin M Murphy, 'Vertical Integration as a Self-enforcing Contractual Arrangement' (1997) 87(2) *The American Economic Review* 415.

[58] G Frank Mathewson and Ralph Winter, 'The Law and Economics of Resale Price Maintenance' (1998) 13 *Review of Industrial Organization* 57, 70.

or VTR do not ensure the required services and other procompetitive effects as they create indirect rather than direct means, while there exist direct means, such as direct compensation or a selective distribution system, which directly provide incentives and/or ensure the existence of required benefits. As Klein and Murphy put it, '[v]ertical restraints, by themselves, do not create a direct incentive for retailers to supply desired services'.[59]

Indeed, RPM or VTR do not directly oblige or motivate retailers to invest in services. As Pitofsky argues, there is no guarantee that retailers know what the manufacturer wants and, even if they do, that they will follow her instruction when RPM or even VTR is used.[60] Therefore, in order to ensure certain services it can be more efficient to use direct means, with direct compensation being only one of them. For instance, in certain cases it is possible for a manufacturer to impose services herself. Comanor points out that if she does so, retailers are not jeopardized by free riders and the manufacturer's profit increases, as does the price charged to retailers.[61] However, many services cannot be performed by the manufacturer, such as those related to shop assisting.

Another possible way to avoid free riding and ensure services, quality and the reputation of products is the manufacturer's refusal to deal with non-suitable retailers. This can be done by adopting a selective distribution system, as illustrated previously in the example with the bicycle manufacturer, which would include particular services and/or quality when choosing retailers. This means that all retailers have to provide specified services without being restricted in their competing strategies, as is the case with RPM and VTR.[62]

III. PROCOMPETITIVE THEORY OF FACILITATING ENTRY

Another procompetitive explanation which is, however, not related to the free riding theory, is that RPM and VTR can assist a new firm to

---

[59] Note 52, Klein and Murphy, 265–6.

[60] Note 15, Pitofsky, 1493.

[61] Note 55, Comanor, 994–7; see also Robert L Steiner, 'How Manufacturers Deal with the Price-Cutting Retailer: When Are Vertical Restraints Efficient?' (1997) 65 *Antitrust Law Journal* 409, 416.

[62] For instance, see *AEG – Allgemeine Elektricitäts – Gesellschaft AEG – Telefunken AG v. Commission* (Case 107/82) [1983] ECR 3151, [1984] 3 CMLR 325, CMR 14018, [33]–[34].

penetrate the market or a firm to penetrate a new market. If it does so, it is positive for the market and competition as it increases competition for a new product. This assistance happens in two forms. First, RPM or VTR provide an incentive to sell and take the risks associated with selling a new product with no reputation and thus motivate distributors and retailers to get involved and sell new products. In general, the risks of unknown profit are reduced if RPM or absolute territories are introduced.[63] Indeed, RPM offers some certainty for retailers that their investment in the new product will be profitable and allows them to better predict risks and returnability of investment.

Second, RPM and VTR assist with building the reputation of the new product and save promotional costs. In this regards, the Chicago School explains that promotional costs create a barrier to entry for new competitors who want to penetrate a market, as the promotional costs are an extra expenditure that might discourage a new competitor from entering the market. In this sense, imposing RPM can be a useful business strategy for new competitors. It can be used as a tool to assist new competitors to overcome this entrance barrier by securing the retail price to retailers and, thus, securing a return on their promotional investment.[64] RPM used by a penetrating company could also eliminate or minimize slotting allowances, in other words fees paid for the retailer's shelf space, in the case of a manufacturer seeking large retail stores. Slotting allowances can be very high if a manufacturer is new to the market.[65]

This theory has been well recognized and implemented in both US and EU approaches to VTR.[66] In particular, the EU objective of free trade

---

[63] Roger van den Bergh and Peter D Camesasca, *European Competition Law and Economics: A Comparative Perspective* (2nd edn, Sweet & Maxwell 2006) 222; Note 61, Steiner, 430, 446; Patrick Rey and Jean Tirole, 'The Logic of Vertical Restraints' (1986) 76(5) *The American Economic Review* 921; Basil S Yamey, *The Economics of Resale Price Maintenance* (Sir Isaac Pitman & Sons 1954) 52–6.

[64] Note 5, Posner, 930; see also Greg Shaffer, 'Slotting Allowances and Resale Price Maintenance: A Comparison of Facilitating Practices' (1991) 22(1) *RAND Journal of Economics* 120, 120–35; Kenneth G Elzinga and David E Mills, 'The Economics of Resale Price Maintenance' in Wayne Collins, *Competition Law and Policy* (American Bar Association 2008) 1–15.

[65] See Organisation for Economic Co-operation and Development, 'Buying Power of Multiproduct Retailers' 7 OECD (Policy Roundtables 1998) DAFFE/CLP(99)21, 38–9 <http://www.oecd.org/competition/abuse/2379299.pdf> (3 August 2015).

[66] Territorial Restraints: EU: C-56/65 *Société La Technique Minière v. Maschinenbau Ulm GmbH* [1966] ECR 235, 250 ('*Minière*'); *Nungesser (LC)*

plays an important role in connection with this theory. A restriction such as VTR in the form of an agreement which can facilitate entering the market of another Member State is justified under Article 101(3) TFEU if it is necessary to penetrate the market.[67] Similarly, in *Leegin*, the US Supreme Court found that RPM can assist new companies in entering the market and in that way increase interbrand competition.[68] In the EU, Guidelines 2010 refers to this justification with regards to RPM.[69]

IV. PROCOMPETITIVE EFFECTS ON CONSUMER WELFARE, OUTPUT AND EFFICIENCY

The advocates of the above-discussed procompetitive theories and of vertical restrictions in general argue that vertical restrictions have procompetitive effects in the form of increased efficiency, output, consumer welfare and indeed competition. These arguments, most notably the arguments on efficiency, are rooted in the transaction cost theory. VTR and RPM are more efficient because they are less costly than their alternatives in situations where VTR or RPM is utilized to introduce certain benefits such as services. Furthermore, VTR can, in certain situations, minimize distribution costs and create the most efficient method for distribution.[70]

Therefore, RPM and VTR and other vertical restraints should not be prohibited only on the basis that there are possible alternatives that do not restrict competition. As Areeda and Hovenkamp explain, the fact that

---

KG and Kurt Eisele v. Commission (Case 258/78) [1982] ECR 2015, [1983] 1 CMLR 278, [44]–[68]; Note 36, Guidelines 2010, [61], [107(b)–(c)]; European Commission, *Green Paper on Vertical Restraints in EC Competition Policy*, (Cm 721, 1996) point 12; US: Note 32, *Sylvania*, 55; *White Motor Co. v. United States*, 372 U.S. 253 (1963) 269; Note 20, Areeda and Hovenkamp, 16, 424–6, 430–2; RPM: Note 20, Areeda and Hovenkamp, 17–18; 308; Note 19, *Leegin*, 891; Note 36, Guidelines 2010, [225]; Regulation 772/2004 on technology transfer agreements [2004] OJ L123/11, 11–17, article 4(2)(b)(ii); Guidelines on the application of Article 81 to technology transfer agreements [2004] OJ C101/27 at 2-42, [101]; see discussions in previous chapters.

[67] Note 66, *Minière*, 250.
[68] Note 19, *Leegin*, 892.
[69] [225].
[70] This justification was confirmed in the US cases of *McDaniel v. Greensboro News Co.*, 679 F.2d 883 (4th Circuit 1983); and *Newberry v. Washington Post. Co.*, 438 F. Supp. 470, 475 (D.D.C. 1977) with regard to the personally delivered newspaper market.

vertical restraints, in particular RPM, have been used in practice (even though some forms of vertical restraints are illegal and RPM has been illegal per se for a long time) means that, in some cases, these restraints are more effective than their alternatives, or the alternatives are not always available.[71] Indeed, any available alternatives can have excessive transaction costs while RPM or VTR can be more efficient.[72]

However, even if RPM or VTR is less costly in a certain situation than its alternatives, there is another issue faced by implementing VTR and RPM in comparison with some potential alternatives. As I have explained above in connection with procompetitive theories, one of the major weaknesses of procompetitive theories is that a number of alternatives directly address issues which the manufacturer aims to address, while RPM and VTR are indirect means (unless VTR itself is utilized because it is a more efficient distribution system and not because it will motivate buyers to introduce services).

Indeed, RPM and VTR do not guarantee any procompetitive aims, such as providing services, but they guarantee the restriction of intrabrand competition. Therefore, two questions remain unanswered. First, how would a manufacturer calculate the cost of RPM if she wants to use it for a procompetitive reason when she does not even have the certainty of such an effect? Second, why would she use such vertical restraints for procompetitive reasons if she cannot assume such results? The answer to the second question could be because she assumes it is less costly and easy to monitor, as explained previously. However, even if we accept this explanation, it leads us back to the first question, which involves uncertainty in the final outcome and thus the effectiveness of using RPM or VTR in order to introduce certain benefits, such as services.

Therefore, how do we determine that the implied VTR or RPM was effective? There are a number of elements which can assist with the determination of the effectiveness of RPM or VTR. First, we can see whether RPM or VTR was introduced for a procompetitive reason, such as the introduction of procompetitive services. Second, we can look at whether these services were introduced or maintained after the implementation of RPM or VTR. Finally, we can analyze the impacts on output and consumer welfare.

---

[71] Note 20, Areeda and Hovenkamp, 22–3.
[72] Ibid., 24; see also Note 9, Williamson, 123–60. I have already elaborated this argument above.

Output

The proponents of the procompetitiveness of vertical restrictions such as RPM and VTR argue that despite the increased price that can follow the introduction of RPM or even VTR,[73] RPM or VTR is procompetitive and efficient if the output increases. Bork believed that anticompetitive theories of vertical restraints result, in general, in a restriction of output.[74] He claimed that output increases when imposing RPM (as well as other vertical restraints) because additional services increase the interest of consumers to buy the product concerned. Therefore, vertical restraints are procompetitive.[75]

There are two drawbacks to this argument. First, output does not always increase. If a vertical restriction results in increased prices and lower output, the restriction is likely not efficient and effective.[76] If output decreases, it is likely that the manufacturer's strategy in the form of a vertical restraint did not work.[77] However, even in situations where output increases, this does not mean that consumers and society have benefited. Indeed, the second reason is that even if output increases, the restriction is not necessarily procompetitive because the vertical restriction did not introduce any procompetitive benefits, such as services and/or it did not increase output at the interbrand level.

Therefore, there are two groups of situations where RPM or VTR leads to increased output. The first one is procompetitive. For instance, when a new company enters the market with the assistance of VTR or RPM, output will increase because, before the introduction of the new product, output of this product was equal to zero, and at the same time competition is enhanced because there is a new product in the market and consumers benefit from an increased choice of products. If RPM is introduced in order to facilitate pre-sale services and output increases, this indicates that the majority of consumers value such services in connection with the RPM product. They benefit from the service and thus

---

[73] Both procompetitive and anticompetitive theories admit that the price will increase or remain the same once RPM is introduced. See Note 4, Wright, 16.

[74] Robert H Bork, *The Antitrust Paradox: A Policy at War with Itself* (The Free Press 1978) 295.

[75] Ibid., 295–7; Note 32, Bork, 403; also see the discussion in Note 4, Areeda and Hovenkamp, 238–9, 243.

[76] See ibid., Areeda and Hovenkamp; William S Comanor, 'Antitrust Policy toward Resale Price Maintenance Following *Leegin*' (2010) 55(1) *Antitrust Bulletin* 59; Note 4, Easterbrook, 163.

[77] Unless, for instance, she simultaneously increased wholesale prices.

the increased output indicates increased competition, in particular, non-price competition. However, if it leads to a decrease in output, it means that RPM was not successful because, for example, the majority of customers valued price over services (or RPM did not lead to increased services) and thus the majority of consumers lost interest in the product with RPM. Prices increase but services do not or they are not of interest to the majority of consumers.

However, there are reasons other than procompetitive ones as to why output can increase with no procompetitive effect. As I explained above, not every procompetitive theory involves benefits for consumers. This can be illustrated in situations where RPM is utilized as an incentive to sell, because, in these cases, RPM is not connected with any extra consumer benefit. In these situations, output is increased simply because the retailers prefer to sell the products from the manufacturer who maintains RPM over her rivals. Other situations where output is increased or remains the same but no procompetitive benefit is introduced include when the brand was so popular or so dominant that the increase in price did not have an obvious impact on consumer choice or the manufacturer simultaneously introduced other strategies or started to advertise more. Therefore, unless an increase in output arises from the vertical restriction itself and is based on valuable services, innovation and improvements of the product or because RPM or VTR facilitated entering a new market, the increase in output does not, on its own, prove the existence of a procompetitive effect.

Furthermore, in situations where there is no consumer benefit but output increases, such an increase is likely at the expense of a decreased output of the competing products. For instance, if RPM is successfully utilized as an incentive to sell and retailers primarily offer this product to consumers because they do not face intrabrand price competition and thus a higher margin is ensured, the increased output will result in a decrease in the output of competing products. These competing products may be cheaper and even of better quality, but retailers will prefer to sell the product with RPM due to the higher potential profits. This is a successful strategy for the manufacturer with RPM which, however, is to the detriment of competition and will decrease total welfare as consumers spend more money on the product with RPM which they could otherwise purchase for less. Indeed, it is important to evaluate the effects on output from the interbrand-competition perspective, especially in a regime such as the US, which focuses on the restriction of interbrand competition. The increase of output at the intrabrand level does not necessarily (and usually will not) lead to increased output at the interbrand level.

Restriction of Competition and Consumer Welfare

Proponents of the procompetitiveness of vertical restrictions such as RPM and VTR argue that VTR and RPM increase interbrand competition and in that way increase consumer welfare. Furthermore, RPM increases non-price competition and is thus beneficial for consumers as it motivates distributors to compete in different areas than just price, such as competing in services, innovation, quality and reputation.[78] As Bork puts it, RPM increases competition in services, which subsequently increases consumer demand and, hence, RPM is 'highly pro-competitive and enhance[s] consumer welfare by stimulating interbrand rivalry'.[79]

This presumption does not apply to the same extent to VTR, as distributors, especially in absolute territories, are not necessarily motivated to increase non-price competition within one brand. Being the only distributors in their territories, they are not motivated to compete at all at the intrabrand level but they may be interested in competing at the interbrand level if there is intensive interbrand competition.

From the interbrand competition point of view, the proponents of procompetitive theories argue that manufacturers have a choice to either implement vertical restraints such as RPM and VTR or to leave it up to free competition, such as price competition. Manufacturers of, for instance, luxury products will have a tendency to implement RPM or even VTR while manufacturers of 'lower end' products will be interested in vigorous price competition. The appropriate mix of price and quality is ideal.[80] The same argument was used in *Leegin* where the Supreme Court stated that, when arguing that RPM increases interbrand competition, RPM can provide more options for consumers in the interbrand market where RPM is utilized for procompetitive reasons, because consumers can choose from 'low-price, low-service brands; high-price, high-service brands; and brands that fall in between'.[81]

Whether RPM or VTR is efficient and increases competition depends on many factors, one of them being market structure.[82] Not every market

---

[78] See Note 17, Kneepkens, 658; Note 14, Telser, 86.
[79] Note 32, Bork, 403.
[80] See Shubha Ghosh 'Vertical Restraints, Competition and the Rule of Reason' in Keith Hylton (ed.), *Antitrust Law and Economics* (Edward Elgar Publishing 2010) 224.
[81] Ibid., 890.
[82] Rey and Stiglitz argue in their economic study that the standard theory of consumer behavior or Posner's test of the presence of 'efficiency-enhancing' costs causing a shift in the demand curve does not exactly apply in reality

is competitive and offers a wide range of products differentiated by their price, quality and services. Even in a competitive market, a vertical restriction does not have to lead to increased efficiency, consumer welfare and competition.[83] In situations where the market is concentrated or even monopolistic, consumers do not have the same choice as presented above. The introduction of a vertical restriction can generally have a negative impact on consumer welfare, as, in the case of RPM, for instance, consumers searching for lower-price products would be worse off. Even in a competitive market, RPM or VTR can lead to a domino effect (or follow-the-leader effect) as described above, which has a restrictive effect on interbrand competition.

The argument that RPM and VTR increase both competition and consumer welfare if introduced by the supplier, such as a manufacturer, is further supported by the claim that manufacturer interests are the same as consumer interests. Therefore, it is in the interest of manufacturers to increase consumer welfare.[84] However, this has many opponents. Adam Smith recognized that manufacturers were driven only by their own interests, primarily profit-making interests.[85] Despite the fact that in order to make a profit manufacturers must attract consumers (and also retailers), the highest possible profit for a manufacturer does not exactly mirror the best interests for a consumer. Furthermore, retailers do not

---

because the structure of different markets is more complicated and includes a number of different aspects. Patrick Rey and Joseph Stiglitz, 'The Role of Exclusive Territories in Producers' Competition' (1995) 26 *RAND Journal of Economics* 431.

[83] For example, in their model, Mathewson and Winter show that simple uniform price maintenance is not efficient in a competitive market. Note 23, Mathewson and Winter, 27; see also Note 58, Mathewson and Winter, 67. On the contrary, Fisher and Overstreet obtained the opposite results in their economic study. Alan A Fisher and Thomas R Overstreet, 'Resale Price Maintenance and Distributional Efficiency: Some Lessons from the Past' (1985) 3 *Contemporary Policy Issues* 43, 49–50.

[84] Note 32, Bork, 403; Note 4, Easterbrook, 135, 147; Brief for the United States as Amicus Curiae in Support of Petitioner, *Monsanto Co. v. Spray-Rite Svc. Corp.*, 465 U.S. 752 (1984) (No 82-914), 1983 U.S. SCt Briefs LEXIS 375, 32–47; see also Note 19, *Leegin*, 889; Case T-168/01 *GlaxoSmithKline v. Commission* [2006] ECR II-2969, [171]–[172]; Note 17, Kneepkens, 658.

[85] Adam Smith, *The Wealth of Nations*, Books I–III edited by Andrew Skinner (Penguin Group 1999) Book I, Chapter II.

want the best profit for manufacturers but for themselves and, understandably, consumers do not want the highest profit for the manufacturers and retailers but the best price, quality and services for themselves.[86]

As we have already seen in Chapter 2, the entity with the best bargaining power on the vertical chain, either the manufacturer or her retailers, will be able to dictate the conditions in the vertical relationship and will thus likely make the better profit. Although both need consumers in order to make profits, they are driven by maximizing their profit, which does not necessarily mean the best possible price, quality or quantity for consumers. Indeed, anticompetitive behavior such as cartels well illustrates that the interests of the manufacturers and retailers do not necessarily correspond with the welfare of consumers. The best price, quality and quantity only occur in a very competitive market, arguably when perfect competition exists,[87] not because the manufacturer and/or retailers are interested in achieving such results on their own, but because the pressure facilitated by competition leads to such results.

Similarly, just because the manufacturer wants and is persuaded that it is best for her profits to introduce certain services, does not mean that all consumers are interested in non-price competition or such services. The procompetitive theories, such as the theory of services, operate on the assumption that the majority of consumers are marginal consumers who are sensitive to any product improvements and services.[88] In other words, they make their choice primarily in relation to extra services – the more services offered, the more products consumers buy or the more consumers that are interested in buying the products – and that RPM (or VTR) increases the choice of such aspects (services).

However, this does not motivate all consumers. The market includes infra-marginal consumers who know the product(s) well, consumers who are only interested in price and consumers interested in qualitative elements other than the services offered. These consumers would be worse off if RPM or VTR were introduced to ensure certain services because they do not need them and they would end up paying more than if they bought the product without the vertical restriction.[89]

Therefore, if the majority of consumers are not interested in services, consumer welfare will decrease. Consumer welfare is only positive if the

---

[86] Note 15, Pitofsky, 1491; compare with Note 4, Easterbrook, 135, 147; Note 32, Bork, 373.

[87] The perfectly competitive conditions are unlikely in reality.

[88] A Michael Spence, 'Monopoly, Quality, and Regulation' (1975) 6(2) *Bell Journal of Economics* 417, 417–19.

[89] See Note 55, Comanor; see also Note 64, Elzinga and Mills, 7–8.

elasticity of demand for the introduced services is high.[90] If only one-half of consumers are marginal and value services, with consumer surplus declining, services will not increase profit and the introduced vertical restraint will be inefficient.[91]

V. EMPIRICAL STUDIES

Advocates of procompetitive and anticompetitive theories agree that RPM increases intrabrand prices and that VTR can lead to the same effect.[92] However, as I have explained in the previous part, the advocates of procompetitive theories argue that other effects of RPM or VTR are procompetitive, as vertical restraints can solve incentive conflicts between suppliers and their buyers leading to increased consumer welfare and efficiency in the form of saved costs, increased output, increased services and increased interbrand competition. Despite the high number of proponents of procompetitive theories, there is no direct empirical evidence to clearly support that applying vertical restraints increases services, the quality of a product or leads to other procompetitive effects.

A few studies which evaluate empirical data argue that RPM (and VTR)[93] leads or can lead to procompetitive outcomes.[94] However, given that these studies are based on assumptions, they do not offer direct evidence that RPM would lead to procompetitive effects. This includes Ippolito's study, which I discussed in Chapter 3. Ippolito surveyed 203 litigated US cases reported from 1975 to 1982. She found that between

---

[90] Note 6, Durand.
[91] Note 55, Comanor, 997–8. Furthermore, the way of purchasing of individual consumers also differs. Some purchase products spontaneously, while others do research before purchasing certain products. This also plays its role in the success and efficiency of RPM or VTR in relation to procompetitive theories. See Norbert Schulz, 'Resale price maintenance and the service argument: Efficiency effects' (2005) Wuerzburg Economic Working Paper No. 53, 1–23.
[92] See, e.g., Note 4, Wright, 16.
[93] There are fewer studies on VTR than on RPM, including the empirical one.
[94] See, e.g., Francine Lafontaine and Margaret Slade, *Exclusive Contracts and Vertical Relationships: Empirical Evidence and Public Policy* (MIT Press 2008); Pauline M Ippolito, 'Resale Price Maintenance: Empirical Evidence from Litigation' (1991) 34 *Journal of Law & Economics* 263, 292–3; Pauline Ippolito, 'Resale price maintenance: empirical evidence from litigation' (Economic Report, FTC, 1983); Thomas R Overstreet, 'Resale price maintenance: Economic theories and empirical evidence' (Bureau of Economics Staff Report, FTC, 1983).

42–50 percent of analyzed cases on RPM involved 'complex products', which, according to the author, are products where quality and information are important attributes. Based on this finding, she argued that the 'majority' of RPM cases could be explained by the services theory. Obviously, this is just an assumption. It does not prove that RPM in all or some of these cases increased services or that it led to any other procompetitive effects. It only shows that RPM at that time was almost equally spread between complex and simple products.

Ippolito also found that the majority of all cases were vertical-agreement cases where only 13.1 percent of all cases and 9.8 percent of private cases involved allegations of horizontal price fixing and thus the majority did not involve horizontal collusion. Overstreet, who examined 68 FTC cases from mid-1965 to 1982, also concluded that a significant majority of cases were not related to horizontal cartels. He focused on the concentration of the market and *assumed* that 80 percent of the analyzed cases could not have involved a collusion of buyers due to the high number of buyers in those cases. Moreover, he assumed that it is not likely that the cases included anticompetitive intentions where the market was structurally competitive.[95] Again, both of Overstreet's findings are assumptions that were made based on analyzed empirical data.

A recent study undertaken by Giovanneti and Magazzini, published in 2013, analyzed 72 RPM complaints lodged with the Office of Fair Trading[96] in the UK from 2007 to 2009.[97] Giovanneti and Magazzini *assume* that the majority of these complaints could be explained using the free riding theory because all retailers who complained operated online, with around 40 percent only online and 60 percent online and high street stores.[98] Furthermore, some complaint proceedings involved the 'justification' of RPM. Thirty-seven percent of respondents said they used RPM to protect themselves from free riding (on customer support activities, training or advertising) and 20 percent to protect brand image.[99] However, these data do not provide direct evidence that RPM in these cases led to procompetitive effects and/or that the provided

---

[95] Ibid, Overstreet, 73, 78–80.

[96] The Office of Fair Trading was abolished in 2014 and replaced by the Competition and Market Authority.

[97] Emanuele Giovanneti and Laura Magazzini, 'Resale Price Maintenance: An Empirical Analysis of UK Firms' Compliance' (2013) 123 *The Economic Journal* 582, 585.

[98] Ibid., 589.

[99] Ibid., 590.

justifications were the real reasons and that the potential procompetitive effects were utilized by RPM.[100]

In contrast, some empirical evidence shows that RPM and VTR increase prices.[101] Furthermore, the study of the US music industry, for instance, as well as other studies, indicates that VTR and RPM led to welfare losses.[102] This is also confirmed by one the most recent studies, an empirical study undertaken by MacKay and Smith, which provides empirical evidence of negative effects on consumer welfare, prices and output in US states which implemented the rule of reason after the case of *Leegin*.

MacKay and Smith did not find any 'broad support' for well-accepted procompetitive theories and anticompetitive theories.[103] They studied the

---

[100] However, what it shows is the importance of online sales, which play a role in the current retail market. As I have explained above, the involvement of online sales can increase competition and lead to procompetitive effects.

[101] RPM: Alexander MacKay and David A Smith, 'The empirical effects of minimum resale price maintenance' (16 June 2014) Kilts Booth Marketing Series, Paper No. 1-009; FTC Press Release, 'Record companies settle FTC charges of restraining competition in CD music market' (10 May 2000) <http://www.ftc.gov/opa/2000/05/cdpres.shtm> accessed 1 June 2015; Note 26, Ornstein and Hanssens, 1–16; Hearings on S. 408 before the Subcommittee on Antitrust and Monopoly of the Senate Committee on the Judiciary, 94th Cong., 1st Sess., 173 (1975); Statement of Keith I Clearwaters, Deputy Assistant Attorney General, Antitrust Divisions, Hearings on HR 2384 before the Subcommittee on Monopolies and Commercial Law of the House Committee on the Judiciary, 94th Cong., 1st Sess., 122 (1975); see also Note 54, Grimes, 134–42; Note 101, FTC Press Release, 'Record Companies Settle'; VTR in US market with malt beverages: Note 26, Sass and Saurman, 153–77; W Patton Culbertson and David Bradford, 'The Price of Beer: Some Evidence from Interstate Comparisons' (1991) 9 *International Journal of Industrial Organization* 275; W Patton Culbertson, 'Beer-Cash Laws: Their Economic Impact and Antitrust Implications' (1989) 34 *Antitrust Bulletin* 209; W John Jordan and Bruce L Jaffee, 'The Use of Exclusive Territories in the Distribution of Beer: Theoretical and Empirical Observations' (1987) 32 *Antitrust Bulletin* 137; US car market: Note 6, Durand; US mattresses market – VTR reduced output and increased prices: Willard F Mueller and Frederick E Gaithman, 'An empirical test of the free rider and market power hypothesis' (unpublished manuscript, 12 April 1989).

[102] Ibid., FTC Press Release; see also Note 54, Grimes, 134–42; Note 26, Ornstein and Hanssens, 1–16; ibid., Hearings on S. 408 before the Subcommittee on Antitrust and Monopoly of the Senate Committee; ibid., Statement of Keith I Clearwaters; Note 6, Durand; ibid., Mueller and Gaithman; ibid., Culbertson and Bradford; ibid., Culbertson; ibid, Jordan and Jaffee.

[103] Note 101, MacKay and Smith, 17–22. The anticompetitive theories of manufacturers' cartels and retailers' cartel are explained below.

price of various products and their quantity after the delivery of the 2007 judgment in *Leegin* in the US in states which had been applying the rule of reason and states which continued to apply the per se rule. They compared these data and found that RPM likely had a negative impact on price and output because prices have increased and output has decreased in states applying the rule of reason. In these states, the estimated overall price increase was 0.33 percent (the price of 8.4 percent of products increased significantly and 9.4 percent of products led to a decrease in quantity) and the decrease of quantity was 3.8 percent. These resulted in a negative impact on consumer welfare with consumer welfare decreasing by 3.1 percent.[104]

Empirical data also indicate that even the implementation of RPM by one manufacturer could lead to anticompetitive restrictions and/or effects across the industry,[105] especially in the situation where the manufacturer with RPM is a leading brand. This impact could be further illustrated by the jeans industry in the US in the 1970s. Levi Strauss, a well-established brand of jeans in the US, stopped using RPM in 1977 after a complaint to the FTC. This resulted not only in a lower retail price for Levi jeans but the retail price decreased across the US jeans market, leading to increased consumer welfare, where consumer surplus gained roughly US$200 million over the 18 months following Levi's elimination of their RPM policy.[106]

Both RPM and VTR can have a negative impact not only on intrabrand competition, but also on interbrand competition in situations where RPM or VTR is implemented across the industry. This can occur, for instance, due to the domino effect, explained above, and not necessarily because there is any explicit agreement between manufacturers. Giovanneti and Magazzini's empirical study on RPM indicates that this is not unusual but rather a common situation with regards to RPM. The studied complaints on RPM in the UK in the period of 2007 to 2009 show that

---

[104] Ibid. Also Steiner explains that when RPM was eliminated in the toy industry in the early 1960s, the output increased and prices decreased. Robert L Steiner, 'Vertical Competition, Horizontal Competition and Market Power' (2008) 53(2) *Antitrust Bulletin* 251, 261.

[105] See, e.g., discussions on the 'interlocking' vertical relationships in Patrick Rey and Thibaud Vergé, 'Resale Price Maintenance and Interlocking Relationships' (2010) LVIII(4) *The Journal of Industrial Economics* 928; Thibaud Vergé, 'Minimum Resale Price Maintenance and Concentrated Markets' (2008) 54(3) *Applied Economics Quarterly* 161, 165–70.

[106] Note 104, Steiner, 260–61.

RPM was utilized across the industry in an impressive 69 percent cases of the studied complaints.[107]

VI. ANTICOMPETITIVE EFFECTS

The number of economic studies analyzing anticompetitive effects of RPM and VTR is lower than those analyzing the possible economic explanations of procompetitive effects.[108] Nevertheless, the sparse empirical studies, primarily on the effects of RPM (and a few existing studies on VTR), show that RPM (and VTR) can lead to anticompetitive effects. These effects involve increased prices,[109] decreased consumer welfare, innovation and efficiency and even decreased output.

Obviously, RPM prevents price decreases because buyers, for instance retailers, are prevented from lowering their sale prices for the product with RPM leading to increased price, especially in situations where the minimum price or fixed price is high. With regard to VTR, a retailer of a certain brand who does not compete with other retailers due to territorial restrictions is not motivated to decrease the price if, for example, the demand curve for the product has the tendency to be inelastic.

RPM and VTR can even decrease output, rather than increase it, as argued by the advocates of procompetitive theories. This decrease in output has been shown in the above-discussed MacKay and Smith's empirical study. At the interbrand level, if prices increase, output decreases as consumers are not able to purchase as many products for the same price. Even in particular situations where RPM is utilized only for one product in a competitive market leading to the successful promotion of the product with RPM (for instance, where RPM operates as an incentive to sell), the output at the interbrand level can decrease. Because RPM increases the price for the RPM product and the number of consumers purchasing the RPM product increase due to its successful

---

[107] Note 97, Giovanneti and Magazzini, 589.

[108] Matthew Bennett, Amelia Fletcher, Emanuele Giovannetti and David Stallibrass, 'Resale price maintenance: explaining the controversy, and small steps towards a more nuanced policy' (2010) MPRA Paper No. 21121, 17, 20 available at <http://mpra.ub.uni-muenchen.de/21121/> accessed 1 June 2015.

[109] Also in situations with VTR: see generally Note 101; Note 36, Guidelines 2010, [224]; Lucas Peeperkorn, 'Resale Price Maintenance and Its Alleged Efficiencies' (2008) June *European Competition Journal* 201, 207; Robert Pitofsky, 'Are Retailers Who Offer Discounts Really "Knaves"?: The Coming Change to the *Dr. Miles* Rule' (2007) *Antitrust Law Journal* 61, 64; Note 6, Burns, 597.

promotion, overall, consumers will likely pay more. If consumers pay more, they might purchase fewer products at the interbrand level. If the successful 'promotion' increases sales of the product with RPM, it will likely decrease sales of competing products because consumers will be persuaded that they should purchase the product with RPM.

This restrictive impact on interbrand competition is even more obvious in situations where RPM or VTR leads to increased prices across the industry, at the interbrand level, for instance, due to the domino effect. Indeed, for the first economic-policy model to be satisfied RPM or VTR must appear across the industry and/or it must affect horizontal competition. Although VTR and RPM are vertical restrictions they can restrict interbrand competition and increase prices at the interbrand level. There are (at least) two ways this can happen.

The first situation is the already discussed domino or follow-the-leader effect, where other competitors decide to implement RPM or VTR after the first manufacturer has done so. They do so in order to keep up with the first manufacturer and provide an incentive to sell to their retailers: they do not want their competitor with RPM or VTR to have a 'selling advantage' as this could have a negative impact on their own profits. This is well illustrated in the recent situation with lens manufacturers in the US as described above and supported by Giovanneti and Magazzini's empirical study, which shows that in 69 percent of RPM complaints in the UK from 2007 to 2009 RPM was utilized across the industries.[110] With regard to VTR, the US automobile-sales market provides a good example where, in particular, exclusive territories are implemented across the industry. VTR in this industry has rather an anticompetitive impact resulting in low consumer welfare and decreased interbrand competition despite the technicality and high price of the relevant products.[111]

The second situation relates to RPM. RPM can lead to the restriction of interbrand competition due to 'interlocking' vertical relationships, which means that retailers sell competing goods. This can occur even when interbrand competition is intensive. RPM limits competition between retailers and due to the interlocking situation, interbrand competition is softened and even eliminated leading to monopoly prices and profits.[112]

---

[110] Note 97, Giovanneti and Magazzini, 589.
[111] See Note 6, Durand.
[112] Note 105, Rey and Vergé; Note 105 Vergé, 165–70.

Furthermore, RPM and VTR can lead to anticompetitive impacts other than increased prices and decreased output such as decreases in innovation, consumer choice and efficiency.[113] One of the most obvious examples of RPM or VTR leading to decreased efficiency is that by increasing retail prices and thus buyers' profit, they can prevent efficient distributors from growing, thus leading to reduced dynamism and innovation at the distribution level.[114] More efficient distributors benefit from free and intensive intra and interbrand competition because these can increase their profit while decreasing the profits of less efficient distributors. In a competitive environment, including intrabrand competition, distributors try to determine how to improve their distribution by, among other things, lowering the cost of distribution, in order to reach more consumers and make a higher profit. However, by introducing RPM, distributors know that they are not competing on price anymore and that a certain profit is ensured. Although they can still compete on non-price services, they do not compete on selling price and thus are not as motivated as they would be without RPM to lower their costs.

With regard to VTR, distributors are not motivated to increase efficiency and innovation due to a restriction of both intrabrand price and non-price competition. They have the exclusivity of selling a particular product in a certain territory. Only intensive intrabrand competition would provide an incentive to lower their costs and improve distribution in order to attract customers.

With regard to RPM, Steiner provided an example of the Japanese market, where RPM prevented more efficient distributors from performing as highly and efficiently as in the US and established barriers to entry.[115] Steiner claimed that when vertical restraints prevent more efficient distributors from being rewarded for their capacity to be efficient, several restrictive results occur at the vertical level. First, distribution costs are higher because less efficient distributors benefit from such conduct. Secondly, the total costs in the vertical system remain higher because of the elimination of the option of allocating functions between manufacturers and more efficient distributors. Thirdly, advertising has a tendency to be lower as the cost of distribution is higher, which

---

[113] See, e.g., Note 42, Gundlach, Manning and Cannon, 18, 18–20.
[114] RPM: Note 109, Peeperkorn, 208; Richard M Brunell, 'Overruling *Dr. Miles*: The Supreme Trade Commission in Action' (2007) 52 *Antitrust Bulletin* 475, 475–529; Note 61, Steiner, 407; see also Note 54, Grimes, 101–49.
[115] Note 61, Steiner, 439.

has a negative impact on output. And, finally, innovation, product quality and consumer choice are restricted.[116]

Another anticompetitive effect with regard to RPM and VTR is the foreclosure of competition and reduction of consumer choice. Increasing final prices restricts consumer choice of potentially cheaper products or services. RPM or VTR can also restrict consumer choice of products that utilize more innovative forms of distribution, as potentially more efficient distributors do not face the pressure of intrabrand competition as a motivating force to improve their distribution.[117] By providing an incentive to sell and thus influencing retailers or distributors to promote or choose manufacturer's products at the expense of the manufacturer's competitors, consumer choice is, at the very least, influenced. Consumer choice would be restricted if this leads to a refusal to sell products other than the RPM or VTR products by retailers. Indeed, as I explained with regards to procompetitive theories, in particular the incentive to sell, if not limited, consumer choice will be at least influenced by the retailers' favoritism for products with RPM or VTR due to the better profits they can receive when selling these products.

VII. ANTICOMPETITIVE THEORY OF SUPPLIER (INTERBRAND) CARTEL

Well-established anticompetitive theories include the theories of manufacturer (supplier) and retailer cartels. These theories focus on the form of conduct rather than the above-discussed anticompetitive effects. In general, they recognize horizontal collusion as anticompetitive. Retailer cartels create horizontal intrabrand collusion unless more than one brand is involved, while supplier cartels are based on interbrand horizontal collusion.

Supplier or retailer cartels with regards to RPM are rare in practice, as shown in Overstreet's, Ippolito's, and MacKay and Smith's empirical studies.[118] A survey of the US and EU cases reveals that supplier cartels

---

[116] Ibid., 439–40.
[117] Ibid., 407; Note 46, Consumer Focus, 'Focus Response', 11–12; see also Note 46, statement of Daniel J Schuler; Note 46, Retail Competition Enforcement Act, hearing before Senate Commission on the Judiciary.
[118] Note 94, Overstreet; Note 94, Ippolito, Journal article, 292–3; Note 94, Ippolito, 'FTC Report'; Note 101, MacKay and Smith.

are even more rare than retailer cartels, with few cases being litigated on these bases.[119]

Unlike any horizontal cartel, a supplier horizontal cartel also has a vertical dimension as it involves a vertical restraint such as RPM or VTR, including both interbrand horizontal and vertical arrangements. In general, RPM assists with maintaining supplier cartels by ensuring not only that wholesale prices remain the same or in the same range, but also retail prices by maintaining the price at the retailers' level and, simultaneously, by preventing cheating. Suppliers might introduce RPM as part of their cartel to assist with monitoring and enforcing collusion and enhancing price transparency.[120] Such arrangements restrict interbrand competition, strengthen the manufacturer cartels and prevent manufacturers from cheating.[121] VTR can also be used to maintain supplier cartels, as territorial restrictions ensure transparency and also strengthen the manufacturers' and retailers' power if a cartel divides the market not just among manufacturers, but also among retailers.[122]

Bork provides some arguments as to why this theory would not apply in practice. Indeed, these arguments can assist with an explanation as to why RPM or VTR as part of a supplier cartel is not common. He argues that RPM is totally unnecessary for supplier cartels, considering the outlet reports and opportunities and reasons for cheating inside the cartels.[123] A cartel consisting of manufacturers and retailers would, logically, have more members and would thus create more opportunities to cheat. However, it could be counterargued that a price cartel further facilitated by the application of RPM is also more transparent, because using vertical restraints in a horizontal cartel makes it easier to determine whether somebody has cheated and could therefore be more easily monitored. This would, arguably, result in less inclination to cheat.

---

[119] VTR: *Service Merchandise Co. v. Boyd Corp.*, 722 F.2d 945 (1st Circuit 1983); RPM: *Toledo Mack Sales & Service, Inc. v. Mack Trucks, Inc.*, 530 F.3d 204 (3d Circuit 2008). Unsuccessful case involving supplier cartel: In re *Online Travel Company Hotel Booking Antitrust Litigation*, 2014 WL 626555 (NDTex).

[120] Note 36, Guidelines 2010, [224]; Note 108, Bennett et al., 21; Note 109, Peeperkorn, 206; Note 17, Kneepkens, 661; Note 64, Elzinga and Mills, 6; Frederic M Scherer and David Ross, *Industrial Market Structure and Economic Performance* (3rd edn, Houghton Mifflin 1990) 550; Note 94, Ippolito, Journal article, 281; see also Note 101, FTC Press Release; Note 54, Grimes, 134–42.

[121] Note 20, Areeda and Hovenkamp, 19–20, 321; Note 17, Shores, 377, 402–3; see Note 36, Guidelines 2010, [100(b)].

[122] See Note 36, Guidelines 2010, [151]; Note 20, Areeda and Hovenkamp, 439–41.

[123] Note 74, Bork, 293–5; see also Note 64, Elzinga and Mills, 6.

Bork also argued that RPM attracts government attention and, therefore, RPM would be used as part of cartel collusion only very rarely.[124] Under the current US regime, RPM would not raise much concern among the DOJ and FTC while horizontal cartel behavior would. Indeed, a horizontal cartel attracts suspicion from a government notwithstanding whether it is in the US or the EU. Despite this attention given to cartels and their strict approach, horizontal cartels occur frequently in reality.

VIII. ANTICOMPETITIVE THEORY OF RETAILER (INTRABRAND) CARTEL

A retailer cartel is, as the name suggests, one initiated by the retailers. Retailer cartels involve anticompetitive intentions and also probably anticompetitive effects. Retailers are interested in softening competition to keep higher profits and to stop more efficient retailers and other price cutters from taking their profits.[125] Retailers with bargaining power may fear intrabrand competition, particularly if they are less efficient, and may thus pressure their manufacturer to utilize RPM.[126] However, the theory of the retailer cartel only applies if the pressure comes from a number of retailers who collude in order to pressure their supplier to enforce a vertical restraint.

Nevertheless, such pressure can also come from only one retailer with bargaining power who can force her supplier to enforce RPM or VTR.[127] Although the effects and reasons are the same in both situations, a retailer cartel or an individual retailer initiation, the theory of the retailer cartel applies only to the first situation and the approach, most notably in the US, differs. The first situation is per se illegal in the US because of the existence of horizontal collusion, while the rule of reason applies to the second situation.

Unlike manufacturer cartels, VTR and RPM in the form of a retailer cartel will primarily foreclose intrabrand competition if it concerns only one product or service. As Bork puts it, vertical restraints 'would not

---

[124] Ibid.
[125] Note 64, Shaffer, 120–36.
[126] Note 76, Comanor, 60–63, 67–9, 75–7; Note 109, Peeperkorn, 206; Note 20, Areeda and Hovenkamp, 20; Note 64, Elzinga and Mills, 5; Note 9, Williamson, 123–60.
[127] A buyer forcing her supplier to introduce RPM: *McDonough v. Toys 'R' Us*, 638 F. Supp.2d 461, 492 (EDPa2009); *Euromodas, Inc. v. Zanella, Ltd.*, 368 F.3d 11 (1st Circuit 2004); Note 4, *Business Electronics*.

eliminate the rivalry of resellers of other manufacturers' products'.[128] However, RPM or VTR can also have an impact on interbrand competition in whatever form it takes, vertical agreements or horizontal retailer cartels, if it involves more than one competing product, in situations where the domino or follow the leader effects occur or with regards to RPM due to the 'interlocking' vertical relationships.

A retailer cartel based on vertical arrangements is also likely to be more stable than an interbrand horizontal agreement because, in addition to collusion among retailers, the cartel is managed by their supplier.[129] Furthermore, with regards to VTR, exclusive territories limit the number of retailers, which makes it easier to engage in tacit collusion, as opposed to a competitive retailer market, where collusion would be less possible and likely.[130]

IX. ANTICOMPETITIVE MOTIVATIONS BY RETAILER

We have seen in this chapter that a number of procompetitive theories exist with regard to RPM and VTR where the supplier initiates a vertical restraint. In contrast, there is no procompetitive explanation for RPM or VTR when a buyer, such as a retailer or a group of retailers, forces the supplier to apply RPM or VTR, notwithstanding whether it is in the form of a retail cartel or such initiation comes from one retailer or a number of retailers unilaterally and simultaneously.

Indeed, it appears to be common that RPM is initiated by a retailer or retailers, as illustrated by Giovanneti and Magazzini's empirical study on RPM claims in the UK from 2007 to 2009, where 42.5 percent of claims involved RPM being introduced due to a downstream member persuading the supplier to impose RPM.[131] The reason for retailers' interest in RPM or VTR is that these represent better profit for retailers due to the foreclosure of intrabrand competition and ensured profit margin. Therefore, the motivation for retailers is either to protect or increase their profit. If retailer(s) possess significant bargaining power with regard to their relationship with the supplier, then they are able to force the supplier to introduce RPM even if there is no benefit for the supplier

---

[128] Note 74, Bork, 292; see also Note 64, Elzinga and Mills, 5–6.
[129] Note 108, Bennett et al., 21–2; Note 66, Gellhorn, Kovacic and Calkins, 342; Note 15, Pitofsky, 1490.
[130] Note 82, Rey and Stiglitz, 446.
[131] Note 97, Giovanneti and Magazzini, 590.

other than to keep her retailer(s) happy and ensure they continue selling her products.

There are two obvious reasons why retailers would start pressuring their supplier to utilize RPM or VTR: either intrabrand competition becomes too intensive, cutting retailers' profits, or there is a new retailer who starts to sell below other retailers' prices. A retailer with bargaining power or a group of retailers would be interested in preserving their power and profit by preventing the entry of new, especially lower cost, retailers via VTR or protecting their profit from lower cost retailers via RPM. If there is a retailer who is able to sell at a discount, because he is, for instance, more efficient than other retailers or is trying to establish himself in the market, other retailers lose their profit. Despite the fact that more retailers and/or intensive vertical competition is usually more profitable for the supplier, the retailer with bargaining power can successfully force his supplier to apply RPM or even stop supplying the discounting retailer, as the supplier fears losing the significant turnover that the sales to this powerful retailer represent.[132]

With regard to intensive intrabrand competition, this situation means that if retailers are continually decreasing the retail prices of a certain product as part of competing, then they are highly motivated to restrict intrabrand competition, for instance by introducing RPM to stop the price and profit decrease. They can even threaten the supplier to decrease her wholesale price or threaten to stop selling her product. Thus, the supplier herself could be motivated to introduce a vertical restraint in order to stop this pressure.

The retailers' reason for introducing RPM or VTR is even more profound in situations where the product they have been vigorously competing in is a well-established brand. As we saw in Chapter 2, retailers such as grocery stores are interested in selling the well-established brands with significant customer loyalty for the best prices possible. If a retail store has higher prices on well-established brands, consumers will assume that such a store has higher prices on all products in general. RPM and potentially VTR can ease this competitive pressure and thus could be of interest to retailers. RPM will ensure that no one will sell such a brand for less, thus ensuring a certain level of profit for retailers, while VTR ensures the elimination of intensive intrabrand competition.

---

[132] See Chapter 2.

X. (ANTI)COMPETITIVE MOTIVATIONS BY SUPPLIER

Motivations Based on Procompetitive Theories

We have seen that there are a number of procompetitive theories and thus procompetitive reasons why a supplier would be motivated to introduce RPM or VTR. The procompetitive theories are well reflected in the US approach. For instance, in *Leegin*, the Supreme Court stated that if RPM is introduced by a retailer(s) it will likely be for an anticompetitive reason, while if it is introduced by a supplier it will most likely be for a procompetitive reason.[133] We have seen that the Supreme Court is correct with regard to the retailers' reasons for introducing RPM. However, the situation is more complicated with regard to suppliers' reasons, as can be detected from the above discussion on procompetitive theories and a number of counterarguments pointing at the weaknesses in these theories.

The above-discussed procompetitive theories provide procompetitive reasons for suppliers to introduce RPM or VTR. However, we have seen two problems with regard to procompetitive motivations arising from procompetitive theories: empirical data and some theoretical drawbacks of some of these theories.

First, the scarce empirical studies do not provide explicit evidence on the existence of procompetitive theories in practice and, indeed, there is no evidence as to how often these theories are utilized in practice. However, a number of the EU cases show that vertical restraints, in particular VTR, can play an important role when a manufacturer is trying to enter a new market.[134]

Second, as we have seen, some so-called procompetitive explanations can have rather anticompetitive effects and/or provide a reason for introducing a vertical restraint which could be either procompetitive or anticompetitive depending on the angle of view. RPM used as an incentive to sell simply because it ensures profit margin to the retailers provides a certain advantage to the manufacturer which is not based on her extra competitive effort. Indeed, unless there is a consumer benefit leading to increased competition and efficiency, profit maximizing which leads to increased prices cannot, on its own, be a procompetitive explanation. The same explanation can be used by the members of cartels and other anticompetitive practices.

---

[133] Note 19, *Leegin*, 890, 896, 898.
[134] See, e.g., Note 66, *Minière*; Note 34, *Consten and Grundig*.

One of the questionable procompetitive theories is the theory which explains RPM or VTR as a tool for maintaining a luxurious image based on high prices. Although high price is one of the attributes of luxury, luxury can be connected with other and rather qualitative aspects, such as high quality and/or uniqueness of a product. Unless some consumers prefer to purchase expensive products purely for the fact that they are expensive, RPM does not involve any benefit for consumers. It could even mislead consumers who expect something more from luxurious products than just high price, as high price is one of the aspects that makes consumers believe that they are buying a luxurious and/or high quality product. Furthermore, any supplier introducing RPM could use the justification that it was protecting and/or creating the reputation of a luxurious product because, aside from high prices, there is no qualitative element that a supplier would have to show in order to apply this theory.

The theory of luxurious image and RPM (or VTR) as an incentive to sell can be utilized as a 'justification argument'; however, without the necessary merits anyone can claim that he/she applied RPM or VTR for this reason. Free riding, which is connected with these and also other procompetitive theories, is then not necessarily free riding but rather discounting.[135] Indeed, any form of discounting and selling for lower price can be referred to as free riding.

For instance, discounting was referred to as free riding even in the case of *Leegin* where the Supreme Court overruled the per se rule on the basis of the existence of procompetitive theories and explanations. In this case, the manufacturer, Leegin, first introduced a selective system ensuring that every retailer was compliant with Leegin's preferred quality of sales. All of Leegin's retailers were selected based on certain qualities and all of them fulfilled these quality conditions, including PSKS, the discounting retailer in question. There was no indication that RPM was necessary to ensure services and other qualities and indeed PSKS was not free riding, instead PSKS was decreasing prices as a result of intensive competition in the local, geographical market, while still providing the 'services' required under the selective system. Thus, there was no free riding on consumer benefits which would have to be prevented by RPM.

---

[135] For instance, Avishalom Tor and William J Rinner argue that some forms of 'free riding' are de facto mere discounting in 'Behavioral Antitrust: A New Approach to the Rule of Reason after *Leegin*' (2011) 3 *University of Illinois Law Review* 805, 822.

Other Motivations

A general reason as to why suppliers would be interested in introducing RPM and VTR reflected in the discussion in this chapter and also in Chapter 2 is that suppliers can be interested in maintaining resale prices to motivate their buyers and thus maintain or even increase their profits. Besides procompetitive theories, this reason involves other explanations, which can be divided into four different forms.

First, the manufacturer can use RPM or VTR to more easily maintain or introduce higher wholesale prices, as RPM and even VTR guarantee retail margins and thus ease the negotiation of higher wholesale prices. By easing intrabrand competition, RPM or VTR also prevents decreasing wholesale prices especially in situations where the manufacturer does not have bargaining power. As Peeperkorn puts it:

> the manufacturer generally prefers [intrabrand] competition not to be so fierce that it also starts to put pressure on its own margins, in other words that the downstream competition means that important buyers demand lower purchase prices.[136]

Second, manufacturers may be motivated to introduce RPM or VTR to create or maintain the loyalty of their retailers. If intrabrand competition among retailers who sell different products is intense, the distributors can reach the point where they cease to make a profit from the product in question and can refuse to buy the product, particularly if the brand does not have a well-established reputation.[137] Usually, it is not in the interest of manufacturers to lose their retailers, as they do not want to decrease their output and/or profit.

Third, RPM can be a useful tool for manufacturers for lobbying existing or potential retailers, improving their selling positions and increasing bargaining power. For example, a smaller manufacturer may fear even being considered by a large retailer and/or she may need to lobby for better shelf position. Therefore, introducing RPM (and in

---

[136] Note 109, Peeperkorn, 207; see also Note 54, Grimes, 148.
[137] Note 46, Steiner, 31–4; Note 104, Steiner, 258; Robert L Steiner, 'Exclusive Dealing + Resale Price Maintenance: A Powerful Anticompetitive Combination' (2004) 33 *Southwestern University Law Review* 447, 454–5, 464–5; Note 61, Steiner, 411; see also Note 46, Harbour and Price, 240–42; Michael Lynch, 'Why Economists Are Wrong to Neglect Retailing and How Steiner's Theory Provides an Explanation of Important Regularities' (2004) 49(4) *Antitrust Bulletin* 911, 926–40.

certain circumstances VTR)[138] can benefit her in the bargaining process. This reason is not necessarily anticompetitive given that it could be utilized by a small manufacturer who faces difficulties in remaining in the market due to small output and/or establishing herself in the market. In this case, the situation is very similar to the penetrating-the-market procompetitive explanation.

Finally, RPM or VTR could be used by a manufacturer in order to persuade retailers to maintain another vertical restraint, such as tying. Tying can assist with increasing the sale of the tied product and thus increase the manufacturer's profit, while RPM or VTR can lead to increased retailer profits.[139]

Nevertheless, the list of reasons is even longer given that there have been other reasons provided in EU and US cases. For instance, a reason typified for the pharmaceutical companies in the EU is to prevent parallel imports as pharmaceutical companies lose their profit if other distributors sell their pharmaceutical products for less in Member States with higher retail and, indeed, wholesale prices.[140]

Unfortunately, many EU and US cases do not include reference to the initiation of RPM or VTR by retailer(s) or to justifications based on procompetitive theories. This could be due to the previous per se rule in the US and the strict approach in the EU. However some cases, particularly the oldest cases, reveal other potential motivations for introducing RPM or VTR. For instance, they show that the manufacturer believed it was simply her right to do so and, as Grundig explained in *Consten and Grundig*, VTR was utilized in order to plan business in advance.[141]

This reasoning and the whole process that takes place when the initiator decides whether to use a vertical restraint, including RPM and VTR, could be explained by methodological individualism. Individuals such as manufacturers are driven by private goals. These goals can be

---

[138] For instance, in the grocery retail market, it is unlikely that a small manufacturer would offer VTR as a successful incentive to lobby.

[139] However, this combination is not common based on the analyzed US and EU cases.

[140] See, e.g., C-501/06 P, C-513/06 P, C-515/06 P, C-519/06 P, *GlaxoSmithKline Services Unlimited v. Commission of the EC* [2009] 4 CMLR 2; *Sot. Lelos kai Sia EE and others v. GlaxoSmithKline AEVE Farmakeftikon Proionton* (Case C-468 to 478/06) [2008] ECR I-7139, [2008] 5 CMLR 20; C-2/01 P and C-3/01 P *Bundesverband der Arzneimittel-Importeure EC and Commission v. Bayer AG* [2004] ECR I-00023; T-41/96, *Bayer v. Commission* [2000] ECR II-3383.

[141] Note 34, *Consten and Grundig*, 348.

anticompetitive or procompetitive, as described above. However, the procompetitive goals and also other explanations could be joint under one common goal, for example some manufacturers wish to decide for themselves how and for how much their products should be sold to customers, rather than leaving it up to the market and their retailers. While such a rationale involves procompetitive theories, where RPM or VTR is used as a manufacturer's method to guide this process, it is broader than that. This broadness is supported by the explanations provided in early cases, in particular those that were not necessarily influenced by specified legal approaches and economic theories. These cases reveal that manufacturers (defendants) argued it was their 'right' to utilize RPM or VTR and/or believed that it was profitable for them,[142] helped them to control sales[143] and/or assisted them to plan their business in advance.[144]

Therefore, RPM or VTR is perceived by those manufacturers as a form of business strategy. This view is supported by some scholars. For instance, Williamson argues that vertical restraints promote the strategic purposes of a manufacturer; however, Williamson does not name these strategic purposes. Aside from explanations based on procompetitive theories, VTR and/or RPM can be a useful business tool to assist a manufacturer in maximizing production and profit. For instance, if retail prices are set and maintained, it can be easier for a manufacturer to predict the market and adjust future business strategies, including a correct assumption of future output, the most profitable retail price in relation to the output and the conditions in the market. Therefore, RPM and/or setting vertical territories can be useful tools in this sense for assisting the manufacturer to set the most effective production and price to maximize her profit.

When considering vertical restraints as business strategies, Williamson argues that manufacturers determine the different transaction costs of these strategies. By utilizing transaction cost theory, Williamson claims that manufacturers' strategic decisions are usually more effective as they save rather than increase transaction costs, unless they lead to dependent oligopolies or monopolies, or such 'restraints', most notably exclusive

---

[142] See, e.g., US: Note 12, *Park & Sons*; Note 28, *Colgate*; *United States v. Parke, Davis & Co.*, 362 U.S. 29 (1959); EU: Case 107/82 *Allgemeine Elektrizitäts-Gesellschaft AEG-Telefunken AG v. Commission of the EC* [1983] ECR 3151.
[143] *Dr. Miles Medical Co. v. John D. Park & Sons Co.*, 220 U.S. 373 (1911).
[144] Note 34, *Consten and Grundig*, 348.

dealing including exclusive territories, are used in monopolistic or oligopolistic markets.[145]

In summary, Williamson argues that, aside from the aforementioned situations, vertical restraints could restrict competition only seemingly, as such restrictions can save transaction costs and subsequently lead to more effective competition, which is procompetitive rather than anticompetitive. Hence, each situation must be economically analyzed based on the transaction costs to determine whether it is pro or anticompetitive.[146] Whether the effect is procompetitive is arguable. For instance, although Steiner agrees with the conclusion that each situation must be economically analyzed, he illustrates in several examples why vertical restraints, in particular RPM but also territorial restraints, lead to less rather than more efficient competition and higher transaction costs.[147] Gundlach, Cannon and Manning also argue in their marketing study that the existence of free riding and thus unrestricted competition leads to lower costs.[148] A few of the empirical studies discussed previously show the negative impact of RPM in the form of increased prices, impacts across industries and even decreased output and consumer welfare.

Indeed, there are two issues with this procompetitive explanation of vertical restraints used as a business strategy leading to decreased transaction costs. First, the manufacturer introduces RPM or VTR to save her own costs and not the costs of other participants on the vertical chain; she uses it for her own benefit, without including any extra benefit for consumers. She is driven by her own profit, as I explained above. She introduces RPM or VTR merely to increase her profit based on the ability to make strategic business decisions that concern other players on the vertical chain: her distributors and retailers. This does not mean that it will result in saved costs for the retailers or that efficiency will be maximized at the downstream level. As we have seen in the part on anticompetitive effects, RPM and VTR demotivate rather than motivate retailers to be more efficient and cost effective.

In that regard, Grimes shows in several cases on RPM that RPM decreased social welfare and was anticompetitive in these cases because this cost-saving concerned only the manufacturer and, for that reason, she

---

[145] Note 9, Williamson, 123–60.
[146] Ibid.
[147] Note 61, Steiner, 'How Manufacturers Deal?', 407–48; see also Note 54, Grimes, 'Dynamic Analysis', 101.
[148] Note 49, Gundlach, Cannon and Manning, 420–21.

was interested in RPM.[149] Indeed, if such RPM or VTR is successful, it will primarily increase the manufacturer's own welfare. However, when we consider the Kaldor-Hicks efficiency and Pareto optimality, this does not necessarily mean that it also will increase total welfare, including consumer welfare, the welfare on which competition law and policy stands, as competition law does not protect and promote the welfare of individual firms.

Indeed, the argument that VTR or RPM is used as a strategic business method which can, for instance, assist with the determination and use of the most profitable output and price, is not on its own a procompetitive explanation. As the CJEU noted in *Consten and Grundig*, risks are part of business and the restriction of competition to eliminate potential risks is not on its own a reasonable, procompetitive justification.[150] What really matters is the overall impact on competition and not individual profit maximization, which drives both procompetitive and anticompetitive decisions such as cartels and abuses of dominant positions.

The second issue is that, in reality, business strategies introduced by the manufacturers (or retailers) do not necessarily lead to expected outcomes. All decisions driven by individual goals have one important element: the decision process made by the manufacturers (or retailers) is not necessarily economically perfect or correct. Indeed, despite the fact that methodological individualism assumes that these individuals, such as manufacturers, are rational, it also recognizes that this rationality is not objectively perfect. This is because these individuals, suppliers, are rational but 'not in the sense that they always choose the best options, but that they choose what they think is good for them'.[151]

Similarly, Williamson refers to bounded rationality and opportunism, which drive all decisions including manufacturers' decisions on RPM or VTR. As we saw in Chapter 2, bounded rationality means that firms are not absolutely capable of making the most efficient decisions because there are simply too many aspects and too much information that they must consider. Furthermore, their ability to obtain information is limited. Opportunism means that if firms recognize an opportunity they will do

---

[149] Note 54, Grimes, 101–49.
[150] Note 34, *Consten and Grundig*, 348; see also the US case Note 44, *Professional Engineers*.
[151] Suri Ratnapala, *Jurisprudence* (2nd edn, Cambridge University Press 2013) 272–3.

whatever they can not to miss it and, therefore, they do not necessarily provide truthful information.[152]

Thus, a manufacturer does not necessarily choose the most effective business strategy for herself as her decision-making process is based on bounded rationality, which is restricted by the information that she possesses. This manufacturer's bounded rationality could be influenced by the opportunism (and also by bounded rationality) of her retailer who might, for example, claim that he will stop selling the manufacturer's products if the manufacturer appoints another retailer in his territory. Such a statement can simply be opportunistic as, in the end, the retailer may not stop selling the manufacturer's product. However, the retailer makes this statement in order to protect his profit. The manufacturer then makes her decision based on the opportunistic statement, which is not necessarily truthful.

The term 'bounded rationality' is used in behavioral economics, which recognizes bounded rationality[153] as the missing element in the economic approach to vertical restraints, in particular RPM. As Tor and Rinner put it,

> There is evidence that real manufacturers – like other decision makers – are not perfectly rational. Instead, they possess limited cognitive resources and are affected by motivation and emotion – that is, they are 'boundedly rational.' To function in a complex world, manufacturers use mental and emotional heuristics when making judgements under uncertainty and rely on situations cues to guide their choices.[154]

Simultaneously, '[c]omplaining dealers clearly have an incentive to dramatize price-cutting, which harms their profits'.[155] This and bounded rationality, which, according to behavioral economists, involves 'emotional heuristics', then influence manufacturers' decisions regarding vertical restraints.

As summarized by behavioral economists, the real world is based on bounded rationality which leads to manufacturers overestimating the potential negative effects of price-cutting and overusing RPM which can lead to economic harm, decreased consumer welfare and efficiency

---

[152] Note 9, Williamson, 126–7; see also Note 54, Grimes, 101–49; Herbert A Simon, 'Theories of Bounded Rationality' in CB McGuire and Roy Radner (eds), *Decisions and Organizations* (North-Holland Publishing Company 1972).

[153] Note 135, Tor and Rinner; see also Herbert A Simon, 'A Behavioural Analysis of Law' (1955) 69 *Quarterly Journal Economics* 99.

[154] Note 135, Tor and Rinner, 819–20.

[155] Ibid., 823.

losses.[156] Therefore, even the procompetitive motivations for manufacturers to implement RPM or VTR do not, on their own, ensure that the effect will be procompetitive.

XI. CONCLUSION

Procompetitive theories have their roots in the transaction cost theory and most are based on the theory of free riding. These, together with the traditional anticompetitive theories, have played a significant role in forming the current US approach to VTR and RPM. However, both procompetitive and anticompetitive theories have a number of pitfalls. Anticompetitive theories focus on just the form, advocating that horizontal collusion is, in general, anticompetitive, without analyzing the effect, in particular the effect of the retailer cartel, which, although it has anticompetitive motivations, will not differ from the effect of RPM or VTR initiated by one retailer: it will primarily restrict intrabrand competition. The effect of a particular intrabrand restriction differs depending on the industry, especially the market structure, as well as other restrictions introduced simultaneously with RPM or VTR; however, whether it was introduced by a group of retailers or one retailer will not determine the effect on interbrand and intrabrand competition.

The discussed procompetitive theories and argued procompetitive effects involve six significant drawbacks to the general underlining concept of these theories: that RPM and VTR are procompetitive as they increase interbrand and non-price competition, consumer welfare and efficiency. First, RPM or VTR, when used for a procompetitive reason, such as pre-sale services, does not necessarily ensure that these services will be implemented in practice. RPM and VTR can lead to these qualities only indirectly as incentives, unlike other alternatives, such as direct compensation or selective distribution systems, which address these procompetitive services directly.

Second, using RPM or VTR as mere incentive to sell and promote these products does not include any extra benefit for consumers in the form of increased non-price competition. Due to the lack of specific consumer benefits, a luxurious image based solely on high prices maintained via RPM is arguably not beneficial either unless the high prices are recognized as beneficial on their own by some consumers. In other words, they satisfy the needs of some consumers who are not

---

[156] See, ibid.

interested in quality and other consumer benefits but merely want to purchase products because they are expensive.

Third, consumer welfare can be increased only if VTR or RPM lead to a desired service or other consumer benefit valued by the majority of consumers.

Fourth, the phenomenon of free riding, which is the basis for the majority of procompetitive theories, can have many procompetitive rather than anticompetitive benefits and can be used for synergistic (mutually complementing) effects, as argued in marketing studies. Dealing with free riding by using RPM or VTR can lead to a decrease in online sales, decreased distribution innovation and consumer choice and higher prices, especially in domino-effect situations, where the whole industry implements vertical restraints. Furthermore, RPM and VTR in such situations can paradoxically result in free riding.

Fifth, RPM and VTR do not always lead to higher output, but even if they do, this does not mean that the increased output leads to increased competition and consumer welfare. If the increased output does not arise from the vertical restriction itself and is not based on valuable services, innovation and product improvements, or it does not facilitate entering a new market, the increase in output does not on its own prove procompetitive effects, because RPM or VTR in these situations leads to a restriction of intrabrand competition and increased prices. The increased output in situations where RPM or VTR does not introduce any benefit for consumers but merely provides an incentive to sell to retailers leads to higher prices and output is increased at the expense of competing products which could be cheaper, of the same quality or even of better quality. Thus, increased output does not occur at the interbrand level.

Finally, RPM and VTR do not necessarily lead to increased interbrand competition as advocated by the US approach to RPM and VTR but, on the contrary, they can decrease interbrand competition. Depending on the market and other circumstances, RPM or VTR as an incentive to sell could lead to the domino effect (or follow-the-leader effect) where RPM or VTR is implemented across the industry. The market is never perfect and situations are never ideal. Therefore, it is unlikely that RPM or VTR will be utilized by only a few firms for procompetitive reasons leading to consumers having the ideal choice in a market where all their needs are met. For instance, RPM or VTR introduced in a monopolistic or concentrated market can lead to less choice for consumers, as well as a decrease in consumer welfare and detriment to competition as a whole.

RPM and VTR can lead not only to the restriction of intrabrand competition, but they can also restrict interbrand competition. Both forms involve a number of anticompetitive effects, some of which have been confirmed by the sparse empirical studies. The most obvious anticompetitive effect is that RPM and also VTR increase prices at the intrabrand level but could even increase prices at the interbrand level. Other anticompetitive effects involve decreased consumer choice and welfare, decreased output, efficiency and distribution innovation.

Another element of the current US approach to RPM and VTR agreements is the assumption arising from the procompetitive theories that if RPM or VTR is introduced by a supplier it will most likely be for a procompetitive reason, while buyers at the downstream market, such as retailers, will be interested in RPM or VTR for anticompetitive reasons. While the findings in this chapter support the anticompetitive motivations of retailers, the arguments I have put forward conclude that the fact that RPM or VTR is initiated by the supplier should not automatically lead to the conclusion that it is for a procompetitive reason. There are two reasons for this. First, we have seen that it is unlikely that procompetitive theories are as common in practice as perceived by some of their advocates, and some of these theories, in particular where RPM is used as an incentive to sell RPM products, could be perceived as anticompetitive rather than procompetitive. Second, there are explanations other than the one based on procompetitive theories as to why a supplier would be motivated to initiate RPM or VTR. These explanations are not procompetitive given that they do not lead to increased competition and consumer welfare (and usually not even total welfare) with some of them being clearly anticompetitive, for instance, where RPM or VTR is utilized in order to increase a supplier's wholesale price.

6. Jurisprudential arguments and the economic concept of RPM and VTR

I. INTRODUCTION

We have seen that economics, in particular welfare economics, have played a pivotal role in the current approach to VTR and RPM, especially in the US. Although, when taking into consideration the nature of this area of law, economics provides absolutely essential background for understanding relationships and the operation of the market and competition, the law itself is not and should not be purely an economic discipline; it should incorporate the rights and responsibilities (duties, obligations and liabilities) of the parties concerned. Thus, legal principles must be core to any area of the law, including competition/antitrust law.

The principal legal question is the determination of which behaviors or conduct are right and which are wrong. One way of finding an answer to this question is by distinguishing between fair and unfair conduct. Sometimes, however, the situation is not necessarily black and white. In these situations, when deciding between two options, the question should be: which behavior is fairer and which is less fair. With regards to vertical restraints, one could ask whether it is fairer for the manufacturer to determine retail price rather than the owner, the retailer. In economics, the question revolves around welfare and efficiencies: is behavior or situation A more efficient than behavior or situation B? Is it more efficient for the manufacturer to maintain the retail price or is it more efficient if the retail price is determined by the retailer?

The outcomes could differ depending on the approach we choose: legal or economic. It is possible that the way the principal legal question is determined does not correspond with the outcomes of the economic question. It could be that the legal question is set on the value or the legal analysis of a value which does not correspond with the economic principles and vice versa. It could also be that the economic principle or analysis does not reflect the reality, principles and values set by the law or vice versa.

All areas of the law are based on values which are then reflected in the objectives and principles of the law. The nature of competition law should involve principles arising from economic values, such as economic welfare and efficiency, and social and political values, such as fairness and freedom. These values and related principles should then be reflected in the legal approach. However, as we have seen in previous chapters, economic values have dominated the legal approach to RPM and VTR.

In this short final chapter I briefly explore values other than the economic. I start with determining the economic standpoint to RPM and VTR, in particular the way it is reflected in the US approach, from the legal theoretical perspective. I argue that the economic-theoretical approach as it applies to RPM and VTR is focused on outcomes and is thus rather a consequentialist approach, while the objective of competition law requires the analysis of the process and thus the incorporation of the deontological account. On the basis of the deontological account, I outline which values are or should be establishing the legal approach to RPM and VTR and utilize these values in order to answer a number of questions arising from previous chapters with regards to RPM and VTR.

II. OUTCOMES: CONSEQUENTIALIST APPROACH

Competition/antitrust analysis can involve two principal elements: process and outcomes. When undertaking an economic analysis of certain areas of competition law, one element can prevail over the other. The analysis of the process element focuses on finding whether the competitive process has been distorted, while the outcomes element aims at determining the final outcomes of certain practices, such as economic harm, efficiency and welfare. The focus on outcomes reflects the consequentialist approach, which sees the rightness in conduct when such conduct leads to good outcomes – consequences, while the process element reflects the deontological approach, which focuses on the character of the conduct when determining its rightness.

The consequentialist approach to economic theories is reflected in a number of aspects: economic harm, welfare, efficiency and output. Anticompetitive harm occurs if there is a decrease in welfare and efficiency. Besides focusing on efficiency and welfare, the Chicago and Post-Chicago Schools emphasized the restriction of output, which is one possible way of measuring whether competition has been restricted or increased.

Bork and Bowman summarize the importance of output in the following way:

> [T]he chief glory of competition [is] that it gives society the maximum output that can be achieved at any given time with the resources at its command ... Output is seen to be maximized because there is no possible rearrangement of resources that could increase the value to consumers of total output.[1]

We have seen that in the economic theories regarding RPM and VTR, in particular procompetitive theories, which have significantly impacted the current US approach, outcomes have played a principal role. Vertical restraints, in particular RPM, are procompetitive if they increase output.[2] RPM is procompetitive and efficient and increases consumer welfare if it, for instance, leads to increased services which increases output.

Rights and Freedoms

We have seen that procompetitive theories justify a number of situations where RPM or VTR is introduced, based on the increased outcome, consequentialist aspect, which argues that welfare increases when the manufacturer introduces RPM or VTR usually for certain procompetitive reasons. The current US approach reflects this thinking. The related question as it follows from the difference between understanding competition of the majority and the dissenting minority of judges in *Leegin*,[3] according to Ghosh, is the issue of whose right it is to determine retail prices – the manufacturer's or retailers'?[4]

The ruling majority of the Supreme Court argued in line with procompetitive economic theories that if RPM is introduced by a manufacturer (a supplier), it will most likely be for a procompetitive

---

[1] Robert H Bork and Ward S Bowman Jr, 'Crisis in Antitrust' (1964) 9(5) *Antitrust Bulletin* 587, 589.

[2] Robert H Bork, *The Antitrust Paradox: A Policy at War with Itself* (The Free Press 1978) 295–7; Phillip E Areeda, and Herbert Hovenkamp, *2009 Supplement to Antitrust Law: An Analysis of Antitrust Principles and Their Application* (Aspen Publishers 2009) 238–9, 243; Frank H Easterbrook, 'Vertical Arrangements and the Rule of Reason' (1984) 53 *Antitrust Law Journal* 135, 163.

[3] *Leegin Creative Leather Products Inc. v PSKS Inc. DBA Kay's Kloset ... Kays' Shoes*, 551 U.S. 877 (2007) ('*Leegin*') 898.

[4] Shubha Ghosh 'Vertical Restraints, Competition and the Rule of Reason' in Keith Hylton, *Antitrust Law and Economics* (Edward Elgar Publishing 2010) 223.

reason in the form of increased services. The Supreme Court also provided further arguments as to why the introduction of RPM by a manufacturer would be procompetitive and not anticompetitive and thus why the manufacturer should not be restricted in doing so.[5]

This issue of whose right it is to determine resale prices is evident from previous cases, most notably *Colgate* and *Dr. Miles*. Unlike in *Leegin*, the majority of judges in *Dr. Miles* were of the opinion that it should be the retailers who are free to determine their retail price, unlike dissenting Justice Holmes, who argued for the right of the manufacturers to determine retail prices.[6]

The question of rights could be seen as a question of, or conflict between, contractual freedom or freedom to deal and ownership freedom. The older US case of *Dr. Miles* is based on ownership freedom. In *Dr. Miles*, the Supreme Court ruled that every person should be free and unrestricted in his/her own business.[7] The Supreme Court explained that only the owners of the products were entitled to determine their prices. Indeed, the owners of the products must be free to determine their business and to compete. In this case, the wholesalers and retailers should have been free to do whatever they wanted to with the products they owned.[8]

In *Colgate*, the Supreme Court ruled that suppliers should be free to choose their business partners, in other words, with whom they would deal. This also included the announcement of conditions, such as RPM, under which the suppliers would sell.[9] It referred to the case of *United States v. Trans-Missouri Freight Association*, where the Supreme Court also stated that traders were free to sell to whomever they wished.[10] In these cases, the freedom to trade or to deal refers to contractual freedom. Suppliers are free to decide with whom to deal and under what conditions, in other words, with whom to conclude a trading or dealership contract.

---

[5] In particular, the free riding theory and justification on the basis of entering a new market. The Supreme Court also referred to two empirical studies to further support its arguments. See Chapter 3, 'RPM: *Leegin*: rule of reason'.

[6] *Dr. Miles Medical Co. v. John D. Park and Sons* 220 U.S. 373 (1911) ('*Dr. Miles*') 412.

[7] Ibid., 406.

[8] Ibid., 404–6.

[9] Ibid., 307; the *Colgate* doctrine was confirmed in the case of *Russell Stover Candies Inc. v. FTC*, 718 F.2d 256 (8th Circuit 1983).

[10] *United States v. Trans-Missouri Freight Association* 166 U.S. 290 (1897) ('*Trans-Missouri*') 320.

Under the *Leegin* ruling, contractual freedom is justified and the right to determine prices is in the hands of manufacturers/suppliers given that the supplier most likely introduces RPM for procompetitive reasons. However, this contractual freedom, including the freedom described in *Colgate*, is rather one sided. As Ghosh puts it, this is rather the 'freedom of manufacturers to set the terms of a contract',[11] while ownership freedom is always on the side of the owner.

This creates a tension leading to the question as to which freedom should prevail. If contractual freedom prevails, then once a retailer becomes the owner of a specific product, he must follow the obligations set in contracts and is thus not free to determine the retail price. If ownership freedom prevails, the retailer is free to determine his retail price despite the existence of a price-restrictive contract.

Indeed, the jurisprudential question is which freedom should be protected in this case? A related question which can assist in determining which freedom we should protect, is whether we can refer to 'freedom' in situations where one party forces the other to do something. Let us address the general question of which freedom should prevail; both economics and jurisprudence can assist with providing an answer.

The economic approach would focus on the harm. It would try to determine whether it is more harmful to promote contractual freedom or ownership freedom. In that regard, we could refer to Coase and his discussion on the 'problem of social cost' and ask the same question he asked in connection with harm, legal disputes and liability and the cost of market transaction in his article from 1960. Coase's question revolves around the issue of which harm is more serious: 'should A be allowed to harm B or should B be allowed to harm A?'[12] He refers to the rights in this matter: '[t]he cost of exercising a right ... is always the loss which is suffered elsewhere in consequence of the exercise of that right',[13] and concludes that '[i]n devising and choosing between arrangements we should have regard for the total effect'.[14]

Indeed, the issue of freedoms with regards to RPM and VTR has reciprocal bases. Choosing one freedom over the other will harm the party whose freedom has not been chosen. We cannot simultaneously choose both because these freedoms can be conflicting; they could lead to a situation where the contract between a manufacturer and her retailer

---

[11] Note 3, Ghosh, 230.
[12] Ronald H Coase, 'The Problem of Social Cost' (1960) 3(1) *The Journal of Law & Economics* 1, 2.
[13] Ibid., 1, 44.
[14] Ibid.

states that the manufacturer determines retail or minimum retail price and ownership freedom means that the retailer, once he becomes the owner, can determine the price of the product in question. In doing so, the retailer would violate his obligation arising from the contract stating that it is the manufacturer and not the retailer who should determine the retail price. One party will be harmed depending on which freedom we prefer. So, which freedom should we prefer? Coase would say that we should take 'regard for the total effect'.[15]

Thus, we are back to determining which situation will result in higher efficiency, higher welfare and less economic harm. However, there is no simple answer for this. The absolute protection of the interests of one or the other does not serve economic efficiency.[16] If the genuine pro-competitive theories on RPM and VTR apply, then contractual freedom should prevail. However, as dissenting Justice Breyer noted in *Leegin*, the question is open as to how often and to what extent this occurs in practice.[17] The deontological account discussed in the next part provides a different way of addressing this issue and in general determining the antitrust/competition law approach to RPM and VTR.

III. PROCESS: DEONTOLOGICAL ACCOUNT

In the current economic approach to RPM and VTR, the focus is not on the process of competition but on the anticompetitive and procompetitive outcomes. Thus, competition is restricted if the final outcome leads to decreased competition in the forms of decreased output, efficiency and welfare, which can take the form of decreased innovation and services.

This approach, as the only approach to RPM and VTR, involves three issues, two of which relate to certainty. The first issue is an economic issue. We have seen that opinions on the effects of RPM and VTR on competition differ and that outcomes are unsure, some more than others.[18] In particular, trying to predict future outcomes is never certain. This is even more pronounced with regard to empirical evidence, which

---

[15] Ibid.
[16] See, also, Richard M Brunell, 'United States: *Dr Miles*' Last House Call' in Barry Rodger (ed.), *Landmark Cases in Competition Law: Around the World in Fourteen Stories* (Wolters Kluwer 2012) 366–7.
[17] Note 4, *Leegin*, 917.
[18] For instance, the negative impact of RPM and VTR on price is highly probable with almost certainty that RPM will increase intrabrand price.

shows that procompetitive outcomes are perhaps not as common as advocated by the supporters of these theories.

With regard to output, many neoclassical US theorists, for instance Bork, have argued that vertical restraints, including RPM and VTR, increase rather than decrease output and are therefore procompetitive. However, in Chapter 5, arguments were introduced showing that RPM and VTR do not always lead to higher output and, in situations where they do, the increased output on its own does not mean that competition and consumer welfare have also increased. A deontological approach could provide legal clarity by providing a clearer answer not with regards to the final outcomes of RPM and VTR but with regards to finding arguments for or against their prohibition. The deontological approach would focus on whether certain conduct arises from competition and its competitive process or whether this process has been hindered by the restrictive conduct.

The second issue, related to the first, is that the economic approach focuses on outcomes, including proving the restriction of interbrand competition with regards to RPM and VTR agreements, which does not assist with legal certainty and transparency. As dissenting Justice Breyer argued in *Leegin*, the current approach introduced in *Leegin* is highly costly, highly technical and time-consuming in litigation.[19] However, the law differs from the economy. Successful litigation must be achievable, it must reveal the wrongness or rightness of the conduct in question and must be based on clear rules. This does not mean that the law will always get it right in individual cases, but the law and litigation should almost always get it right.

The standpoint for determining what is right and what is wrong under competition/antitrust law is understanding what such law intends to do, in other words, what the objective of competition/antitrust law is. As I explain below, the mere consequentialist (outcome-focused) approach does not necessarily reflect the objective of competition law, which is the third issue.

Competition as Process: Objective of Competition/Antitrust Law

The objective of competition/antitrust law is primarily centered around process. Although words such as consumer welfare and efficiency have

---

[19] Note 4, *Leegin*, 918.

often been used with regard to the goal of competition/antitrust law,[20] the main focus has been placed on competition itself. For instance, EU law is clear in this regard when it uses the connotation in Article 101(1) TFEU of 'the prevention, restriction or distortion of competition'.

In the US, the Clayton Act prohibits any conduct that may 'substantially lessen competition' under Section 7, while Section 5 of the Federal Trade Commission (FTC) Act refers to 'unfair methods of competition'. Sections 1 and 2 of the Sherman Act refer to restrictions of trade and commerce rather than competition. Nevertheless, the reference to unrestricted trade is also present in the TFEU and in EU law in general, where free trade is the EU framework principle assisted by competition law and its protection. Indeed, EU competition law has seen notable usage of the phrases 'effective competition'[21] and 'fully-effective internal market'.[22]

Although it could be argued that legislation prohibits anticompetitive conduct usually or partially in the forms of outcomes,[23] these anticompetitive outcomes arise from a process which is not competitive. This is directly reflected in some definitions of competition law. For instance,

---

[20] Connotations such as 'restraint of trade or competition' or 'substantial lessening of competition' could either be seen as final outcomes, whether certain conduct leads to the outcome of restricting or lessening competition, or it could be seen as part of a process. For the purposes of Section 2 of the Sherman Act, 'monopolization' is rather focused on the process and dynamism of certain actions or a group of ongoing actions.

[21] See, e.g., Case 85/76 *Hoffmann-La Roche & Co. AG v. Commission* [1979] ECR 461, [38]; Case 2/76, *United Brands v. Commission* [1978] ECR 207, [65]; Commission Notice 2009/C45/02 Guidance on the Commission's enforcement priorities in applying Article 82 of the EC Treaty to abusive exclusionary conduct by dominant undertakings [2009] OJ C45/7, C(2009)864 final ('Guidance on Article 82'), [6], [10], [18], [27]; Council Regulation (EC) No 139/2004 of 20 January 2004 on the control of concentrations between undertakings (the EC Merger Regulation) [2004] OJ L24/1 arts 2, 3; Commission, 'Evaluation Report on the Operation of Regulation No 1400/2002 Concerning Motor Vehicle Distribution and Services' (2008) 3; Commission Notice 2004/C 31/03 Guidelines on the assessment of horizontal mergers under the Council Regulation on the control of concentrations between undertakings [2004] OJ C31/03 [76]; European Commission, *Competition Policy in Europe, The Competition Rules for Supply and Distribution Agreements* (European Union Publications Luxembourg, 2012) 5; Simon Bishop and Mike Walker, *The Economics of EC Competition Law* (2nd edn, Sweet & Maxwell 2002) 11–12.

[22] TFEU, *Protocol 27 on the internal market and competition.*

[23] For instance, restriction of competition could be interpreted in the way that competition is restricted if the outcomes of the conduct in question are unwanted.

Furse states that competition law must prevent free competition from being disturbed to protect the entire competitive process.[24] Additionally, ordoliberalism, an important ideological stream that has influenced EU competition law, believes that competition law should protect the process of competition as a means of protecting individual economic freedoms. Therefore, competition should be free and best performing for all of society, with competition law and a competition authority acting as the watchdogs for this process.[25] This view reflects, for instance, the situation in the European Community in 1985 when the European Commission focused its policy on effective competition, protecting the freedom of participants in the competitive process and free competition.[26] Likewise, the Antitrust Division of the US DOJ states that: 'The goal of the antitrust laws is to protect economic freedom and opportunity by promoting free and fair competition in the marketplace.'[27] The process of competition and competition itself are not static but dynamic, thus the view of competition when we try to determine whether certain conduct is anticompetitive or procompetitive should go beyond a static view. Moreover, even from an economic standpoint, we can divide efficiency between dynamic and static, where, given that competition is a process, the dynamic efficiency is the one which determines the impact of a particular conduct on competition. However, dynamic efficiency is based on a changeable and ongoing process in the market and is therefore difficult to measure precisely.[28] Indeed, it is impossible to measure dynamic efficiency as complex and ongoing static moments. One way of

---

[24] Mark Furse, *Competition Law of the EC and UK* (6th edn, Oxford University Press 2008) 1.

[25] Wernhard Möschel, 'Competition Policy from an Ordo Point of View' in Alan Peacock and Hans Willgerodt (eds), *German Neo-Liberals and the Social Market Economy* (Palgrave Macmillan 1989); Walter Eucken, *The Foundations of Economics* (Terence Wilmot Hutchison (tr.), William Hodge 1950) 314.

[26] European Commission, *XV Annual Report on Competition Policy* (European Union Publications Luxembourg, 1986).

[27] Antitrust Division, 'About the Division – Mission' (Department of Justice) <http://www.justice.gov/atr/about/mission.html> accessed 5 August 2015.

[28] Doris Hildebrand, 'The European School in EC Competition Law' (2002) 25 *World Competition* 3, 8–9; George J Stigler, 'Perfect Competition, Historically Contemplated' (1957) 65(1) *The Journal of Political Economy* 1; John Maurice Clark, 'Toward a Concept of Workable Competition' (1940) 30 *The American Economic Review* 241; See also, Pamela Jones Harbour and Laurel A Price, 'RPM and the Rule of Reason: Ready or Not, Here We Come?' (2010) 55(1) *Antitrust Bulletin* 225, 240–41.

measuring the anticompetitiveness of a particular conduct is by analyzing situations at the beginning of a restriction's application and at any time after this compared with situations in a market without restrictions.[29] However, such an approach takes us back to the consequentialist, outcome-orientated approach, which does not fully reflect the dynamic nature of competition as a process.

The following questions commonly asked with regard to competition law also have a dynamic nature, reflecting the view of competition as a process rather than a static moment: Are companies competing or colluding? Are they playing a fair game or are they trying to cheat and/or benefit from restricting competition? Do RPM and VTR hinder the competitive process or are they in line with the competitive process? And how do we determine the answers to these questions? Taking into consideration the nature of these questions, the consequence-orientated, economic approach is not satisfactory. Instead, a deontological approach based on legal principles should be part of competition law, its policy and enforcement.

Like any area of law, competition law is based on certain values that determine the content of the law, its objectives and its application. We have seen that competition law is focused on competition as a process. This process is an economic, commercial process. Indeed, competition and competition law must include economic values (such as social welfare and efficiency); however, it must also involve other, rather social, political and ethical values.

Words used by legislators such as restrictions of competition and/or trade indicate that the objective of competition/antitrust law should be based on unrestricted competition and/or trade; in other words, free competition and trade. Furthermore, the protection of 'free competition' has been one of the essential principles of EU law. This principle was referred to as early as in the Treaty of Rome. The Maastricht Treaty[30] and current TFEU, Article 120, also place an obligation on the EU and Member States to act in accordance with the 'principle of an open market economy with free competition'.

---

[29] EU Courts have clarified that situations with and situations without a particular restriction should be compared to determine the effects on competition: see Case 56/65 *Société La Technique Minière v Maschinenbau Ulm GmbH* [1966] ECR 235.

[30] See, Article G of the Treaty on the European Union which amends the Treaty of Rome (the EC Treaty): arts 3(a), 102(a), 105 of the consolidated version of the Treaty of Rome (1992) – the Treaty Establishing the European Community.

In addition, US policy tends to refer to free competition as part of the goal of US antitrust law.[31] Another value commonly referred to by the competition/antitrust authorities and even law is 'fair competition'. The US Antitrust Division of the DOJ states that antitrust law should promote 'free and fair competition in the marketplace'.[32] Antitrust practices prohibited by the Sherman Act and enforced by the US FTC are 'unfair methods of competition' under Section 5 of the FTC Act.

European Union and Community policies likewise involve fairness with regard to competition law. For example, the Preamble of the Treaty of Rome stresses the importance of 'steady expansion, balanced trade and fair competition'. The Green Paper on vertical restraints from 1996 refers to the efficiency and fairness of competition as the primary objectives of the EU (at the time, EC) competition law.[33] In 2015, the current EU Commissioner, Margrethe Vestager, proclaimed that competition enforcement must ensure that the game for competitors is *fair*.[34]

These values of free and fair competition can assist with regard to the deontological, legal approach to RPM and VTR. One of the ways of determining these values is by referring to ordoliberalism, which focuses on the process element of competition and includes the concepts of freedom and fairness. It also promotes the benefits arising from the competitive process, arguing that the law should be used to protect such a process.

Free Competition and Economic Freedom

We have seen that both EU and US law and policy refer to free competition and/or trade. Free trade and free competition can correlate, as is the case in the EU where free trade means that there should not be any private or public obstacles in trade between nations. Free competition then forms part of free trade focusing on restrictions to compete. Free trade is a general objective of EU law, including EU competition law. By

---

[31] Note 27, Antitrust Division, 'Mission'.
[32] Ibid.
[33] Commission, 'Green Paper on Vertical Restraints in EC Competition Policy' COM (1996) 721 final, [10]–[13], [25].
[34] Margrethe Vestager, 'Competition policy in the EU: Outlook and recent developments in antitrust' (Speech delivered at Peterson Institute for International Economics, Washington DC, 16 April 2015), available at <http://ec.europa.eu/commission/2014-2019/vestager/announcements/competition-policy-eu-outlook-and-recent-developments-antitrust_en> accessed on 14 May 2015.

establishing the protection of competition (the process) as an underlining objective of competition/antitrust law, the focus must be placed on free competition (rather than free trade) given that free trade has a broader meaning.[35]

Free competition has been promoted by ordoliberalism, which has influenced EU competition law. Ordoliberals see free competition in a market as a value that enhances economic welfare and efficiency and respects individual economic freedoms.

The theory of ordoliberalism provides a theoretical framework for a deontological account of the meaning of free competition and its significance for competition law. According to Eucken, free competition is an underlining principle arising from a salient convention, the Economic Constitution, based on a transaction economy. The Economic Constitution provides normative rules for legal and political decision-making regarding the economy.[36] The 'transaction economy' (in other words, market economy) is an economy primarily driven by economically free private entities, in contrast to the 'centrally administered economy' where economic decisions are made by a central authority: the government.[37] The Economic Constitution arising from the transaction economy involves the principles of free and fair competition ensuring the economic freedoms of individuals to compete as an integral part of political freedom[38] and protecting individuals from potential restrictions that may have been put in place by the government or a private power. Thus, competition law prevents the exercising of powers that would hinder the economic freedom of individuals to compete, where, with regards to private power, no private entity should exercise his/her economic power to dominate his/her competitors and/or prevent them from competing in the market.[39]

---

[35] As is the case under EU law.
[36] Note 25, Eucken, 208–13, 242–73. Walter Eucken, 'What Kind of Economic and Social System?' in Note 25, Peacock and Willgerodt, *German Neo-Liberals*, 27–45; David J Gerber, 'Constitutionalizing the Economy: German Neo-Liberalism, Competition Law and the "New" Europe' (1994) 42 *American Journal of Comparative Law* 25, 44–5.
[37] Note 25, Eucken, 152–6.
[38] Note 36, Gerber, 36.
[39] Note 25, Eucken, 269–70; Note 36, Gerber, 43. The ordoliberal doctrine recognizes that not every market can reach an equally competitive level; factors such as barriers to entry and levels of demand determine the maximum potential for competitiveness. Some markets (such as the bread market) can be highly competitive, while others (such as the jet plane production market) can reach only a low level of competition.

The ordoliberalistic understanding of freedom is in line with Sen's explanation of freedom. Sen divides freedom into two aspects: 'substantive opportunities' and 'process consideration'. Substantive opportunities represent the opportunities for an individual to achieve those objectives valued by her. It does not mean that she will reach these objectives, just that she should be free to try; in other words, she should have the opportunity to do so. The opportunities represent not just quantity but also diversity.[40] The competitive process naturally creates these opportunities, reflected primarily in consumer choice.

The process consideration aspect of freedom involves the decisional autonomy of choices and protection from the interference of others. In other words, competitors must have opportunities to choose their subject and form of competition (this does not include restricting competition) and their decisions must be autonomous without disruption from others.[41] These disruptions or interference may come through others abusing or using their economic power in the form of restrictions of competition.

Both ordoliberalism and Sen promote the freedom-based approach as opposed to the economic outcome-focused evaluation. The concepts of free competition and economic freedom can assist with providing answers to two questions specific to RPM and VTR, which have arisen in the previous chapters:

- What form of competition should be protected under competition law with regards to vertical restraints, in particular RPM and VTR?
- Which rights should prevail: ownership or contractual rights?

Forms of protected competition
We have seen that the current US antitrust regime protects interbrand competition and horizontal competition but not necessarily vertical and intrabrand competition. However, ordoliberalism does not differentiate between intrabrand and interbrand competition, horizontal and vertical competition and other forms of competition, such as price and non-price competition, but protects competition as whole, emphasizing the protection of the competitive process and free competition. Thus, protecting free competition and competition as a process should involve many forms of competition.

---

[40] Amartya Sen, 'Markets and Freedoms: Achievements and Limitations of the Market Mechanism in Promoting Individual Freedoms' (1993) 45 *Oxford Economic Papers*, 519, 522–5, 527–32.

[41] Ibid., 522–7.

Free competition is based on the economic freedom of individuals. This freedom ensures that individuals can enter the market to compete, in other words, have the opportunity to compete, and leave the market. Because the emphasis is placed on the process and not the outcome, the exact number of competitors is irrelevant as long as the competing process is preserved and thus opportunities to compete exist. Nevertheless, the competitive process has its social value not only because it ensures the economic freedom to compete but because this freedom leads to increased efficiency and greater overall welfare.[42] Thus, free competition allows and ensures that anyone can compete in the market and if he/she is efficient and innovative enough within the competitive process, he/she will remain in the market.

Firms compete at both the interbrand and intrabrand level and, as we have seen in Chapter 2, intrabrand competition can be vigorous, in particular where the brand is well established. Protecting and providing the economic freedom to compete means that firms should be free to compete at both levels.[43] EU competition law and the CJEU's approach reflect this standpoint, protecting both forms of competition while placing the emphasis on interbrand competition due to the more severe anticompetitive effects of this form of competition.

Protected rights

The overall protection of competition as a process, which ensures that competition is free, involves the rights and responsibilities of the individuals. We have seen that there can be a conflict between allowing both manufacturers and retailers to determine and set retail prices. This can be determined as a conflict between ownership rights and freedom and contractual freedom. Free competition contains economic freedoms such as the freedom to compete. This freedom can solve the conflict between contractual and ownership freedom, which encompasses the objective view and the individual freedom view.

From the objective point of view, free competition, as an essential value of antitrust law, indicates that competition should determine retail prices and thus it should not be set by a supplier. In other words, it must be left up to competition, which also involves intrabrand competition. Similarly, whether price or non-price competition is more important

---

[42] See, e.g., Note 36, Eucken, 27–45; Note 36, Gerber, 41–3. Law should not protect the outcomes but the process of competition.

[43] The same could apply to vertical competition only if vertical competition is recognized as a form of competition, which is currently not the case in the US or the EU.

should be left up to free competition to decide; it should not be RPM that favors non-price competition over price competition but free competition based on owners' and consumers' preferences.

Indeed, economic freedom which arises from free competition supports that the owner should have the autonomy to determine his/her prices and business. In order to compete, an entity must be free to conduct his/her own business and determine the conditions of his/her own business, in particular how, to whom, where and for how much he/she will sell particular products or services. Having this economic freedom then means that the entity is either better, worse or equally successful as his/her competitors. If he/she is better, he/she remains in the market. If he/she is not successful conducting his/her business, he/she will be forced to leave the market. The most efficient and innovative competitors remain in the market profiting from competition, while the less efficient competitors leave. If economic freedom is restricted due to a restriction of competition, competitors will lose the motivation to be better competitors, in other words more efficient and innovative. It will not be the power of competition in the market but private power with regards to restrictions of competition that will dictate certain market conditions.

Indeed, in situations where conduct restricts the competitive process, including intrabrand and interbrand competition and price and non-price competition, the freedom to compete prevails over contractual freedom in situations where contractual freedom places restrictions in the market. VTR places a restriction on intrabrand competition in the form of where to sell, while RPM restricts in the form of how much to sell for, eliminating intrabrand price competition. The protection of ownership rights then supports economic freedom and free competition as it gives owners the right to determine his/her own business, which involves the freedom to conduct his/her own business once he/she becomes the owner of the product in question.

Fairness

Another value at the center of the ordoliberalistic understanding of competition is fairness. Fairness, with regards to RPM and VTR, assists with determining three questions: whether the use of RPM or VTR is fair; whether it is fair if the supplier determines retail prices and other retail conditions and, finally, if RPM or VTR is found anticompetitive, who should be liable? In order to answer these questions I must first explain the meaning of fairness, which, as with other, previously discussed, principles, I will determine with regard to the process rather than the outcome.

Böhm from the Ordoliberal School refers to fairness as equal opportunities, explaining that the competitive process based on free competition ensures that all participants have equal opportunities in the market.[44] (We have seen that Sen associates his opportunities aspect with freedom rather than fairness.) However, this does not mean that they should equally share the benefits arising from competition in the market. On the contrary, competition leading to fairness through its process does not mean equal rewards for all competitors but, instead, the competitive process distributes rewards fairly according to competitors' respective merits, such as their efficiency and innovation. This means that more efficient and innovative competitors will receive greater profit than less efficient competitors.[45] This naturally leads to efficiency and welfare maximization and fair distribution of profit based on free competition.

Unlike the Chicago School, ordoliberalism reaches efficient outcomes and the maximization of social welfare via the competitive process based on fairness and freedom. In contrast, the Chicago School does not focus on what is fair or unfair but tries to determine which outcomes are more efficient. Ordoliberalism is based on process (jurisprudential) principles, fairness and free competition, which lead to increased efficiency. Restrictions of competition, therefore, hinder this natural economic process arising from free competition. Indeed, the aim of competition law under ordoliberalism is to ensure fairness and the economic freedom of individuals by prohibiting private (and also public) economic powers from interfering with the natural competitive process.[46]

With regard to vertical restrictions, we have seen in previous chapters that RPM and VTR can lead to decreased efficiency. They can also result in unfair distribution of benefits due to their negative impact on the motivation to compete. RPM eliminates price intrabrand competition and thus the incentive to be cost effective, which leads to a decrease in efficiency. Unless RPM has merits in genuine free riding leading to increased non-price competition (or other genuine procompetitive reasons), it cannot be justified on the basis of fairness. For instance, if the

---

[44] Franz Böhm, 'Rule of Law in a Market Economy' in Alan Peacock and Hans Willgerodt (eds), *Germany's Social Market Economy: Origins and Evolution* (Palgrave Macmillan 1989) 51–4; Note 36, Gerber, 38.

[45] Such a conception of fairness is in line with Aristotle's distributive justice under which participants share the benefits according to their abilities and inputs. The method of distribution is based on a comparison of the participants' respective merits. Thus, Aristotle's distributive justice leads to proportional equality and not absolutely equal equality.

[46] Note 36, Gerber, 37–8.

used justification on the basis of free riding has merits in mere discounting based on vigorous competition, using RPM will lead to an unfair distribution of profits. The entity which was (or could be) more effective and/or was competing more vigorously will likely be worse off than in a situation without RPM, while less efficient or 'greedy' entities trying to avoid competition will benefit from a situation with RPM. RPM then decreases efficiency and leads to the distribution of profits on a restrictive basis rather than on the merits of free competition. Such a situation is unfair from the competitive process perspective because the competitive process is hindered by RPM. However, the situation where some retailers genuinely free ride on services required by consumers can be perceived as unfair due to the advantages unfairly taken by free riders. RPM or VTR can then be utilized to re-establish fairness in the intrabrand market by providing fair opportunities for retailers.

The same concept applies to VTR, although VTR differs to RPM. Unlike RPM, which is aimed at price competition, absolute vertical territorial restrictions eliminate both price and non-price intrabrand competition. Unless there is vigorous interbrand competition and the situation in the market is such that buyers will compete as intensively as if there were no VTR, competition will be restricted[47] and thus the process of fair distribution of profit based on competition will be hindered.

A question related to the issue of whether RPM and VTR can be perceived as fair under the competitive process is whether the upstream entity or the downstream entity should determine the downstream price and business. In other words, whether the freedom to conduct business based on ownership rights or contractual freedom should prevail. Which situation is fairer?

Considering that the competitive process leads to fairness as it ensures the fair distribution of profit based on fair opportunities for all participants, participants should be free to conduct their business with regard to competition. If this right is hindered by, for instance, contractual obligations in the form of RPM or VTR, the distribution of profit will not arise from participants' freedom to compete but will be influenced by the particular restriction. Under this conception, it is not fair that those participants who are more efficient than others will not benefit from a

---

[47] Unlike the consequentialist account, the Chicago School and the US approach to VTR and RPM, the principle of free competition does not presume that the restriction of intrabrand competition results in increased interbrand competition, but instead focuses on the protection of competition as a process, including all forms of competition.

higher number of customers due to RPM or VTR.[48] Thus, the principle of fairness supports the concept of free competition in that regard.

The fair distribution of benefits that arises from participants having equal opportunities in the competitive process should also have consequences in situations where such fairness is hindered. This leads us to the question of liability. The participant in the market who initiated and maintained the restrictive practice, if such an entity can be individualized, should be liable. We have seen that both the US and EU regimes require proof of the existence of an agreement. However, an analysis of the cases shows that it is typical for RPM or VTR to be initiated either by a supplier or a buyer or group of buyers and that the success of such an initiation depends on bargaining power. The US and EU requirement for the existence of an agreement holds liable not only the initiators but also other participants who did not initiate RPM or VTR, even in situations where they were forced to comply.[49]

IV. CONCLUSION

The economic approach to RPM and VTR is outcome-orientated; however, final outcomes are uncertain. It cannot be said that RPM and VTR are always procompetitive or anticompetitive. Whether a particular VTR or RPM practice is anticompetitive or procompetitive differs from case to case and, moreover, also depends on the method and theory used for the outcome measurement. An approach fully based on economics can be overcomplicated and overtechnical when dealing with restrictions on vertical chains such as RPM and VTR, and this does not serve legal certainty and transparency. Furthermore, the mere outcome-focused approach does not necessarily reflect the objective of competition law, which is focused on competition as a process rather than the final outcomes. Therefore, a process-orientated, deontological approach should form part of a competition/antitrust law and policy regime and, indeed,

---

[48] If a participant is more cost efficient than others, she will receive higher profit per item than others if RPM or VTR is used. However, this on its own does not justify the fairness rooted in the competitive process because such a process is hindered by RPM or VTR, leading to a distorted distribution of benefits based on the particular vertical restriction and not on the pure merits of free competition.

[49] See, e.g., Joined Cases C-2/01 P and C-3/01 P *Bundesverband der Arzneimittel-Importeure EC and Commission v. Bayer AG* [2004] ECR I-23; *Business Electronics Corp. v. Sharp Electronics Corp.* 485 U.S. 717 (1988).

such an approach can assist with legal certainty and transparency with regards to RPM and VTR.

A process-orientated approach based on free competition accompanied by the economic freedom of individuals and fairness leads to consequences desired by the economic approach, such as increased welfare and efficiency, because it protects the competitive process in order to reach these positive economic outcomes. Freedom under the deontological account means that the protection of competition, including economic freedom, ensures decisional autonomy of competitive choices including the way an owner conducts his/her business in a competitive manner, and simultaneously provides protection from the interference of others. Fairness represents distributive fairness, where competitors obtain benefits arising from competition, primarily profits, according to their respective merits.

On these bases, RPM and VTR cannot be allowed in general because such practices interfere with the competitive process and free competition and they are often not in accordance with the principles of fairness and economic freedom. Nevertheless, there are a few situations where RPM and VTR would promote rather than repress these principles. For instance, in situations involving genuine free riding, RPM and VTR solve the problem of fairness and are thus in agreement with the principle of fairness. Unlike free riding, which is de facto discounting that reflects vigorous price competition, in genuine free riding the free riders benefit from an unjust advantage in the form of saved costs created by, usually, pre-sale services offered by competitors and which are required by consumers. Free riders obtain unfair profits, which thus decreases the profit of competitors who provide such benefits to consumers. RPM and VTR solve this problem of unfair distribution of profit. However, given that RPM and VTR restrict intrabrand competition and subsequently the free-competition process, the principle of proportionality should apply in order to determine whether other, less competition-restrictive methods could be used to re-establish fairness among competing buyers.

The underlining principle of the competitive process, free competition, including economic freedom, allows RPM or VTR in situations where such a restraint is used in order to enter the market and start competing. In particular, in situations where a new competitor would not be able to enter the market without the assistance of RPM or VTR, these tools allow for the opportunity to start competing and simultaneously enhance competition through the entrance of a new competitor. In any other situation, free competition implies that it should be the competitive process and not the restrictions that decides who stays in the market and who leaves and, with regards to RPM, which form of competition will prevail: price or non-price competition.

7. Conclusion

The discussion in this book leads to the conclusion that both extremes, either the absolute prohibition or absolute legalization, including the de facto legalization, of RPM and VTR would not reflect the nature of these restrictions, nor would it be the right approach to serve justice under competition/antitrust law. This conclusion is supported by both the outcome- and process-orientated approaches. The outcomes of RPM and VTR show that both of these vertical restraints can have procompetitive explanations in some cases, while in other cases they can restrict competition, primarily intrabrand competition. Such a restriction can lead to increased prices and, based on a case-by-case evaluation, other restrictive, anticompetitive results, such as decreased consumer welfare, efficiency and even interbrand competition. By protecting the competitive process, the process-orientated, deontological approach protects all forms of competition, including intrabrand competition, and provides a limited number of situations where RPM or VTR should be allowed. Situations such as these include when the principle of proportionality does not offer less restrictive and more efficient options to solve the problem of penetrating the market, thus increasing competition, or where the fair distribution of benefits is hindered due to the problem of genuine free riding. Although justification should be allowed if it forms a true reason for introducing RPM or VTR in an individual case, determining how often these procompetitive situations occur in practice remains a complex and complicated empirical question.

Competition law and policy regimes can implement a variety of models. In this book, I have differentiated between two. The first model protects horizontal competition while placing an emphasis on interbrand competition, while the second model recognizes that vertical restrictions go beyond horizontal market structure and include vertical market structure and its vertical interaction and relationships. By recognizing this, it also protects other forms of competition. The process-orientated approach supports the second model, while the first model stands on the outcome-orientated approach implemented by the Chicago and Post-Chicago Schools.

The optimal approach should primarily reflect the process-orientated approach because the objective of competition/antitrust law is to protect the competitive process and the values arising from such a process: fairness, economic freedom and free competition, thus protecting all forms of competition not just horizontal and interbrand competition, as is the case in the first policy model. Therefore, it should prohibit RPM and VTR unless they can be justified in particular cases. This allows for the potential justification of RPM and VTR, while applying the principle of proportionality: primarily protecting the competitive process ensures the prohibition of practices that could hinder such a process. RPM and VTR disturb the competitive process; therefore, they should be prohibited unless one of them is the least restrictive method assisting with a procompetitive aim, such as penetrating the market.

The optimal approach should recognize that either the supplier or her buyer(s) initiate RPM or VTR, and sometimes both parties simultaneously, for various reasons, and it is the supplier who could (but does not always have) procompetitive reasons. If RPM or VTR is implemented by either an upstream or downstream player(s), the supplier or the buyer(s), he/she will succeed if he/she holds the bargaining power. The optimal approach should also reflect these findings in relation to liability, holding liable the entity who initiates it. Bargaining power can assist with the determination of this liability.

Neither of the two regimes analyzed in this book fully accommodates the optimal approach to RPM and VTR. Both the US and EU provisions that apply to RPM and VTR, in particular Article 101 TFEU and Section 1 of the Sherman Act, involve two general issues. The first is the issue of proving an 'agreement', in other words, whether a particular practice of RPM or VTR has the form of a bilateral/multilateral conduct, prohibited under Section 1 of the Sherman Act or Article 101(1) TFEU. The second issue is whether RPM or VTR restricts (unreasonably, appreciably) competition (or trade).

The issue of establishing an agreement is related to the fact that both Article 101 TFEU and Section 1 of the Sherman Act were not necessarily drafted with vertical restrictions in mind, rather they were introduced to capture horizontal collusion. Therefore, these provisions do not fully reflect the nature of vertical restraints because RPM and VTR are not always (and probably only sometimes) initiated through a mutually beneficial agreement between at least two parties. On the contrary, RPM and VTR are usually in the interest of one party or some parties who, if they have bargaining power, initiate RPM or VTR and even succeed in forcing others to comply.

Despite the application of Section 1 of the Sherman Act to RPM and VTR and thus proof of the existence of an agreement, the US approach involves elements that indicate that it is or can be one party who introduces RPM or VTR. It presumes the existence of procompetitive reasons in situations where the supplier initiates RPM or VTR and provides an alternative to proving the restriction of interbrand competition in situations where one buyer, a retailer, introduces RPM. If the RPM is introduced by the retailer, it allows for the court to be satisfied that the second element is fulfilled – the restriction of competition – if the retailer has significant market power. However, in such situations, Section 2 could be better suited because it does not require the existence of an agreement. Similarly, Article 102 could theoretically apply to RPM and VTR if such practices are recognized as forms of an abuse of a dominant position. The dominant position could actually have a broader meaning and could also mean position on the vertical chain, where one entity holds the dominant bargaining power. However, the determination of the relevant market, in particular, when the vertical nature is taken into consideration, can be questionable and complicated as we can see in recent US cases and the discussion in Chapter 3.

A related issue is whether it is the manufacturer's or the retailer's right in a manufacturer–retailer relationship to set resale price and other business conditions. In other words, whether contractual or ownership rights prevail. We have seen that the current US approach has a preference for the right of the supplier to set buyers' prices and territories. However, as I argued in Chapter 6, it follows from the deontological account, given that the objective of competition/antitrust law is to protect the competitive process in the form of free competition, that it should be the owner, in this case the retailer, who is free to decide how to conduct his/her own business, including setting his/her own prices.

The second issue of proving a restriction of competition involves different ways of evaluating these restrictions, which in turn depend on the meaning of the term 'competition' and how the restriction of competition is determined, whether it is based on outcomes or process. I have differentiated between two potential policy models, where understanding of the term 'competition' is narrow in the first and broad in the second. The first policy model reflects the Chicago School. It understands competition as horizontal competition, placing the emphasis on interbrand competition. The current US approach to VTR and RPM arises from the Chicago and Post-Chicago Schools and is thus similar to this model. The second model involves other forms of competition as well, including intrabrand competition and potentially even vertical competition. It accommodates better the nature of vertical restraints, taking into consideration not only horizontal relationships but also vertical relationships and recognizes that even vertically related entities compete in order to obtain better profit and that there are economically beneficial reasons for protecting intrabrand competition.

The protection of competition as a process leads to the conclusion that the competitive process is beneficial and thus needs to be protected. Such protection does not differentiate between different forms of competition, meaning that some forms of competition should be protected while other forms should not. Thus, this view supports the second policy model.

The outcome-orientated approach can be more complicated in this matter because it is difficult to precisely determine the outcomes of RPM and VTR, especially their impact on interbrand competition. The presumption, which we have seen in Chapter 3, that the restriction of intrabrand competition can lead to an improvement in interbrand competition is not necessarily correct. Chapters 2 and 5 provide a number of examples where intrabrand restrictions in the form of RPM or VTR do not lead to increased interbrand competition but, on the contrary, lead to its restriction.

However, when analyzing a particular VTR or RPM case in isolation, the primary result is the restriction of intrabrand competition, which is not a concern under the first policy model. Indeed, VTR and RPM primarily restrict intrabrand competition because they occur on the vertical chain. Proving the restriction of interbrand competition can be overcomplicated and overtechnical because it is not only the relationship between a particular manufacturer and his retailers which must be analyzed in isolation but also their horizontal competition. Thus, all players on all parts of the vertical chain in question and the effect, the interbrand effect, which is not the primary effect of RPM or VTR, must be evaluated. This means that under the first policy model, it is difficult and even impossible, in particular for the private litigant, to prove a restriction of competition. This also means that the first policy model could lead to the de facto legalization of RPM and VTR if it is applied in practice, as is the case for VTR in the US. On the contrary, under the second policy model, it would be enough to prove the restriction of intrabrand competition, while the defendant could provide evidence that such a restriction increased interbrand competition. (This is already applicable in the EU regime.) Such an approach would better balance the burden of proof and would make litigation, in particular private litigation, workable and the law clear.

The US approach is predominantly based on the first policy model, finding horizontal agreements per se illegal and focusing on proving the restriction of interbrand competition in situations where RPM or VTR is arranged vertically. Despite the drawbacks related to the first policy model, if the first policy model is the preferable policy, then the US approach involves only a few issues. The first is that it should not insist on the tendency to presume that if RPM or VTR is introduced by a supplier, it is for procompetitive reasons and that a restriction of intrabrand competition leads to increased interbrand competition. A number of arguments disprove these statements. VTR or RPM can either increase or decrease or have no impact on interbrand competition. Additionally, a supplier can have an anticompetitive reason for introducing RPM or VTR. The second issue is liability and the application of Section 1 in situations where RPM or VTR is initiated and forced upon others by one party with bargaining power. Such situations are not based on the same voluntary agreements as horizontal agreements between competitors.

The EU approach involves the same issue of proving an agreement in RPM and VTR and thus also holds both parties liable. However, unlike the US approach, it has some similarities with the second policy model and also the optimal approach involving aspects from the process-focused, deontological account. Nevertheless, it does not fully reflect the nature of vertical restraints and with it the associated meaning of competition and the application of bargaining power. It only recognizes intrabrand competition, interbrand competition and horizontal competition. Indeed, the TFEU does not include a direct provision for vertical restraints, which would stand on bargaining power. Furthermore, the recent development of the Brussels policy shows signs of applying the economic approach based on the Post-Chicago and Chicago Schools, which focuses on outcomes rather than the process. The arguments presented in this book recommend not departing from the process-orientated approach; instead, the EU regime should ideally further accommodate the second policy model.

Bibliography

BOOKS

Amato G, *Antitrust and the Bounds of Power* (Hart Publishing, 1997)
American Bar Association, *Antitrust Law Development* (5th edn, vol I, ABA Book Publishing, 2002)
Areeda PE and Hovenkamp H, *Antitrust Law: An Analysis of Antitrust Principles and Their Application* (2nd edn, vol VIII, Aspen Publishers, 2004)
Areeda PE and Hovenkamp H, *2009 Supplement to Antitrust Law: An Analysis of Antitrust Principles and Their Application* (Aspen Publishers, 2009)
Areeda PE, Kaplow L and Edlin A, *Antitrust Analysis: Problems, Text and Cases* (7th edn, Aspen, 2004)
Bain JS, *Barriers to New Competition* (Harvard University Press, 1956)
Bain JS, *Industrial Organisation* (2nd edn, Wiley, 1968)
Bain JS, *Essays on Price Theory and Industrial Organization* (Little, Brown and Company, 1972)
Barounos D, Hall DF and Rayner JJ, *EEC Antitrust Law, Principles and Practice* (Butterworths, 1975)
van den Bergh R and Camesasca PD, *European Competition Law and Economics, A Comparative Perspective* (2nd edn, Sweet & Maxwell, 2006)
Besanko D et al, *Economics of Strategy* (5th edn, John Wiley & Sons, 2010)
Bishop S and Walker M, *The Economics of EC Competition Law: Concepts, Application and Measurement* (2nd edn, Thomson, Sweet and Maxwell, 2002)
Bork RH, *The Antitrust Paradox: A Policy at War with Itself* (The Free Press, 1978)
Bouterse RB, *Competition and Integration – What Goals Count?: EEC Competition Law and Goals of Industrial, Monetary, and Cultural Policy* (Kluwer Law and Taxation Publishers, 1994)
Buttigieg E, *Competition Law: Safeguarding the Consumer Interest: A Comparative Analysis of US Antitrust Law and EC Competition Law* (Kluwer Law International, 2009)

Chalmers D, Davies G and Monti G, *European Union Law: Text and Materials* (2nd edn, Cambridge University Press, 2010)
Chamberlin E, *The Theory of Monopolistic Competition* (Harvard University Press 1933)
Clark JB, *The Philosophy of Wealth* (Ginn, 1886)
Colino SM, *Vertical Agreements and Competition Law: A Comparative Study of the EU and US Regimes* (Hart Publishing, 2010)
Eucken W, *The Foundations of Economics, History and Theory in the Analysis of Economic Reality* (William Hodge, 1950)
Ezrachi A and Bernitze U, *Private Labels, Brands and Competition Policy: The Changing Landscape of Retail Competition* (Oxford University Press, 2009)
Fisher I, *The Works of Irving Fisher* (Barber WJ et al (eds), Pickering & Chatto, 1997)
Furse M, *Competition Law of the EC and UK* (6th edn, Oxford University Press, 2008)
Galbraith JK, *American Capitalism: The Concept of Countervailing Power* (Transaction Publishers, 1993)
Gerber D, *Law and Competition in Twentieth Century Europe: Protection Prometheus* (Clarendon Press, 1998)
Goyder J and Albors-Llorens A, *Goyder's EC Competition Law* (5th edn, Oxford University Press, 2009)
Green N, Hartley TC and Usher JA, *The Legal Foundations of the Single European Market* (Oxford University Press, 1991)
Großmann-Doerth H, *Selbstgeschaffenes Recht der Wirtschaft und Staatliches Recht* (Wagner'sche Universitätsbuchhandlung, 1933)
Hildebrand D, *Vertical Analyses of Vertical Agreements – A Self-Assessment* (Kluwer Law International, 2005)
Hovenkamp H, *The Antitrust Enterprise: Principle and Execution* (Harvard University Press, 2005)
Hovenkamp H, *Federal Antitrust Policy, The Law of Competition and Its Practice* (4th edn, Thomson West, 2011)
Hylton KN, *Antitrust Law: Economic Theory and Common Law Evolution* (Cambridge University Press, 2003)
Jevons WS, *The Theory of Political Economy* (3rd edn, Macmillan, 1888)
Jones A and Sufrin B, *EU Competition Law: Text, Cases, and Materials* (5th edn, Oxford University Press, 2014)
Kaysen C and Turner DF, *Antitrust Policy, an Economic and Legal Analysis* (Harvard University Press, 1959)
Kobel P. Këllezi P and Kilpatrick B (eds), *Antitrust in the Groceries Sector & Liability Issues in Relation to Corporate Social Responsibility* (Springer, 2015)
Korah V, *Guide to Competition* (9th edn, Hart Publishing, 2007)

Kwoka JE and White LJ, *The Antitrust Revolution* (4th edn, Oxford University Press, 2004)
Lafontaine F and Slade M, *Exclusive Contracts and Vertical Relationships: Empirical Evidence and Public Policy* (MIT Press, 2008)
MacGregor DH, *Economic Thought and Policy* (Oxford University Press, 1949)
Marshall A, *Principles of Economics* (Macmillan, 1890)
Marshall A, *Industry and Trade* (Macmillan, 1920)
Mason ES, *Economic Concentration and the Monopoly Problem* (Harvard University Press, 1957)
Monti G, *EC Competition Law* (Cambridge University Press, 2008)
Neale AD and Goyder DG, *The Antitrust Laws of the United States of America: A Study of Competition Enforced by Law* (3rd edn, Cambridge University Press, 1980)
Palamountain J, *The Politics of Distribution* (Harvard University Press, 1955)
Pareto VFD, *Manuale d'economia politico* (Milan, 1906)
Posner RA, *Antitrust Law* (2nd edn, University of Chicago Press, 2001)
Ratnapala S, *Jurisprudence* (2nd edn, Cambridge University Press, 2013)
Ricketts M, *The Economics of Business Enterprise: An Introduction to Economic Organization and the Theory of the Firm* (Edward Elgar Publishing, 2002)
Rodger BJ and MacCulloch A, *Competition Law and Policy in the EC and UK* (4th edn, Routledge-Cavendish, 2009)
Rose V and Bailey D (eds) *Bellamy & Child: European Community, Law of Competition* (7th edn, Oxford University Press, 2013)
Scherer FM and Ross D, *Industrial Market Structure and Economic Performance* (3rd edn, Houghton Mifflin, 1990)
Smith A, *The Wealth of Nations* (Books I–III, A Skinner (ed.), Penguin Group, 1999)
Stigler G, *The Theory of Price* (4th edn, Prentice Hall, 1987)
Stocking GW and Watkins MW, *Monopoly and Free Enterprise* (Twentieth Century Fund, 1951)
Sullivan TE et al, *Antitrust Law, Policy and Procedure: Cases, Materials, Problems* (7th edn, LexisNexis, 2014)
Thaler RH and Sunstein CR, *Nudge: Improving Decisions about Health, Wealth and Happiness* (Yale University Press, 2008)
Thorelli HB, *The Federal Antitrust Policy: Origination of an American Tradition* (P. A. Norstedt & Söner, 1954)
Viscusi WK, *Economics of Regulation and Antitrust* (2nd edn, MIT Press, 1995).
Williamson OE, *Antitrust Economics: Mergers, Contracting, and Strategic Behaviour* (Basil Blackwell, 1987)

Yamey BS, *The Economics of Resale Price Maintenance* (Sir Isaac Pitman, 1954)

BOOK CHAPTERS

Bell D, 'The Business Model for Manufacturers' Brands' in Ezrachi A and Bernitze U (eds), *Private Labels, Brands, and Competition Policy* (Oxford University Press, 2009)

Böhm F, 'Rule of Law in a Market Economy' in Peacock A and Willgerodt H (eds), *Germany's Social Market Economy: Origins and Evolution* (Palgrave Macmillan, 1989)

Böhm F, Eucken W and Grossmann-Doerth H, 'The Ordo Manifesto of 1936' in Peacock A and Willgerodt H (eds), *Germany's Social Market Economy: Origins and Evolution* (Palgrave Macmillan, 1989)

Brunell RM, 'United States: *Dr. Miles'* Last House Call' in Rodger B (ed.), *Landmark Cases in Competition Law: Around the World in Fourteen Stories* (Wolters Kluwer, 2012)

Elzinga KG and Mills DE, 'The Economics of Resale Price Maintenance' in Collins W (ed.), *Competition Law and Policy* (American Bar Association, 2008)

Eucken W, 'What Kind of Economic and Social System?' in Peacock A and Willgerodt H (eds), *German Neo-Liberals and the Social Market Economy* (Palgrave Macmillan, 1989)

Ghosh S, 'Vertical Restraints, Competition and the Rule of Reason' in Hylton K (ed.), *Antitrust Law and Economics* (Edward Elgar Publishing, 2010)

Gilo D, 'Private Labels, Dual Distribution, and Vertical Restraints – An Analysis of the Competitive Effects' in Ezrachi A and Bernitze U (eds), *Private Labels, Brands, and Competition Policy* (Oxford University Press, 2009)

Hay D and Vickers J, 'The Economics of Market Dominance' in Hay D and Vickers J, (eds), *The Economics of Market Dominance* (Oxford University Press, 1987)

Hayek FA, 'The Meaning of Competition', in *Individualism and Economic Order* (University of Chicago Press, 1996)

Herbert R, 'Private Labels – What Drives Them Forward?' in *Private Labels, Brands, and Competition Policy* (Oxford University Press, 2009)

Jedličková B and Clarke J, 'Antitrust in the Groceries Sector: Australia' in Kobel P, Këllezi P and Kilpatrick B (eds), *Antitrust in the Groceries Sector & Liability Issues in Relation to Corporate Social Responsibility* (Springer, 2015)

Lianos I, 'The Vertical/Horizontal Dichotomy in Competition Law: Some Reflections with Regard to Dual Distribution and Private Labels' in Ezrachi A and Bernitze U (eds), *Private Labels, Brands, and Competition Policy* (Oxford University Press, 2009)
Macedo BG 'Economics and Law: Interaction between Equals' in *The Handbook of Competition Economics* (Global Competition Review, 2009)
Möschel W, 'Competition Policy from an Ordo Point of View' in Peacock A and Willgerodt H (eds), *German Neo-Liberals and the Social Market Economy* (Palgrave Macmillan, 1989)
Simon HA, 'Theories of Bounded Rationality' in McGuire CB and Radner R (eds), *Decisions and Organizations* (North-Holland Publishing Company, 1972)
Smith H and Thanassoulis J, 'Bargaining between Retailers and Their Suppliers' in Ezrachi A and Bernitze U (eds), *Private Labels, Brands, and Competition Policy* (Oxford University Press, 2009)
Tumlir J, 'Franz Böhm and Economic-Constitutional Analysis' in Peacock A and Willgerodt H (eds), *German Neo-Liberals and the Social Market Economy* (Palgrave Macmillan, 1989)
Willgerodt H and Peacock A, 'German Liberalism and Economic Revival' in Peacock A and Willgerodt H (eds), *Germany's Social Market Economy: Origins and Evolution* (Palgrave Macmillan, 1989)

ARTICLES

Achrol RS and Kotler P, 'Marketing in the Network Economy' (1999) 63 *Journal of Marketing* 146
Ackert GR, 'An Argument for Exempting Prestige Goods from the *Per Se* Ban on Resale Price Maintenance' (1995) 73 *Texas Law Review* 1185
De Alessi L, 'Property Rights, Transaction Costs, and X-Efficiency: An Essay in Economic Theory' (1983) 73(1) *The American Economic Review* 64
Bailey EM and Leonard GK, 'Minimum Resale Price Maintenance: Some Empirical Evidence from Maryland' (2010) 10 *The BE Journal of Economic Analysis & Policy* 1
Bain JS, 'The Sherman Act and "the Bottlenecks of Business"' (1941) 5 *Journal of Marketing* 254
Baker JB, 'Competition Policy as a Political Bargain' (2005–2006) 73 *Antitrust LJ* 483
Baumol WJ, 'Contestable Markets and Uprising in the Theory of Industry Structure' (1982) 72 *American Economic Review* 1
Baxter W, 'Vertical Practices – Half Slave, Half Free' (1983) 52 *Antitrust LJ* 743

Baxter W, 'The Viability of Vertical Restraints Doctrine' (1987) 75 *California Law Review* 933

Baxter W and Kessler DP, 'Toward a Consistent Theory of the Welfare Analysis of Agreements' (1995) 47 *Stanford Law Review* 615

Benham L, 'The Effect of Advertising on the Price of Eyeglasses' (1972) 15 *Journal of Law and Economics* 337

Blair RD and Harrison JL, 'Antitrust Policy and Monopsony' (1990–1991) 76 *Cornell L Rev* 297

Blair RD and Haynes JS, 'The Plight of Online Retailers in the Aftermath of *Leegin*: an Economic Analysis' (2010) 55(1) *Antitrust Bulletin* 245

Bork RH, 'Legislative Intent and the Policy of the Sherman Act' (1966) 9 *Journal of Law & Economics* 7

Bork RH, 'The Rule of Reason and Per Se Concept: Price Fixing and Market Division' (1966) 75(2) *Yale LJ* 373

Bork RH, 'The Goals of Antitrust Policy' (1967) 57 *American Economic Review* 242

Bork RH and Bowman WS, 'Crisis in Antitrust' (1964) 9(5) *Antitrust Bulletin* 587

Bowman WS, 'Resale Price Maintenance – A Monopoly Problem' (1952) 25(3) *Journal of Business* 141

Bowman WS, 'Toward Less Monopoly' (1953) 101 *University of Pennsylvania Law Review* 577

Bowman WS, 'The Prerequisites and Effects of Resale Price Maintenance' (1955) 22 *The University of Chicago Law Review* 825

Boylaud O and Niccoleti G, 'Regulatory Reform in Retail Distribution' (2001) 32 *OECD Economic Studies* 254

Brodley JF, 'The Economic Goals of Antitrust: Efficiency, Consumer Welfare, and Technological Progress' (1987) 62 *New York University Law Review* 1020

Brunell RM, 'Overruling *Dr. Miles*: The Supreme Trade Commission in Action' (2007) 52 *Antitrust Bulletin* 475

Burns JW, 'Vertical Restraints, Efficiency, and the Real World' (1993) 62 *Ford L Rev* 597

Callery C, 'Should the European Union Embrace or Exorcise *Leegin*'s "Rule of Reason"?' (2011) 32(1) *ECLR* 42

Cann WA, 'Vertical Restraints and the "Efficiency" Influence – Does Any Room Remain for More Traditional Antitrust Values and More Innovative Antitrust Policies?' (1986) 24(4) *American Business Law Journal* 483

Carstensen PC, 'Buyer Power, Competition Policy, and Antitrust: the Competitive Effects of Discrimination among Suppliers' (2008) 53(2) *Antitrust Bulletin* 271

Chen Z, 'Defining Buyer Power' (2008) 53(2) *Antitrust Bulletin* 241

Choi YS and Fuchikawa K, 'Comparative Analysis of Competition Laws on Buyer Power in Korea and Japan' (2010) 33(3) *World Competition* 499

Clark JM, 'Toward a Concept of Workable Competition' (1940) 30(2) *American Economic Review* 241

Coase RH, 'The Nature of the Firm' (1937) 4(16) *Economica* 386

Coase RH, 'The Problem of Social Cost' (1960) 3 *Journal of Law and Economics* 1

Comanor WS, 'Vertical Territorial and Customer Restrictions: *White Motor* and Its Aftermath' (1968) 81(7) *Harvard Law Review* 1419

Comanor WS, 'Vertical Price-Fixing, Vertical Market Restrictions, and the New Antitrust Policy' (1985) 98(5) *Harvard Law Review* 983

Comanor WS, 'The Two Economics of Vertical Restraints' (1992) 21 *Sw UL Rev* 1265

Comanor WS, 'Antitrust Policy Toward Resale Price Maintenance Following *Leegin*' (2010) 55(1) *Antitrust Bulletin* 59

Culbertson WP, 'Beer-Cash Laws: Their Economic Impact and Antitrust Implications' (1989) 34 *Antitrust Bulletin* 209

Culbertson WP and Bradford D, 'The Price of Beer: Some Evidence from Interstate Comparisons' (1991) 9 *International Journal of Industrial Organization* 275

Deacon D, 'Vertical Restraints under EC Competition Law: New Directions' (1995) *Fordham Corporate Law Institute* 307

Dethmers F and Posthuma de Boer P, 'Ten Years On: Vertical Agreements under Article 81' (2009) 30(9) *ECLR* 424

Dobson P, 'Exploiting Buyer Power: Lessons from the British Grocery Trade' (2005) 72(2) *Antitrust LJ* 529

Dobson P and Waterson M, 'Retailer Power: Recent Developments and Policy Implications' (1999) 28 *Economic Policy* 135

Dobson P and Waterson M, 'The Competition Effects of Industry-Wide Vertical Price Fixing in Bilateral Oligopoly' (2007) 25 *International Journal of Industrial Organization* 935

Easterbrook FH, 'Vertical Arrangements and the Rule of Reason' (1984) 53 *Antitrust LJ* 135

Easterbrook FH, 'Workable Antitrust Policy' (1986) 84(8) *Michigan Law Review* 1696

Elzinga KG and Mills DE, 'Leegin and Procompetitive Resale Price Maintenance' (2010) 55(2) *The Antitrust Bulletin* 349

Fisher AA, Johnson FI and Lande RH, 'Do the DOJ Vertical Restraints Guidelines Provide Guidance?' (1987) 32 *The Antitrust Bulletin* 609

Fisher AA and Overstreet TR, 'Resale Price Maintenance and Distributional Efficiency: Some Lessons from the Past' (1985) 3 *Contemporary Policy Issues* 43

Fox EM, 'The Modernization of Antitrust: A New Equilibrium' (1981) 66 *Cornell L Rev* 1140

Frank LK, 'The Significance of Industrial Integration' (1925) 33(2) *Journal of Political Economy* 179

Gavil A, 'Resale Price Maintenance in the Post-*Leegin* World: A Comparative Look at Recent Developments in the United States and European Union' (2010) 1 *The CPI Antitrust Journal* 1

Gerber DJ, 'Constitutionalizing the Economy: German Neo-Liberalism, Competition Law and the "New" Europe' (1994) 42 *American Journal of Comparative Law* 25

Gerber DJ, 'Europe and the Globalization of Antitrust Law' (1999) 14 *Connecticut Journal of International Law* 15

Ginsburg DH, 'Vertical Restraints: De Facto Legality under the Rule of Reason' (1991) 60 *Antitrust LJ* 67

Giovanneti E and Magazzini L, 'Resale Price Maintenance: An Empirical Analysis of UK Firms' Compliance' (2013) 123(Nov) *The Economic Journal* 582

Goldberg VP, 'Featuring the Three Tenors in La Traviata' (2005) 1(1) *Review of Law and Economics* 55

Gould JR and Preston LE, 'Resale Price Maintenance and Retail Outlets' (1965) 32(127) *Economica* 302

Grimes WS, 'Buyer Power and Retail Gatekeeper Power: Protecting Competition and the Atomistic Seller' (2005) 72 *Antitrust LJ* 563

Grimes WS, 'A Dynamic Analysis of Resale Price Maintenance: Inefficient Brand Promotion, Higher Margins, Distorted Choices, and Retarded Retailer Innovation' (2010) (55) 1 *Antitrust Bulletin* 101

Gundlach GT, 'Overview and Contents of the Special Issue: Antitrust Analysis of Resale Price Maintenance after *Leegin*' (2010) 55(2) *Antitrust Bulletin* 1

Gundlach GT, 'Overview of the Symposium' (2013) 58(1) *The Antitrust Bulletin* 1

Gundlach GT, Cannon JP and Manning KC, 'Free Riding and Resale Price Maintenance: Insights from Marketing Research and Practice' (2010) 55(2) *The Antitrust Bulletin* 381

Gundlach GT and Loff AG, 'Dual Distribution Restraints: Insights from Business Research and Practice' (2013) 58(1) *The Antitrust Bulletin* 69

Gundlach GT, Manning KC and Cannon JP, 'Resale Price Maintenance and Free Riding: Insights from Multi-channel Research' (2011) 1 *Academy of Marketing Science Review* 18

Hammer PJ, 'Antitrust Beyond Competition: Market Failures, Total Welfare, and the Challenge of Intramarket Second-Best Tradeoffs' (2000) 98 *Michigan Law Review* 849

Handler M, 'Introduction' (1990) 35(1) *Antitrust Bulletin* 13

Harbour PJ, 'An Enforcement Perspective on the Work of Robert L. Steiner: Why Retailing and Vertical Relationships Matter' (2004) 49 *Antitrust Bulletin* 985

Harbour PJ and Price LA, 'RPM and the Rule of Reason: Ready or Not, Here We Come?' (2010) 55 *Antitrust Bulletin* 225

Hawk BE, 'System Failure: Vertical Restraints and EC Competition Law' (1995) 32 *Common Market Law Review* 973

Hawley E, 'Herbert Hoover and the Sherman Act, 1921–1933: an Early Phase of a Continuing Issue' (1989) 74 *Iowa L Rev* 1067

Heyer K, 'A World of Uncertainty: Economics and the Globalization of Antitrust' (2005) 72 *Antitrust Law Journal* 375

Heyer K, 'Consumer Welfare and the Legacy of Robert Bork' (2014) 57 *Journal of Law and Economics* 1

Hicks J, 'The Foundations of Welfare Economics' (1939) 49(196) *Economic Journal* 696

Hildebrand D, 'The European School in EC Competition Law' (2002) 25 *World Competition* 3

Houben PH, 'The Merger of the Executives of the European Communities' (1965) 3 *Common Market Law Review* 37

Hovenkamp H, 'Chicago and Its Alternatives' (1986) 34 *Duke Law Journal* 1014

Hovenkamp H, 'Harvard, Chicago, and Transaction Cost Economics in Antitrust Analysis' (2010) 55(2) *Antitrust Bulletin* 613

Hovenkamp H, 'The Law of Vertical Integration and the Business Firm: 1880–1960' (2010) 95 *Iowa Law Review* 863

Hughes DE and Ahearne M, 'Energizing the Reseller's Sales Force: The Power of Brand Identification' (2010) 74 *Journal of Marketing* 81

Ippolito PM, 'Resale Price Maintenance: Empirical Evidence from Litigation' (1991) 34 *Journal of Law & Econ* 263

Ippolito PM, 'RPM Myths that Muddy the Discussion' (2010) 55 *The Antitrust Bulletin* 157

Jakobsen PS and Broberg M, 'The Concept of Agreement in Article 81 EC: On the Manufacturers' Right to Prevent Parallel Trade within the European Community' (2002) 23(3) *ECLR* 130

Jedličková B, 'Boundaries between Unilateral and Multilateral Conducts in Vertical Restraints' (2008) 10 *ECLR* 600

Jedličková B, 'Vertical Issues Arising from Conduct between Large Supermarkets and Small Suppliers in the Grocery Market: Law and Industry Codes of Conduct' (2015) 36(1) *ECLR* 19

Jones A, 'Completion of the Revolution in Antitrust Doctrine on Restricted Distribution: *Leegin* and Its Implications for EC Competition Law' (2008) 53(4) *Antitrust Bulletin* 903

Jones A, 'Resale Price Maintenance: A Debate about Competition Policy in Europe?' (2009) 5(2) *European Competition Journal* 479

Jones A, 'Left Behind by Modernisations? Restrictions by Object under Article 101(1)' (2010) 6(3) *European Competition Journal* 649

Jordan WJ and Jaffee BL, 'The Use of Exclusive Territories in the Distribution of Beer: Theoretical and Empirical Observations' (1987) 32 *Antitrust Bulletin* 137

Kahneman D, Knetsch JL and Thaler RH, 'Experimental Tests of the Endowment Effect and the Coase Theorem' (1990) 98 *Journal of Political Economy* 1325

Kahneman D and Tversky A, 'Prospect Theory: An Analysis of Decision Under Risk' (1979) 47 *Econometrica* 263

Kaldor N, 'Welfare Propositions in Economics and Interpersonal Comparisons of Utility' (1939) 49(195) *Economic Journal* 549

Kallaugher J and Witbrecht A, 'Developments under the Treaty on the Functioning of the European Union, Articles 101 and 102, in 2008/2009' (2010) 31(8) *ECLR* 307

Kelly K, 'The Role of the Free Rider in Resale Price Maintenance: The Loch Ness Monster of Antitrust Captured' (1988) 10(2) *George Mason Law Review* 327

Kirkwood JB, 'Buyer Power and Exclusionary Conduct: Should *Brooke Group* Set the Standards for Buyer-Induced Price Discrimination and Predatory Bidding?' (2005) 72 *Antitrust LJ* 625

Kirkwood JB, 'Rethinking Antitrust Policy toward RPM' (2010) 55(2) *Antitrust Bulletin* 423

Klein B, 'Competitive Resale Price Maintenance in the Absence of Free-Riding' (2009) 76(2) *Antitrust LJ* 431

Klein B and Murphy KM, 'Vertical Restraints as Contract Enforcement Mechanisms' (1988) 31 *Journal of Law and Economics* 265

Klein B and Murphy KM, 'Vertical Integration as a Self-enforcing Contractual Arrangement' (1997) 87(2) *The American Economic Review* 415

Klick J and Mitchell G, 'Government Regulation of Irrationality: Moral and Cognitive Hazards' (2006) 90 *Minnesota Law Review* 1620

Kneepkens M, 'Resale Price Maintenance: Economic Call for a More Balanced Approach' (2007) 28(12) *ECLR* 656

Komninos AP, 'Public and Private Antitrust Enforcement in Europe: Complement? Overlap?' (2006) 3 *Competition Law Review* 1

Kotsiris L, 'An Antitrust Case in Ancient Greek Law' (1988) 22(2) *International Lawyer* 451

Kovacic WE, 'Failed Expectations: the Troubled Past and Uncertain Future of the Sherman Act as a Tool for Deconcentration' (1989) 74 *Iowa L Rev* 1105

Kovacic WE, 'The Modern Evolution of U.S. Competition Policy Enforcement Norms' (2004) 71 *Antitrust LJ* 377

Kuenzler A, 'Presumptions as Appropriate Means to Regulate Resale Price Maintenance: in Defence of Structuring the Rule of Reason' (2012) 8(3) *European Competition Journal* 497

Kwoka JE, 'Advertising and the Price and Quality of Optometric Services' (1984) 74(1) *American Economic Review* 211

Lafontaine F and Slade ME, 'Transaction Cost Economies and Vertical Market Restrictions – Evidence' (2010) 55 *Antitrust Bulletin* 608

Lambert TA, 'A Decision-Theoretic Rule of Reason for Minimum Resale Price Maintenance' (2010) 55(1) *Antitrust Bulletin* 167

Lao M, 'Resale Price Maintenance: The Internet Phenomenon and Free Rider Issues' (2010) 55 *The Antitrust Bulletin* 473

Leibenstein H, 'Allocative Efficiency vs. "X-Efficiency"' (1966) 56(3) *American Economic Review* 392

Liebeler WJ, 'Resale Price Maintenance and Consumer Welfare: Business Electronics Corp. v. Sharp Electronics Corp.' (1989) 36 *UCLA Law R* 889

Loozen E, 'The Application of a More Economic Approach to Restrictions by Object: No Revolution After All (*T-Mobile Netherlands*, C-8/08)' (2010) 31(4) *ECLR* 146

Lopatka JE, 'Stephen, Breyer and Modern Antitrust: A Snug Fit' (1996) 40 *Antitrust Bulletin* 1

Lynch MP, 'Why Economists Are Wrong to Neglect Retailing and How Steiner's Theory Provides an Explanation of Important Regularities' (2004) 49(4) *Antitrust Bulletin* 911

McGuire N, 'An Antitrust Narcotic: How the Rule of Reason is Lulling Vertical Enforcement to Sleep' (2012) 45 *Loyola of Los Angeles Law Review* 1225

Mann HM, 'Seller Concentration, Barriers to Entry, and Rates of Return in Thirty Industries, 1950–1960' (1966) 48 *Review of Economics and Statistics* 296

Marvel HP, 'Resale Price Maintenance and Resale Prices: Paying to Support Competition in the Market for Heavy Trucks' (2010) 55 *Antitrust Bulletin* 79

Marvel HP and McCafferty S, 'Resale Price Maintenance and Quality Certification' (1984) 15(3) *RAND Journal of Economics* 346

Mason ES, 'The Current Status of the Monopoly Problem in the United States' (1949) 62(8) *Harvard Law Review* 1265

Mathewson GF and Winter RA, 'An Economic Theory of Vertical Restraints' (1984) 15(1) *RAND Journal of Economics* 27

Mathewson GF and Winter RA, 'The Law and Economics of Resale Price Maintenance' (1998) 13 *Review of Industrial Organization* 57

Meese AJ, 'Property Rights and Intrabrand Restraints' (2003) 89 *Cornell Law Review* 553

Miller WT and Shaw KN, 'Pricing Practices: A Comparative Perspective' (2009) *The Antitrust Review of the Americas* 14

Monti G, 'Article 81 EC and Public Policy' (2002) 39(5) *Common Market Law Review* 1057

Muris TJ, 'The FTC and the Law of Monopolization' (2000) 68 *Antitrust L.* 325

Nazzini R and Nikpay A, 'Private Actions in EC Competition Law' (2008) 4(2) *Competition Policy International* 107

Nelson RP, 'Comments on a Paper by Posner' (1979) 127 *University of Penn LR* 949

Noll RG, '"Buyer Power" and Economic Policy' (2005) 72(2) *Antitrust Law Journal* 589

Nunes PF and Cespedes FV, 'The Customer Has Escaped' (2003) 81(11) *Harvard Business Review* 96

Orbach BY, 'The Image Theory: RPM and the Allure of High Prices' (2010) 55 *Antitrust Bulletin* 277

Ornstein SI and Hanssens DM, 'Resale Price Maintenance: Output Increasing or Restricting? The Case of Distilled Spirits in the United States' (1987) 36(1) *Journal of Industrial Economics* 1

Paldor I, 'RPM as an Exclusionary Practice' (2010) 55 *Antitrust Bulletin* 309

Peeperkorn L, 'Resale Price Maintenance and Its Alleged Efficiencies' (2008) 5(3) *European Competition Journal* 201

Peritz RJ, 'A Genealogy of Vertical Restraints Doctrine' (1988–1989) 40 *Hastings LJ* 511

Phillips A, '*Schwinn* Rules and the "New Economics" of Vertical Relations' (1975) 44 *Antitrust LJ* 573

Piraino TA, 'A Proposed Antitrust Approach to Buyers' Competitive Conduct' (2004–2005) 56 *Hastings Law Journal* 1121

Pitofsky R, 'In Defense of Discounters: The No-Frills Case for a Per Se Rule against Vertical Price Fixing' (1983) 71 *Georgetown LJ* 1487

Pitofsky R, 'Proposals for Revised United States Merger Enforcement in a Global Economy' (1992) 81 *Georgetown Law Journal* 195

Pitofsky R, 'Are Retailers Who Offer Discounts Really "Knaves"?: The Coming Change to the *Dr. Miles* Rule' (2007) 21(2) *Antitrust* 61

Posner RA, 'The Rule of Reason and the Economic Approach: Reflections on the *Sylvania* Decision' (1977) 45 *University of Chicago Law Revue* 1

Posner RA, 'The Chicago School of Antitrust' (1979) 127 *University of Pennsylvania Law Review* 925

Posner RA, 'The Next Step in the Antitrust Treatment of Restricted Distribution: Per Se Legality' (1981) 48 *University of Chicago Law Review* 6

Pozdnakova A, 'Buyer Power in the Retail Trading Sector: Evolving Latvian Regulation' (2009) 30(8) *ECLR* 387

Ratliff J, 'Major Events and Policy Issues in E.C. Competition Law, 2000: Part 2' (2001) 12 *International Company and Commercial Law Review* 72

Rey P and Stiglitz J, 'Vertical Restraints and Producers' Competition' (1988) 32 *European Economic Review* 561

Rey P and Stiglitz J, 'The Role of Exclusive Territories in Producers' Competition' (1995) 26(3) *RAND Journal of Economics* 431

Rey P and Tirole J, 'The Logic of Vertical Restraints' (1986) 76(5) *The American Economic Review* 921

Rey P and Vergé T, 'Bilateral Control with Vertical Contracts' (2004) 35(4) *RAND Journal of Economics* 728

Rey P and Vergé T, 'Resale Price Maintenance and Interlocking Relationships' (2010) 58(4) *The Journal of Industrial Economics* 928

Ridyard D and Bishop S, 'EC Vertical Restraints Guidelines: Effects Based on Per Se Policy?' (2002) 23(1) *ECLR* 35

Rill JF and Turner SL, 'Presidents Practicing Antitrust: Where to Draw the Line?' (2014) 79 *Antitrust Law Journal* 577

Salop SC, 'What Consensus? Why Ideology and Elections Still Matter to Antitrust' (2014) 79(2) *Antitrust Law Journal* 601

Sass TR and Saurman DS, 'Mandated Exclusive Territories and Economic Efficiency: An Empirical Analysis of the Malt-Beverage Industry' (1993) 36(1) *Journal of Law and Economics* 153

Schmidt ILO, 'The Suitability of the More Economic Approach for Competition Policy: Dynamic vs. Static Efficiency' (2007) 28(7) *ECLR* 408

Se-Hak C et al, 'Emerging Dual Channel System and Manufacturer's Direct Retail Channel Strategy' (2011) 20 *International Review of Economics & Finance* 812

Sen A, 'Markets and Freedoms: Achievements and Limitations of the Market Mechanism in Promoting Individual Freedoms' (1993) 45 *Oxford Economic Papers* 519

Shaffer G, 'Slotting Allowances and Resale Price Maintenance: A Comparison of Facilitating Practices' (1991) 22(1) *RAND Journal of Economics* 120

Shores DF, 'Vertical Price-Fixing and the Contract Conundrum: Beyond Monsanto' (1985) 54 *Fordham Law Review* 377

Silcock TH, 'Some Problems of Price Maintenance' (1938) 48 *Economic Journal* 42

Simon HA, 'A Behavioural Analysis of Law' (1955) 69 *Quarterly Journal Economics* 99

Skitol RA, 'Concerted Buying Power: Its Potential for Addressing the Patent Holdup Problem in Standard Setting' (2005) 72 *Antitrust Law Journal* 727

Spence AM, 'Monopoly, Quality, and Regulation' (1975) 6(2) *Bell Journal of Economics* 417

Steiner RL, 'Does Advertising Lower Consumer Prices?' (1973) 37(4) *Journal of Marketing* 19

Steiner RL, 'The Nature of Vertical Restraints' (1985) 30 *Antitrust Bulletin* 157

Steiner RL, 'Sylvania Economics – A Critique' (1991) 60 *Antitrust Law Journal* 41

Steiner RL, 'The Effect of GTE Sylvania on Antitrust Jurisprudence: Sylvania Economics – A Critique' (1991) 60 *Antitrust Law Journal* 59

Steiner RL, 'How Manufacturers Deal with the Price-Cutting Retailer: When Are Vertical Restraints Efficient?' (1997) 65 *Antitrust Law Journal* 407

Steiner RL, 'Exclusive Dealing + Resale Price Maintenance: A Powerful Anticompetitive Combination' (2004) 33 *Southwestern University Law Review* 447

Steiner RL, 'Vertical Competition, Horizontal Competition and Market Power' (2008) 53(2) *Antitrust Bulletin* 251

Steiner RL, 'The *Leegin* Factors – a Mixed Bag' (2010) 55(1) *Antitrust Bulletin* 25

Stigler G, 'Perfect Competition, Historically Contemplated' (1957) 65 *The Journal of Political Economy* 1

Stucke ME, 'Behavioral Economics at the Gate: Antitrust in the Twenty-First Century (2007) 38 *Loyola University Chicago Law Journal* 513

Taussig FW, 'Price Maintenance' (1916) 6 *American Economic Review* 172

Telser LG, 'Why Should Manufacturers Want Fair Trade?' (1960) 6 *Journal of Law and Economics* 86

Tor A and Rinner WJ, 'Behavioral Antitrust: A New Approach to the Rule of Reason after *Leegin*' (2011) 3 *University of Illinois Law Review* 805

Van Baal S and Dach C, 'Free Riding and Customer Retention across Retailers' Channels' (2005) 19(2) *Journal of Interactive Marketing* 75

Varney A, 'A Post-*Leegin* Approach to Resale Price Maintenance Using a Structured Rule of Reason' (2010) 24 *Antitrust* 22

Vatiero M, 'The Ordoliberal Notion of Market Power: An Institutionalist Reassessment' (2010) 6(3) *European Competition Journal* 689

Velez M, 'The Tenuous Evolution of Resale Price Maintenance' (2011) 32(6) *ECLR* 297

Vergé T, 'Minimum Resale Price Maintenance and Concentrated Markets' (2008) 54(3) *Applied Economics Quarterly* 161

Verhoef PC, Neslin SA and Vroomen B, 'Multichannel Customer Management: Understanding the Research-Shopper Phenomenon (2007) 24 *International Journal of Research in Marketing* 129

Vettas N, 'Developments in Vertical Agreements' (2010) 55(4) *Antitrust Bulletin* 843

Vinhas AS and Anderson E, 'How Potential Conflict Drives Channel Structure: Concurrent (Direct and Indirect) Routes to Market' (2005) 42 *Journal of Marketing Research* 507

Voorhees T, 'Reasoning Through the Rule of Reason for RPM' (2013) 28(1) *Antitrust* 58

Voorhees T, 'The Political Hand in American Antitrust – Invisible, Inspirational, or Imaginary?' (2014) 79 *Antitrust Law Journal* 557

Walton SR, 'Antitrust, RPM and the Big Brands: Discounting in Small-Town' (1983) 25 *Antitrust Law & Econ Rev* 16

Weitbrecht A, 'From Freiburg to Chicago and Beyond, the First 50 Years of European Competition Law' (2008) 29(2) *ECLR* 81

Werden GJ, 'Antitrust's Rule of Reason: Only Competition Matters' (2014) 79(2) *Antitrust Law Journal* 713

Wickihalder U, 'The Distinction between an "Agreement" within the Meaning of Article 81(1) of the EC Treaty and Unilateral Conduct' (2006) 2(1) *European Competition Journal* 87

Williamson OE, 'Economies as an Antitrust Defense: The Welfare Tradeoffs' (1968) 58 *The American Economic Review* 18

Wills RL and Mueller WF, 'Brand Advertising and Pricing' (1989) 56 *Southern Economic Journal* 383

Wils WPJ, 'The Relationship between Public Antitrust Enforcement and Private Actions for Damages' (2009) 32 *World Competition* 3

Wright JD and Stone JE, 'Misbehavioral Economics: The Case against Behavioral Antitrust' (2012) 33 *Cardozo Law Review* 1517

HEARINGS

DJ Schuler's statement, *Consumer Protection Against Price Fixing,* hearings on S. 429 before the Subcommission on Antitrust, Monopolies and Business Rights of the Senate Commission on the Judiciary, 102d Cong., 1st Sess. 66 (1991)

KI Clearwater's statement (Deputy Assistant Attorney General, Antitrust Division), hearings on H.R. 2384 before the Subcommittee on Monopolies and Commercial Law of the House Committee on the Judiciary, 94th Cong., 1st Sess., 122 (1975)

Retail Competition Enforcement Act, hearing before Senate Commission on the Judiciary, 100th Cong., 1st Sess. 281 (1987)

TE Kauper's statement (Assistant Attorney General, Antitrust Division), hearing on S. 408 before the Subcommittee on Antitrust and Monopoly of the Senate Committee on the Judiciary, 94th Cong., 1st Sess., 173 (1975)

OFFICIAL PUBLICATIONS OF ANTITRUST AGENCIES

Almunia J, 'Competition – what's in it for consumers?' (Speech delivered at European Competition and Consumer Day, Poznan, 24 November 2011), available at <http://europa.eu/rapid/press-release_SPEECH-11-803_en.htm?locale=en>

Clark DS, Secretary of the Federal Trade Commission, 'The Robinson-Patman Act: General Principle, Commission Proceedings and Selected Issues, Retail Channel Conference for the Computer Industry' (speech delivered at San Jose, 7 June 1995) <https://www.ftc.gov/es/public-statements/1995/06/robinson-patman-act-general-principles-commission-proceedings-and-selected>

Department of Justice, Antitrust Division, *Corporate Leniency Policy* (08/10/1993), http://www.justice.gov/atr/public/guidelines/0091.htm

Department of Justice, Antitrust Division, *Guidelines on Vertical Restraints*, issued on 23 January 1985 and published at 50 Fed. Reg. 6,263 (14 Feb. 1985) and 4 TRADE REG. REP. (CCH) P 13,105 (1988)

Department of Justice, Antitrust Division, *Guidelines on Vertical Restraints*, issued on 27 March 1995, reprinted in 4 TRADE REG. REP. (CCH) P 13,400; Section 605 of Public Law No. 99-180,99 Stat. 1169 (13 Dec. 1985)

Department of Justice, Antitrust Division, *Individual Leniency Policy* (08/10/1994), http://www.justice.gov/atr/public/guidelines/0092.htm

Department of Justice, Antitrust Division, 'Overview' (29/07/2015), <http://www.usdoj.gov/atr/overview.html>

Department of Justice, Antitrust Division, Press Release, 'Justice Department Reaches Settlement with George's Inc.' (Washington, 23/06/2011), <http://www.justice.gov./atr/public/press_releases/2011/272510.htm>

Donahau J, Chief Deputy Attorney General of the Antitrust Section 'The Antitrust Fall Forum' (Speech delivered at the American Bar Association, Section of Antitrust Law Washington DC, 13 November 2009)

Dullien S and Guérot U, 'The Long Shadow of Ordoliberalism: Germany's Approach to the Euro Crisis' (European Council on Foreign Relations, 2012) <http://www.ecfr.eu/page/-/ECFR49_GERMANY_BRIEF.pdf>

European Commission, XV Annual Report on Competition Policy [1986] <http://ec.europa.eu/competition/publications/annual_report/>

European Commission, XXIII Report on Competition Policy [1993] <http://ec.europa.eu/competition/publications/annual_report/>

European Commission, Annex to Commission Recommendation of 6 May 2003 concerning the definition of micro, small and medium-sized enterprises, OJ L 124, 20.5.2003

European Commission, Commission Evaluation Report on the Operation of Regulation (EC) No 1400/2002 Concerning Motor Vehicle Distribution and Services

European Commission, Delors White Paper on Growth, Competitiveness and Employment: the Challenges and Ways Forward into the 21st Century, COM(93)700, 1993

European Commission, Green Paper on vertical restraints in EC competition policy, COM (1996) 721, January 1997

European Commission, Green Paper on damages actions for breach of the EC antitrust rules, COM (2005) 672 final, IP/05/1634 and MEMO/05/489, 20 December 2005

European Commission, Guidance on the Commission's enforcement priorities in applying Article 82 of the EC Treaty to abusive exclusionary conduct by dominant undertakings [2009] OJ C 045, 24/02/2009 P

European Commission Press Release, 'Antitrust: Commission adopts revised competition rules for vertical agreements: frequently asked questions', MEMO/138, Brussels, 20 April 2010

European Commission Press Release IP/10/2; Competition Handbooks <http://ec.europa.eu/competition/antitrust/legislation/legislation.html>

European Commission, White Paper on completing the internal market, COM (1985) 310, 28 and 29 June 1985

European Commission, White Paper on modernisation of the rules implementing Articles 81 and 82 of the EC Treaty [1999] OJ C132/1

European Commission, White Paper on private damages actions, COM(2008) 165, 2 April 2008

Federal Trade Commission Press Release, 'Record Companies Settle FTC Charges of Restraining Competition in CD Music Market' (10 May 2000) <http://www.ftc.gov/opa/2000/05/cdpres.shtm>

Italianer A, 'EU Priorities and Competition Enforcement' (speech, Dublin, 25/03/2011), <http://ec.europa.eu/competition/speeches/text/sp2011_03_en.pdf>

Overstreet TR, 'Resale Price Maintenance: Economic Theories and Empirical Evidence' (Staff Report, Bureau of Economics Staff of the Federal Trade Commission, 1983)

Rogers RP, 'Staff Report on the Development and Structure of the US Electric Lamp Industry' (2/1980) Bureau of Economics, Federal Trade Commission

Rosch JT, 'Managing Irrationality: Some Observations on Behavioral Economics and the Creation of the Consumer Financial Protection Agency' (Federal Trade Commission, Speech delivered at the Conference on the Regulation of Consumer Financial Products, New York, 6 January 2010) <http://www.ftc.gov/public-statements/2010/01/managing-irrationality-some-observations-behavioral-economics-and-creation>

Varney CA, Assistant Attorney General, Antitrust Division, DOJ, 'Antitrust Federalism: Enhancing Federal/State Cooperation' (Speech, 7 October 2009) <http://www.justice.gov/atr/public/speeches/250635.pdf>

Varney CA, Assistant Attorney General, Antitrust Division, DOJ, 'Vigorously Enforcing the Antitrust Laws: Developments at the Division' (speech delivered in Washington DC, 24 June 2011) <http://www.justice.gov/atr/public/speeches/272536.pdf>

Vestager M, 'Competition policy in the EU: Outlook and recent developments in antitrust' (Speech delivered at Peterson Institute for International Economics, Washington DC, 16 April 2015) <http://ec.europa.eu/commission/2014-2019/vestager/announcements/competition-policy-eu-outlook-and-recent-developments-antitrust_en>

CONFERENCE AND RESEARCH PAPERS AND OTHER MATERIALS

American Chamber of Commerce to the European Union, 'AmCham EU Response to the European Commission's Consultation on the Review of the Vertical Restraints Block Exemption Regulation and Guidelines' (Response to Draft Commission Regulation, 2009)

Bennett M et al, 'Resale Price Maintenance: Explaining the Controversy, and Small Steps Towards a More Nuanced Policy' (MPRA Paper No. 21121, 2010)

Brief for the United States as Amicus Curiae in Support of Petitioner, *Monsanto Co v Spray-Rite Svc Corp*, 465 U.S. 752 (1984), No 82-914

Brief for William S Comanor and Frederic M Scherer as Amici Curiae Supporting Neither Party, *Leegin Creative Leather Products, Inc. v. PSKS, Inc DBA Kay's Kloset ... Kays' Shoes*, 551 U.S. 877 (2007), No. 06-480

Consumer Focus 'Consumer Focus Response to Vertical Restraints Block Exemption Regulation' (Discussion Paper, Consumer Focus Group, London, 2009)

Dobson P, Waterson M and Chu A, 'The Welfare Consequences of Exercise of Buyer Power' (Office of Fair Trading, Research Paper 16, 1998)

Durand D, 'On the Efficiency of VTR' (Thesis, Boston College, The Department of Economics, May 2000)

European Federation of Pharmaceutical Industries and Associations (representing 31 national pharmaceutical industry associations and 44 leading pharmaceutical companies in Europe), 'The Proposal to Revise the Vertical Restraints Block Exemption Regulation' (2009)

Gundlach GT et al 'The Changing Landscape of Supply Chain Management, Marketing Channels of Distribution, Logistics and Purchasing' (American Antitrust Institute 2014 Annual Conference: The Inefficiencies of Efficiency, 19 June 2014)

ICC (International Chamber of Commerce) Commission on Competition 'Review of EC Competition Rules Applicable to Vertical Agreements' (Document No. 225/662, 28 September 2009)

Lande R, 'Market Power without a Large Market Share: The Role of Imperfect Information and Other "Consumer Protection" Market Failures' (Paper, 8 March 2007) <http://www.justice.gov/atr/market-power-without-large-market-share-role-imperfect-information-and-other-consumer-protection> accessed 17 August 2015

LAWIN, 'Review of the Competition Rules Applicable to Vertical Agreements: Response to Consultation' (Response to Draft Commission Regulation, 2009)

MacKay A and Smith DA, 'The Empirical Effects of Minimum Resale Price Maintenance' (Kilts Booth Marketing Series Paper 1-009, 16 June 2014)

Moss DL and Taylor RC, 'Short End of the Stick: The Plight of Growers and Consumers in Concentrated Agricultural Supply Chains' (American Antitrust Institute 2014 Annual Conference: The Inefficiencies of Efficiency, 19 June 2014)

Mueller WF and Gaithman FE, 'An Empirical Test of the Free Rider and Market Power Hypothesis (12 April 1989) (unpublished manuscript, on file with the University of Wisconsin)

Obama The Hon B, 'Statement of Senator Barack Obama for the American Antitrust Institute' (27 September 2007) <www.antitrustinstitute.org/node/10883>

Office of Fair Trading (UK), 'Competition in Retailing' (Research Paper 13, London, 1997)

Organisation for Economic Co-operation and Development, 'Buying Power of Multiproduct Retailers' (OECD Policy Roundtables DAFFE/CLP(99)21, 1998) <http://www.oecd.org/competition/abuse/2379299.pdf>

Schulz N, 'Resale Price Maintenance and the Service Argument: Efficiency Effects' (Wuerzburg Economic Working Paper 53, 2005)

Senator John Sherman's speech, 25 January (1889) 20 *Congressional Record* 1167

Senator John Sherman's speech, 21 March (1890) 21 *Congressional Record* 3: 2457, 2456, 2455

The American Antitrust Institute, 'Action Needed to Address Resale Price Maintenance in Contact Lenses – and Countless Other Markets', Letter sent to FTC and DOJ (24 October 2014) <http://www.antitrustinstitute.org/content/aai-urges-action-minimum-price-policies-contact-lens-industry> accessed 2 June 2015

Wegener RJ, 'Dancing with Dinosaurs: Using Legal Analysis to Determine the Role of Vertical Non-Price Restraints in Competition Strategy' (American Law Institute, ALI-ABA Course of Study, 6 March 1997)

Wright JD, 'The Economics of Resale Price Maintenance & Implications for Competition Law and Policy' (Speech delivered at British Institute of International and Comparative Law, 9 April 2014, London, UK)

Index

Note: Author has used bold formatting on page numbers to indicate where a term is discussed in particular detail.

advertising **29–31**, 36, 78, 132, 213, 283
agents 18–19, 152
agreement 5, 17, 52–3
   ancillary **56–7**, 63, **64–5**, 89
   horizontal **1**, 52, 97–9, 121, 130, **134**, 137–8, 140, 145–7, 151, 156, 174, 183, 218, 245, 278, **284–7**, 297, 321, 324
   naked 56, 64, 117
   tacit 52, 146, 148, 151, 152, 191, 202, 206, 237, 287
   vertical **1**, **53**, 61, 66, **94–5**, 98, 100, 109, 111, 123, 125, 138, 142, 147, 157, 160–61, 176, 180, 196–7, 207, 218, **234–7**, 240, 287
Almunia, Joaquín 207
anticompetitive effect and anticompetitive/restrictive object *see* effect
appreciable objective advantage **179**, 214, 225–6, 240–41

balancing test 179, 211, 236, **241**, 243
bargaining 5, 8–9, 11, 36
   bargaining power *see* power
barriers to entry 109, 140, 172, 178, 196, 269, 283
behavioral economics **119–20**, 247, 296–7
Böhm, Franz 165, 315
Bork, Robert H **91–2**, 272, 274, 285–6, 302, 306
bounded rationality **9**, 14, 24–5, 247, **295–7**
Brunell, Richard M 126, 130, 133

Bush, George W 94, 117–18

cartel
   retailer 122, 131, 135, 138, 141–2, 156, **286–7**, 297
   supplier 131, 248, **284–6**, 289
causal link 151, 225–6
Chicago School 6, 7, 28, 55, 57, **71–2**, 91, 98, 100–101, 108, 114, 117, 120, 140, 161, 175, 184, 201, 246, 252, 269, 302, 315, 320, 323, 324
   see also liberalism, neoliberalism; Post-Chicago School
class action 124, 142–5, 147, 151
Clinton, William J 117–18
Coase, Ronald H 9, 58, 247
Coase theorem 58, 127, 160, 247, 304
Colgate doctrine 62, **69–71**, 73, **76–80**, 81–2, 111, 124
collusion *see* agreement
Comanor, William S 24, 268
combination 52–3, 63, 79, 81, 125, 134, 136, 148, 152
common law 50–52, 56–7, 64, 66–8, 113, 125, 133, 178
community interest **211–12**
competition
   downstream vertical 33, 43, 45, 102, 213, 235, 253, 287, 291, 294, 299, 316, 321
   fair 162, 168, 242, 308, **310–11**
      see also fairness
   free 68, 162, 168, 170, 194, 208, 264, 274, 308–9, **310–19**, 321–2

horizontal 7, **27–8**, 36–7, 41, 45, 47, 102, 114, 122, 144, 160–61, 248, 282, 312, 320, **322–4**
horizontal intrabrand **34**, 140, 284
interbrand 5, 7–10, 16, 26–7, **28–31**, 34, 39–40, 45, 47, 69, 86–7, 96–8, **101–2**, **103–10**, 122–3, 126–8, 131–2, 134–5, 140, **145–8**, 154–7, **159–61**, 175–7, 184, 196, 200–201, 210, 214, 219, 221–2, 224, **241–5**, 255, 258, 270, 273–5, 277, 280, 282–3, 285, 287, 298, 306, **312–14, 320–24**
intrabrand 1, 5, 7, 10, 12, 16–17, 21, 23, **25–31**, 34, 37, 40, 47, 66, 69, 83, 87, 96–100, **101–2**, **103–9**, 121–2, 126, 128, 131–2, 140, 142–5, 148, 154–5, 157, **159–61**, 162, 177, 197, 199–200, 210, 214, 221–2, 224, 241–3, 245, 251, 255–6, 271, 280, 283–4, 286–8, 291, **297–8, 312–18, 320–24**
vertical 5, 12, 26, 28, **34–7, 102**, 131, 288, 312–13, 323
vertical intrabrand 34, 143
concerted practice 171, 186, 198, 201–2, 207, 216–17, 236
concurrence of wills 198, **205–6**, 216–19, **220–21**
conduct
 bilateral 52–3, 63, 69, 77, 80, 171, 198, 236–7, 321
 multilateral 52–3, 63, 69, 70, 77, 80, 171, 186, 191, 198, **201**, 232, 236–7, 321
 parallel 145, 148, **150–53**
 unilateral 52–3, 61–2, **69–71**, 77–81, 83, 110–11, 116, 121, 124, 148, 150, 152–3, 171, 186, 191, 198, **201**, 205, 236, 287
consequentialist approach **301–6**, 309
conspiracy 52–3, 63, 88, 95, 110, 138–9, 148–52

Court of Justice of the European Union 168, 173–92, 194, 198, 202–6, 208–9, 214–19, 221, 223–32, 236, 238–9, 241, 244, 259, 263, 295, 313
customer allocation 17, 77, **233–4**

damages 52, 151, 209, 231
decision by association of undertakings 171, 186
deontological approach 301, **305–18**, **320–24**
Department of Justice, Antitrust Division 49, 56, 60–61, **92–6**, 112, 118, 120, 134, 255, 286, 308, 310
distribution
 channel **13**, 265–6
 cost 40, 122, 135, 270, 283
 dual 17, **18–22**, 99, 140, 145–47, 154, 161
 dynamically organized distribution **14**
 ecosystems **14**
 exclusive **16–17**, 77, 175–7, 184, 189, 204, 213, 216, 233
 networks **14–15**, 43, 190
 online **15, 18–19**, 46, 142, 147–51, 213–14, **226–9**, 239, **259–65**, 278, 298
 selective **16–17**, 126, **183–97**, 211, 214, **226–30**, 233–4, 243, 260–61, 268, 297
 systems 7, **13–14**, 15–20, 63, 75, 77, 85, 87, 88–100, 110, 136, 139, 144–5, 154, 161, 175, 183–6, 189–92, 195–7, 204, 211, 213–14, 226–9, **233–4**, 243, 249, 260–61, 268, 271
doctrine of conspiracy 50
dominant market position 13, 39, 42–3, 46, 76, 101, 135, 141–3, 156, 166, 171–2, 209–11, 215, 226, 230, 273, 295, 322
dominant undertaking 171
dual-stage factors 34–5

Easterbrook, Frank H 11, 267
economic approach 5, 49, **93**, 98, 162, 174, 193–7, 199, 201, 207–13, 221, 224, 296, 304–6, 309, 317–18
economic entity 8, 18, 152, 199
  integrated entity **7–20**, 46, 51, 60, 76, 91, 99, 139, 152, 154, 247
  non-integrated entity 9–10, 12, 17, 19
economic integration 162, 166, 167, **172–81**, 194–6, 208, 235
economic union 169
economies of scale 8–9
effect
  anticompetitive/restrictive effect or object 171, 175, 177, **180–82**, **198–200**, 213–19, 221–4, **226–9**, 233, **236–9**, 240, 242–3, 259–61, 281–4
  appreciable 57, 236, 237–8
  direct 167, 231
  domino/follow-the-leader **255**, 275, 280, 282, 287, 298
  interlocking (situation, relationships) 282, 287
  procompetitive **22–4**, 29, 49, 72, 86, **99–104**, 122, **127–31**, 188, 195–9, 219, 224–6, 243, 244–8, 248–69, **270–77**, 278–81, 302–8, 315–17, 320–24
  triple stage effects **34–5**, 46
efficiency 11, 25, 43, 58, 71–2, **90–91**, 92–3, 99, 103, 122, 127, 166, 183, **193–5**, 201, 208, 214, 224, 226, 235, 239, 241, 244, 248, 250, 264, **270**, 275, 277, 281, 283, 289, 294, 296–9, 301, **305–19**, 320
  allocative 92, 239, 244
  dynamic 308–9
  economic 71, 91–2, 194, 214, 244, 305
empirical studies 2, 5–6, 71, 119, 126, **129–32**, 247–8, **277–81**, 282, 284, 287, 289, 294, 299, 305
enforcement 10, 55, 59–60, 94, 118–19, 138, 145, 148–50, **151–9**, 162–3, 170, 173, 193, 207–12, **230–42**, 309–10

  in Europe 162–3, 170, 173, 193, 207–12, **230–42**
  in the United States 55, 59–60, 94, 118–19, 138, 145, 148–50, **151–9**
equilibrium 58, 92
equitable relief 66, 125
Eucken, Walter 165, 311
European Commission 16–17, 163, 172, 210–13, **230–31**, 244, 259, 308
European Competition Network 193, 232
evidence
  of an agreement or collusion 63, 112, 121, 123, 137–8, 145, **148–53**, 187, 202, 218
  circumstantial **145–52**
  direct 112, 123
  empirical *see* empirical studies
  of free-riding 107, 115, 130
  of market power or the abuse thereof 123, 135, 142, 156
  prima facie evidence 151
  of restriction of interbrand competition 107–8, 110, 141, 146, 155, 245, 323
  of restriction of intrabrand competition 98, 113–14, 190, 216–17
exclusive dealing **16–17**, 59, 74–6, 98, 176, 182, 187–8, 254
exclusive sourcing 16
exclusive supply agreement 16–17

fair trial 169
fairness 21, 33, **59–61**, 68, 86, 162, 166, 172, **195**, 208, 242, **300–312**, **314–17**
  see also competition, fair
Federal Trade Commission 49, **60**, 92, 94, 118–23, 129–30, 158, 255, 278, 280, 286, 307, 310
foreclosure 16, 26, 40, 66, **69**, 125, 284, 286–7
franchising **16**, 40, 75, **86–103**, 109, 183–5, 213

free movement of goods 57, 162, 167–8, 172, 228
free riding 18, **22**, 58, **63**, 64–5, 72, 82, 103, 105, 107, 111, 115–16, **126–30**, 139, 153, 160, 213, 246–55, **256–68**, 278, 290, 294, 297–8, 315–18, 320
free trade 162, 167, 172, 177, 245–6, 263–4, 269, 307, **310–11**
freedom 165, 197, 213, **302–5**, 321
   to compete **67–9**
   to conduct business 199–201
   contractual 50, 160
   to deal **70–71**, 74, 83
   economic 165, 246, 308, **310–12**, **314**
   ownership 313
Freiburg School 165
French Revolution 165
further factual enhancement 148–50

game theory 39, 46
General Court 183, 187, 194, 198, 202–6, 211, 213–14, 217–26, 231–2, 236
Ghosh, Shubha 160, 302, 304
Grossmann-Doerth, Hanns 165
Gundlach, Gregory T 13, 18, 21, 294

hard-core restriction 2, 3, 199, 212–13, 227, **233–4**, 240, 243, 260
harm
   anticompetitive 8, 27, 29, 37, 53, 58, 108–9, 119, 121, 123, 140–43, 146, 195, 238, 244–5
   economic 26, **209–11**, 244–5
   potential 129, 146
Harvard School **71–2**, 164, 246–7
horizontal restrictions 7, 12, 27, 100, 134, 146, 161
Hovenkamp, Herbert 8, 20, 44, 91, 135, 139, 271

intellectual property rights 16, **64**, **66–7**, 178, 187–8, 313
information technology 12, 196, 265
injunction 52, 151

innovation 10, 26, 36, 41, 72, 91, **213–16**, **224–6**, 245, **263–4**, 273–4, 281, 283–4, 298–9, 305, 315
interlocking vertical relationship *see* effect
Internet sale *see* distribution, online

Kaldor-Hicks efficiency 58, 244, 295
know-how 16, **184–5**, 251
   see also intellectual property rights

laissez-faire 164
liberalism
   classical 164–5
   European 164–5
   neoliberalism **10–13**, **20**, 28–9, 44, 58, 160, 165
   ordoliberalism **164–8**, 173, 246, 308, 310, 311, 312, 314, 315
   social **165**

marginalist theory 24, **58**, 276–7
marginalization 24, **43–4**, 58
market
   common 166, 167, 172, 173, 174, 181, 183, 191, 211, 238
   downstream 33, 102, 299
   foreclosure *see* foreclosure
   free 71, 164, 246, 259, 263
   integration 168, 173–4, 182, 195–6, 206, 209, 215
   internal 3, **166–70**, 183, **207**, 214–15, 307
   intrabrand 26, 316
   monopolistic 28–9, 38, 40, 43–5, 50, 53, 84, 134, 141, **155–60**, 275, 294, 298
   relevant 102, 109, 140–41, 146, 155, 158, 211, 238, 322
   share 30, 33, 35, 37, 87–8, 98, 100, 102, 104, 107, 119, 127, 130, 135, 156, 195, 197, 200, 235, 237, 243
   single 169, 174, 177, 183, 194–8, 207–8, 215
single-stage market (horizontal market) 34

structure 7, 12, 24, 27, **37–48**, 196, 223, 235, 246, 274, 297, 320
upstream 41, 43, 45, 102, 144, 213, 235, 316, 321
meeting of the minds 148, 202–3
monetary union 169
monopolization 52, 53, 97, 161
monopoly 38–41, 70, 71, 83, 84, 101, 135
  bilateral **43–5**
  profit 131, 282
monopsony **40–43**
Monti, Mario 194
most-favored-nation clause 147–8
motivations
  anticompetitive 39, 143–4, 204, 248, 254–5, **287–96**, 297, **299**, 314–15
  procompetitive 143, 204, 248–70, **289–96**, 297

national competition authorities (NCA) **193**, 210–11, 230–33, 235, 241
national courts 193, 230–32
national procedural autonomy 231
notification procedure 173–4, 181, 193, 199, 210

Obama, Barack H 118–20
objective of antitrust/competition law 4, 6, 92, 162, 167, 169, 172–3, 195, 207–8, 214–15, 226, 242, 245, 301, **306–10**, 311, 317, 321–2
opportunism 9, 14, 24–5, **295–6**
oligopoly **38–40**, 41
  bilateral **43–5**
oligopsony **40–43**, 45
ordoliberalim *see* liberalism
Overstreet, Thomas R **129–30**, 278, 284
ownership 44, 62, **67–71**, **89–90**, 160, 178, **303–5**, 312–14, 316, 322

parallel trade 162, 174–7, 180, 188–9, 196, 198, 202–4, **214–25**, 230, 242, 242
parent firm 11, 18
Pareto optimality **58**, 92, 244, 295

passive sale 3, 212–14, 217–18, 229, 233, 239
per se rule 2–3, 34, 48–51, 56, 61–2, **65–6**, 73–80, **81–91**, 93–101, 103, **111–17**, 118, 121–9, 132–7, 154–9, 160–61, 201, 212, 239–42, 271, 280, 286, 290, 292, 324
Pitofsky, Robert 54, 132, 263–4, 268
plus factors 150–51
Posner, Richard A 103, 157
Post-Chicago School 91, 117, 120, 140, 161, 175, 184, 301, 320, 322, 324
power
  bargaining 8, 11, 15, 18, 20–23, **25–30**, **31–4**, 37–8, 40–47, 113, 115–16, 142, 144, 203, 276, 286–9, 291, 317, 321–2, 324
  buyer **31–2**, 42, 44, 123
  countervailing 31
  economic **166**, 311–12, 315
  market (horizontal) 37, 98, **213**, 224–5, 234, 243, 245, 258, 322
  seller **31–2**, 37
predatory pricing 53, 60–61
preliminary ruling 180, 186, 215, 226, 230, 232
price-cutting 30, 64, 95, 105, 107, 110, 112–13, 115–17, 120–21, 153, 249, 268, 286, 296
price fixing
  horizontal 74, 95, 121, 131–2, 134, 141, **145–6**, 149, 232, 234, 278
  maximum 74
  minimum 74, 95, 121, 131–2, 134, 141, **145–6**, 149, 232, 234, 278
  vertical **25**, 29, 34, 39, **44–5**, **48–9**, **61–2**, **65–6**, 74, 77, **80–84**, 85, 88–9, 117, 121–2, 124, 126, 147, 186, 212, 232, 234
  maximum 44–5, 48–9, 74, **80–84**, 121–2
  minimum **25**, 29, 34, 39, **62**, **65–6**, 77, 117, **124**, **126**, **147**, 186, 212, 234
principal **18–19**, 51
private labels **17**, 29, 31, **41**

procompetitive justification 102–4, **248–76**
  exclusivity justification **248–68**
  facilitating entry justification 105, 107, 127, 175, 180–81, 185–6, 189, 195–6, 240, **268–70**, 292, 320–21
  incentive to sell 21, **253–6**, 257–9, 269, 273, 281–2, 284, 289–90, 297–9
  protection of brand reputation 24, 29–31, 65, 77, 129, 184, 197, 228, **251–3**, 249, 257–62, 268, 274, **290–91**, 297
  theory of quality certification **251–3**
  theory of services 58, 82, 103, **249–51**, 271, 276, 297
progressive school **20–22**, 120, 140
proportionality 86, **187–9**, 214, 219, **224–6**, 240, 243, 259–61, 266, 316, 320–21
public interest 57, 61, 66–7

restraint of trade 50, 90, 104, 106
right of defence 169
Roosevelt, Theodore 59
rule of reason **2–5**, 11, 48–50, 55–8, 66, 74–5, 86, 90, 92–9, **100–111**, **113–17**, **117–36**, 138, 140–41, 143, 146, **153–61**, 201, 243, 255, 279–80, 286

safe harbour **234–5**
Sen, Amartya 312
Sherman, John 51, 54
single-branding **16–17**, 186
social justice 165–6
standard of reasonableness 51, 57, 62–4, 89
stare decisis 125–6, **133–4**
Steiner, Robert 29–30, 34–5, 46, 115, 126, 283, 294
subsidiary 18, 104, 220
sufficient degree of probability 181, 225, 238, 240–41
supply chain **14**

supremacy 167

Taft, William Howard 59
Telser, Lester G 72, 250–51, 267
territorial vertical restrictions
  absolute territory 1, 3, 26, 38, 139, **176–80**, 186, 188–9, 198, 216–19, 235, 236, 242, 254, 269, 274, 316
  exclusive territory 80, 89, 100, 174–5, 234
trade secret 63–7, 178
  see also intellectual property rights
transaction cost 8–9, 13, 23, 45, 58, 91, 127, 243, 247, 267, 270–71, **293–4**, 297
transaction economy 165, 311
tying 16, 23, 59, 172, 292

unfair methods of competition 59–60, 307
unfair pricing **60**
United States Congress 50–51, 54, 59–61, 93–6, 112, 118, 133–4
unreasonable restraint of trade **51–2**, 53, 56–7, 90, 104, 106, 109, 143, 154, 243

vertical integration **8–12**, 14, 17, 61
vertical restraints/restrictions **1–3**, **5**, **7–8**, **10**, **12**, **14**, **16–17**, **19–24**, **26–31**, **33–6**, **39**, **42–3**, **45–7**, 48–50, 52–4, 59, 61, 64, 66, 72, 76–7, 85–6, 90, **93–6**, 99, 101, 111, 113–17, 127, 134, 138–9, 142, 144, 146, 153–5, 160–61, 162, 171–2, 174–5, 178, 183–4, 186–7, **192–201**, 204, **206–13**, 216, 219, **230–35**, **241–8**, 250–51, 253–6, 258–9, 262–6, **268–77**, 282–3, 285–9, **292–8**, **300–302**, **306**, **310**, **312**, **315**, **317**, **320–24**
  complex vertical restrictions **76–7**, **80–81**, **84–5**, 89, 129, 139
vertical non-price restraints 20, 23, 26, 84, **93–4**, 96, 110–11, **113–17**, 139, 147, 153, 155, 175, 192, 204, 251

see also customer allocation; exclusive dealing; exclusive sourcing; exclusive supply agreement; franchising; territorial vertical restrictions; tying
vertical price restraints 1, 3, 84, 93–4, 111, 117, **122–5**, 128, 138, 153, 186, 200
see also price fixing
Vestager, Margrethe 207–8, 310

welfare
consumer 12, 23, 30, 40, 58, **91–3**, 122, 127, 162, **193–5**, 207–9, 214, 219, 222–4, 241–2, 244–5, 248, 250, 255, 270–73, **274–7**, 279–82, **295–9**, 302, 306, 320
total 10, 12, 26, 58, 92, 119, 273, 294–5, 299, 309, 315
Williamson, Oliver E 1, 4, 9, 38, 45, 91, 247, 293–5
Woodrow, Wilson 59